SPSS®
Statistics

4th Edition

by Jesus Salcedo
and Keith McCormick

for
dummies®

A Wiley Brand

SPSS® Statistics For Dummies®, 4th Edition

Published by: **John Wiley & Sons, Inc.**, 111 River Street, Hoboken, NJ 07030-5774, www.wiley.com

Copyright © 2020 by John Wiley & Sons, Inc., Hoboken, New Jersey

Published simultaneously in Canada

For general information on our other products and services, please contact our Customer Care Department within the U.S. at 877-762-2974, outside the U.S. at 317-572-3993, or fax 317-572-4002. For technical support, please visit https://hub.wiley.com/community/support/dummies.

Wiley publishes in a variety of print and electronic formats and by print-on-demand. Some material included with standard print versions of this book may not be included in e-books or in print-on-demand. If this book refers to media such as a CD or DVD that is not included in the version you purchased, you may download this material at http://booksupport.wiley.com. For more information about Wiley products, visit www.wiley.com.

Library of Congress Control Number: 2020941201

ISBN 978-1-119-56083-8 (pbk); ISBN 978-1-119-56087-6 (ebk); ISBN 978-1-119-56082-1 (ebk)

Manufactured in the United States of America

SKY10020237_080320

Contents at a Glance

Table of Contents

Introduction

Good news! You don't have to know diddlysquat about the math behind statistics to be able to come up with well-calculated conclusions and display them in fancy graphs. You won't be doing any calculations by hand. All you need is the IBM SPSS Statistics software and a bunch of numbers. This book shows you how to type the numbers, select options in the menus, and produce brilliant statistics. And interpret them properly, too! It really is as simple as that.

About This Book

Some sections of the book are written as stand-alone tutorials to make it easy for you to get into whatever you're after. After you're up and running with SPSS, you can skip around and read just the sections you need. You really don't need to read straight through the entire book. However, the book's chapters are organized in parts, and it's generally a good idea to read the chapters in a part in sequence. And you should start with Part 1 if you are brand new to SPSS.

This book is not about math. It's about statistics. You don't derive anything. You don't do any math by hand or look up numbers in statistical tables. You won't find one explanation of how calculations are performed under the hood. This book is about the things you can do to command SPSS to calculate statistics for you. You can avoid all of those fancy formulas with lots of sigmas in them and still use SPSS to produce some nifty stats!

However, if you decide to study the techniques of statistical calculation, you'll be able to understand what SPSS does to produce numbers. Your main advantage in understanding the process to that degree of detail is that you'll be able to choose a calculation method that more closely models the reality you're trying to analyze. Although SPSS rescues you from the stress that some associate with manual calculations, it still leaves it up to you to interpret the results. We spend a lot of pages on carefully preparing you for that responsibility.

Throughout the book are examples that use data stored in files. These files are freely available to you. Some files are installed with IBM SPSS Statistics in the SPSS installation directory, which is \Program Files\SPSS (unless you chose another location during installation). Other files are available via the Welcome dialog when you launch SPSS. Most of the files, however, were designed for this book and are available on the book's companion website (see "Beyond the Book" for more information). In every case, the files were carefully curated to demonstrate some specific capability of SPSS.

And a technical note: The official name of the product is IBM SPSS Statistics. Throughout this book, we refer to it simply as *SPSS*. Outside this book, that shortcut can be risky because other related products are also called SPSS — notably, IBM SPSS Modeler, which, though powerful and part of the same brand, is not the subject of this book.

About the Fourth Edition

The authors wrote this fourth edition using IBM SPSS Statistics version 27. The technical editor checked all tasks against his concurrent version of SPSS Statistics Subscription and the instructions were consistent on both platforms. The third edition of this book was written using IBM SPSS Statistics version 23. Even if you use a version of SPSS prior to version 27, we urge you to use this fourth edition because its more than 100 pages of new content better prepare new users and meet the needs of intermediate users, as well as cover statistical analytic procedures to a much greater extent.

Foolish Assumptions

This book is for anyone new to SPSS. No prior knowledge of statistics is needed or even expected. In specific terms, we made a few assumptions about you, the reader of this book:

>> You may be a student who isn't majoring in statistics but has been instructed to use SPSS by one of your professors.

>> You may have an interest in statistical analysis but are new to using SPSS.

>> You may work in an office setting and have been asked to use SPSS to analyze some data.

For most people who generate statistics, the complexity of using the software becomes an obstacle. Our purpose in writing this book is to show you how to move that obstacle out of the way with minimum effort.

Icons Used in This Book

Throughout this book, we use icons in the margins to grab your attention. Here's what those icons mean:

REMEMBER

You should keep this information in mind. It's important to what you're doing.

TECHNICAL STUFF

This icon highlights unnecessarily geeky information, but we had to include it to complete the thought. You can skip anything marked with this icon unless the text makes you curious.

TIP

This icon highlights a point that can save you time and effort.

WARNING

Anything marked with this icon offers information about something that can sneak up and bite you.

Beyond the Book

In addition to the material in the print or e-book you're reading right now, this product also comes with some access-anywhere goodies on the web. Check out the free cheat sheet at www.dummies.com/cheatsheet/spss for information on variable levels of measurement, commonly used procedures in the Analyze menu, and possible conclusions that you can reach after conducting a statistical test. Finally, for the examples, you can download the data files that don't come with SPSS at www.dummies.com/go/spss or keithmccormick.com/SSFD4E.

Where to Go from Here

If you're new to SPSS, we recommend starting out by reading Part 1, so you understand what SPSS is. If you haven't already gained access to a copy of SPSS, check out Chapter 2. Chapter 3 introduces the software and goes through a typical session using SPSS. Read the stuff in Chapter 4 about defining variables and declaring metadata — it all makes sense once you get the hang of it, but the process seems kind of screwy until you see how it works. The material in Chapter 4 covers areas in which some new users of SPSS go astray, so read it carefully. And from there, use the table of contents and index to find the things you want to do!

Two chapters are worthy of special mention. Chapter 22 helps you navigate statistical techniques covered in Parts 5 and 6 and beyond. If you know the name of the statistical procedure you want to use, you should be okay without Chapter 22. But what if you don't know the name of the statistical procedure? How are you supposed to look it up? This is when you should try Chapter 22.

Sometimes things seem amiss, but you simply don't know what's wrong. Chapter 30 addresses this issue. How are you supposed to find out how to fix an issue when SPSS isn't working as it's supposed to? In this case, check out Chapter 30, which covers the most common reasons why SPSS acts strangely.

If you have a question, you can reach Jesus Salcedo at jesussalcedo@yahoo.com and Keith McCormick at keithmc123@keithmccormick.com. We will post information about updates, joining our mailing list, and the latest SPSS news at keithmccormick.com/SSFD4E.

1
Getting Started with SPSS

Chapter **1**

Introducing SPSS

A *statistic* is a number, but it's a special kind of number. A statistic is a measurement of some sort. It's fundamentally a count of something — occurrences, speed, amount, or whatever. A statistic is calculated using a sample. In a sense, a sample is the keyhole you have to peer through to see the population, which is what you're trying to understand. The value at the population level — the average height of an American male, for instance — is called a *parameter.* Unless you've got all the data there is, and you've collected a census of the population, you have to make do with the data in your sample. The job of SPSS is to calculate. Your job is to provide a good sample. Together you try to understand the population even though all you have is a sample.

In this chapter, we discuss the importance of having accurate, reliable data, and some of the implications when this is not the case. We talk also about how best to organize your data in SPSS and the different kinds of files that SPSS creates. We take a trip down memory lane and discuss the origins of SPSS so you can understand all of its many names. We discuss what can be done in the program and the different ways of communicating with the software. Finally, we spend some time discussing different ways in which you can get help when navigating SPSS.

SPSS's Job, Our Job, and Your Job

It's important to have appropriate expectations. In this section, we discuss the various roles that all parties play with regard to learning to use SPSS.

SPSS's job

After you give SPSS data and instructions, it will perform the calculations for you. The data and the *metadata* — the information about the data — have to be correct. (We have a lot to say about metadata.) The instructions have to be correct as well. Correct data processed with the wrong technique won't give you the results you need.

SPSS won't make math errors. That's not the kind of errors computers make. They always do *exactly* what we tell them to do, and sometimes that's the problem. SPSS's job is to take data that has been declared correctly and produce statistical results in the form of tables and charts that allow you to draw conclusions about your data — if you know how to interpret those results.

Our job

Your authors, Jesus and Keith, have had so many hours using SPSS that we've lost count. You may have heard of the somewhat controversial *10,000 hour rule*, which states that you need that many hours of "deliberate practice" to truly master a complex subject. Well, you'll be pleased to know that Jesus and Keith each have more than 10,000 classroom hours teaching SPSS in addition to decades of using it on our own projects.

As the authors, we are primarily responsible for the following:

» **Making the book easy to read:** We know where to focus your attention when you're getting started because we've helped thousands of SPSS beginners get started.

» **Walking you through how to set up everything properly:** Parts 1 and 2 focus on getting started with SPSS as well as how to define data files, variables, and their attributes.

» **Acclimating you regarding how SPSS works:** Getting you familiar with the software is our number one focus and mission. We hope to get you to a point where you stop worrying about the software so you can concentrate on your analysis.

» **Explaining how to tell SPSS to do basic tasks:** This edition has a greatly expanded section in Parts 5 and 6 on understanding the basic theory, choosing the right technique, and interpreting results. We realize that if you're confused about SPSS, it may be because you're confused about statistics. However, we spend the rest of the book helping you understand the software.

» **Starting you on your SPSS Statistics journey:** You won't master statistics when you reach the end of this book, but you will be much more comfortable with SPSS software. No book of this length could cover all statistical techniques, but we selected the most important procedures for new users of SPSS.

Your job

Your number one job is to relax. You might be reading this book because you're up against a deadline or something in SPSS is causing you stress. However, if you take a little time now to understand how to work in SPSS efficiently, it will pay off in the long run. You have some other responsibilities:

>> **Know your data.** SPSS can't put your data into context — only you can. SPSS will trust everything you give it. It will never second-guess the data you give it, and it will never ask you about it. Only you can ensure that the data is trustworthy.

>> **Declare your data and set it up properly.** Declaring and setting up yourdata is a critical responsibility that we cover thoroughly, especially in Chapters 3 and 4. Setting up data is not just about declaring the metadata but also about other data management tasks that we cover in Part 3.

>> **Choose the correct statistical technique.** The toughest task for you may be to choose the correct statistical technique. Dozens of techniques are available, but we know which ones are the most important to learn. We've given you a life preserver. If you feel stuck and don't know which chapter to refer to, check out Chapter 22, where we provide an overview for analyzing data and a larger context of where in the research process various statistical techniques are typically used.

>> **Know how to interpret the results.** Finally, Parts 5 and 6 have many examples of how to interpret statistical output.

Garbage In, Garbage Out: Recognizing the Importance of Good Data

SPSS doesn't warn you when there is something wrong with your sample. Its job is to work on the data you give it. If what you give SPSS is incomplete or biased, or if there is data that doesn't belong in there, the resulting calculations won't reflect the population very well. Not much in the SPSS output will signal to anyone that there is a problem. So, if you're not careful, you can conclude just about anything from your data and your calculations.

Consider the data in Table 1-1. What if you calculated the survival rate of *Titanic* passengers based on this small sample? What if you calculated what fraction of the passengers were in each class of service? You can easily see that you'd be in real trouble.

TABLE 1-1   ## Sample of *Titanic* Passengers

Survived or Died	Class	Name	Sex	Age	Fare Paid	Cabin	Embarkation
Died	1	Andrews, Mr. Thomas, Jr.	Male	39	0.00	A36	Southampton
Died	1	Parr, Mr. William Henry Marsh	Male		0.00		Southampton
Died	1	Fry, Mr. Richard	Male		0.00	B102	Southampton
Died	1	Harrison, Mr. William	Male	40	0.00	B94	Southampton
Died	1	Reuchlin, Mr. John George	Male	38	0.00		Southampton
Died	2	Parkes, Mr. Francis "Frank"	Male		0.00		Southampton
Died	2	Cunningham, Mr. Alfred Fleming	Male		0.00		Southampton
Died	2	Campbell, Mr. William	Male		0.00		Southampton
Died	2	Frost, Mr. Anthony Wood "Archie"	Male		0.00		Southampton
Died	2	Knight, Mr. Robert J.	Male		0.00		Southampton
Died	2	Watson, Mr. Ennis Hastings	Male		0.00		Southampton
Died	3	Leonard, Mr. Lionel	Male	36	0.00		Southampton
Died	3	Tornquist, Mr. William Henry	Male	25	0.00		Southampton
Died	3	Johnson, Mr. William Cahoone, Jr.	Male	19	0.00		Southampton
Died	3	Johnson, Mr. Alfred	Male	49	0.00		Southampton

However, consider this: Would you be tempted to drop these cases from your analysis because their fare information appears to be missing? What if fare information were provided for all the other passengers? You might drop the cases in Table 1-1 but use everyone else. You'd be dropping only a handful of passengers out of hundreds, so that would be okay, right? The answer is no, it would not be okay. As it turns out, there is a good reason that each of these passengers didn't pay a fare (for example, Mr. Thomas Andrews, Jr., designed the ship), and if this was your data, your job would be to know that.

Sampling is a big topic, but here's the quick version:

>> The data points in your sample should be drawn at random from the population.

>> There should be enough data points.

>> You should be able to justify the removal of any data points.

THE ORIGIN OF SPSS

In 2018, IBM SPSS Statistics turned 50. That makes it older than Windows and older than the first Apple computer, so in the early days SPSS was run on mainframe computers using punch cards.

At Stanford University in the late 1960s, Norman H. Nie, C. Hadlai (Tex) Hull, and Dale H. Bent developed the original software system named Statistical Package for the Social Sciences (SPSS). They needed to analyze a large volume of social science data, so they wrote software to do it. The software package caught on with other folks at universities, and, consistent with the open-source tradition of the day, the software spread through universities across the country.

The three men produced a manual in the 1970s, and the software's popularity took off. A version of SPSS existed for each of the different kinds of mainframe computers in existence at the time. Its popularity spread from universities into the public sector, and it began to leak into the private sector as well.

In the 1980s, a version of the software was moved to the personal computer. In 1992, Jack Noonan became CEO of SPSS, Inc. (replacing Nie) and a period of acquisition of smaller software companies began. Many of those products are still part of the SPSS family, such as IBM SPSS AMOS (for structural equation modeling) and IBM SPSS Modeler (originally called Clementine). In 2009, SPSS, Inc. was acquired by IBM, and the name of the product became IBM SPSS Statistics to differentiate it from the other products.

The official name of the software today is still IBM SPSS Statistics, and it's available in several formats and versions. We discuss these different options in Chapter 2.

REMEMBER

This book is not about the accuracy, correctness, or completeness of the input data. Your data is up to you. This book shows you how to take the numbers you already have, put them into SPSS, crunch them, and display the results in a way that makes sense. Gathering valid data and figuring out which cases to use is up to you.

WARNING

Your data is your most valuable possession. If you're the only one in the world with your data, be sure to back it up before you start working with it. Make sure you have multiple copies, ideally with one copy in the cloud. At key milestones in your analysis and data modifications, remember to save it again. The last thing you want is to lose your data.

Talking to SPSS: Can You Hear Me Now?

More than one way exists for you to command SPSS to do your bidding. You can use any of three approaches to perform any of the SPSS functions, and we cover them all in this section. The method you should choose depends not only on which interface you prefer, but also (to an extent) on the task you want performed.

The graphical user interface

SPSS has a window interface. You can issue commands by using the mouse to make menu selections that cause dialog boxes to appear. This is a fill-in-the-blanks approach to statistical analysis that guides you through the process of making choices and selecting values. The advantage of the graphical user interface (GUI) approach is that, at each step, SPSS makes sure you enter everything necessary before you can proceed to the next step. This interface is preferred for those just starting out — and if you don't go into depth with SPSS, this may be the only interface you ever use.

Syntax

Syntax is the internal language used to command actions from SPSS. It's the command syntax of SPSS (hence, its name). Syntax is often referred to as the "command language." You can use the Syntax command language to enter instructions into SPSS and have it do anything it's capable of doing. In fact, when you select from menus and dialog boxes to command SPSS, you're actually generating Syntax commands internally that do your bidding. In other words, the GUI is nothing more than the front end of a Syntax command-writing utility.

Writing (and saving) command-language programs is a good way to create processes that you expect to repeat. You can even grab a copy of the Syntax commands generated from the menu and save them to be repeated later.

Programmability

Programmability refers to the myriad ways of customizing SPSS with extensions. These *extensions* are new capabilities that the user community adds to SPSS using the programming languages Python and R. Learning to write these powerful new features is beyond the scope of this book, but you should know that they exist. (SPSS has an entire menu called Extensions.) When you allow SPSS to do so, a number of these extensions are installed during installation.

How SPSS works

The developers of SPSS have made every effort to make the software easy to use. SPSS prevents you from making mistakes or even forgetting something. That's not to say it's impossible to do something wrong in SPSS, but SPSS software works hard to keep you from running into the ditch. To foul things up, you almost have to work at figuring out a way of doing something wrong.

You always begin by defining a set of *variables*; then you enter data for the variables to create a number of *cases*. For example, if you're doing an analysis of automobiles, each car in your study would be a case. The variables that define the cases could be things such as the year of manufacture, horsepower, and cubic inches of displacement. Each car in the study is defined as a single case, and each case is defined as a set of values assigned to the collection of variables. Every case has a value for each variable. (Well, you *can* have a missing value, but that's a special situation described later.)

There are different types of variables. These types describe how the data is *stored* — for example, as letters (strings), as numbers, as dates, or as currency (see Chapter 4 for more information on data types). Each variable is defined as containing a certain kind of number, so you also have to define the variable's level of measurement. For example, a *scale* variable is a numeric measurement, such as weight or miles per gallon. A *categorical* variable contains values that define a category; for example, a variable named gender could be a categorical variable defined to contain only values 1 for female and 2 for male. Things that make sense for one type of variable don't necessarily make sense for another. For example, it makes sense to calculate the average miles per gallon, but not the average gender.

After your data is entered into SPSS — your cases are all defined by values stored in the variables — you can easily run an analysis. You've already finished the hard part. Running an analysis on the data is simple compared to entering the data. To run an analysis, you select the analysis you want to run from the menu, select the appropriate variables, and click OK. SPSS reads through all your cases, performs the analysis, and presents you with the output as tables or graphs. Of course, you have to know which analysis to choose. For that information, see Parts 5 and 6.

You can instruct SPSS to draw graphs and charts directly from your data the same way you instruct it to do an analysis. You select the desired graph from the menu, assign variables to it, and click OK.

TIP

When you're preparing SPSS to run an analysis or draw a graph, the OK button is unavailable until you've made all the choices necessary to produce output. Not only does SPSS require that you select a sufficient number of variables to produce output, but it also requires you to choose the right kinds of variables. If a categorical variable is required for a certain slot, SPSS won't allow you to choose any other kind of variable. Whether the output makes sense is up to you and your data, but SPSS makes sure that the choices you make can be used to produce some kind of result.

NUMBERS NOT WORDS

SPSS works best with numbers. Whenever possible, try to have your SPSS data in the form of numbers. If you give SPSS names and descriptions, it'll seem like they're being processed by SPSS, but that's because each name has been assigned a number. (Sneaky.) That's why survey questions are written like this:

- How do you feel about rhubarb? Select one answer:
  - A. I love it!
  - B. It's okay.
  - C. I can take it or leave it.
  - D. I don't care for it.
  - E. I hate it!

A number is assigned to each of the possible answers, and these numbers are fed through the statistical process. SPSS uses the numbers — not the words — so be careful about keeping all your words and numbers straight. We cover this subject in some detail in Chapter 4.

Remember: Keep accurate records describing your data, how you got the data, and what it means. SPSS can do all the calculations for you, but only you can decipher what it means. In *The Hitchhiker's Guide to the Galaxy,* a computer the size of a planet crunched on a problem for generations and finally came out with the answer, 42. But the people tending the machine had no idea what the answer meant because they didn't remember the question. They hadn't kept track of their input. You must keep careful track of your data or you may later discover, for example, that what you've interpreted to be a simple increase is actually an increase in your rate of decrease. Oops!

All output from SPSS goes to the same place — a window named SPSS Statistics Viewer. This window displays the results of whatever you've done. After you've produced output, if you perform some action that produces more output, the new output is displayed in the same window. And almost anything you do produces output. Of course, you need to know how to interpret the output — SPSS will help you, and so does this book.

Getting Help When You Need It

You're not alone. Some immediate help comes directly from the SPSS software package. More help can be found online. If you find yourself stumped, you can look for help in several places:

>> **Topics:** Choosing Help ⇨ Topics from the main window of the SPSS application is your gateway to immediate help. The help is somewhat terse, but it usually provides exactly the information you need. The information is in one large Help document, presented one page at a time. Choose Contents to select a heading from an extensive table of contents, choose Index to search for a heading by entering its name, or choose Search to enter a search string inside the body of the Help text.

TIP

In the Help directory, the titles in all uppercase are descriptions of Syntax language commands.

>> **SPSS Support:** Choose Help ⇨ Support to open a browser window for the support page at IBM. This area is primarily to report potential bugs or to check

if anyone else has encountered the same bug. It's not the best option if you're struggling with a task on the first try.

>> **SPSS Support Forums:** Choose Help ⇨ SPSS Forums to open a browser showing the various support forums. IBM is putting a lot of resources into SPSS communities, which might have more activity over time than these forums.

>> **PDF Documentation:** Choose Help ⇨ Documentation in PDF Format if you want to access the many user's guides for SPSS. This resource is online, but you can download them all to a folder on your machine if you want offline access to them.

>> **Command Syntax Reference:** Choose Help ⇨ Command Syntax Reference to display more than 2,000 pages of references to the Syntax language in your PDF viewer. The regular help topics, mentioned previously, provide a brief overview of each topic, but this document is more detailed.

>> **Compatibility Report Tool:** Choose Help ⇨ Compatibility Report Tool to answer a series of queries online to determine the compatibility of your software and hardware. If you're having trouble getting SPSS to install, access this information at www.ibm.com/software/reports/compatibility/clarity/index.html.

>> **SPSS Statistics Community:** Choose Help ⇨ IBM SPSS Predictive Analytics Community to visit a huge collection of IBM blogs and forums for every need. It will take a little time to get registered and settled in, but it's designed to be your free, go-to resource for the latest news and a chance to interact with other users. Be sure to sign up for the SPSS Stats group, in the IBM Data Science community. Hundreds of thousands of people are in this community, so it should be your first stop, before the support forums.

Chapter **2**

Finding the Best SPSS for You

In this chapter, we discuss the surprising variety of options in acquiring your own copy of SPSS, with a focus on the different ways of licensing SPSS. If you have your own copy of SPSS or have access to it through work or school, you may safely skip this chapter. However, if you either need to secure a copy or simply want to better understand what's out there, this chapter will help you find the best version of SPSS for you. Licensing is not the only choice, but it is the first big choice you have to make.

Four licensing options are available:

» Free trial

» Campus editions

» Subscription plan

» Commercial editions

Let's get the easiest choice out of the way first. If you want a way to practice the exercises in this book and you haven't had a trial version of SPSS within the last year, you'll want to start with the free trial. The rules of the trial differ from year to year, but typically the length of the trial is either 14 days or 30 days. The only other choice you'll have to make is the operating system: Windows or Mac.

TECHNICAL STUFF

There is also a server version of SPSS which gives you a third operating system option: Linux. Also, there are both 32-bit and 64 bit-versions. IBM provides good documentation for system compatibility issues on its website.

The free trial is always the subscription version of SPSS and always has all the add-on modules. We have more to say about add-on modules in this chapter and in Chapter 29, which has a detailed list of the add-on modules. One more warning about the free trial: The subscription version, while fully downloaded to your machine, needs to maintain access to the Internet. So SPSS may give you trouble if you are consistently offline.

TIP

Because the free trial includes access to all add-on modules, make sure to take them out for a spin. At some point, the decision to include a module might add hundreds of dollars to your investment, so familiarize yourself with the modules while you can.

In the rest of the chapter, we describe the other three licensing options and the additional choices you have to make. Here is a quick summary of how to choose among them after you've exhausted your access to a free trial:

>> Campus editions with their academic pricing are always the most cost-effective option, but you must be eligible to purchase them.

>> The subscription plans allows you to change your mind from month to month, which is handy if your needs might change.

>> Consider commercial plans with their term or perpetual license if you're prepared to commit to SPSS for multiple years, without version updates.

These options are also summarized in Figure 2-1.

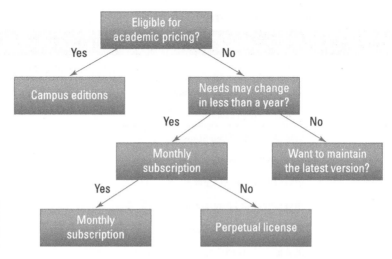

FIGURE 2-1:
Choosing an SPSS
Statistics licensing
option.

Campus Editions

IBM's campus editions are an order of magnitude cheaper than any other option. If you're eligible for this option, you should absolutely pursue it. You must have an academic affiliation as an instructor or a student. Some academic researchers may also qualify.

IBM does not sell this option directly. Often referred to as a GradPack or a Faculty Pack, you must purchase it through a third-party vendor. The vendors aren't difficult to find on the Internet. In addition, IBM lists some partner companies at www.ibm.com/us-en/marketplace/spss-statistics-gradpack/details.

Naturally, you'll want to first double-check to see if you have free university access as a student or faculty member through a campus-wide license. If you don't have access, you'll have to decide whether to buy the base, standard, or premium edition. We list the add-on modules in each edition in Table 2-1. You may be able to find terms that extend longer than 12 months in some cases.

TIP

Our advice is to buy the feature-rich premium edition and for the longest possible term. The equivalent of the premium campus edition would cost thousands of dollars per year with any other licensing arrangement. This your chance to try the add-on modules at a much reduced cost to determine which ones you find useful. In particular, we think that the Custom Tables module is useful to everyone who uses SPSS. The academic pricing option is so much lower that it may even be cost-effective to take a university course to both sharpen your skills and get access to academic pricing.

TABLE 2-1   **Campus Editions and Terms**

Edition	Add-On Modules	Terms
Base	None	6 or 12 months
Standard	IBM SPSS Advanced Statistics	6 or 12 months
	IBM SPSS Regression	
Premium	IBM SPSS Advanced Statistics	12 months
	IBM SPSS Regression	
	IBM SPSS Custom Tables	
	IBM SPSS Data Preparation	
	IBM SPSS Missing Values	
	IBM SPSS Forecasting	
	IBM SPSS Decision Trees	
	IBM SPSS Direct Marketing	
	IBM SPSS Complex Sampling	
	IBM SPSS Conjoint	
	IBM SPSS Neural Networks	
	IBM SPSS Bootstrapping	
	IBM SPSS Categories	
	IBM SPSS Exact Tests	

TIP

If you see a listing for the AMOS campus edition, realize that IBM SPSS AMOS is not an add-on module. It's stand-alone software for performing Structural Equation Modeling.

Subscription Plans

When purchasing a monthly subscription, you don't have to worry about the version number. For example, while writing this book, we used an offline desktop term license with version number 27, but the subscription has no such version number. Because you're paying each month, you simply download updates on an ongoing basis. Clearly a major advantage of a subscription is that the software is always up to date.

Although the subscription option requires that you download the software to your machine, the licensing requires access to the Internet. If you use this version of SPSS offline, it may stop working because it has to periodically check the license.

TIP

Periodically visit the Help menu and click Check for Updates. You've paid for the updates, so be sure to download them.

TIP

With a subscription plan, IBM makes it fairly easy to add and drop modules. For example, you could purchase an add-on module for a special project for as short a time as one month and then drop the module the next month.

TIP

IBM sometimes offers an annual payment of your monthly subscription in exchange for a discount. But even if you pay annually, it's still the subscription version — not the perpetual or term versions, which we describe in the next section.

The subscription also has some bundled options with increasing access to add-on modules. Watch out, however. Unlike the trial license or the academic pricing, the add-on modules can double or triple your monthly investment. If you haven't familiarized yourself with the modules it will be tough to decide what you need from the names alone. Chapter 28 will help as it describes each of the modules, and what they are useful for. You could also consider getting the full version for one month as long as you can commit to spending some time during that month trying them.

WARNING

Be careful. IBM has given the upgraded subscription options nicknames such as *Custom tables and Adv. Stats* on its website, but don't take these nicknames literally because they don't refer to every add-on module included in the option. Refer to Table 2-2 for a listing of the add-on modules included in each option.

TABLE 2-2   ## Subscription Plans

Subscription Pricing Option	Add-On Modules Included
Base	SPSS Statistics Base
	Data Preparation
	Bootstrapping
Custom tables and Adv. Stats	All modules in the base edition
	Advanced Statistics
	Regression
	Custom Tables

(continued)

TABLE 2-2 *(continued)*

Subscription Pricing Option	Add-On Modules Included
Forecasting and Decision Trees	All modules in the Custom tables and Adv. Stats edition
	Forecasting
	Decision Trees
	Direct Marketing
	Neural Networks
Complex sampling and testing	All modules in the Forecasting and Decision Trees edition
	Missing Values
	Neural Networks
	Categories
	Complex Samples
	Conjoint
	Exact Tests

Commercial Editions

Commercial editions offer two license options that are more traditional: a term license, where you purchase SPSS for a year, and a perpetual license, where you are an owner, not a renter, of SPSS, which has both advantages and disadvantages. For these styles of license, you need to contact IBM and speak to a representative, who will be able to give you a license code. Although you need to be online to process the license code, you don't need to be online when you're using SPSS.

Approximately once each year, SPSS offers a new updated version and assigns a version number. During the writing of this book, the authors used version 27 (which is just a bit lower than the number of years since SPSS has been available on personal computers). A number of members of the SPSS community opt to skip a version from time to time, or lag behind the latest version. If you do so strategically, it might represent a cost savings. This strategy requires that you make a substantial upfront investment and go awhile without an update. If the notion of missing out on updates and new features is unappealing, a monthly subscription might be the best option for you.

You also have to decide which add-on modules you need. The add-on modules substantially increase the cost of your term or perpetual license, much like the subscription option. You might want to keep Chapter 28 handy during a call to a sales representative because he or she will ask you which modules you need. Table 2-3 shows the add-on modules associated with the four editions of the perpetual and term licenses.

Note when comparing Tables 2-2 and 2-3 that the bundles in the subscription plans are different than those in the commercial editions.

TABLE 2-3   **Commercial Editions**

Edition	Add-On Modules Included
Base	SPSS Statistics base only
Standard	All modules in the base edition
	Advanced Statistics
	Regression
	Custom Tables
Professional	All modules in the standard edition
	Data preparation
	Missing Values
	Forecasting
	Categories
	Decision Trees
Premium	All modules in the professional edition
	Direct Marketing
	Complex Samples
	Conjoint
	Neural Networks
	Bootstrapping
	Exact Tests

TIP

Most introductory SPSS books, including this one, don't provide examples using the add-on modules. Introductory books must assume that you have access only to SPSS base. However, there are books that cover add-on modules. For example, in the book *SPSS Statistics for Data Analysis and Visualization* (Wiley), we dedicate hundreds of pages to several add-on modules. In fact, the inspiration for writing the book was to provide some badly needed coverage of the modules.

What's New in Version 27

Hot off the press! SPSS version 27 has just been released! This new edition features statistical enhancements for quantile regression, effect sizes, and MATRIX commands and two new statistical procedures: power analysis and Cohen's weighted Kappa, as well as various productivity and usability enhancements. Most relevant to this chapter are the licensing changes. Starting in version 27, the Custom Tables module is part of the standard edition and the Bootstrapping and Data Preparation modules are part of the base edition.

Chapter 3

Getting to Know SPSS by Running a Simple Session

This chapter introduces the SPSS environment and demonstrates a typical session. You use SPSS to read a previously defined SPSS data file, manipulate data, and then produce a simple statistical summary and chart. You also learn the roles of the primary windows in SPSS. More detailed instruction about many of the topics in this chapter follow in later chapters. Here, a basic framework is given for understanding and using SPSS.

Opening a Dataset

In this example, you start SPSS and then open up the bankloan.sav data file. We also briefly discuss the SPSS graphic user interface.

To begin, follow these steps:

1. **Choose Start ➪ All Programs ➪ IBM SPSS Statistics ➪ SPSS Statistics 27.**

   The SPSS Welcome dialog shown in Figure 3-1 appears. This is where you can see what's new in the software, provide user feedback, and navigate to data files. You'll open one of the sample SPSS data files.

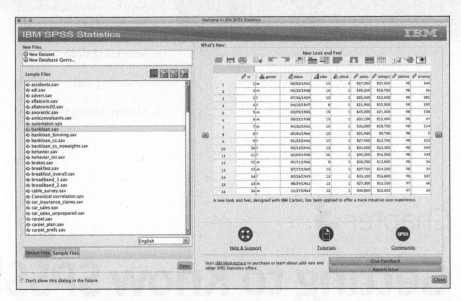

FIGURE 3-1:
The SPSS
Welcome dialog.

2. **Click the Sample Files tab in the lower-left corner of the dialog.**

3. **Select the bankloan.sav data file and then click Open.**

The bankloan dataset consists of 12 variables and 850 cases. Figure 3-2 shows the first few lines of the dataset. Note the structure of the data. Respondents who participated in the research make up the rows, and information about the respondents such as age and income constitute the columns. Typically, SPSS uses not *rows* and *columns* for the data, but *cases* and *variables*, respectively. *Cases* represent the units of analysis, and *variables* represent the items that have been measured.

FIGURE 3-2:
The bankloan
dataset.

In SPSS, the Data Editor window makes up only one of the three main windows in the program. The others follow:

>> **Data Editor:** Contains the data to be analyzed

>> **Output Viewer:** Displays the results of an analysis or graph

>> **Syntax Editor:** Contains the code used to modify or create variables, as well as the commands to run analyses or graphs

In this chapter, you spend most of your time working with the Data Editor and Output Viewer windows. Chapters 26 and 27 cover the Syntax Editor window in detail.

The Data Editor window is comprised of two views:

>> **Data view:** Displays data with cases in rows and variables in columns

>> **Variable view:** Displays detailed variable information, with variables represented in rows and variable attributes represented in columns

The data view of the Data Editor window has various menus:

>> **File:** Opens various types of files

>> **Edit:** Performs the standard cut, copy, and paste Windows functions

>> **View:** Changes fonts and gridlines

>> **Data:** Performs data manipulations that modify the number of cases

>> **Transform:** Performs data manipulations that modify the number of variables

>> **Analyze:** Runs reports and statistical tests

>> **Graphs:** Creates charts

>> **Utilities:** Improves efficiency

>> **Extensions:** Allows for SPSS to be used with programming languages

>> **Window:** Toggles between windows

>> **Help:** Provides assistance

Running an Analysis

After you bring data into SPSS, the next step is to select a procedure. The Analyze menu contains a list of reporting and statistical analysis categories. Most of the categories are followed by an arrow, which indicates that several analytical procedures are available in the category; these appear on a submenu when the category is selected. To select a procedure, choose Analyze, an analysis category, and then the procedure. The procedure dialog will open.

Most data files contain many variables and it's not always easy to remember the properties of each one. You may want to produce documentation, often referred to as a *codebook*, listing all the information about the variables in the data. SPSS provides the Codebook procedure for viewing variable attributes and reporting summary descriptive tables for each variable.

To create a Codebook, choose Analyze ⇨ Reports ⇨ Codebook, as shown in Figure 3-3.

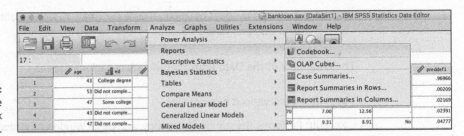

FIGURE 3-3:
Choosing the
Codebook
procedure.

Figure 3-4 shows the Codebook dialog. You'll need to select the variables of interest and then run the analysis from the procedure dialog. Most procedure dialogs have the same basic components and contain a number of common features.

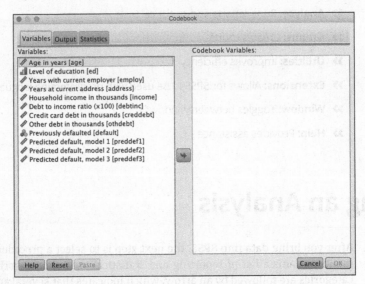

FIGURE 3-4:
The Codebook
dialog.

Each procedure dialog contains the following components:

>> **Source variables** are variables available for the procedure.

>> **Target variables** are variables used in the procedure. You'll need to move the source variable(s) to the target variables box.

>> **Control buttons** run, reset, or cancel the procedure.

>> **Dialog tabs or buttons** control optional specifications.

In the source and target variable lists, the variable label is shown, followed by the variable name in square brackets. If a variable doesn't have a label, only the variable name appears.

TIP

You can resize any SPSS dialog. If you make it larger, it's easier to see the variable list. In addition, right-click any variable in the source list to display a description of that variable. And if you are having trouble finding a variable in the source list, in most dialogs, you can type the first letter of the label to display matching variable labels. Repeatedly typing the letter will allow you to move through the list to each variable label beginning with that letter. If you're a fast typist, you can include multiple letters to better narrow your search for variables.

REMEMBER

The icons displayed next to variables in the dialog provide information about the variable type and measurement level. See the Chapter 4 for details.

Because SPSS procedures provide a great deal of flexibility, the dialog often can't display all possible choices. The main dialog contains the minimum information required to run the procedure. You can make additional optional specifications in subdialogs. The subdialogs are accessed from the buttons located on the right side of the main dialog or tabs at the top of the dialog.

TECHNICAL
STUFF

The name of a subdialog is often similar to the name of the equivalent subcommands in SPSS Syntax. SPSS Syntax is discussed in Chapters 26 and 27.

Instead of an OK button, subdialogs have a Continue button, to return to the main dialog. The control buttons that appear along the bottom of the dialog instruct SPSS to perform an action:

>> **OK** runs the procedure. The OK button is disabled (appears dimmed) until the minimum dialog requirements are completed.

>> **Reset** resets all specifications made in the dialog and associated subdialogs and keeps the dialog open.

>> **Cancel** cancels the selections and closes the dialog without running the procedure.

>> **Help** opens the SPSS Help facility with help relevant to the current dialog.

>> **Paste** pastes SPSS syntax for commands into the Syntax Editor window.

In the Codebook procedure, you'll need to select the variables to display. You can run the codebook on selected variables or on all variables in the file.

1. **In the Variables box, click the first variable, hold down the shift key, and click the last variable.**

2. **Click the arrow to move all the variables to the Codebook Variables box, as shown in Figure 3-5.**

3. **Click OK to run the analysis.**

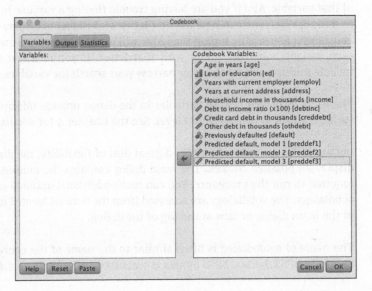

FIGURE 3-5: The completed Codebook dialog.

After you move the variables (Step 2), you can make selections on the Output and Statistics tabs. Optionally on the Output tab, you can select variable attributes to display in each table and the order of the tables. By default, all variable attributes are displayed and the tables are in the order shown in the Codebook Variables list. On the Statistics tab, you can select statistics to display in the tables. By default, counts and percents are displayed for variables defined as nominal or ordinal measurement level. For scale variables, the mean, standard deviation, and quartiles are displayed.

Interpreting Results

When a procedure has been run, the results are displayed in the Output Viewer window. The Viewer window has two sections, or panes: the outline pane and the contents pane. The outline pane, on the left side, contains an outline or list of all items displayed in the contents pane, on the right side. You can quickly go to any table or chart in the Viewer by selecting it in the outline pane. Let's examine some results.

The Codebook procedure uses the measurement level defined for each variable to determine the summary statistics produced in the table. Be sure that the appropriate measurement attribute has been defined for each variable before running Codebook. A table is displayed for each selected variable. Counts and percentages are displayed for variables of nominal or ordinal measurement level; means, standard deviations, and quartiles are displayed for scale variables.

Figure 3-6 shows a codebook table for the education variable, which is defined as an ordinal variable, and a table for the age variable, which is defined as a scale variable. Summary statistics appropriate for the measurement level are displayed in each table and the set of tables document the variable information associated with each variable, as well as a summary of the data values for each variable.

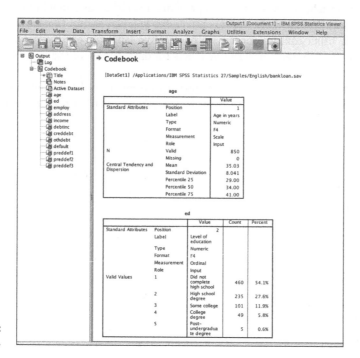

FIGURE 3-6:
Codebook output.

Now go back to the Data Editor window by clicking the Window menu and selecting bankloan.sav, as shown in Figure 3-7, or by clicking the star icon (shown in the margin).

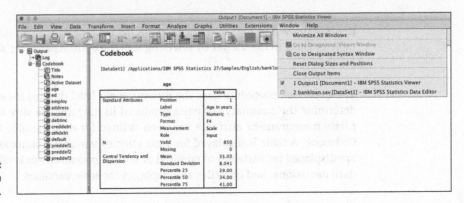

Previously, we mentioned that the Data Editor window has two views. Let's take a look at variable view, where metadata is controlled. Click the Variable View tab, which is in the lower-left corner of the Data Editor window.

In variable view, each row represents a variable, as show in Figure 3-8. The columns represent the various attributes you can assign to a variable. For example, the Label column contains a descriptive label for each variable, and the Values column contains descriptive labels for data values for the variable.

Although many of these attributes are optional, you'll no doubt find many of them useful. In Chapter 4, we describe the variable attributes and how to assign them.

Creating Graphs

Now that you've run an analysis, it's time to create a graph. To create a graph, follow these steps:

1. Choose Graphs ⇨ Chart Builder.

As shown in Figure 3-9, a warning appears, informing you that before you use this dialog, the measurement level should be set properly for each variable in your chart. We set the correct measurement level for the variables (nominal for the `default` variable, ordinal for the `ed` variable, and scale for the `income` variable), so you can proceed.

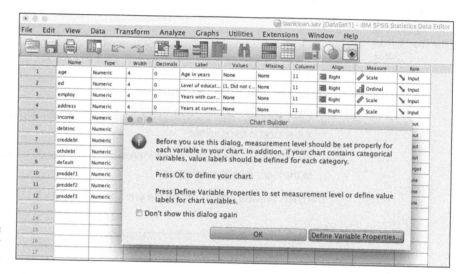

FIGURE 3-9:
A Chart Builder warning.

2. Click OK.

Figure 3-10 shows the Chart Builder dialog. For this example, you'll build a prefabricated graph. We have more to say about building graphs in Chapters 12 and 13.

3. Make sure the Gallery tab is selected.

4. In the Choose From list, select Bar as the graph type.

Various types of bar charts appear in the gallery to the right of the list.

5. Choose the first bar graph (Simple bar) and drag it to the large chart preview panel at the top.

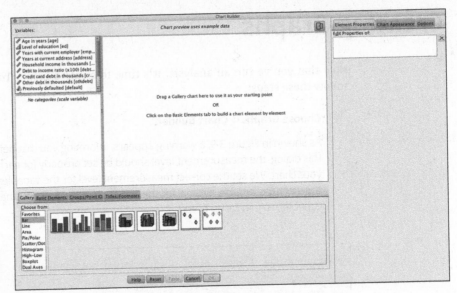

FIGURE 3-10:
The Chart Builder
dialog.

6. **In the Variables list in Chart Builder:**

   a. Select the Previously defaulted (default) variable and drag it to the
   X-Axis label in the diagram.

   b. Select the Household income in thousands (income) variable and drag it
   to the Y-Axis label in the diagram.

   The chart preview now looks like the one shown in Figure 3-11.

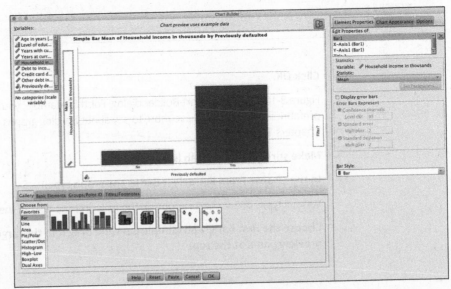

FIGURE 3-11:
The chart preview
after assigning
the x- and y-axes.

WARNING

The graphic display in the Chart Builder preview window *never* represents your actual data, even after you insert variable names. This preview window simply displays a diagram that demonstrates the composition and appearance of the graph that will be produced.

7. **Click the OK button to produce the graph.**

The SPSS Viewer window appears, containing the graph shown in Figure 3-12. This graph is based on the actual data. It shows the average household income for those who had and had not previously defaulted on a loan.

FIGURE 3-12:
Household
income by
previous loan
defaults.

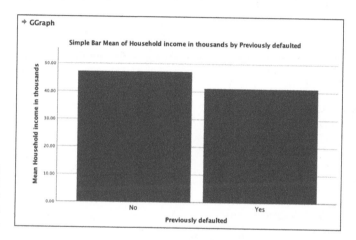

Now suppose that you want to add another variable to the graph. Do the following:

1. **Choose Graphs ⇨ Chart Builder.**

2. **Click OK.**

3. **Because you generated a graph previously, click the Reset button to clear the Chart Builder display.**

4. **Make sure the Gallery tab is selected. In the Choose From list, select Bar as the graph type.**

5. **Choose the second bar graph (Clustered bar) and drag it to the large chart preview panel at the top.**

6. In the Variables list in Chart Builder:

a. Select the Previously defaulted (default) variable and drag it to the X-Axis label in the diagram.

b. Select the Household income in thousands (income) variable and drag it to the Y-Axis label in the diagram.

c. Select the Level of education (ed) variable and drag it to the Cluster on X: set color box.

The chart preview now looks like the one shown in Figure 3-13.

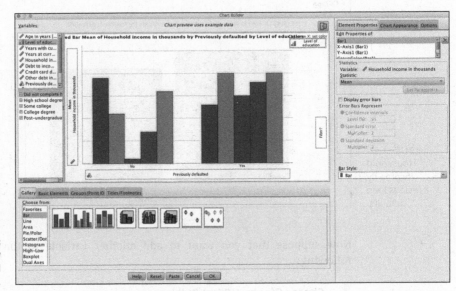

FIGURE 3-13: The chart preview for a clustered bar chart.

FIGURE 3-13:
The chart preview for a clustered bar chart.

7. Click the OK button to produce the graph.

Figure 3-14 is showing interesting results. It seems that people who have not previously defaulted on a loan and have more than a college degree have household incomes that are about twice as large as the household incomes of those with less education.

This result seems worthy of additional investigation. Let's go to the Data Editor window to get a better view of the data.

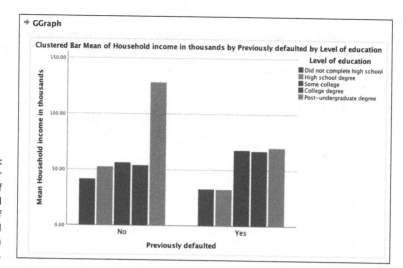

FIGURE 3-14:
A clustered bar chart of household income by level of education and previous loan defaults.

Investigating Data

You can change the order of your cases (rows) in just about any way you want. In the next example, you simply sort cases directly in Data Editor based on the income variable. We go into much more detail on ordering data in Chapter 8.

To begin, click the Window menu and select bankloan.sav. Then, to sort cases, right-click the income variable in the Data Editor window and choose Sort Descending, as shown in Figure 3-15.

FIGURE 3-15:
Right-click options in the Data Editor window.

Figure 3-16 shows the data sorted in descending order based on the income variable. Interestingly, several individuals with very high household incomes do not have a high school degree and some of these people (rows 2 and 4) also have missing data for the `default` variable. Might there be a pattern with the missing data? That would be problematic because statistical analyses assume that data is missing randomly.

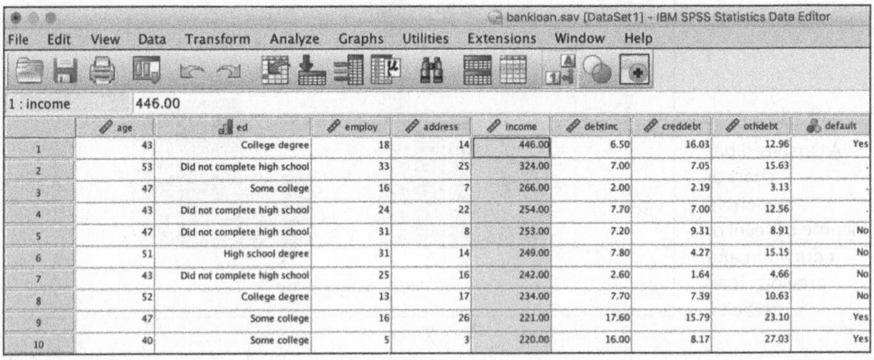

	age	ed	employ	address	income	debtinc	creddebt	othdebt	default
1	43	College degree	18	14	446.00	6.50	16.03	12.96	Yes
2	53	Did not complete high school	33	25	324.00	7.00	7.05	15.63	.
3	47	Some college	16	7	266.00	2.00	2.19	3.13	.
4	43	Did not complete high school	24	22	254.00	7.70	7.00	12.56	.
5	47	Did not complete high school	31	8	253.00	7.20	9.31	8.91	No
6	51	High school degree	31	14	249.00	7.80	4.27	15.15	No
7	43	Did not complete high school	25	16	242.00	2.60	1.64	4.66	No
8	52	College degree	13	17	234.00	7.70	7.39	10.63	No
9	47	Some college	16	26	221.00	17.60	15.79	23.10	Yes
10	40	Some college	5	3	220.00	16.00	8.17	27.03	Yes

FIGURE 3-16: Data sorted in descending order based on income.

It can be useful to know what type of missing data you have. SPSS allows for two types of missing data:

- **System missing:** If no value is present for a numeric variable, it's assigned the system-missing value, which is indicated by a period in the data view of Data Editor.
- **User missing:** Coded values are used to defined missing data. For example, a code of 99 might mean *Not Applicable* for a variable.

We discuss missing data further in Chapter 4. For now, take a closer look at how missing data might affect data interpretation. For this example, you use the Crosstabs procedure. To perform a crosstabulation between two variables, do the following:

1. **Choose Analyze ⇨ Descriptive Statistics ⇨ Crosstabs.**

   The Crosstabs dialog appears. Chapter 17 describes the options of this procedure in detail. For now, you will use crosstabs only to investigate the relationship between `Level of education (ed)` and `Previously defaulted (default)`.

2. **Select the `Level of education (ed)` variable and place it in the Row(s) box.**
3. **Select the `Previously defaulted (default)` variable and place it in the Column(s) box, as shown in Figure 3-17.**
4. **Click OK.**

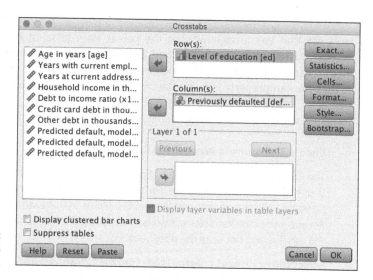

FIGURE 3-17:
The Crosstabs
dialog.

The Case Processing Summary table shown in Figure 3-18 displays the number of valid and missing cases for the variables requested in the crosstabulation. Only valid cases are displayed in the crosstabulation table. Note that the dataset has 850 cases, but only 700 cases have complete data and are therefore the only ones used in the crosstabulation table. If the amount of missing data is substantial, as in this situation where almost 18 percent of cases are missing from an analysis, you may want to question why the data is missing and how your analysis will be affected.

➡ Crosstabs

Case Processing Summary

	Cases					
	Valid		Missing		Total	
	N	Percent	N	Percent	N	Percent
Level of education * Previously defaulted	700	82.4%	150	17.6%	850	100.0%

Level of education * Previously defaulted Crosstabulation

Count

		Previously defaulted		Total
		No	Yes	
Level of education	Did not complete high school	293	79	372
	High school degree	139	59	198
	Some college	57	30	87
	College degree	24	14	38
	Post-undergraduate degree	4	1	5
Total		517	183	700

FIGURE 3-18:
Crosstabulation
results.

Let's say that you discovered that the people with missing information on the default variable have new loans and therefore you can't know the outcome yet (with regard to defaulting). This information would allow you to recode your data so that you can properly identify the cases with missing data as new loans.

To recode the data, follow these steps:

1. **Choose Transform ⇨ Recode into Same Variables.**

   WARNING

   The Recode into Same Variables option does not allow you to make changes to your data if you make a mistake. For this reason, it's safer to use Recode into Different Variables as demonstrated in Chapter 8. In this example, you use the Recode into Same Variables option because you want to permanently change the variable and not keep the prior version.

2. **Select the Previously defaulted (default) variable and place it in the Numeric Variables box, as shown in Figure 3-19.**

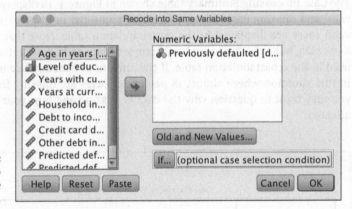

FIGURE 3-19:
The Recode into
Same Variable
dialog.

3. **Click the Old and New Values button.**

4. **In the Old Value box, select the System-Missing radio button.**

5. **In the New Value box, select the Value radio button and type -9.**

6. **Click the Add button, so that the system missing values will be recoded into -9, as shown in Figure 3-20.**

7. **Click Continue and then click OK to create the new recoded variable.**

Now that the default variable has been recoded, add the appropriate metadata, in this case a label for the value of -9, so you can better interpret the results of the prior analysis, that is, the crosstabulation. To define a label for a value, do the following:

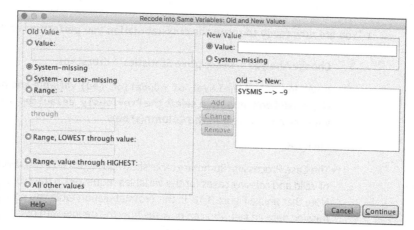

FIGURE 3-20:
The Old and New
Values dialog.

1. **Click the Variable View tab in the lower-left corner of the Data Editor window.**

2. **Click the Value box for the `default` variable (depending on where you click in the Value box, you might need to also click the . . .).**

3. **In the Value box type** -9.

4. **In the Label box, type** New Loan.

5. **Click the Add button.**

   The value and label appear in the large text block, as shown in Figure 3-21.

6. **To save the value labels and close the dialog, click OK.**

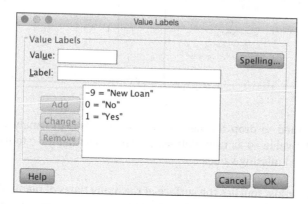

FIGURE 3-21:
The Value
Labels dialog.

You are now ready to rerun the crosstabulation you performed earlier. To do so:

1. **Choose Analyze ⇨ Descriptive Statistics ⇨ Crosstabs.**

2. **If needed, select the** Level of education (ed) **variable and move it in the Row(s) box, and then select the** Previously defaulted (default) **variable and move it in the Column(s) box.**

3. **Click OK.**

   The Case Processing Summary table shown in Figure 3-22 displays the number of valid and missing cases for the variables requested in the crosstabulation. Note that unlike Figure 3-18, in this crosstabulation table you no longer have missing data. In fact, you can now see how the people with new loans are distributed across education level.

➡ Crosstabs

Case Processing Summary

	Cases					
	Valid		Missing		Total	
	N	Percent	N	Percent	N	Percent
Level of education * Previously defaulted	850	100.0%	0	0.0%	850	100.0%

Level of education * Previously defaulted Crosstabulation

Count

		Previously defaulted			Total
		New Loan	No	Yes	
Level of education	Did not complete high school	88	293	79	460
	High school degree	37	139	59	235
	Some college	14	57	30	101
	College degree	11	24	14	49
	Post-undergraduate degree	0	4	1	5
Total		150	517	183	850

FIGURE 3-22: Crosstabulation results with the new loan category.

TIP

If you wanted to drop the new loan category from the analysis again, simply declare the value –9 as user-defined missing. See Chapter 4 to learn more about user-defined missing values.

This chapter just touches the surface of the many types of manipulations, graphs, and analyses you can perform in SPSS. Subsequent chapters go into much greater detail on a variety of SPSS topics.

2

Getting Data into and out of SPSS

Set up a new dataset like a pro.

Get data into SPSS.

Get results out of SPSS.

Master all the SPSS data types.

Chapter **4**

Understanding SPSS Data: Defining Metadata

To process your data, you have to get it into the computer, but that's not enough: You also have to declare metadata. *Metadata* are your variable attributes, and tell SPSS how variables are defined and can be used.

SPSS data has three major components: cases, variables, and metadata. When you receive data, you will rarely have a problem with the cases, occasionally have a problem with the variables, but almost always have a problem with the metadata. In this chapter, you focus on SPSS metadata. (In the next chapter, you see how to bring in cases. We start in this chapter by bringing in the metadata because it's something you always have to do.)

SPSS can read data from a variety of formats, including databases, text files, Microsoft Excel, and SAS. You can also type directly into SPSS — and, if you want, copy the data to places other than SPSS later.

In SPSS, data is organized as cases, and each case is made up of a collection of variables. First, you define the characteristics of the variables that make up a case, and then you enter the data into the variables that make up the contents of the cases. This chapter shows you how to work with this technique of getting data into your system.

Entering Variable Definitions on the Variable View Tab

To enter data into SPSS, use the Variable View tab, which is in the lower-left corner of the Data Editor window. As you can see in Figure 4-1, variable attributes (such as Name, Type, and Width) are defined at the top of the window. All you have to do is enter something in each column for each variable.

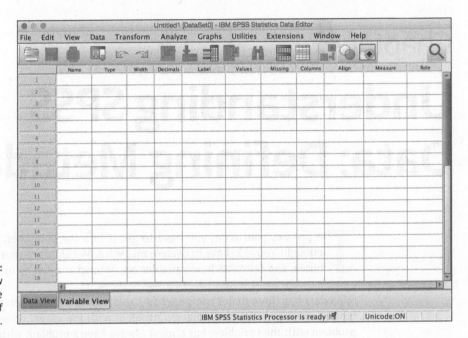

FIGURE 4-1: The Variable View tab defines the characteristics of variables.

The predefined set of 11 characteristics are the only ones needed to completely specify all the attributes of any variable. When you add a new variable, you'll find that reasonable defaults appear for most characteristics.

TECHNICAL STUFF

The Variable View tab is just for defining variables. The entry of the numbers comes later (see "Entering and Viewing Data Items on the Data View Tab," later in this chapter).

REMEMBER

Each variable characteristic has a default, so if you don't specify a characteristic, SPSS fills one in for you. However, what SPSS selects may not be what you want, so let's look at all the possibilities.

Name

The cell on the far left is where you enter the name of the variable. Just click the cell and type a short descriptor, such as **age**, **income**, **sex**, or **odor**. (A longer descriptor, called a *label*, comes later.) You can type longer names here, but you should keep them short because they'll be used in named lists and as identifier tags on the data graphs and such — where the format can be crowded. Names that are too long might garble or truncate the output from SPSS.

If the name you assigned to a variable turns out to be too long or is misspelled, you can always change it on the Variable View tab. One of the nice things about SPSS is that you can correct mistakes quickly.

TIP

Here are some handy hints about names:

>> **You can use characters in a name, such as @, #, and $, as well as the underscore character (_) and numbers.** But if you use these types of characters in a variable name, you may live to regret it. For example, you can't start variable names with these special characters. And in some advanced features, these characters denote special variables. An underscore in the middle of a name is a great way to make a name more readable, but otherwise, it's best to keep your names simple.

>> **Be sure to start every name with a letter, not a number.**

>> **You can't include spaces anywhere in a name, but an underscore is a good substitute.**

REMEMBER

If you want to export data to another application, make sure the names you use are in a form acceptable to that application. Watch out for special characters.

Spaces are not allowed in variable names!

WARNING

Type

Most data you enter will be just regular numbers. However, data such as currency must be displayed in a special format, and data such as dates require special procedures for calculation. For this type of data, you simply specify what type you have, and SPSS takes care of the details for you.

In this section, you look at all data types. (For advice about some special types, see Chapter 7.)

Click the cell in the Type column you want to fill in, and a button with three dots appears on its right. Click that button to display the Variable Type dialog, shown in Figure 4-2.

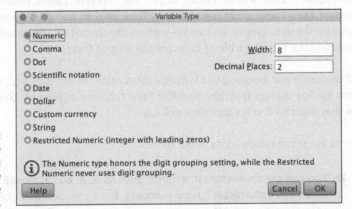

FIGURE 4-2:
The Variable Type
dialog allows you
to specify the
type of variable
you're defining.

You can choose from the following predefined types of variables:

>> **Numeric:** A numeric is a standard number in any recognizable form. The values are entered and displayed in the standard form, with or without decimal points. Values can be formatted in standard scientific notation, with an embedded *E* to represent the start of the exponent. The Width value is the total number of all characters in a number — including any positive or negative signs and the exponent indicator. The Decimal Places value specifies the number of digits displayed to the right of the decimal point, not including the exponent.

>> **Comma:** This type specifies numeric values with commas inserted between three-digit groups. The format includes a period as a decimal point. The Width value is the total width of the number, including all commas and the decimal point. The Decimal Places value specifies the number of digits to the right of the decimal point. You may enter data without the commas, but SPSS will insert them when it displays the value. Commas are never placed to the right of the decimal point.

>> **Dot:** This type is the same as the Comma option, except a period is used to group the digits into threes, and a comma is used for the decimal point.

>> **Scientific notation:** This option refers to a numeric variable that always includes *E* to designate the power-of-ten exponent. The *base* (the part of the number to the left of the *E*) may or may not contain a decimal point. The *exponent* (the part of the number to the right of the *E*, which also may or may not contain a decimal) indicates how many times 10 multiplies itself,

after which it's multiplied by the base to produce the number. You may enter D or E to mark the exponent, but SPSS always displays the number using E. For example, the number 5,286 can be written as 5.286E3 or 5.286D3. To represent a small number, the exponent can be negative. For example, the number 0.0005 can be written as 5E–4. This format is useful for very large or very small numbers.

» **Date:** This type represents a variable that can include the year, month, day, hour, minute, and second. When you select Date, the available format choices appear in a list on the right side of the dialog, as shown in Figure 4-3. Choose the format that best fits your data. Your selection determines how SPSS will format the contents of the variable for display. This format also determines, to some extent, the form in which you enter the data. You can enter the data using slashes, colons, spaces, or other characters. The rules are loose — if SPSS doesn't understand what you enter, it tells you, and you can reenter it another way. For example, if you select a format with a two-digit year, SPSS accepts and displays the year that way, but it will use four digits to perform calculations. The first two digits (the number of the century) will be selected according to the configuration you set by choosing Edit ⇨ Options and then clicking the Data tab.

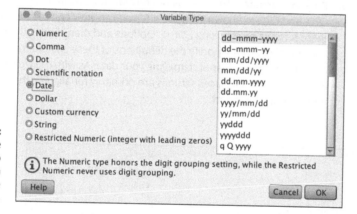

FIGURE 4-3: Selecting a date format also selects which items are included.

» **Dollar:** When you select the Dollar option, the available format choices appear in a list on the right side of the dialog (see Figure 4-4). Dollar values are always displayed with a leading dollar sign and a period for a decimal point; for large values, commas are included to collect the digits in groups of threes. You select the format and its Width and Decimal Places values. The format choices are similar, but it's important that you choose one that's compatible with your other dollar-variable definitions so they align when you print and display monetary values in output tables. The Width and Decimal Places settings help with vertical alignment in the output, no matter how many digits you include in the format itself. You can enter values without the dollar sign and the commas; SPSS inserts those for you.

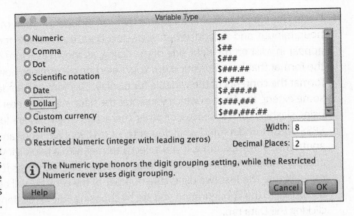

FIGURE 4-4:
The different dollar formats mostly specify the number of digits to be included.

>> **Custom currency:** The five custom formats for currency are CCA, CCB, CCC, CCD, and CCE, as shown in Figure 4-5. You can view and modify the details of these formats by choosing Edit ⇨ Options and then clicking the Currency tab. Fortunately, you can modify the definitions of these custom formats as often as you like without fear of damaging your data. As with the Dollar format, the Width and Decimal Places settings are primarily for aligning the data when you're printing a report.

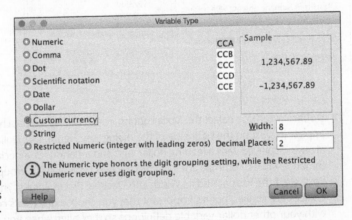

FIGURE 4-5:
Five custom currency formats are available.

>> **String:** This type is a freeform non-numeric item (see Figure 4-6). The only good time to use a string is when the data truly is a string, such as an address, a proper name, or a product code (SKU). Avoid using the string type when the data should be labeled numeric. Something such as favorite color, sex, or state should *not* be a string because it has a finite list of possibilities that are known in advance. (See the "Values" section later in this chapter.) SPSS allows a very large number for the size of the string — so large that you could fit a paragraph, which is exactly what you would do if you were doing text mining. Open-ended response items in a survey are an example of a string.

>> **Restricted Numeric:** A restricted numeric is perfect for numbers that sometimes have leading zeros, such as ZIP codes and Social Security numbers. These variables aren't really numbers because you don't perform arithmetic on them. Back in the day, this type of number had to be declared as a string.

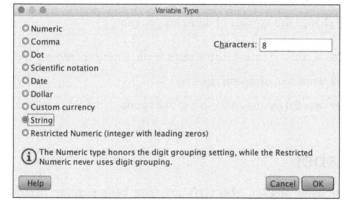

FIGURE 4-6: Strings are text such as addresses, names, and open-ended responses.

Width

The Width column in the definition of a variable determines the number of characters used to display the value. If the value to be displayed is not large enough to fill the space, the output will be padded with blanks. If it's larger than you specify, it will be reformatted to fit or asterisks will be displayed.

TIP

Certain type definitions allow you to set a Width option. The value you enter is the same as the one you enter in the Width column when you define the type. If you make a change to the value in one place, SPSS changes the value in the other place automatically. The two values are the same.

To change variable width, you can

>> Accept the default (or the number you entered previously under Type).

>> Enter a number and move on.

>> Use the up and down arrows that appear in the cell to select a numeric value.

Decimals

The Decimals column contains the number of digits that appear to the right of the decimal point when the value appears onscreen. You may have specified this value as the Decimal Places value when you defined the variable type. If you entered a number there, it appears in the Decimals column as the default. If you enter a number in the Decimals column, it changes the Decimal Places value. They're the same.

To change the number of decimals you can

>> Accept the default (or the number you entered previously under Type).

>> Enter a number and move on.

>> Use the up and down arrows that appear in the cell to select a numeric value.

Label

The name and the label serve the same basic purpose: They're descriptors that identify the variable. The difference is that the *name* is the short identifier and the *label* is the long one. You need one of each because some output formats work fine with a long identifier and other formats need the short form.

You can enter just about anything in the Label column. What you choose has to do with how you expect to use your data and what you want your output to look like. For example, the variable name might be *Address* and the longer label might be *Number of years living at current address.*

TIP

The length of the label isn't determined by a software requirement. However, output looks better if you use short names and somewhat longer labels. Variable names and labels should make sense standing alone. After you produce some output, you may find that your label is lousy for your purposes. That's okay; it's easy to change the label. Just pop back to the Variable View tab and make the change. The next time you produce output, the new label will be used.

You can also skip defining a label. If you don't have a label defined for a variable, SPSS will use the variable name you defined for everything.

Values

The Values column is where you assign labels to all possible values of a variable. If you select a cell in the Values column, a button with three dots appears. Click that button to display the dialog shown in Figure 4-7.

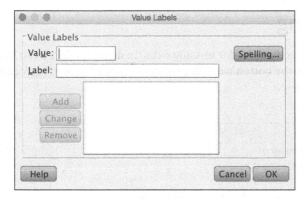

FIGURE 4-7:
You can assign a name to each possible value of a variable.

Normally, you make one entry for each possible value that a variable can assume. For example, for a variable named Sex you could assign the value 1 to the Male label and 2 assigned to the Female label. Or, for a variable named Committed, you could have 0 for No, 1 for Yes, and 2 for Undecided. If you define labels, your output can display labels instead of values.

To define a label for a value, do the following:

1. In the Value box, enter the value.

2. In the Label box, enter a label.

3. Click the Add button.

   The value and label appear in the large text block.

4. To change or remove a definition, simply select it in the text block, make your changes, and then click the Change button.

5. Repeat Steps 1–4 as needed.

6. To save the value labels and close the dialog, click OK.

You can always come back and change the definitions using the same process you used to enter them. The dialog will reappear, filled in with all the definitions; then you can update the list.

TECHNICAL STUFF

Sometime, you'll have a bunch of strings and not want to make them all values because you think it will be a lot of work. For example, suppose you have a college major variable. If you dread setting up 1 as Astrophysics, 2 as Biology, 3 as Chemistry, and so on, you can use a special dialog called Automatic Recode (under the Transform menu) to do the work for you.

Missing

You can specify codes for missing data. To do this, select a cell in the Missing column. Click the button with three dots to display the Missing Values dialog, shown in Figure 4-8.

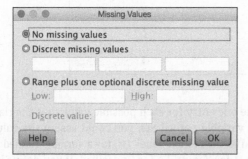

FIGURE 4-8:
You can specify what is entered for a missing value.

For example, suppose you're entering responses to questions, and one of the questions is, "How many cars do you own?" The normal answer to this question is a number, so you define the variable type as a number. If someone chooses to ignore this question, this variable won't have a value. However, you can specify a placeholder value. Perhaps 0 seems like a good choice for a placeholder here, but it's not because lots of people don't have cars. Instead, a less likely value, such as 99, is a better choice.

You can even specify unique values to represent different reasons for missing values. In the preceding example, you could define −99 as the value entered when the answer is "I don't remember," and −98 could be used when the answer is "None of your business." If you specify that a value is representing a missing value, that value is not included in general calculations. During your analysis, however, you can determine how many values are missing for each of the different reasons. You can specify up to three specific values (called *discrete values*) to represent missing data, or you can specify a range of numbers along with one discrete value, all to be considered missing. The only reason you would need to specify a range of values is if you have lots of reasons why data is missing and want to track them all.

TIP

One of the many reasons why you don't want to use the string type is because it is case sensitive. For example, suppose you have a Gender variable and values of Female and Male. But if you get entries such as m, M, and Male, and even crazy unexpected ones such as H and mail, these responses will all be considered separate categories. Do what all experienced users do: Use numeric codes with values!

Columns

The Columns attribute is where you specify the width of the column you'll use to enter the data. The folks at SPSS could have used the word *Width* to describe it, but they already used that term for the width of the data itself. A better name may have been the two words *Column Width*, but that would have been too long to display nicely in this window, so they just called it *Columns*. To specify the number of columns, select a cell and enter the number.

Align

The Align column determines the position of the data in its allocated space, whenever the data is displayed for input or output. The data can be left aligned, right aligned, or centered. You've defined the width of the data and the size of the column in which the data will be displayed; the alignment determines what happens to any space left over.

Aligning to the left means inserting all blanks on the right; aligning to the right inserts all the extra spaces on the left; centering the data splits the spaces evenly on each side.

Measure

Your value for the Measure attribute specifies the level of measurement of your variable. In Chapter 14, we discuss how level of measurement determines the kinds of summary statistics you can obtain. Following are the level of measurement options in SPSS:

>> **Nominal:** A value that specifies a category or type of thing. You can have 0 represent Disapprove and 1 represent Approve. Or you can use 1 to mean Female and 2 to mean Male.

>> **Ordinal:** A value that specifies the position (order) of something in a list. For example, *first, second,* and *third* are ordinal numbers.

>> Scale: A number that specifies a magnitude. The scale can be distance, weight, age, or a count of something.

Role

Some SPSS dialogs select variables according to the *role* of a variable, or how it will be used in an analysis. You don't need to worry about the Role column for now. Just note that it can be handy when you have some experience with SPSS and understand how defaults are chosen.

When you click a cell in the Role column, you can select one of six choices:

>> Input: An independent variable. This is the default role.

>> Target: A dependent variable.

>> Both: A variable used as both input and target.

>> None: A variable that does not have a role assignment.

>> Partition: A variable used to split data into separate samples for training, testing, and validation.

>> Split: A variable used to build separate models for each possible value of the variable. This capability should not be confused with file splitting (see Chapter 8).

TIP

You can use the Define Variable Properties procedure in the Data menu to specify the same variable attributes that can be defined in the Variable View window of Data Editor. It is typically faster to define variable properties in the Variable View window of Data Editor, but the Define Variable Properties procedure allows you to create syntax that can be saved, which allows you to reuse variable attribute definitions. Note that you can also reuse variable attribute specifications by using the Copy Data Properties procedure under the Data menu.

Entering and Viewing Data Items on the Data View Tab

After you've defined the variables, you can begin typing the data. Click the Data View tab of the Data Editor window. At the top of the columns, you see the variable names. Entering data into one of these cells is straightforward: You simply click the cell and start typing.

If something is already in a cell and you want to change it, you can. You can do all the normal mouse and keyboard stuff there, too. For example, use the Backspace key to erase characters, or select the entire value and type right over it.

If your data is already in a file, you may be able to avoid typing it in again by reading that file directly into SPSS. For more information, see Chapter 5.

REMEMBER

Entering data into SPSS is a two-step process. First, you define what sort of data you'll be entering, and then you enter the numbers. This process may sound time-consuming, but nifty software is available to help you.

WARNING

Don't take chances. As soon as you type a few values, save your data to a file by choosing File ⇨ Save As. Then continue saving your data by choosing File ⇨ Save throughout the data-entering process, in case your computer crashes unexpectedly.

Chapter **5**

Opening Data Files

You don't need to put your data into the computer more than once. If you have your data in another program, you can import it from there into SPSS — because every program worth using has some form of output that can serve as input to SPSS. This chapter discusses ways to transfer data into and out of SPSS.

REMEMBER

Sometimes you won't get variable names when you import data from other software, but you can fix that problem in variable view.

Getting Acquainted with the SPSS File Format

SPSS uses its own format, the .sav extension, for storing data and writing files. The file format contains special codes and usually can't be used to export your data to another application. Instead, the file format is used only for saving SPSS data that you want to read back into SPSS at a later time.

The tremendous advantage of using SPSS data format is that it contains not only the cases and variables but also the metadata. For every other type of file that you bring into the software, you'll need to go back to the variable view to set up the metadata, as explained in Chapter 4.

Several example files in this format are copied to your computer as part of the normal SPSS installation. These files are in the same directory as your SPSS installation. To load one of these files, choose File ➪ Open ➪ Data and select the file to be loaded. When you do so, the variable names and data are loaded into SPSS.

If you have data in SPSS, you can save it as a .sav file by choosing File ➪ Save As and providing a name for the file. Or if you've loaded the information from a file, or previously saved a copy of the information to a file, simply choose File ➪ Save to overwrite the previous file with a fresh copy of both variable definitions and data.

WARNING

It's easy to be fooled by the way the SPSS documentation uses the word *file*. If you've defined data and variables in your program, SPSS documentation often refers to it all as a file, even though it may never have been written to disk. SPSS also refers to the material written to disk as a file, so watch the context.

When you write your file to disk, if you don't add the .sav extension to the filename; SPSS adds it for you. When you choose File ➪ Open ➪ Data to display the list of files, you may not see the filename extension (depending on how your Windows system is configured), but it's there.

TIP

When you drag a data file to the SPSS Data Editor window, SPSS chooses the appropriate format and begins reading the data file.

Reading Simple Data from a Text File

This section contains an example of a procedure you can follow to read data from a simple text file into SPSS. The example reads this text file and inserts it into the cells of SPSS. Along the way, SPSS keeps you informed about what's going on so there won't be any big surprises at the end.

Follow these steps:

1. **Choose File ➪ Import Data ➪ Text Data.**

   The file is in the SPSS installation directory.

2. **Select the demo.txt file, and then click Open.**

   The Text Import Wizard appears, as shown in Figure 5-1, allowing you to load and format your data.

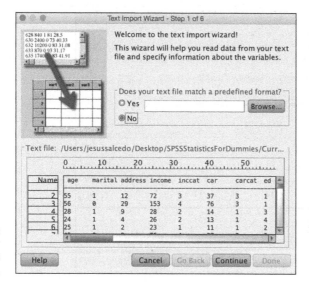

FIGURE 5-1:
Make sure your data looks reasonable.

3. **Examine the input data.**

   The screen lets you peek at the contents of the input file so you can verify that you've chosen the right file. Also, if your file uses a predefined format (it doesn't in this example), you can select it here and skip some of the later steps. If your data doesn't show up nicely separated into values the way you want, you may be able to correct it in a later step. Don't panic just yet.

4. **Click Continue.**

5. **Specify that the data is delimited and the names are included, as shown in Figure 5-2.**

   As you can see in this example, SPSS takes a guess, but you can also specify how your data is organized. It can be divided using spaces (as in this example), commas, tabs, semicolons, or some combination. Or your data may not be divided — it may be that all the data items are jammed together and each has a fixed width. If your text file includes the names of the variables, you need to tell SPSS.

6. **Click Continue.**

7. **Specify how SPSS should interpret the text.**

   For this example, the correct settings are shown in Figure 5-3. You can tell SPSS something about the file and which data you want to read.

   Perhaps some lines at the top of the file should be ignored — this happens when you're reading data from text intended for printing and header information is at the top. By telling SPSS about it, those first lines can be skipped.

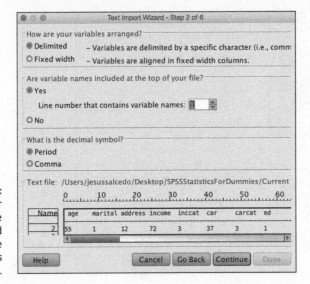

FIGURE 5-2:
Specify whether the fields are delimited and whether the variable names are included.

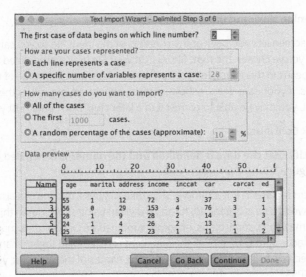

FIGURE 5-3:
Specify where the data appears in the file.

Also, you can have one line of text represent one case (one row of data in SPSS), or you can have SPSS count the variables to determine where each row starts.

And you don't have to read the entire file — you can select a maximum number of lines to read starting at the beginning of the file, or you can select a percentage of the total and have lines of text randomly selected throughout the file. Specifying a limited selection can be useful if you have a large file and would like to test parts of it.

8. Click Continue.

9. Specify tab as the delimiter, as shown in Figure 5-4.

SPSS knows how to use commas, spaces, tabs, and semicolons as delimiting characters. You can even use some other character as a delimiter by selecting Other and then typing the character into the blank. You can also specify whether your text is formatted with quotes (which is common) and whether you use single or double quotes. Strings must be surrounded in quotes if they contain any of the characters being used as delimiters.

TIP

You can specify that a data item is missing in your text file. Simply use two delimiters in a row, without intervening data.

```
● ● ●          Text Import Wizard - Delimited Step 4 of 6

Which delimiters appear between variables?      What is the text qualifi...
  ☑ Tab              ☐ Space                      ◉ None
  ☐ Comma            ☐ Semicolon                  ○ Single quote
  ☐ Other:                                        ○ Double quote
                                                  ○ Other:
Leading and Trailing Spaces
  ☐ Remove leading spaces from string values
  ☐ Remove trailing spaces from string values

Data preview
  age    marital  address  income  inccat  car   carca
  55     1        12       72      3       37    3
  56     0        29       153     4       76    3
  28     1        9        28      2       14    1
  24     1        4        26      2       13    1
  25     1        2        23      1       11    1
  45     0        9        76      4       37    3
  44     1        17       144     4       72    3
  46     1        20       75      4       37    3
  41     0        10       26      2       13    1
  29     0        4        19      1       10    1

   Help                        Cancel   Go Back   Continue    Done
```

FIGURE 5-4: Specify the delimiters that go between data items and which quotes to use for strings.

10. Click Continue.

11. Change the variable name and data format (if needed), as shown in Figure 5-5.

You can change the variable names and specify their types. Here you see that SPSS has made a guess for the type of each variable. If you did not have variables names, SPSS would assign the variables the names V1, V2, V3, and so on. To change a name, select it in the column heading at the bottom of the window, and then type the new name in the Variable Name field at the top. You can select the format from the Data Format drop-down list, if you need to change it.

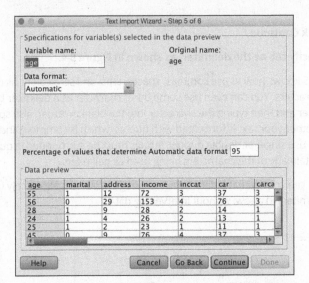

FIGURE 5-5:
Name your
variables and
select their data
types.

REMEMBER

This step is optional. If you need to refine your data types, you can do so later in the Variable View tab of the Data Editor window. The point here is to get the data into SPSS.

12. **Click Continue.**

13. **In the Would You Like to Save This File Format for Future Use? section, click No, as shown in Figure 5-6.**

Saving the file format for future use is something you would do if you were loading more files of this same format into SPSS — it reduces the number of questions to answer and the amount of formatting to do next time.

TECHNICAL
STUFF

In the Would You Like to Paste the Syntax? section, you have the chance to grab a copy of the Syntax language instructions that do all these data manipulations. But unless you know about the Syntax language (as described in Chapters 26 and 27), it's best to pretend that this option doesn't exist for now.

14. **Click the Done button.**

Depending on the type of data conversions and the amount of formatting, SPSS may take a bit of time to finish. Be patient. The Data View tab of the Data Editor window will eventually display your data.

15. **Look at the data. Correct your data types and formats, if necessary. Then save it all to a file by choosing File ➪ Save As.**

You're instructed to enter a file name. You can just call it **Demo**. The new file will have the .sav extension, which indicates that it's a standard SPSS file.

After you complete Step 6 of 6 in the wizard, the data appears in SPSS as shown in Figure 5-7.

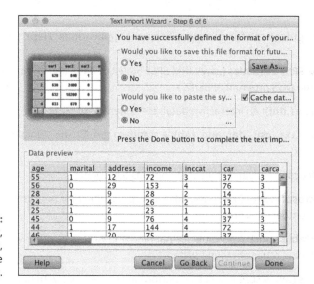

FIGURE 5-6:
Save the format, grab the syntax, or enable caching.

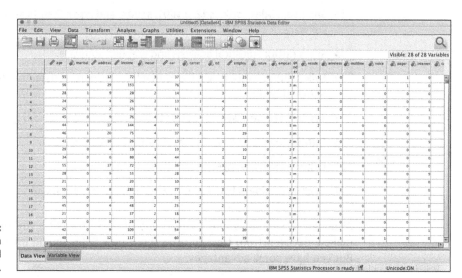

FIGURE 5-7:
The data formatted in SPSS.

Transferring Data from Another Program

You can get your data into SPSS from a file created by another program, but it isn't always easy. SPSS knows how to read some file formats, but if you're not careful, you'll find your data stored in an odd file format. Deciphering some file formats can be as confusing as Klingon trigonometry. SPSS can read only from file formats it knows.

SPSS recognizes the file formats of several applications. Here's a complete list:

>> **IBM SPSS Statistics (.sav):** IBM SPSS Statistics data, and also the format used by the DOS program SPSS/PC+

>> **dBase (.dbf):** An interactive database system

>> **Text (.txt, .csv, .dat, and .tab):** A standard text file that contains unformatted text

>> **CSV (.csv):** A plain text file that contains a list of data

>> **Microsoft Excel (.xls, .xlsx, .xlsm):** A spreadsheet for performing calculations on numbers in a grid

>> **Portable (.por):** A portable format read and written by other versions of SPSS, including other operating systems

>> **Lotus (.w):** A spreadsheet for performing calculations with numbers in a grid

>> **SAS (.sas7bdat, .sd7, .sd2, .ssd01, ssd04, and .xpt):** Statistical analysis software

>> **Stata (.dta):** Statistical analysis and graphics software

>> **Sylk (.slk):** A symbolic link file format for transporting data from one application to another

>> **Systat (.syd and .sys):** Software that produces statistical and graphical results

>> **Database:** Any database with an ODBC connection

>> **Cognos TM1:** A budgeting and forecasting program

>> **Cognos Business Intelligence:** A web-based reporting tool

Although SPSS knows how to read any of these formats, you may still need to make a decision from time to time about how SPSS should import your dataset. But you have some advantages:

>> You know exactly what you want — the form of data appearing in SPSS is simple, and what you see is what you get.

>> SPSS has some reasonable defaults and makes some good guesses along the way.

>> You can always fiddle with things after you've loaded the data.

REMEMBER

You're only reading from the data file, so you can't hurt it. Besides, you have everything safely backed up, don't you? If the process gets hopelessly balled up, you can always call it quits and start over. That's the way we do it — we think of it as a learning process.

Reading an Excel file

SPSS knows how to read Excel files directly. If you want to read data from an Excel file, we suggest you read the steps in "Reading Simple Data from a Text File," earlier in this chapter, because the two processes are similar. If you understand the decisions you have to make in reading a text file, reading from an Excel file will be duck soup.

Do the following to read this data into SPSS:

1. **Choose File ⇨ Import Data ⇨ Excel.**

2. **Select the demo.xls file and then click Open.**

The file is in the SPSS installation directory.

3. **Select the data to include.**

An Excel file can contain more than one worksheet, and you can choose the one you want from the drop-down list, as shown in Figure 5-8.

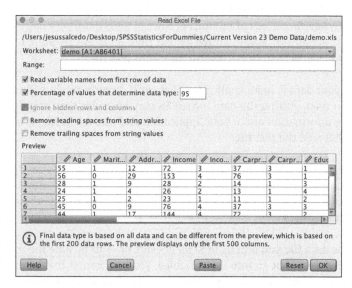

FIGURE 5-8:
Select which data in the spreadsheet to include.

Also, if you've elected to read only part of the data, enter the Excel cell numbers of the upper-left and lower-right corners here. You can specify if the names of variables appear in the first row and what percentage of data to use to determine the variable type. Finally you can remove any leading or trailing spaces.

It's a good idea to inspect the data preview to make sure the variables and data are read properly.

4. Click OK.

Your data appears in the SPSS window.

5. Switch to the Variable View tab to examine the variable definitions and make any changes.

SPSS makes a bunch of assumptions about your data, and some of those assumptions are probably wrong.

6. Save the file using your chosen SPSS name, and you're off and running.

Reading from an unknown program type

SPSS can import most file types, but there are exceptions. However, almost any file format in current use can be exported as a text file and then imported into SPSS.

REMEMBER

SPSS has been around for more than a half century, and organizations, such as the IRS, have hundreds of millions of rows of SPSS data. Very large files or older datasets are almost always stored as text files. So if you're going to be an SPSS power user, you'll need to get comfortable with text files.

If your data is in an application that can't directly create a file of a type that SPSS can read, getting the data into SPSS may be easier than you think. If you can get the information out of your application and into a text file, it's fairly easy to have SPSS read the text file.

TECHNICAL STUFF

Years ago, it was not uncommon that an unusual proprietary format could not be exported to a text format but could be easily imported into SPSS. Although this situation is now rare, expert users of SPSS syntax can import even the most arcane data formats.

The data file you output to SPSS doesn't have to include the variable names, just the values that go into the variables. You can format the data in the file by using spaces, tabs, commas, or semicolons to separate data items. Such dividers are known as *delimiters*. Another method of formatting data avoids delimiters. In that method, you don't have to separate the individual data items, but you must make each data item a specific length, because you have to tell SPSS exactly how long each item is.

The most intuitive format is to have one *case* (one row of data) per line of text. That way, the data items in your text file are in the same positions they'll be in when they're read into SPSS. Alternatively, you can have all your data formatted as one long stream, but you'll have to tell SPSS how many items go into each case.

Always save this kind of raw data as simple text; the file you store it in should have the .txt extension so SPSS can recognize it for what it is.

An even more roundabout way to bring in data from another application is by selecting, copying, and pasting the data you want, but we don't recommend doing this method. The places you're copying from and pasting to are usually larger than the screen, so highlighting and selecting can be tricky. You must be ready to choose Edit ⇨ Undo when necessary.

A better method is to write the data to a file in a format understood by SPSS, and then read that file into SPSS. SPSS knows how to read some file formats directly. Using such a file as an intermediary means you'll have an extra backup copy of your data, and that's never a bad idea.

When you drag a data file to the SPSS Data Editor window, SPSS chooses the appropriate format and begins reading the data file.

Saving Data

Writing data from SPSS is easier than reading data into SPSS. All you do is choose File ⇨ Save As, select your file type, and then enter a file name.

You have lots of file types to choose from. You can write your data not only in 3 plain-text formats, but also in 3 Excel spreadsheet formats, 3 Lotus formats, 3 dBase formats, 9 SAS formats, 1 SYLK format, 1 Portable format, and 18 Stata formats.

If you'll be exporting data from SPSS into another application, find out what kinds of files the other application can read, and then use SPSS to write in one of those formats.

Chapter **6**

Getting Data and Results from SPSS

SPSS analyzes your data and displays information in easy-to-understand tables and graphs. But the time comes when you want to take these results and use them in another application. You might want to send output to the printer or to another program, such as Microsoft Word or Excel. This chapter explains how to get your data out of SPSS and into the forms that other programs need.

Exporting Data to Another Program

You can export SPSS data directly to another program. Simply go to the Data View tab of the Data Editor window, and choose File ⇨ Export. Then choose the program to which you would like to export the data.

You can export data to the following programs and file types:

>> Databases

>> Microsoft Excel file

>> CSV (comma-separated values) file

>> Tab-delimited file

>> Fixed-text file

>> SAS

>> Strata

>> dBase file

>> Lotus

>> Cognos TM1

>> SYLK

If you want to use a database system that isn't listed, choose File ⇨ Export ⇨ Database. When the Export to Database Wizard appears, click the Add ODBS Data Source button.

To export the data, simply follow the onscreen instructions for selecting the variables to be written and choosing whether to append new data or to overwrite existing data.

Navigating SPSS Statistics Viewer

When you run an analysis, produce a graph, or do anything that generates output (even loading a file), the SPSS Statistics Viewer window pops up automatically to display what you've created. Understanding the features available in this window is key to customizing output and exporting output to other applications.

Let's take a look at a previously saved SPSS output file. Choose File ⇨ Open ⇨ Output, and open the file Example Output.spv. The file is not in the SPSS installation directory. You have to download it from the book's companion website at www.dummies.com/go/spss4e.

Figure 6-1 displays part of the Example Output.spv file. The Output Viewer window is divided into two panes:

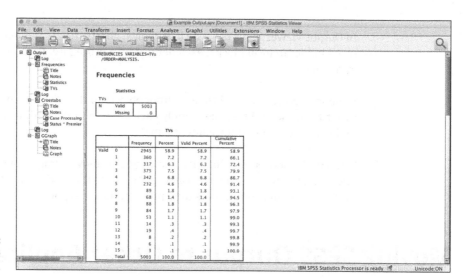

FIGURE 6-1:
The Example
Output.spv file.

>> The outline pane, on the left, contains an outline of all the information stored in Output Viewer.

>> The content pane, on the right, contains the statistical tables, charts, and text output.

You can easily browse the output by navigating to individual tables or charts. You can also manage and manipulate the output to create a document that contains the required results, arranged and formatted appropriately.

To allocate more or less space to each pane, left-click and drag the divider between the two panes.

In the outline pane, an open book icon appears in front of items visible in the content pane and a closed book icon in front of items not shown in the content pane. To hide an object in the content pane:

>> Double-click the open book icon in the outline pane.

>> Select the item and use the hide tool on the toolbar.

>> Choose View ➪ Hide.

Hiding items without deleting them allows the user to more easily concentrate on the results of interest while retaining all the results.

In Output Viewer, objects — such as tables, charts, titles, and notes — are organized in hierarchical blocks, each defined by a procedure. Each block is identified by a name.

Although you can scroll through output objects in the content pane, navigation is easier from the outline pane. Simply click an item in the outline pane to navigate to the selected item in the content pane.

Standard Windows functionality allows you to move (drag), copy, or delete any selected item. In this way, you can organize output generated by different statistical and graphical procedures for a presentation or report.

Moving SPSS Output to Other Applications

Often you'll want to report the results of your analyses using another application, such as Microsoft Word or Microsoft PowerPoint, and include relevant tables or charts to illustrate key findings. Or you might need to perform post-processing of the results using an application such as Microsoft Excel. Or perhaps you want to distribute tables and charts to colleagues who do not have SPSS.

You can bring SPSS output to another application in two ways. If you have a single table or a small number of tables, copy and paste the objects directly into a file opened in the other application. Or you can export large numbers of tables and charts into a file in a variety of common formats: Excel, Portable Document Format (PDF), HTML, text, Microsoft Word, PowerPoint, or Excel.

Copying and pasting output

When you've run an analysis or produced a graph in SPSS, the simplest way to transfer the object to another application is to copy and paste. To copy output items from SPSS to the clipboard, you have two options: Copy and Copy Special.

Copy copies the output table onto the clipboard by default into the plain text, RTF, or Biff format. RTF is the default format used when pasting into Microsoft Word, and Biff is the default format when pasting into Microsoft Excel. Plain text is another option that's available in various programs, including Microsoft Word and Excel.

Copy Special allows you to select the format copied to the clipboard. The output is pasted into the other application as a picture image. You can save your Copy Special selection as the default to be used by Copy for future operations.

Use Paste Special or Paste options in the destination application. The Paste operation pastes the default format for the application. Paste Special gives you all the copy formats appropriate for the destination application. For example, Microsoft Word offers text and RTF formats as the default formats used for Copy in SPSS, whereas Microsoft Excel will offer text and Biff formats. You select from the available formats the one to paste.

To copy and paste an object, right-click the image and click Copy or Copy Special, as shown in Figure 6-2. Then open an application, such as Microsoft Word, and use Paste Special to transfer the object to the application, as shown in Figure 6-3.

TVs

		Frequency	Percent	Valid Percent	Cumulative Percent
Valid	0	2945	58.9	58.9	58.9
	1	360	7.2		
	2	317	6.3		
	3	375	7.5		
	4	342	6.8		
	5	232	4.6		
	6	89	1.8		
	7	68	1.4		
	8	88	1.8		
	9	84	1.7		
	10	53	1.1		
	11	14	.3		
	12	19	.4	.4	99.7
	13	8	.2	.2	99.8
	14	6	.1	.1	99.9
	15	3	.1	.1	100.0
	Total	5003	100.0	100.0	

Context menu overlay:
- Cut
- Copy
- Copy Special...
- Paste After
- Create/Edit Autoscript...
- Style Output...
- Export...
- Edit Content ▶

FIGURE 6-2: Copying an object in SPSS Statistics Viewer.

REMEMBER

Charts will always paste as images that cannot be edited regardless of the clipboard format.

Exporting output

Copying and pasting tables one-by-one might not be a good option if you have many tables to transfer. Instead, use the Export Output facility, which provides several file formats appropriate for use by other applications.

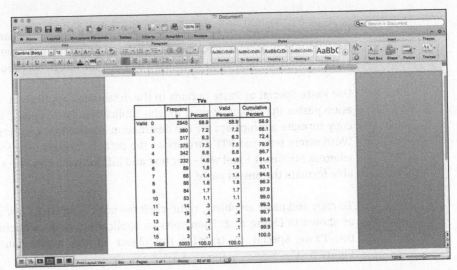

FIGURE 6-3:
Pasting an object in Microsoft Word.

As an example you'll export the Example Output.spv file to Microsoft Word:

1. Choose File ➪ Export.

The Export Output window appears, as shown in Figure 6-4.

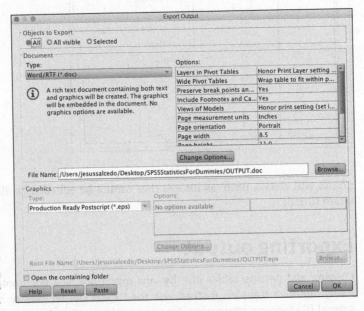

FIGURE 6-4:
The main control window for exporting from SPSS Statistics Viewer.

2. **In the Objects to Export section, select which items to include in the output:**

- *All:* Exports all the information that SPSS Statistics Viewer contains, regardless of whether the information is currently visible.

- *All Visible:* Includes only those objects currently displayed by SPSS Statistics Viewer.

- *Selected:* Allows you to select which objects to export.

To follow along with the example, choose All Visible.

WARNING

The set of selections available in the Export Output dialog is determined by the types of objects displayed by SPSS Statistics Viewer, which (if any) objects are selected, and your choice in the Document section's Type drop-down list. The only combinations of options available are those that produce output.

3. **In the Document section's Type drop-down list, choose the file type that you want to export to:**

- *Excel 97–2004 (*.xls):* Excel files can include text, tables, and graphics, with the graphics embedded in the 1997–2004 workbook. You can create a new file or add to an existing workbook. No graphic options are available.

- *Excel 2007 and higher (*.xlsx):* Excel files can include text, tables, and graphics, with the graphics embedded in the 2007 and higher workbook. You can create a new file or add to an existing workbook. No graphic options are available.

- *Excel 2007 and higher macro enabled (*.xlsm):* Excel files can include text, tables, and graphics, with the graphics embedded in the 2007 and higher macro-enabled workbook. You can create a new file or add to an existing workbook. No graphic options are available.

- *HTML (*.htm):* HTML files can be used for text both with and without graphics. If graphics are included, they will be exported separately and included as HTML links. You must also choose the graphic file type.

- *Web Reports (*.htm or *.mht):* Creates an interactive document compatible with most browsers, including Cognos Active Report.

- *Portable Document Format (*.pdf):* PDF documents will include not only text but also any graphics existing in the original. No graphic options are available.

- *PowerPoint (*.ppt):* PowerPoint documents can be written as text with graphics embedded in the TIFF format. No graphic options are available.

- *Text-Plain (*.txt):* Text files can be output with graphic references included, and the graphics written to separate files. The reference is the name of the graphic file. The graphic file format is specified by choosing options in the lower section of the window.

- *Text-UTF8 (*.txt):* UTF-8 is Unicode text encoded as a stream of 8-bit characters. Graphics are handled the same as they are for text files.

- *Text-UTF16 (*.txt):* UTF-16 is Unicode text encoded as a stream of 16-bit characters. Graphics are handled the same as they are for text files.

- *Word/RTF (*.doc):* Word documents are written in rich text format (RTF), which can be copied into a Word document. No graphic options are available.

- *None:* When selected, this option means no text is output — only graphic images. The graphic file format is specified by options in the lower section of the window.

To follow along with the example, choose Word/RFT.

TIP

If you want to share your data with non-SPSS users, typically the best option is to export data to Excel. If you want to share your output with non-SPSS users, we recommend exporting output to PDF.

4. **In the Graphics section, select the image file format, if one is needed, from the Type drop-down list.**

   Some formats (for example, the text-file format) require that graphics be exported in separate files; you can also elect to export *only* graphics files. Graphics can be exported in the following formats:

   - Standard jpeg (JPG)

   - Portable network graphics (PNG)

   - Postscript (EPS)

   - Tagged image file format (TIFF)

   - Windows bitmap (BMP)

   - Enhanced metafile (EMF)

   To follow along with the example, don't change anything here.

5. **To adjust the default format options, click the Change Options button.**

   The Options dialog, which is shown in Figure 6-5, differs depending on the export format. When exporting to the Word/RTF format, you can control how layered tables and pivot tables wider than the page width are exported. You can also choose whether to include captions and footnotes, as well as page breaks, and how models are to be handled. To change the page setup (margins and page orientation), click the Page Setup for Export button.

   To follow along with the example, don't change any of these default options.

6. **Click Continue.**

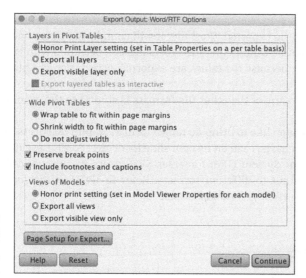

FIGURE 6-5:
Formatting
options for
exporting to
Microsoft Word.

7. **Click the Browse button, select the directory and name of the exported file, and then click Save.**

   The Save button doesn't write the file(s) — it only inserts the selected name into the Export Output window.

8. **Click OK.**

   The file(s) are written— each in the chosen format and at the chosen location.

9. **To view the exported file, open Microsoft Word (see Figure 6-6).**

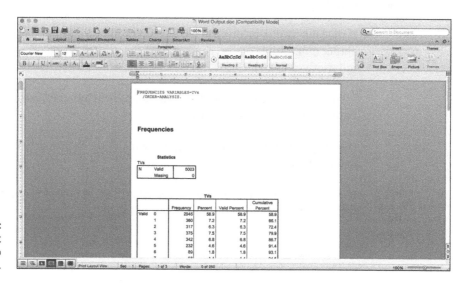

FIGURE 6-6:
SPSS output
exported to
Microsoft Word.

If you open the exported Word file, it will contain the tables and graph that make up the Example Output.spv file. The tables can be edited with the Microsoft Word table editor, because the tables are exported as text, not as a picture.

Exporting to any of the other file formats is similar to the example shown here.

How would you like to bring 40 tables from SPSS into 40 sheets in a workbook? Or bring in 50 charts, each on its own slide in a PowerPoint presentation? The Output Management System (OMS) enables SPSS users to automatically write selected types of output to different formats. Refer to *SPSS Statistics for Data Analysis and Visualization* (Wiley) for an example.

Printing Data

The simplest form of output is to print the numeric rows and columns of the raw data as it appears on the Data View tab of the Data Editor window. To do so, choose File ⇨ Print. A familiar Print dialog appears, where you can select the print settings you need for your system. The table of data will be printed with lines between the rows and columns, the same as they appear onscreen. The printed form has row numbers to the left and variable names at the top.

If you're not sure what your output will look like, you can choose File ⇨ Print Preview and see, on the screen, the layout that will be sent to the printer. The zoom and page-selection controls at the top of the window allow you to examine the output.

If the table you're printing is too wide to fit on the sheet of paper, SPSS splits the output on multiple pages. You can hold the printed sheets side by side to see the full width of the table.

If you want to print the variable definitions, switch to the Variable View tab of the Data Editor window before printing.

If you want to print a table or graph, switch to the SPSS Statistics Viewer window and print from there.

If you go to print and you don't see your printer, you need to specify your printer information in your operating system, not in SPSS.

Chapter 7

More about Defining Your Data

Without a definition, a number serves no purpose. For example, the number 3 could be the number of miles, or an answer to a multiple-choice question, or the number of jelly beans in your pocket. As you can see, a variable's definition is important.

Data type is part of a variable's definition. The data type is more than just a tag — it determines how a value can be manipulated. For example, calculating *date arithmetic* (the distance in time between two dates) would be a nightmare without the proper date format. As soon as you specify the proper date format, you can take advantage of special menus for manipulating dates.

Multiple-response variables — those "check all that apply" questions on surveys — are another kind of variable type that needs extra attention. Again, when you create multiple-response variables properly, you can use a special menu dedicated to this type of variable. Finally, all this data definition stuff can be time consuming, so SPSS includes a special shortcut menu for copying your data and variable definitions from one dataset to another.

Working with Dates and Times

Calendar and clock arithmetic can be tricky, but SPSS can handle it all for you. Just enter date and time variables in whatever format you specify, and SPSS will convert the values internally to do the calculations. Also, SPSS displays the newly created date and time variables in your specified format, so the variable is easy to read.

SPSS understands the meaning of slashes, commas, colons, blanks, and names in the dates and times you enter, so you can write the date and time almost any way you'd like. If SPSS can't figure out what you've typed, it clears away what you typed and waits for you to type something again.

TECHNICAL STUFF

Internally, SPSS keeps all dates as a positive or negative count of the number of seconds from a zero date. Here's a bit of trivia for you. The zero date in SPSS is the birth of the Gregorian calendar in 1582. No kidding! You can choose a display format that includes or excludes the time, but the information is always there. You can even change the display format without loss of data. If the time isn't included in the data you enter, SPSS assumes zero hours and minutes (midnight).

On the Data View tab of the Data Editor window you can determine the data type for each variable. The type is chosen from the list of types shown in Figure 7-1. On the right, you select a format. SPSS uses this format to interpret your input and to format the dates for display.

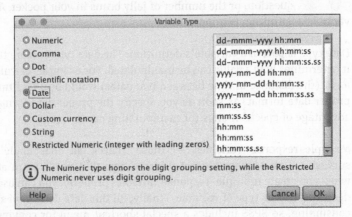

Variable Type	
○ Numeric	dd-mmm-yyyy hh:mm
○ Comma	dd-mmm-yyyy hh:mm:ss
○ Dot	dd-mmm-yyyy hh:mm:ss.ss
○ Scientific notation	yyyy-mm-dd hh:mm
◉ Date	yyyy-mm-dd hh:mm:ss
○ Dollar	yyyy-mm-dd hh:mm:ss.ss
○ Custom currency	mm:ss
○ String	mm:ss.ss
○ Restricted Numeric (integer with leading zeros)	hh:mm
	hh:mm:ss
	hh:mm:ss.ss

ⓘ The Numeric type honors the digit grouping setting, while the Restricted Numeric never uses digit grouping.

Help   Cancel   OK

FIGURE 7-1: Select the data type and the format.

REMEMBER

SPSS uses the format you select for both reading your input and formatting the output of dates and times.

WARNING

The Columns setting of the Date variable on the Variable View tab of the Data Editor window is important. The column width determines the maximum number of characters that can be displayed. If you choose a format that is too narrow to fit, the date will appear as a row of asterisks.

The available formats are defined as a group and change according to the variable type. For example, the Dollar type has a different list of choices than those offered for the Date type.

The list of format definitions you have to choose from are constructed by combining the specifiers listed in Table 7-1. Format definitions look like mm/dd/yy and ddd:hh:mm.

TABLE 7-1 ## Specifiers in Date and Time Formats

Specifier	Means
dd	A two-digit day of the month in the range 01, 02, . . ., 30, 31.
ddd	A three-digit day of the year in the range 001, 002, . . ., 364, 365.
hh	A two-digit hour of the day in the range 00, 01, . . ., 22, 23.
Jan, Feb, . . .	The abbreviated name of the month of the year, as in JAN, FEB, . . ., NOV, DEC.
January, February, . . .	The name of the month of the year, as in JANUARY, FEBRUARY, . . ., NOVEMBER, DECEMBER.
mm	When adjacent to a dd specifier in a format, a two-digit month of the year in the range 01, 02, . . ., 11, 12. When adjacent to an hh specifier in a format, a two-digit specifier of the minute in the range 00, 01, . . ., 58, 59.
mmm	A three-character name of a month, as in JAN, FEB, . . ., NOV, DEC.
Mon, Tue, . . .	The abbreviated name of the day of the week, as in MON, TUE, . . ., SAT, SUN.
Monday, Tuesday, . . .	The name of the day of the week, as in MONDAY, TUESDAY, . . ., SATURDAY, SUNDAY.
q Q	The quarter of the year, as in 1 Q, 2 Q, 3 Q, or 4 Q.
Ss	Following a colon, the number of seconds in the range 00, 01, . . ., 58, 59. Following a period, the number of hundredths of a second.
ww WK	The one- or two-digit number of the week of the year in the range 1 WK, 2 WK, . . ., 51 WK, 52 WK. **Note:** Although week numbers can be one or two digits, the numbers always align when printed in columns because SPSS inserts a blank in front of single-digit numbers.
yy	A two-digit year in the range 00, 01, . . ., 98, 99. The assumed first two digits of the four-digit year are determined by the configuration found at Edit ⇨ Options ⇨ Data.
yyyy	A four-digit year in the range 0001, 0002, . . ., 9998, 9999.

You can change the format of a date variable at any time without fear of losing information. For example, you could enter the data under a format that accepted only the year, month, and day, and then change the format to something that contains only the hours and minutes. The format may not display all the information you entered (in this case, it won't), but when you change the format back to something more inclusive, all your data is still there.

To enter data, choose a format — any format — that contains all the data you have. Later, you can change to a more limited format that displays only the information you want. But you can't go the other way.

Using the Date and Time Wizard

If you have dates that have been properly declared, you can easily do numerous types of calculations. Just follow these steps:

1. **Open the nenana2.sav dataset.**

The file is not in the SPSS installation directory. You have to download it from the book's companion website at www.dummies.com/go/spss4e.

2. **Choose Transform ⇨ Date and Time Wizard.**

The window shown in Figure 7-2 appears.

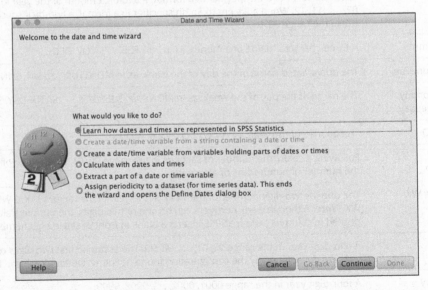

FIGURE 7-2:
The Date and
Time Wizard.

3. Select the **Extract a Part of a Date or Time Variable** radio button, and click **Continue.**

4. In the Date or Time list, choose DateTime. In the Unit to Extract list, choose **Day of Week** (see Figure 7-3) and click **Continue.**

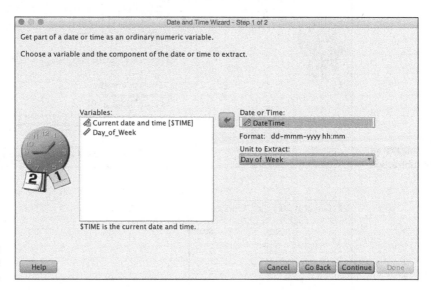

FIGURE 7-3:
Extracting Day
of Week.

5. Call the Result variable Day_of_Week2, **and click Done.**

Let's do a second calculation next.

6. Choose **Transform ⇨ Date and Time Wizard.**

7. Select the **Calculate with Dates and Times** radio button this time, and click **Continue.**

8. Select the **Calculate Number of Time Units between Two Dates** radio button, and click **Continue.**

9. Select Current Date and Time [$Time] and move it to the Date1 field. Then select DateTime and move it to the minus Date2 field.

10. Select the **Retain Fractional Part** radio button, as shown in Figure 7-4, and click **Continue.**

11. Name the Result variable Years_Since2, **and click Done.**

The screen shown in Figure 7-5 appears with the two new variables you created. Note that your Years_Since2 variable will be slightly different than what is shown in the image because the current data and time will be different.

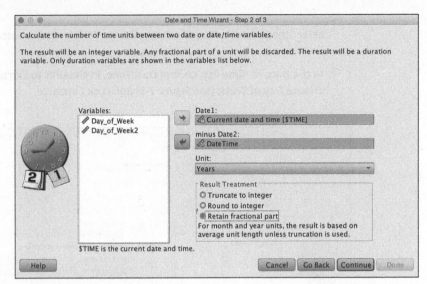

FIGURE 7-4:
Date subtraction.

Day_of_Week2	Years_Since2
Sat	80.02
Mon	22.02
Fri	27.01
Tue	30.01
Sat	16.01
Mon	94.00
Wed	25.01
Wed	32.00
Wed	77.00
Mon	51.00

FIGURE 7-5:
The dataset with
calculations
added.

Creating and Using a Multiple-Response Set

Most survey questions allow respondents to provide only one answer. For example, the question "What is your favorite baseball team?" allows for only one response. Multiple-response questions, on the other hand, allow respondents to provide more than one answer. For instance, the question, "What TV shows have you seen in the last six months?" allows for more than one response.

A *multiple-response set*, or *multiple-response variable*, is much like a new variable made of other variables you already have. A multiple-response set acts like a variable in some ways, but in other ways it doesn't. You define it based on the variables you've already defined, but it doesn't appear on the Variable View tab. It doesn't even show up when you list your data on the Data View tab. But it does appear among the items you can choose when defining graphs and tables.

The following steps explain how you can define a multiple-response set, but not how you can use one — that comes later when you generate a table or a graph. Also, SPSS has three Multiple Response menus: The one in the Data menu is for graphs; the one under the Analyze ⇨ Tables ⇨ Multiple Response Sets is for tables; and the one in the Analyze menu is for using special menus that you see in this example.

Having three menus for declaring this variable type can be a little confusing.

A multiple-response set can contain a number of variables of various types, but it must be based on two or more *dichotomy variables* (variables with just two values — for example, yes or no or 0 or 1) or two or more *category variables* (variables with several values — for example, country names or modes of transportation). For example, suppose you have two dichotomy variables with the value 1 defined as no and the value 2 defined as yes. You can create a multiple-response set consisting of all the cases where the answer to both is yes, where the answer to both is no, or whatever combination you want.

Do the following to create a simple multiple-response set:

1. **Open the Apples and Oranges.sav dataset.**

   The file is not in the SPSS installation directory. You have to download it from the book's companion website at www.dummies.com/go/spss4e. Four dichotomous variables have 1 for Yes and 0 for No as their possible answers. Note in Figure 7-6 that the dataset has only ten respondents.

2. **Choose Analyze ⇨ Multiple Response ⇨ Define Variable Sets.**

   Your variables appear in the Set Definition area. If you previously defined any multiple datasets, they appear in the list on the right.

3. **Select all four variables in the Set Definition box, and then click the arrow to move the selections to the Variables in Set box.**

4. **In the Variable Coding area, select the Dichotomies option and specify a Counted Value of 1.**

5. **Provide a multiple response set name.**

   To follow along with the example, type **Fruit.**

🍎 Apples	🍊 Oranges	🍐 Pears	🍌 Bananas
Yes	No	Yes	No
Yes	Yes	Yes	No
Yes	No	Yes	No
Yes	Yes	Yes	No
Yes	No	Yes	No
Yes	Yes	No	Yes
Yes	No	No	Yes
Yes	Yes	No	Yes
Yes	No	No	Yes
No	Yes	No	Yes

FIGURE 7-6:
The variables are
nominals with
possible values of
1 and 0, which
have been
labeled Yes and
No, respectively.

6. **Click Add.**

    The new multiple-response set is created and a dollar sign ($) is placed before
    the name, as shown in Figure 7-7. The dollar sign in the file name identifies the
    variable as a multiple-response set. The new name will appear in two special
    menus in the Analyze menu.

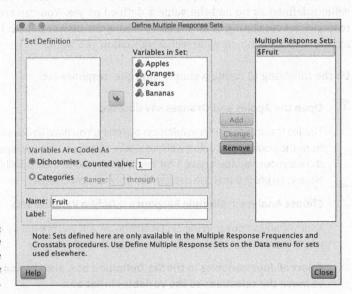

FIGURE 7-7:
The window
showing the
complete
definition.

7. **Click Close.**

    Now that you've created the multiple-response variable, you'll be able to use it
    to obtain frequencies.

8. **Choose Analyze ⇨ Multiple Response ⇨ Frequencies.**

   The new special variable appears. To obtain frequencies, you'll need to place the multiple-response variable in the Table(s) For box.

9. **Move the $Fruit variable into the Table(s) For area, as shown in Figure 7-8.**

   The new special Frequencies report appears in the output window, as shown in Figure 7-9.

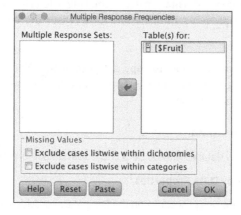

FIGURE 7-8: The Multiple Response Frequencies dialog.

$Fruit Frequencies				
		Responses		Percent of Cases
		N	Percent	
$Fruit^a	Apples	9	37.5%	90.0%
	Oranges	5	20.8%	50.0%
	Pears	5	20.8%	50.0%
	Bananas	5	20.8%	50.0%
Total		24	100.0%	240.0%
a. Dichotomy group tabulated at value 1.				

FIGURE 7-9: The Multiple Response Frequencies table.

This table might look confusing at first. As mentioned, the dataset has only ten people, and you can see that they bought 24 pieces of fruit. Nine pieces of fruit were apples — 37.5 percent of the fruit. Nine out of ten people bought apples — 90 percent of the people. So the difference is the denominator: 9/24 or 9/10. What makes this table special is that what you usually care about are people with multiple responses. In other words, how many people shopping at the store will buy apples along with other purchases?

TIP

If multiple-response sets are a common variable type for you, consider getting the Custom Tables module because it offers lots of options for this kind of variable. You can read more about modules in Chapter 28.

Copying Data Properties

Suppose you have some data definitions in another SPSS file, and you want to copy one or more of those definitions but you don't want the data. (All you want is the metadata.) SPSS enables you to choose from several files and copy only the variable definitions you want into your current dataset.

TIP

If you have a variable of *the same name* defined in your dataset before you run the Copy Data Properties procedure, you can choose to change the existing variable definition by loading new information from another file. The copied definition simply overwrites the previous information. Otherwise, the copying procedure creates a new variable.

The following steps show you how to copy data properties. You start with a new data file and copy the properties from the Apples and Oranges.sav data file, which was used in the previous exercise:

1. **Choose File ⇨ New ⇨ Data.**

You now have a new dataset with no data and no variable information.

2. **Choose Data ⇨ Copy Data Properties.**

The Copy Data Properties procedure on the Data menu provides the facility to copy variable properties from one dataset to another. Dictionary information can be copied to the active data file from an open dataset or from an external SPSS data file.

3. **In the An Open Dataset box, select Apples and Oranges.sav, as shown in Figure 7-10.**

If the Apples and Oranges.sav data file does not appear in the An Open Dataset box, select the An External SPSS Statistics Data File radio button, click the Browse button, locate the file, and click Open.

4. **Click Continue.**

A screen appears with the following options:

- *Apply Properties from Selected Source Dataset Variables to Matching Active Dataset Variables:* This option is the default.

    To update the source list to display all variables in the source data file, also select Create Matching Variables in the Active Dataset If They Do Not Already Exist. If selecting source variables that do not exist in the active dataset (based on variable name), new variables will be created in the active dataset with the variable names and properties from the source data file. If the active dataset does not contain variables (a blank, new dataset), all variables in the source data file are displayed and new variables based on the selected source variables are automatically created in the active dataset.

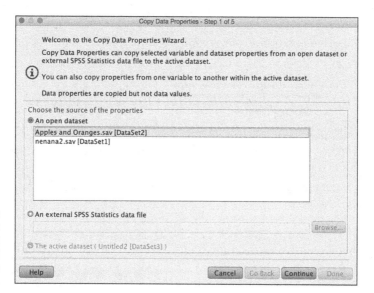

FIGURE 7-10:
Select the file you
want to use as
the source of
variable
definitions.

- *Apply Properties from a Single Source Variable to Selected Active Dataset Variables of the Same Type*: Applies the selected variable properties from one source variable to the selected variables in the active dataset. This option is useful when you're copying value labels or missing value designations to a series of variables.

- *Apply Dataset Properties Only — No Variable Selection:* Applies only file properties to the active dataset. (For example, a dataset can have a file label and this file label will be copied). No variable properties will be applied (this option is not available if the active dataset is also the source data file).

5. **Use the default option.**

   Now you need to specify from which variables you want to copy properties.

6. **Select the variables from which you want copy information.**

   To follow along with the example, select all the variables, as shown in Figure 7-11. (To deselect a variable, hold down the Ctrl key, and click the variable.)

7. **To use the variables you've selected, click Continue.**

   If instead you wanted to copy the complete definitions of all the variables you selected and overwrite what you have, you would click Done. Clicking the Continue button, as in this example, allows you to be more specific about which parts of the variable definitions you want to copy.

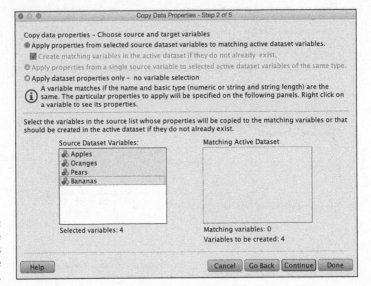

FIGURE 7-11:
Select the source
variable names
you want to use
for definitions.

8. **Choose the properties of the existing variable definitions you want to copy to the variables you're modifying.**

To follow along with the example, copy all the properties. In Figure 7-12, everything is selected by default, but you can deselect any properties you don't want. These selections apply to all variables you've chosen. If you want to handle each variable separately, you'll have to run through this procedure again for each one, selecting different variables each time.

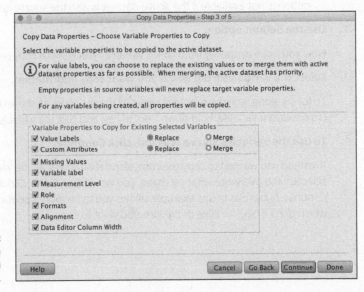

FIGURE 7-12:
Select which
attributes you
want to copy.

9. **Click Continue.**

If you were satisfied with your choices, you could click Finish to complete the process. By clicking Continue, however, you can select from a list of available properties to be copied.

10. **Choose any properties made available in the dialog shown in Figure 7-13.**

Depending on the variable type, different properties are available to be copied. Unavailable properties appear dimmed. By default, none of them are selected. The example dataset does not have any of these properties.

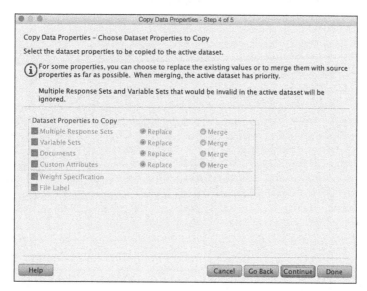

FIGURE 7-13:
Attributes other than variable definitions can be copied from the source.

11. **Click Continue to move to the final dialog.**

The screen displays the number of existing variable definitions to be changed, the number of new variables to be created, and the number of other properties that will be copied.

12. **To execute the copy procedure immediately, click Done.**

You could instead save the set of instructions as a Syntax script so you can execute them later. (Part 8 describes using the Syntax language.)

Using the basic variable types and adding property descriptions as needed, you should be able to concoct any type of variable you want.

3
Messing with Data in SPSS

Transform your data into the form that you need it.

Find out about the Compute Variable command, one of the most important commands in SPSS.

Learn the grammer of functions to manipulate your data efficiently.

Combine data files efficiently.

IN THIS CHAPTER

» **Sorting your cases in different ways**

» **Using some data (and not other data)**

» **Combining counting and case identifying**

» **Recoding variable content to new values**

» **Grouping data in bins**

Chapter **8**

The Transform and Data Menus

After you get your raw data into SPSS, you may find that it contains errors or isn't organized how you'd like. A way to alleviate these problems is to make modifications to your data by configuring the values into a form that's easier to work with and read. This chapter contains some methods you can use to modify your data without losing any information.

A related problem occurs when you want to analyze only some of your data or perform the same analysis more than once. For example, you may want to select the good, complete data and avoid the incomplete, messy data. Or you may want to do a separate analysis for new customers and established customers.

Sorting Cases

You can change the order of your cases (rows) so they appear in just about any order you want. You sort them by comparing the values you entered for your variables. The following example uses the Cars.sav dataset. You sort with two variables, or *sort keys*. The initial sort of the data will simply be by car_id.

You don't need to limit your sorting to one or two sort keys. You can have a third key or more, if necessary, but these keys come into effect only when the keys sorted before them hold identical values. In most cases, two sort keys are enough to get what you want.

You can sort based on variables of any type simply by selecting the variables as keys. For example:

1. **Choose File ▷ Open ▷ Data and select the Cars.sav file.**

The file is not in the SPSS installation directory. You have to download it from the book's companion website at www.dummies.com/go/spss4e. The result is the presentation of a collection of apparently unsorted cases, as shown in Figure 8-1.

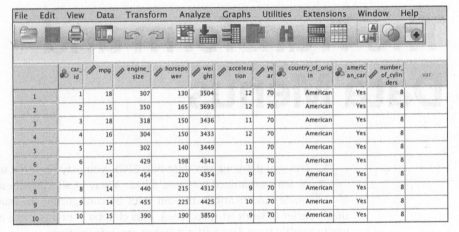

FIGURE 8-1:
The data unsorted, as it's loaded directly from the data file.

2. **Choose Data ▷ Sort Cases.**

The Sort Cases dialog appears.

3. **Select the** country_of_origin **variable and then the** horsepower **variable, in that order, and either click the arrow button or drag the variables to the Sort By box, as shown in Figure 8-2.**

The order of the sort keys is important. If you had chosen Horsepower first and Country_of_Origin second, the results would have been different.

4. **Click OK to sort the data.**

The result is shown in Figure 8-3.

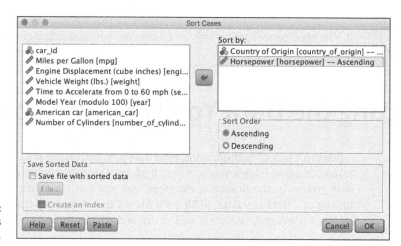

FIGURE 8-2: The Sort Cases dialog.

	car_id	mpg	engine_size	horsepower	weight	acceleration	year	country_of_origin	american_car	number_of_cylinders
1	35	9	4	93	732	9	0 (Missing)	.	.	.
2	39	25	98	.	2046	19	71	American	Yes	4
3	134	21	200	.	2875	17	74	American	Yes	6
4	344	24	140	.	2905	14	80	American	Yes	4
5	383	23	151	.	3035	21	82	American	Yes	4
6	203	29	85	52	2035	22	76	American	Yes	4
7	204	25	98	60	2164	22	76	American	Yes	4
8	245	31	98	63	2051	17	77	American	Yes	4
9	358	35	105	63	2215	15	81	American	Yes	4
10	387	38	105	63	2125	15	82	American	Yes	4

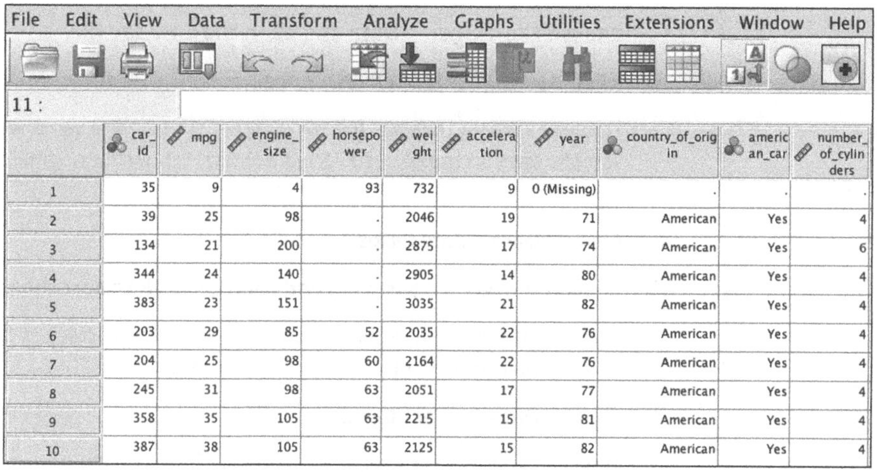

FIGURE 8-3: The data sorted alphabetically by country of origin and then by horsepower.

The order in which data is *displayed* never affects the analysis. You sort data only to better see information in Data Editor. You can get a quick sense of what's going on by sorting your data, but in the end, it isn't a substitute for a proper analysis in the output window.

Also, note that in the top row of data, `year` has a value of `0`, which has been declared as a code for user-defined missing values, and the `country_of_origin`, `american_car`, and `number_of_cylinders` variables have system missing data. System missing values will be sorted to appear before all other values when performing a sort in ascending order. You encounter some functions for handling missing data in Chapter 10.

TIP

If you need to sort using only one variable, you can just right-click the column name.

Selecting the Data You Want to Look At

A powerful way of manipulating your data is to turn some data off. The *select cases* transformation allows you to select a group and then run your analyses on only that group. In the following example, you analyze just European cars, without having to delete any data. SPSS even makes it easy to keep track of what's being counted, averaged, analyzed, and so on, and what's turned off.

Follow these steps:

1. **Choose File ⇨ Open ⇨ Data and open the Cars.sav file.**

   If Cars.sav is already open, that's fine.

   To make sure you see the following screenshots in the same way, you'll first sort the data on the car_id variable (which is how the original data file was sorted).

2. **Choose Data ⇨ Sort Cases.**

3. **Choose the car_id variable, and then click OK to sort the data.**

   Now that the data has been sorted on car_id, you can select the European cars so you can do your analyses just on them.

4. **Choose Data ⇨ Select Cases.**

   The Select Cases dialog appears, as shown in Figure 8-4.

5. **Select the If Condition Is Satisfied radio button and then click the If button.**
   Now you can specify the selection criteria.

6. **Move the country_of_origin variable from the list on the left to the expression box (on the top left).**

   You can move the variable by either dragging it or by selecting it and then clicking the arrow button.

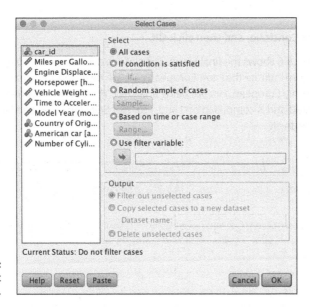

FIGURE 8-4:
The Select
Cases dialog.

7. **Use your keyboard or the onscreen keypad to enter =2 in the expression box, as shown in Figure 8-5.**

You have just told SPSS that you want to select only cases that have a value of 2 for the country_of_origin variable. You type 2, and not the word *European,* because the stored value is 2 even though the label for a value of 2 is European.

WARNING

From this point forward, every piece of output that you generate will use only European cars. To return to using all cases, select the All Cases radio button in the main Select Cases dialog (refer to Figure 8-4).

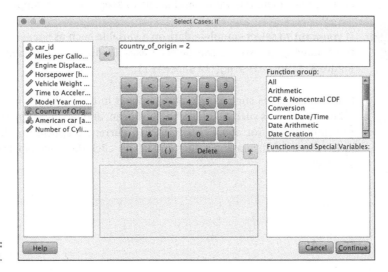

FIGURE 8-5:
The If dialog.

8. Click Continue, and then click OK.

Figure 8-6 shows the final result. The slashes over some row IDs (in the first column) indicate that non-European cars are being ignored (for the time being) and only European cars are being analyzed. The `filter_$` variable is also created and is comprised of 0 and 1 for Not Selected cases and Selected cases, respectively.

File	Edit	View	Data	Transform	Analyze	Graphs	Utilities	Extensions	Window	Help

11 :

	mpg	engine_size	horsepower	weight	acceleration	year	country_of_origin	american_car	number_of_cylinders	filter_$
250	14	454	220	4354	9	70	American	Yes	8	Not Selected
251	14	455	225	4425	10	70	American	Yes	8	Not Selected
252	14	455	225	3086	10	70	American	Yes	8	Not Selected
253	12	455	225	4951	11	73	American	Yes	8	Not Selected
254	16	400	230	4278	10	73	American	Yes	8	Not Selected
255	41	85	.	1835	17	80	European	No	4	Selected
256	35	100	.	2320	16	81	European	No	4	Selected
257	26	97	46	1835	21	70	European	No	4	Selected
258	26	97	46	1950	21	73	European	No	4	Selected
259	.	97	48	1978	20	71	European	No	4	Selected

FIGURE 8-6: The data sorted, indicating selected and unselected cases.

REMEMBER

You should always use values and labels for your category values, as we did with the `country_of_origin` variable in this dataset. This is the way SPSS likes it, and you don't want to make SPSS grumpy, do you? Try typing just strings, and you're likely to get some errors and random happenings. SPSS's bad mood could soon become your own. Use values and labels to keep everyone happy.

TECHNICAL STUFF

If you want to select complete data on a variable such as `horsepower`, you can use the following phrase in the Select Cases IF dialog expression box, shown in Figure 8-5: `not(missing(horsepower))`.

Sometimes values such as 1, 2, and 3 appear in the data view of Data Editor, and other times labels such as American, European, and Japanese appear. In Figure 8-6 the information for `country_of_origin` currently appears as labels. To easily switch between displaying values and labels, click the value labels icon in the data window.

Splitting Data for Easier Analysis

Under some conditions, you can use an even more powerful version of what we've just illustrated with the select cases transformation. For instance, sometimes you might want to run a series of analyses on one group of cases, and then select another group of cases and rerun the same analyses on them. The *split file* transformation allows you to select each group in turn, one at a time, and run all your analyses on each separate group.

1. **Choose File ⇨ Open ⇨ Data and open the Cars.sav file.**

If Cars.sav is already open, that's fine, but you'll be starting with the data sorted on car_id. Make sure that the All Cases radio button is selected in the Select Cases dialog.

2. **Choose Data ⇨ Split File.**

The Split File dialog appears.

3. **Select the Compare Groups radio button.**

4. **Choose country_of_origin as the Compare Groups variable (see Figure 8-7) and click OK.**

Your data window won't have slashes as it did with the Select Cases If filter in the preceding example. Until you run some output, it won't be clear that anything has changed.

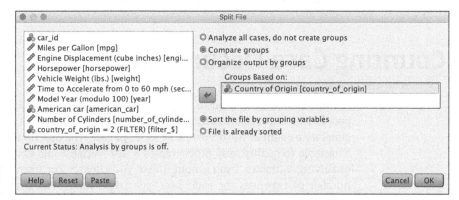

FIGURE 8-7:
The completed
Split File dialog.

5. **Choose Analyze ⇨ Descriptive Statistics ⇨ Frequencies.**

6. **Choose Number of Cylinders and place it in the Variable(s) box.**

7. **Click OK.**

The resulting output, shown in Figure 8-8, is broken down by country of origin. You can stay in split mode as long as you like. Some people spend hours in split mode when producing tables, charts, and statistics for each group.

Number of Cylinders						
Country of Origin			Frequency	Percent	Valid Percent	Cumulative Percent
.	Missing	System	1	100.0		
American	Valid	4	72	28.5	28.5	28.5
		6	74	29.2	29.2	57.7
		8	107	42.3	42.3	100.0
		Total	253	100.0	100.0	
European	Valid	4	66	90.4	90.4	90.4
		5	3	4.1	4.1	94.5
		6	4	5.5	5.5	100.0
		Total	73	100.0	100.0	
Japanese	Valid	3	4	5.1	5.1	5.1
		4	69	87.3	87.3	92.4
		6	6	7.6	7.6	100.0
		Total	79	100.0	100.0	

FIGURE 8-8:
The frequency of number of cylinders while in split mode.

REMEMBER

When you're finished with the split files (or select cases) transformation, turn it off. To turn off a split, choose the Analyze All Cases, Do Not Produce Groups radio button in the Split File dialog (refer to Figure 8-7).

Split by country_of_origin   An indicator in the bottom-right corner of the Data Editor window tells you whether a split or select operation is turned on.

Counting Case Occurrences

If your data is being used to keep track of multiple similar occurrences, such as people who subscribe to any combination of three different magazines, you can generate a count of the occurrences for each case. You specify what value(s) cause a variable to qualify, and SPSS creates a new variable and counts the number of qualifying variables from among those you choose. For example, if you have a number of expenses for each case, you could have SPSS count the number of expenses that exceed a certain threshold.

In the following example, people are listed as subscribers or nonsubscribers to three magazines, which are named simply mag1, mag2, and mag3. The following steps generate a total of the number of subscriptions for each person:

1. **Choose File ⇨ Open ⇨ Data and open the magazines.sav file.**

This file can be downloaded from the book's companion website at www.dummies.com/go/spss. The data is shown in Figure 8-9.

	name	mag1	mag2	mag3	var	var	var	var	var
1	fred	yes	no	no					
2	sam	no	yes	yes					
3	sue	no	no	no					
4	pete	yes	yes	yes					
5									

magazines.sav [DataSet2] –

File Edit View Data Transform Analyze Graphs Utilities Extensions Window Help

FIGURE 8-9: Each magazine has the value 1 for a subscriber and 0 for a nonsubscriber.

2. **Choose Transform ⇨ Count Values Within Cases.**

3. **Do the following for each variable you want to use in the count:**

a. Select the variable.

b. Click the arrow to move it to the Numeric Variables box.

c. In the Target Variable box, give your new variable a name.

When you've finished, the screen will look like Figure 8-10. This operation works only with numerics because it must perform numeric matches on the values. If you want, you can assign both a name *and* a label to the variable that this process creates. In this example, the variable's name is count and the label is Count of subscriptions.

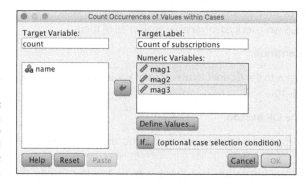

FIGURE 8-10: The chosen variables to be counted, and the name of the new variable.

4. Click the Define Values button.

The screen shown in Figure 8-11 appears. Next, you will count the number of selected variables that have a numeric value of 1, which signifies a subscription.

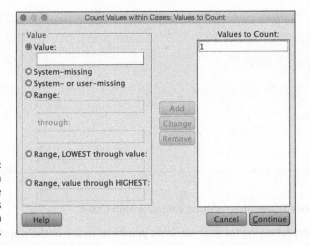

FIGURE 8-11:
Define the criteria
that determine
which values
are included in
the count.

5. In the Value area, type 1 and then click the Add button to move it to the Values to Count box on the right.

After adding the value, you'll have the result shown in Figure 8-11. The new variable contains a count of the variables you named that have a value that matches at least one of the criteria you specified. Each case is counted separately.

As you can also see in figure, the total can also be based on missing values and ranges of values. In the ranges, you can specify both the high and low values, or you can specify one end of the range and have the other end be either the largest or smallest value in the set. In fact, you can select a number of criteria, and SPSS will check each variable against all of them.

6. Click Continue.

You return to the Count Occurrences of Values within Cases screen (refer to Figure 8-10).

7. Click the OK button.

Values appear for the new variable, count, as shown in Figure 8-12.

The count transformation is a great way to assess missing data. You can count missing values across all your variables.

TIP

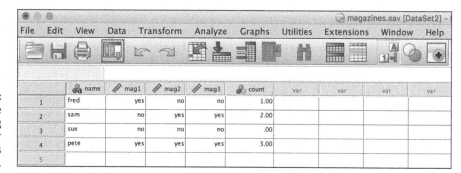

FIGURE 8-12:
A new variable
containing
the total number
of subscriptions
per case.

		name	mag1	mag2	mag3	count	var	var	var	var
1		fred	yes	no	no	1.00				
2		sam	no	yes	yes	2.00				
3		sue	no	no	no	.00				
4		pete	yes	yes	yes	3.00				
5										

Recoding Variables

You can have SPSS change specific values to other specific values according to rules you provide. You can change almost any value to anything else. For example, if you have Yes and No represented by 5 and 6, you could recode the values into 1 and 2, respectively. SPSS has two options for recoding variables:

» **Recode into Same Variables:** Recodes the values in place without creating a new variable

» **Recode into Different Variables:** Creates a new variable and keeps the original variable

You may want to recode to correct errors or to make the data easier to use.

WARNING

If you want to recode values without creating a new variable to receive the new numbers, be sure to create a copy of your data before you start so that you don't accidently lose your data. Chapter 3 has an example of Recode into Same Variables.

Changes to your data can't be automatically reversed, so you could destroy information. For this reason, don't use the Recode into Same Variables option unless you're sure that you want to use it. The main reason to use this option is when you want to change a bunch of variables all at once. It's safer to stick with Recode into Different Variables.

Recoding into different variables

In this section, you use a tiny dataset so that you can see how recoding works. In the dataset, some No responses have been coded 0 and others have been coded –1. You want all No responses to be 0. Duplicate or conflicting values are common in real-world projects when data comes from multiple sources (perhaps different departments) or you have an old system and a new system.

Often you don't want to overwrite existing values — at least not at first. Instead, you want both the old and new versions of the data available. This is always a safe way to recode. You can always delete the original later if you don't need it.

The following steps create the recoded values and stores them in a new variable:

1. **Load the rsvp.sav dataset, as shown in Figure 8-13, and choose Transform ⇨ Recode into Different Variables.**

   This file can be downloaded from the book's companion website at www. dummies.com/go/spss. The Recode into Different Variables dialog appears.

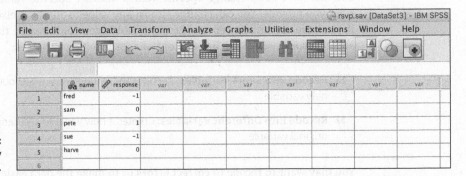

FIGURE 8-13:
The rsvp.sav
data file.

2. **In the left panel, move the** response **variable, which holds the values you want to change, to the center panel.**

3. **In the Output Variable area, enter a name** (attending) **and label** (Attending or not) **for the new variable.**

WARNING

   For the output variable, if you choose a new variable name, a new variable is created. If you choose an existing variable name, its values will be overwritten. Here, you chose a new name to protect the existing data.

4. **Click the Change button.**

   The output variable is defined, as shown in Figure 8-14.

5. **Click the Old and New Values button.**

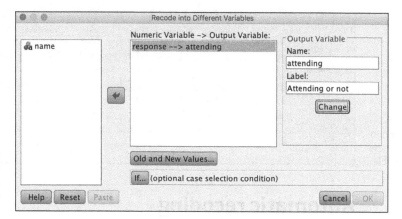

FIGURE 8-14:
Name the
variable to
receive the
recoded values.

6. **Define the recoding:**

   a. *In the Old Value text box, enter an existing value.*

   b. *In the New Value text box, enter the new recoded value.*

   c. *Click the Add button for the Old ⇨ New list (see Figure 8-15).*

   Be sure to map all values — even the ones that don't change — because you're creating a new variable and it has no preset values.

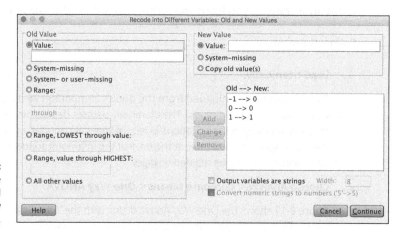

FIGURE 8-15:
All possible
values recoded
for a new
variable.

7. **Click Continue.**

8. **Click OK.**

   The results shown in Figure 8-16 appear. You now have a new variable and the values have been coded in a more useful manner.

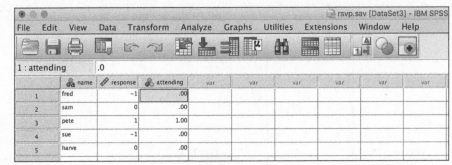

FIGURE 8-16:
Values recoded
into a new
variable.

Automatic recoding

Automatic recoding converts string values into numeric values with labels. String variables can sometimes create confusing behaviors in SPSS because some dialogs, such as One-Way ANOVA, don't recognize string variables, even though these dialogs do accept categorical variables.

In the following example, you work with the Embarked variable, which contains letters that represent where passengers got on the *Titanic*, and convert these string values into numeric values. First, however, you take a brief look at the One-Way ANOVA dialog so you can see an example of when a dialog does not display string variables. We won't discuss the theory behind ANOVA or perform the analysis now — you learn about this statistical technique in Chapter 20.

Follow these steps:

1. **Load titanic.sav.**

   This file can be downloaded from the book's companion website at www.dummies.com/go/spss. The titanic.sav dataset has become famous in machine-learning demonstrations in recent years. It contains a partial list of the passengers on the *Titanic* at the time of the infamous accident, when it hit an iceberg during its maiden voyage.

2. **Choose Analyze ⇨ Compare Means ⇨ One-Way ANOVA.**

   Figure 8-17 shows the One-Way Anova dialog with the Titantic.sav dataset in the background. As you can see, the dataset has 13 variables but only 8 appear in the One-Way ANOVA dialog. The 5 variables missing from the dialog are all string variables, and we would like to use one of them, the Embarked variable, in a One-Way ANOVA. However, note that the previously recoded numeric variable, Embarked_Code, is visible in the One-Way ANOVA dialog. This is because this dialog does not allow string variables, even if a variable is suitable for this technique.

This issue is not common, but it can be confusing when it happens. You won't pursue this analysis now. Instead, you will turn your attention to learning how to quickly and easily convert a string variable to a numeric variable with labels so that you can use the new numeric variable in practically every dialog in SPSS.

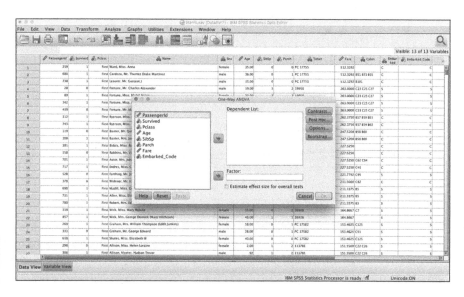

FIGURE 8-17:
ANOVA dialog
with a dataset in
the background.

3. **Click Cancel to exit the One-Way ANOVA dialog.**

4. **Choose Transform ⇨ Automatic Recode.**

   The Automatic Recode dialog appears.

5. **In the list on the left, move the variable you want to recode to the box on the left.**

   To follow along with the example, move the Embarked variable.

6. **In the Variable ⇨ New Name box, enter the name of the variable to receive the recoded values.**

   Type the name Embarked_Code2.

7. **Click the Add New Name button.**

   Embarked_Code2 appears in the box above the new name.

8. **Select the Treat Blank String Values as User-Missing option, as shown in Figure 8-18.**

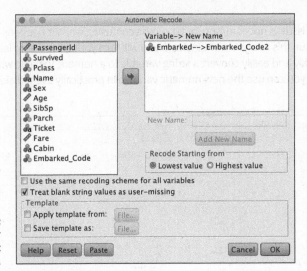

FIGURE 8-18:
The dialog for automatic recoding.

9. Click OK.

Recoding takes place, as shown in the output window shown in Figure 8-19. The M adjacent to the value 4 indicates that not only have the missing values been assigned to the numeric value 4 but SPSS also has declared value 4 as missing.

```
Embarked into Embarked_Code2
Old Value  New Value  Value Label

C                     1  C
Q                     2  Q
S                     3  S
        M             4M
```

FIGURE 8-19:
Autorecoded values.

The values in the new variable, Embarked_Code2, come about from sorting the values of the original variable and then assigning numbers to them in the new sort order. If the input values are a string of characters instead of the digits, the strings are sorted alphabetically (well, almost — uppercase letters come before lowercase).

In the Automatic Recode window (refer to Figure 8-18), you can see the choice for recoding values with new numbers that start with either the lowest value or the highest value. The new numeric values will be the same either way; they're just assigned in the opposite order.

At the bottom of the Automatic Recode window are two choices for the creation of a template file. A *template file* holds a record of the recoding patterns. That way, if you want to recode more data with the same variable names, the new input values will be compared against the previous encoding and be given appropriate values so that the two data files can be merged and the data will all fit. For example, if you have brand names or part numbers in your data, the recoding will be consistent with the original values because it will be assigned the same *pattern* of recoded values.

Binning

If you're using a scale variable, which contains a range of values, you can create groups of those values and organize them in bins. For example, you could use the ages of a number of people and put each one in its own bin, such as one bin for ages 0 to 20, another bin for ages 21 to 40, and so on. You can specify the size and content of bins in several ways. The actual binning process is automatic.

The following steps divide salaries into bins:

1. **Choose File ⇨ Open ⇨ Data and load the salaries.sav file.**

To download the file, go to www.dummies.com/go/spss4e. The file contains a list of ID numbers with a salary for each one, as shown in Figure 8-20.

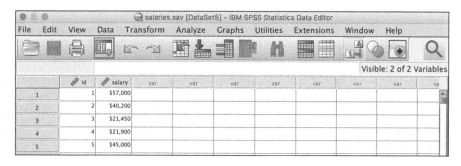

FIGURE 8-20:
A list of employee ID numbers and the salaries corresponding to them.

2. **Choose Transform ⇨ Visual Binning.**

The Visual Binning dialog appears.

3. **Move Current Salary from the Variables box to the Variables to Bin box, as shown in Figure 8-21.**

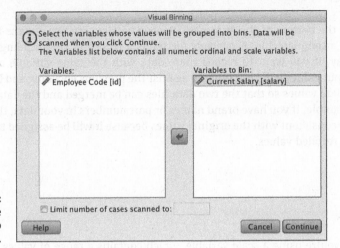

FIGURE 8-21:
Select the name
of the variable to
be binned.

4. **Click Continue.**

   A bar graph displaying the range of values of the salaries appears, as shown in Figure 8-22.

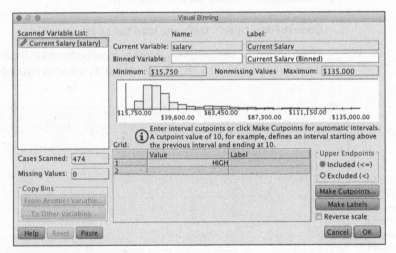

FIGURE 8-22:
How the binning
will be done.

5. **Click the Make Cutpoints button.**

6. **Select the points at which you want to cut the data into parts to create the bins.**

   In this example, we divided the data into even percentiles of numbers of cases — that is, each bin will contain the same number of cases, as shown in Figure 8-23. Note that four cutpoints divide the data into five bins, each holding 20 percent of the cases.

We could have divided the data into equal-width intervals — that is, each bin would contain a range of the same magnitude, which would put different numbers of cases in each bin. Or the cutpoints could have been based on standard deviations, which would create two cutpoints, dividing the data into the three bins — one each of low, medium, and high capacity.

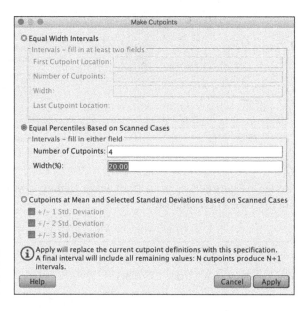

FIGURE 8-23:
Specify how you
want the data
divided into bins.

7. **Click the Apply button, and the cutpoints appear as vertical lines on the bar graph, as shown in Figure 8-24.**

   You can click the Make Cutpoints button repeatedly and cut the data different ways until you get the cutpoints the way you like. Any new cutpoints you define replace previous ones.

8. **In the Binned Variable text box, enter** salary_bin **as the new variable to contain the binning information.**

   Be sure to use an underscore. The default label for the new variable appears in the text box to the right of the name. You can change this if you want.

   The bins are created and numbered from 1 to 5, but if you select the Reverse Scale option (in the lower-right corner), the numbering will be from 5 to 1.

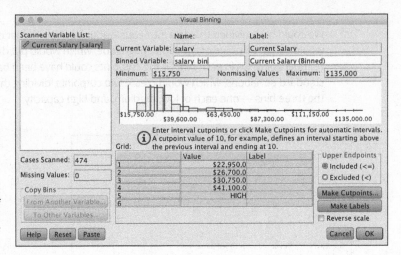

FIGURE 8-24:
A bar graph of
the data with
cutpoints for
binning.

9. Click OK.

The message in Figure 8-25 appears. Don't worry. Nothing is wrong because you want to create a new variable.

FIGURE 8-25:
A message
alerting that you
are about to
create a new
variable.

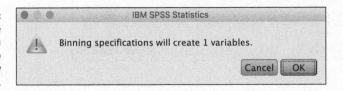

10. Click OK to dismiss the warning message.

The new variable is created and filled with the bin values, as shown in Figure 8-26.

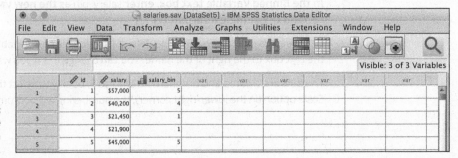

FIGURE 8-26:
The new variable
containing the bin
numbers.

Optimal Binning

Another kind of binning called optimal binning is easy but powerful, using technology similar to that used in machine learning. *Optimal binning* finds the cutpoints that are optimal for predictions.

Follow these steps to perform optimal binning:

1. **Return to the titanic.sav dataset. Choose Transform ⇨ Optimal Binning.**

2. **Move the** Fare **variable to the Variables to Bin box, and move** Survived **to the Optimize Bins with Respect To box, as shown in Figure 8-27.**

The variable in the Optimize Bins with Respect To box doesn't have to be a variable from a previous binning operation. It can be any variable that contains a collection of values that can be separated into bins.

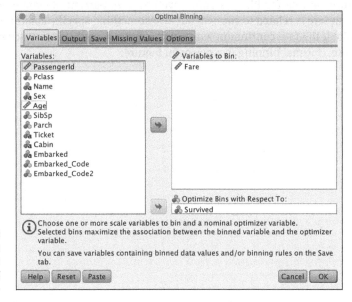

FIGURE 8-27:
Select the bin variable and the optimizing variable.

3. **Click OK.**

The output shown in Figure 8-28 is generated.

Optimal Binning

Binning Summary

Fare

Bin	End Point Lower	End Point Upper	Number of Cases by Level of Survived 0	Number of Cases by Level of Survived 1	Number of Cases by Level of Survived Total
1	a	10.5000	272	67	339
2	10.5000	75.2500	254	201	455
3	75.2500	a	23	74	97
Total			549	342	891

Each bin is computed as Lower <= Fare < Upper.

a. Unbounded

FIGURE 8-28:
The output from optimal binning.

The results are interesting. The fares are in British pounds, but remember that the *Titanic* accident happened in 1912. The upper cutoff of 10.5 for Bin 1 (shown in Figure 8-28), adjusted for inflation, would be over 1,000 British pounds today. The survival rate for Bin 1, the lowest fares, is 67/339, or about 20 percent. The survival rate for Bin 3 is 74/97, well over 75 percent. So you've learned not just that fare is related to survival but also something specific about the optimal points along the fare continuum where you can most easily perceive changes in survival rate. Optimal binning is a powerful feature.

Chapter **9**

Computing New Variables

The Compute Variable dialog, which you access from the Transform menu, is one of the most frequently used dialogs in all of SPSS. Why? This dialog, shown in Figure 9-1, contains dozens of functions as well as numerous arithmetic operators and logical operators that perform all kinds of calculations.

The Compute Variable dialog is also where you go to make new variables out of existing ones. To do so, you build your own formulas in which you combine variables in your dataset with simple arithmetic operators. This process is the focus of the chapter. In the next chapter, we will continue our discussion of the Compute Variable dialog, but with a focus on several of those fancy functions.

Even though you will be getting help from the Compute Variable dialog, at times it will feel like programming, albeit at a basic level. If you don't have much programming experience, it may seem a little tricky, at first. But don't worry — in this chapter, we give you the information you need to get started.

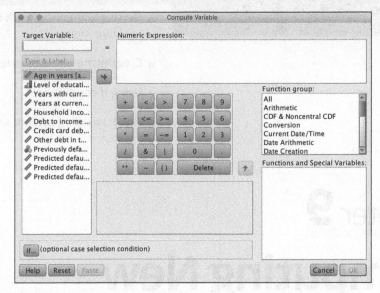

FIGURE 9-1:
The Compute
Variable dialog.

Calculating a New Variable with a Formula

In the first example, you write a simple formula to calculate how long a bank employee has been with the bank. Follow these steps:

1. **Open the bank.sav dataset, shown in Figure 9-2.**

   You can download the file at www.dummies.com/go/spss4e.

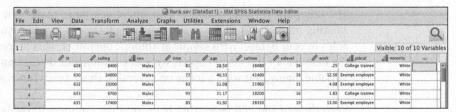

FIGURE 9-2:
The bank.sav
dataset.

2. **Choose Transform ⇨ Compute Variable.**

   The Compute Variable dialog appears.

3. **Drag Current salary (salnow) to the Numeric Expression box.**

   You can instead type **salnow** in the expression box.

4. **Add a minus symbol to the expression using either the dialog's keypad or your keyboard.**

5. Drag `Beginning Salary (salbeg)` to the Numeric Expression box.

You can instead type **salbeg** in the expression box.

6. **In the Target Variable box, type** increase, **which is the name of your new variable.**

The dialog now looks like Figure 9-3.

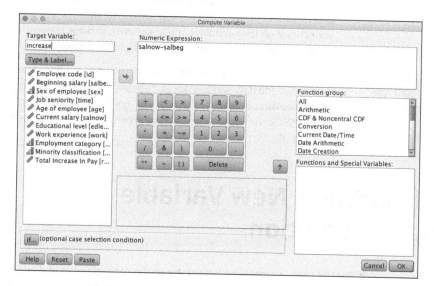

FIGURE 9-3:
A simple
subtraction of
two variables.

7. **Add a label by clicking the Type & Label button, selecting the Label option, and typing** Total Increase In Pay, **as shown in Figure 9-4.**

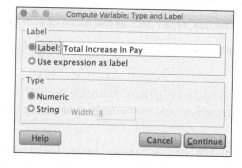

FIGURE 9-4:
The Type and
Label dialog.

8. **Click Continue and then click OK.**

Your new variable appears as shown in Figure 9-5.

FIGURE 9-5:
The dataset
displays
increase, the
new variable.

	id	salbeg	sex	time	age	salnow	edlevel	work	jobcat	minority	increase	var
1	628	8400	Males	81	28.50	16080	16	.25	College trainee	White	7680.00	
2	630	24000	Males	73	40.33	41400	16	12.50	Exempt employee	White	17400.00	
3	632	10200	Males	83	31.08	21960	15	4.08	Exempt employee	White	11760.00	
4	633	8700	Males	93	31.17	19200	16	1.83	College trainee	White	10500.00	
5	635	17400	Males	83	41.92	28350	19	13.00	Exempt employee	White	10950.00	

Remember that the Data View tab of the Data Editor window displays only data
and variables names. If you want to see the variables labels, you'll need to put
your cursor on the variable name or switch to variable view (by clicking the
Variable View tab in the lower-left corner of the window).

WARNING

Unlike in Excel, formulas are not stored in the data window. New variable
columns in the data window are just like any other data columns. This
difference can cause confusion if you're more familiar with Excel than you are
with SPSS. Some of the differences between Excel and SPSS are discussed in
Chapter 30.

Calculating a New Variable with a Condition

For the next example, you continue in the same dataset and add an IF condition to
your toolkit. These steps have a twist: We will make two very common mistakes
so that you will not make these mistakes in the future (we hope) or will know how
to resolve them.

1. **Choose Transform ⇨ Compute Variable.**

2. **In the Target Variable box, type** bonus **as the name of your new variable.**

3. **In the Numeric Expression box, type the following string of characters:** $1,000.

4. **Click OK.**

   The warning shown in Figure 9-6 appears. The dollar sign tells SPSS that the
   formula contains a system variable, not currency. (More on system variables in
   the next section.)

   If you want to indicate that bonus is currency, you use the Variable View tab of
   the Data Editor window and adjust the variable's metadata. (For details, see
   Chapter 3.)

5. **Remove the dollar sign and the comma, leaving the following string of
   characters:** 1000.

6. **Click the If button in the lower-left corner to display the If dialog.**

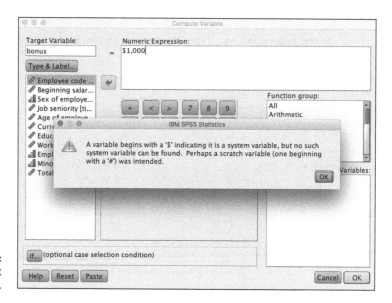

FIGURE 9-6:
A warning about
system variables.

7. **Select the Include If Case Satisfies Condition radio button.**

8. **In the If dialog, right-click the** `Employment Category (jobcat)` **variable and select Variable Information from the menu.**

   The screen looks like Figure 9-7. Another common mistake is to type a variable's category label directly into an expression. The correct way to incorporate a variable's category in an expression is to use a value, not a value label.

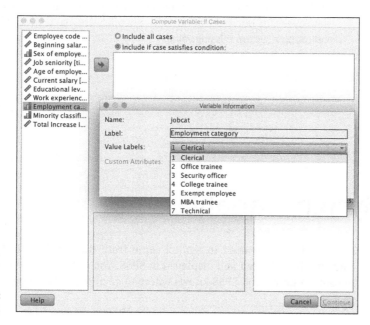

FIGURE 9-7:
The If dialog.

9. In the expression box, type jobcat = 5, as shown in Figure 9-8.

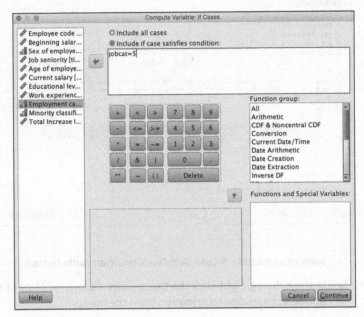

FIGURE 9-8:
Correctly
referencing a
category in an
expression.

10. Click Continue and then click OK.

The result appears in the Data Editor window, as shown in Figure 9-9. A new variable, bonus, is visible and is populated for some cases but not others. The employees for whom the bonus does not apply are marked with a period, indicating a system missing value.

FIGURE 9-9:
The dataset
displays bonus,
the new variable.

Using System Variables

Most of the values used in Syntax come from the variables in the dataset you currently have loaded and displayed in SPSS. You simply use your variable names in your program, and SPSS knows where to go and get the values.

SPSS has another type of variable that is already defined and can be used any-where in a program. Predefined variables are called *system variables* and are shown in Table 9-1. They all begin with a dollar sign ($) and already contain values.

TABLE 9-1   **System Variables**

Variable Name	Description
$CASENUM	The current case number. It's the count of cases from the beginning case to the current case.
$DATE	The current date in international date format with a two-digit year.
$DATE11	The current date in international date format with a four-digit year.
$JDATE	The count of the number of days since October 14, 1582 (the first day of the Gregorian calendar).
$LENGTH	The current page length.
$SYSMIS	The system missing value. This is displayed as a period or whatever is defined as the decimal point.
$TIME	The number of seconds since midnight October 14, 1582 (the first day of the Gregorian calendar).
$WIDTH	The current page width.

WARNING

System variable names are not the only names to carefully avoid. Don't try to name variables AND, OR, or NOT. These logical operators are keywords in the Syntax language and are *also* reserved words. If you try to use a reserved word as a variable name, SPSS will catch it and tell you that you can't do it. Relational operators, which are used in the Syntax language to compare values, are also reserved words. The relational operators are EQ, NE, LT, GT, LE, and GE. Some other reserved words are ALL, BY, TO, and WITH. For more on reserved words, see Chapter 27.

Contrasting $Sysmis with SYSMIS

It's easy to confuse the $Sysmis system variable, with the Sysmis function. We dedicate Chapter 10 to functions, but we want to clarify the difference here with a brief example:

1. **Choose Transform ⇨ Compute Variable.**

2. **In the Numeric Expression box, type $SYSMIS, as shown in Figure 9-10.**

This expression contains the correct grammar if you want all values of a new variable to have the value of system missing. However, it's not the correct grammar in a conditional expression.

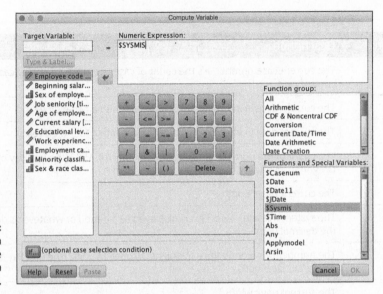

3. **Click the If button to display the If dialog.**

4. **Select the Include If Case Satisfies Condition radio button and type** sysmis(bonus), **as shown in Figure 9-11.**

   This is the correct grammar to use if you want to resolve the logical expression and determine if the expression is true or false.

5. **Click Cancel and then click Cancel again.**

   You don't create a new variable in this example.

In summary, the $Sysmis system variable is used to assign a value of system missing to a new variable. The Sysmis function determines if a particular case in the dataset is system missing or not. We provide another example of the use of the Sysmis function in Chapter 10.

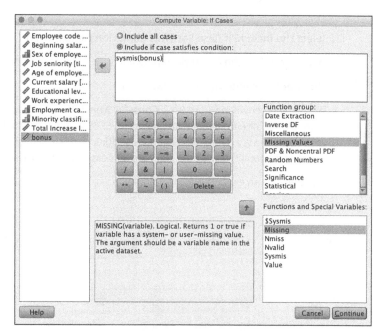

FIGURE 9-11:
An expression using the Sysmis function.

Understanding Missing Data in Formulas

The next example is more elaborate because you start to combine what you've just learned. By building an expression that includes the bonus variable, you explore how SPSS behaves when some variables in an expression are complete but others have missing data.

Follow these steps, using the same dataset:

1. **Choose Transform ⇨ Compute Variable.**

2. **Type** AveRaise **as the target variable.**

3. **In the Numeric Expression box, type** increase/(time/12)+bonus**.**

    The employee's total raise is increase, which you created previously. The time variable is recorded in months, so dividing by 12 converts time to years.

4. **Click the If button to display the If dialog.**

    The If dialog allows us to specify to whom the expression in the compute dialog will apply. In our case, the expression will apply to exempt employees, who have a value of 5 in the variable job category.

5. Select the Include If Case Satisfies Condition radio button.

6. Type jobcat=5 in the Numeric Expression box.

7. Click Continue and then click OK.

The result is shown in Figure 9-12. Consider what SPSS would do with these instructions. For employees with Jobcat=5, SPSS would calculate the new variable, AveRaise. Does SPSS need that additional instruction? What would happen without it? How would SPSS process cases that are missing bonus?

Let's perform an experiment to find out.

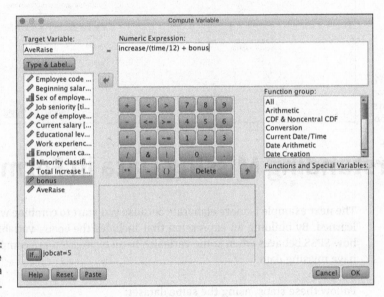

FIGURE 9-12:
The AveRaise
expression with a
condition applied.

8. Choose Transform ⇨ Compute Variable.

9. Click the If button to display the If dialog.

10. Select the Include All Cases radio button.

11. Click Continue.

12. When the dialog asks if you want to change the existing variable, click OK. Click OK again to create the variable.

Note that you're reversing the preceding process. The result is shown in Figure 9-13.

13. Review the results in the data window, as shown in Figure 9-14.

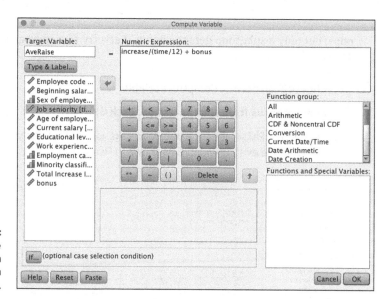

FIGURE 9-13:
The AveRaise
expression
without a
condition.

FIGURE 9-14:
The new
AveRaise
variable in the
data window.

Because bonus is sometimes missing, SPSS must leave certain cases as system missing because the calculation can't be performed. (Remember system missing is indicated with a period.) No warning is generated and the computation proceeds for most cases. You simply see *system missing* for the cases with a value for bonus. In the next example, you use another approach for calculating AveRaise.

Efficiently Calculating with Multiple Formulas

There's a trick to calculating a variable such as AveRaise when you need two different formulas. It's not always necessary to have an IF condition for one group and another IF condition for the other group. Often, the more efficient method is to perform the more basic calculation for everyone, and then return to the Compute Variable dialog a second time for the subgroup. In this example, everyone gets a raise, but only a subgroup gets the bonus. Let's try this approach, using the same dataset:

1. **Choose Transform ⇨ Compute Variable.**

2. **Remove** bonus **from the expression. Click OK.**

Because AveRaise already exists, SPSS asks you confirm that you want to overwrite the existing variable, as shown in Figure 9-15.

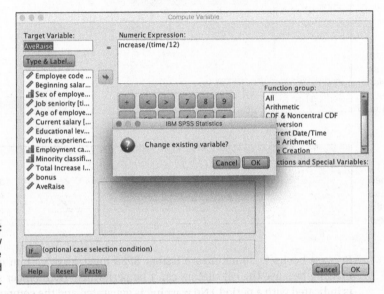

FIGURE 9-15:
The new
AveRaise
variable created
for everyone.

3. **Click OK to confirm and OK again to compute** AveRaise.

The dataset now looks like Figure 9-16.

FIGURE 9-16:
The new
AveRaise
variable created
for everyone in
the data window.

4. Return to the Transform Compute dialog by choosing Transform ⇨ Compute Variable.

5. Click the If button to display the If dialog.

6. Select the Include If Case Satisfies Condition radio button.

7. Type jobcat=5 in the expression box.

8. Click Continue.

9. Add + bonus back into the expression.

The dialog shown in Figure 9-17 appears.

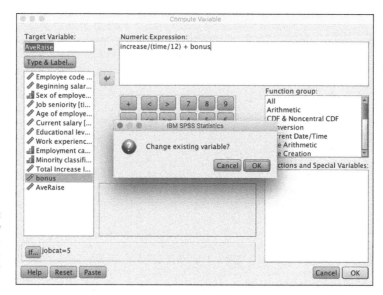

FIGURE 9-17: The new AveRaise variable with a conditional computation.

10. Click OK to confirm that AveRaise is to be overwritten.

11. Click OK.

Your new variable is now populated in all rows of the dataset.

You have now efficiently created a new variable when you needed two different formulas, showing that it's not always necessary to have an IF condition for each group.

IN THIS CHAPTER

» **Learning the language of SPSS functions**

» **Using the** LENGTH **function**

» **Working with the** ANY **function**

» **Making the** MEAN **function work for you**

» **Expanding your toolkit of functions**

Chapter **10**

Some Useful Functions

I n this chapter, we focus on the variety of functions available in the Compute Variable dialog. We won't discuss them all, but we do provide examples of several of the most useful ones. If you use spreadsheet software such as Microsoft Excel or Apple Numbers, you've encountered some of these functions, but SPSS offers a greater variety of statistical options than you'll find in spreadsheet software. We emphasize the functions aligned with the most important SPSS skills.

SPSS divides functions into function groups. Here's just a sampling of the kinds of functions you'll find:

» Arithmetic functions

» Statistical functions

» String functions

» String/numeric conversion functions

» Date and time functions

» Random variable and distribution functions

» Missing value functions

» Logical functions

When you click a function group name such as Arithmetic (refer to Figure 10-1), you see a list of the functions that belong to that function group. In this chapter, you investigate just 12 of these functions, but they're a diverse 12. The idea is to give you a sense of the different kinds of things you can do and to introduce you to the function help system.

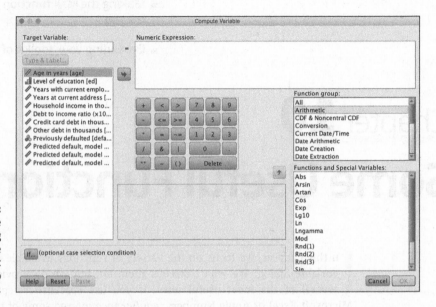

FIGURE 10-1:
The Compute Variable dialog with the Arithmetic function group selected.

The LENGTH Function

For the initial examples, you use the Web Survey.sav dataset. The end of the Web Survey.sav dataset has an open-ended question where respondents can leave a comment. This type of question often prompts a generic answer such as "Not at this time" or "None," but sometimes the responses can be useful.

The goal of this exercise is to identify, as simply as possible, if the respondent provided a comment. That way, you won't clog up your report with lots of blank rows. To do so, you use the LENGTH function.

The LENGTH function identifies the number of characters in a response, so anyone with a value greater than zero provided a response. This function also allows you to review some features of the help that SPSS provides for each function. This simple function is a good place to start because it requires only one argument:

1. **Open the Web Survey.sav dataset.**

   To download the file, go to the book's companion website at www.dummies. com/go/spss4e. (You may stumble upon Web Survey 2.sav, which is what the dataset looks like at the end of the chapter.)

2. **Choose Transform ➪ Compute Variable.**

3. **Select String in the Function Group area in the upper right, and then select the Length function.**

4. **Either drag Length into position in the editing area at the top, or click the up-arrow button on the right.**

   The window should look like Figure 10-2.

FIGURE 10-2: The Compute Variable dialog with the LENGTH function selected.

5. **Select the Comment variable and either drag it into position, replacing the question mark, or click the right-arrow button on the left.**

   Making progress. You could just click OK, but let's take a moment to read the function help at the bottom of the screen, which is visible whenever you click a function's name (as you did for Length in Figure 10-2). You have to scroll to read it onscreen; the complete text is as follows:

   > LENGTH(strexpr). Numeric. Returns the length of strexpr in bytes, which must be a string expression. For string variables, in Unicode mode this is the number of bytes in each value, excluding trailing blanks, but in code page mode this is the defined variable length, including trailing blanks. To get the length (in bytes) without trailing blanks in code page mode, use LENGTH(RTRIM(strexpr)).

Whoa! This information can be intimidating at first, but it is all there for a reason. The function help section has the following consistent structure across all functions in SPSS:

- Function name and grammar

- Type of output

- Description of the function

The first part — *LENGTH(strexpr)* — is the name and grammar of the function. You have to give the command a string expression in parentheses. Next, the word *Numeric* means that the function will return a numeric value. This pattern is repeated for every function. The first two parts are half the battle! The final part, which isn't always easy to read, is the description of how the function works.

In this case, you give the LENGTH function a word, and it gives you a number. Let's try it.

6. **In the Target Variable box, name the new variable** Length **and verify that your screen looks like Figure 10-3.**

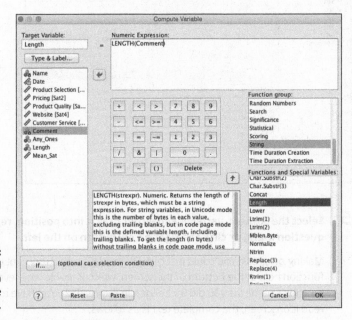

FIGURE 10-3:
The completed LENGTH function in the Compute Variable dialog.

7. **Click OK.**

In the data window, you see a new variable, Length, listing several numbers. Glance at the original Comment variable. Doug, Jack, and Georgia did not leave comments, so they should have a zero value.

The ANY Function

Learning the grammar of a function includes identifying the number of required arguments or components. The LENGTH function has only one argument. Now you move on to a more complex function, the ANY function, which has two arguments.

When analyzing data, it's often useful to identify people who meet certain criteria. For example, you may want to identify employees who have high performance ratings (to keep them in mind for future job openings), or you may want to identify customers who gave your company a low satisfaction rating (to see how you can improve their experience). The ANY function allows you to identify cases that meet the criteria you specify across a series of variables.

In this example, you identify customers who gave a response of 1, the lowest possible value, on the satisfaction variables, so you can contact them and address their concerns.

1. **If the Web Survey.sav dataset is not still open, open it now.**

2. **Choose Transform ⇨ Compute Variable.**

3. **In the Function Group area in the upper right, select Search and then select the Any function.**

4. **Either drag Any into position in the editing area at the top, or click the up-arrow button on the right.**

The window should look like Figure 10-4.

FIGURE 10-4: The Compute Variable dialog with the ANY function chosen.

5. Review the function definition at the bottom of the dialog.

Let's take a moment to read the function help for ANY at the bottom of the dialog:

> ANY(test,value[,value,. . .]). Logical. Returns 1 or true if the value of test matches any of the subsequent values; returns 0 or false otherwise. This function requires two or more arguments. For example, ANY(var1, 1, 3, 5) returns 1 if the value of var1 is 1, 3, or 5 and 0 for other values. ANY can also be used to scan a list of variables or expressions for a value. For example, ANY(1, var1, var2, var3) returns 1 if any of the three specified variables has a value of 1 and 0 if all three variables have values other than 1.

Most people find these definitions difficult at first, but remember: It all means something. The first part — *ANY(test,value[,value,. . .])* — is the name and grammar of the function. Note that it has more arguments than LENGTH, so it's a little more complicated. The next word — *Logical* — tells you that you're going to get a true or false result, which SPSS indicates with 1 and 0, respectively. Finally, the third section describes the purpose of the function. Again, the structure of the help section remains consistent.

So the definition means that you give the ANY function a test value and several variable names, and it will give you a 1 or a 0. Let's try it.

6. In the Target Variable box, name the new variable Any_Ones.

7. In the Numeric Expression box, replace the first question mark with 1.

It looks like you have room for only one more variable because you have only one more question mark, but you can add as many as you like.

8. Drag all the Sat variables (Sat1, Sat2, Sat3, Sat4, and Sat5), separating each with a comma, and replacing the second question mark, as shown in Figure 10-5.

9. Click OK.

The data window displays a new variable, Any_Ones, which is 1 (true) or 0 (false), depending on whether the respondent gave a 1 (the lowest score) for any of the satisfaction variables. You could easily imagine that management at this company wants to know if anyone is upset enough to give a score of 1 on any question.

Before attempting to run any function, make sure you delete all question marks in the function. Otherwise, you will not be able to run the command.

WARNING

FIGURE 10-5:
The dialog with
the completed
ANY function.

The MEAN Function and Missing Data

Next, you calculate the mean of the five satisfaction variables. There is a twist, though — you can include or exclude rows with some missing data. If the respondent didn't answer any of the questions, you don't have much choice, but what if someone answered only some questions? Here's how to calculate a mean in two different ways:

1. If Web Survey.sav isn't open, open it.

2. Choose Transform ⇨ Compute Variable.

3. Select Statistical in the Function Group area, and then select the Mean function.

4. Either drag Mean into position in the editing area at the top, or click the up-arrow button on the right.

5. Review the function definition at the bottom of the dialog.

Here's what it says:

MEAN. MEAN(numexpr,numexpr[,..]). Numeric. Returns the arithmetic mean of its arguments that have valid, nonmissing values. This function requires two or more arguments, which must be numeric. You can specify a minimum number of valid arguments for this function to be evaluated.

The first word is the name of the function. The second part — *MEAN(numexpr, numexpr[,..])* — means you have to provide at least two variables; the two dots indicate that you can provide more than two variables, if needed. The next word — *Numeric* — tells you that the result will be a number. Note that you can specify a minimum number of valid arguments for this function to be evaluated. This functionality will be important in the second example.

To summarize, you give MEAN several variable names (or numbers), and it returns a number.

6. **In the Target Variable box, name the new variable** Mean_Sat.

7. **Drag all the** Sat **variables (**Sat1, Sat2, Sat3, Sat4, **and** Sat5**)), separating each with a comma, to the Numeric Expression box, as shown in Figure 10-6.**

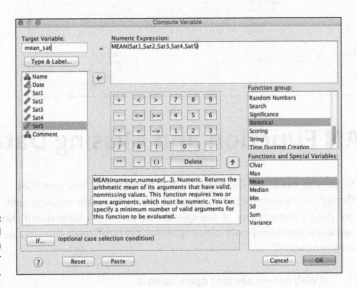

FIGURE 10-6:
The completed
MEAN function
that allows for
missing values.

8. **Click OK.**

The Data Editor window displays the new variable, Mean_Sat, populated for everyone, even though Frank didn't answer all the questions. His average is based on the answers he did provide.

9. **Choose Transform ⇨ Compute Variable.**

The previous expression that you created in the Compute Variable dialog is still there.

10. **Name the new variable** Mean_Sat2.

11. **In the Numeric Expression box, add** .5 **to the function so that it reads** MEAN.5, **as shown in Figure 10-7.**

Don't change the rest of the function.

The .5 (the .n suffix) tells SPSS Statistics that to compute a mean, each case must provide at least five valid values. Here you are specifying the minimum number of valid arguments for this function to be evaluated.

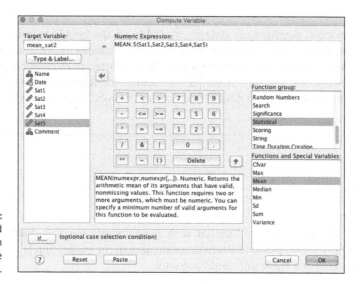

FIGURE 10-7:
The completed
MEAN function
requiring five
valid values.

12. **Click OK.**

The Data Editor window displays the new variable, Mean_Sat2, which is populated for everyone except Frank because he didn't answer all the questions.

This is powerful stuff. Mastering missing values is one of the things that will mark you as an expert in SPSS Statistics.

TIP

Specifying the minimum number of valid arguments for a function to be evaluated (the .n suffix) works with all statistical functions, notably the SUM( ) function.

TIP

If you want to read extended documentation on functions, go to Command Syntax Reference in the Help menu. Make sure look in Chapter 2, "Universals," under "Transformation Expressions." If you look in the section for the Compute command, the information is much more limited and you might not find what you need.

RND, TRUNC, and MOD

SPSS allows you to declare and display numeric variables with up to 16 decimal places, which is far more than you will typically want to report. SPSS uses all of this precision when performing calculations, whether you display them or not. In some instances, you'll want to convert real numbers into integers.

The Arithmetic function group offers a number of options to do this kind of conversion. In this section, you explore three functions: RND (rounds to the nearest integer), TRUNC (truncates the remainder), and MOD (returns the remainder).

The loan_payment.sav dataset, available on the book's website (www.dummies. com/go/spss4e) and shown in Figure 10-8, includes information about how long it's been since loans were originated. It's reported in months because statements are sent out monthly. A simple calculation (dividing by 12) would calculate the number of years, but what if you wanted to report years and months?

	CID	Fullname	Loan_Date	Loan_Income	Current	Late_Payments	Owner	Months
1	101192	Brown, Tim	09/14/1998	$125,000	.	0	1	260
2	101091	Miser, Angus	09/17/2008	$41,000	.	2	9	140
3	101197	Gummage, Bill	01/19/2020	$92,000	$92,000	0	1	4
4	101010	Banker, Jill	02/05/2015	$75,000	$105,000	4	1	63
5	101056	Brown, Edith	07/03/2015	$87,500	$87,500	6	0	59

FIGURE 10-8: The loan_ payment.sav dataset.

At this point, you're familiar with the Compute Variable dialog, so Table 10-1 simply shows possible alternatives to place in the expression box using the simple formula and three different functions.

Note that the MOD( ) function takes two arguments, so it requires a comma to separate the two arguments. The second argument, called the modulus, is 12 because the divisor is 12. As you can see, the best way to report years and months is to use the combination of the TRUNC( ) and MOD( ) functions. For instance, CID 101192 has had a loan for 21 years and 8 months.

TABLE 10-1   Arithmetic Function Results

CID	Months	Months/12	Rnd(Months/12)	Trunc(Months/12)	Mod(Months,12)
101192	260	21.67	22	21	8
101091	140	11.67	12	11	8
101197	4	.33	0	0	4
101010	63	5.25	5	5	3
101056	59	4.92	5	4	11

WARNING

Don't use the Variable View tab of the Data Editor window (see Chapter 3) to attempt to convert real numbers to integers. Changing the number of decimal places in the Variable View tab changes only the decimal places that appear in the Data Editor window; it doesn't change the number of decimal places stored in the variable or in any calculations. The decimal places are still there even if you can't see them. Change the decimal places back again and they will return to view.

TECHNICAL STUFF

A number of arithmetic functions have an optional fuzzbits argument. The vast majority of SPSS users can safely ignore this argument. It relates to significant digits and can become an issue when making calculations and then reporting to many decimal places. When reporting at this level of precision, Excel, SAS, and SPSS can disagree due to subtle little differences in the calculations. If this ever happens, research fuzzbits in the Command Syntax Reference.

Logicals, the MISSING Function, and the NOT Function

Many SPSS functions, such as the ANY function (which you used previously), the MISSING function, and the SYSMIS function, return 1 for true and 0 for false. The 1s and 0s are not labeled, which can be confusing. Most computer programming languages call this kind of variable a Boolean, or binary, variable because it has two possible outcomes.

The MISSING function is true if a value is either user-defined missing or system missing. The SYSMIS function returns true only when the value is system missing.

The SPSS feature of user-defined missing (see Chapter 3) involves an otherwise valid value that has been declared as missing in the Variable View tab of the Data Editor window. In this dataset, the Owner variable has a user-defined missing value of 9, meaning unverified, whereas the Current variable has two system missing values. The results of four different variables created by Compute Variable when using the MISSING and SYSMIS functions are shown in Table 10-2.

TABLE 10-2   **MISSING() and SYSMIS() Function Results**

CID	Missing(Current)	Missing(Owner)	Sysmis(Current)	Sysmis(Owner)
101192	1	0	1	0
101091	1	1	1	0
101197	0	0	0	0
101010	0	0	0	0
101056	0	0	0	0

Another characteristic of Boolean variables is that you can make a logical comparison. Doing a logical comparison does not require a function, but the result will be either 1, 0, or system missing. Table 10-3 shows a logical comparison of the original loan-verified income and a more recent self-reported current income. Note that when the comparison can't be made, the result is system missing.

Table 10-3 also shows the NOT function, which reverses the pattern of 1s and 0s from the logical comparison (this can be beneficial when trying to identify instances when something of interest did not occur).

TABLE 10-3   **Logical Comparison and NOT()**

CID	Loan_Income = Current	Not(Loan_Income = Current)
101192	.	.
101091	.	.
101197	1.00	.00
101010	.00	1.00
101056	1.00	.00

String Parsing and Nesting Functions

In the next example, we introduce two functions related to parsing strings and nesting functions. Nesting functions can seem tricky at first because the expression looks complicated, but you're simply putting a function inside another function. The inside function acts as an argument to the outside function. In this example, you extract a person's last name from the full name.

The CHAR.INDEX function example is shown in Table 10-4. The two arguments in this function are the string in which you're searching (Fullname) and what you're searching for (a comma). Note that the comma is surrounded by single quotes. The comma's location tells you where the last name ends — or more specifically, one character beyond where the last name ends.

TABLE 10-4   **String Parsing Results**

Fullname	CHAR.INDEX(Fullname,',')	CHAR.SUBSTR(Fullname,1,CHAR.INDEX(Fullname,',')-1)
Brown, Tim	6	Brown
Miser, Angus	6	Miser
Gummage, Bill	8	Gummage
Banker, Jill	7	Banker
Brown, Edith	6	Brown

The next expression (in the last column of the table) extracts the last name. It has three arguments:

>> The string in which you are searching, Fullname.

>> The location in the string where you want to start searching, which is the first character, indicated by the number 1.

>> A slight modification of the previous expression, CHAR.
INDEX(Fullname,',')-1. Because the comma is located one character beyond what you need, you add -1.

Because the second expression produces a string result, you must declare the new variable as a string before you can populate the new variable with an expression that produces a string. If you fail to do this, SPSS will assume that you intend to create a numeric variable, and numeric variables are incapable of storing strings. Also, make sure that the string is of sufficient size. A length of 20, shown in Figure 10-9, should be plenty for most last names.

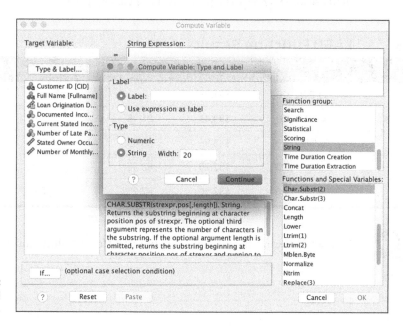

FIGURE 10-9: The Type and Label dialog.

If you're comfortable with these more complex expressions, it's a good indication that you'll be comfortable with Syntax as well, although moving from complex functions in the expression box to writing programs in the Syntax window still requires a small leap in SPSS knowledge. We cover programming with Syntax in

Chapters 26 and 27. If writing code is not your preferred way to work with SPSS, you can generally avoid it and stick to the menus. We discuss the tradeoffs in Chapter 26.

Calculating Lags

A common task is to lag, or shift, values using the LAG function. Perhaps the most common example is transactional data or time series data. The brief example in this section uses the stock_lag dataset, which is available on the book's website (www.dummies.com/go/spss4e) and shows two simple expressions.

Table 10-5 shows the stock closing price for each date. You can also see that the lag of the closing price places the previous day's value in a new column. This allows you to calculate Close-Lag(Close), which represents the price change. For instance, on Tuesday, August 4, our fictional stock rose to $83.45, representing an increase of $1.67 over the previous day's closing price.

TABLE 10-5 ## LAG() Function Results

Stock_Ticker	Date	Close	LAG(Close)	Close-LAG(Close)
X123	08/03/2020	$81.78	.	.
X123	08/04/2020	$83.45	81.78	1.67
X123	08/05/2020	$83.95	83.45	.50
X123	08/06/2020	$82.25	83.95	-1.70
X123	08/07/2020	$82.50	82.25	.25

TIP

You can perform a lag also by using the Transform ⇨ Shift Values menu.

IN THIS CHAPTER

» Combining files by adding cases

» Combining files by adding variables when doing a one-to-one match

» Combining files by adding variables when doing a one-to-many match

Chapter **11**

Combining Files

D
ata is often kept in different files. Sometimes these files are similar (for example, the same customer information just separated by store); other times the files are very different (for example, customer satisfaction information in one file and financial information in another). IBM SPSS Statistics has two facilities available for merging files: Add Cases joins data files that contain similar variables for separate groups of cases; Add Variables joins data files that contain different information for the same cases.

Merging Files by Adding Cases

Add Cases appends cases with the same or similar variables. Figure 11-1 illustrates a simple Add Cases merge of two files containing customer satisfaction records. Both files have the same variables, Satisfaction and Years_Customer. The variables must have the same name, coded values, and type (for example, string vs. numeric) in both files. In this example, there are three cases in each of the files, so the combined file has six cases. In other words, the combined file contains the total number of cases from both files.

TECHNICAL STUFF

Note that although an ID variable is in both files, ID variables are not used as a merge key in an Add Cases merge operation.

ID	Satisfaction	Years_Customer
1	10	5
2	8	7
3	9	7

+

ID	Satisfaction	Years_Customer
101	7	1
102	4	0
103	3	0

=

ID	Satisfaction	Years_Customer
1	10	5
2	8	7
3	9	7
101	7	1
102	4	0
103	3	0

FIGURE 11-1:
An Add Cases merge.

The following example shows you how to combine data files:

1. **Make sure that no other data files are open before you begin the merge operation.**

2. **Choose File ⇨ Open ⇨ Data and load the stroke_invalid file.**

   Download the stroke_invalid file and the stroke_valid file from the book's companion website at www.dummies.com/go/spss4e.

   The stroke_invalid data file, which has 39 variables and 1,183 cases, is shown in Figure 11-2. This file doesn't contain information on whether the patient had a stroke.

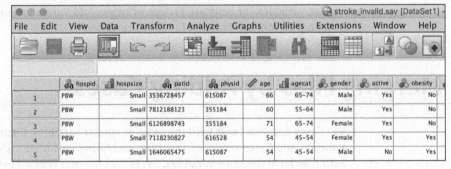

FIGURE 11-2:
The stroke_invalid data file.

3. **Choose File ⇨ Open ⇨ Data and load the stroke_valid file.**

   As mentioned, download the file from the book's companion website. The data file, which has 42 variables and 1,048 cases, is shown in Figure 11-3. This file contains information on whether the patient had a stroke, which is why it has three additional variables.

   Now you want to combine these two files.

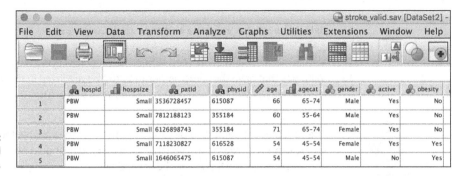

FIGURE 11-3:
The stroke_valid
data file.

4. **Using the Window menu, ensure that the stroke_invalid file is the active dataset (make sure it is selected).**

   It doesn't matter much if you add the second file to the first file or vice versa, but your choice will determine which data is at the top of the file (data from the active dataset appears first in the combined file). Your first attempt at a merge could be confusing if you perform the merge in the reverse order of the book.

5. **Choose Data ⇨ Merge Files ⇨ Add Cases.**

   The dialog shown in Figure 11-4 appears. At this point, you can combine the active dataset (instroke_valid) with any files open in IBM SPSS Statistics or files saved as an IBM SPSS Statistics data file. If you want to combine files in other formats, you must first read the files into SPSS.

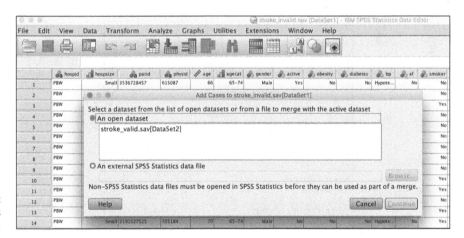

FIGURE 11-4:
The Add Cases
dialog.

6. Select the stroke_valid file and then click Continue.

The dialog shown in Figure 11-5 appears.

Variables that have the same names in both files are listed in the Variables in New Active Dataset box. Variables that do not match are listed in the Unpaired Variables box.

WARNING

The variables are combined by variable name, and the variable formats should be the same. For example, a variable such as gender should not be coded as 1 and 2 in one file and M and F in the second file.

When matching variables that don't have the same name across both files, you have three options on how to proceed:

- Change the name of one of the variables before combining the files.

- Use the rename option in the Add Cases facility.

- Pair any unpaired variables by clicking the Pair button; the new variable's name is taken from the variable in the active data file.

The file legend in the lower-left corner lists the symbol corresponding to each file, which is used to designate the source for unpaired variables.

Variables that are unpaired and don't measure the same thing can be moved to the Variables in New Active Dataset list, and they'll be retained in the combined file.

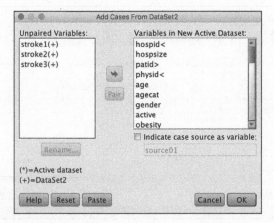

FIGURE 11-5:
Unpaired
variables.

7. Select the stroke1, stroke2, and stroke3 variables and click the arrow to move them to the box on the right.

8. **Select the Indicate Case Source as Variable option and rename the new variable** File.

The Indicate Case Source as Variable option allows you to create a new variable, named source01 by default, which will be coded 0 if the case comes from the active dataset and 1 if the case comes from the other data file. This case source indicator variable can be useful if you don't have a variable in the files that uniquely identifies that file.

9. **Click OK.**

The combined file, with the new File variable, is generated. The result is a new file with 43 variables and 2,231 cases, as shown in Figure 11-6. Note that the stroke1, stroke2, and stroke3 variables have missing information for the cases that came from the stroke_invalid file, which makes sense because these are the unpaired variables. For all other variables, the merge has been successful. Note also that the name of the file is still stroke_invalid.

FIGURE 11-6: The combined data file.

10. **Choose File ➪ Save As. Name the file** combined_stroke **and click Save.**

WARNING

When merging, don't be casual about saving the file after the merge. If you just click Save, the new combined file will overwrite the original active file and you will have lost the original file! Instead, make sure you use Save As (not Save). Remember to do this as soon as you confirm that the new combined file looks correct.

Now you can perform analyses on the combined data file or compare the people in the first file with the people in the second file using the new variable you just created.

TECHNICAL STUFF

Only two data files can be combined simultaneously when using dialogs. However, you can merge an unlimited number of files using Syntax.

Merging Files by Adding Variables

Add Variables joins two data files so that information held for an individual in different locations can be analyzed together. You can perform two types of Add Variables merges: one-to-one and one-to-many. Both types add variables to cases matched on key variables. *Key variables* are case identifiers that exist in both files (for example, a variable such as ID, for the customer ID number).

In a *one-to-one merge,* the basis for the cases is the same in both files and the cases are matched so that one case in the first file corresponds to one case in the second file. In Figure 11-7, for example, ID is the key variable used for the match. The resulting file contains all the variables from both files. All cases are retained from both files. Cases not in a file have system missing values for the variables from that file. In the example, all cases were in both files.

ID	Satisfaction	Years_Customer
1	10	5
2	8	7
3	9	7

+

ID	Product_A	Product_B
1	Yes	No
2	No	Yes
3	Yes	Yes

=

ID	Satisfaction	Years_Customer	Product_A	Product_B
1	10	5	Yes	No
2	8	7	No	Yes
3	9	7	Yes	Yes

FIGURE 11-7:
Adding variables using a one-to-one match.

WARNING

Both input files must be sorted in ascending order on the key variables to get a one-to-one match to work properly.

In a *one-to-many merge,* one file is designated as the table file and cases from that file can match multiple cases in the case file. The case file defines the cases in the merged file. The values of the key variable(s) must define unique cases in the table file but not in the case file.

In Figure 11-8, each case in the case file represents a property with information about the property. Each case in the table file is defined by a zip code with the mean property value for that zip code. Zip_code is the key variable that uniquely identifies each record in this file and is used as the key variable in the one-to-many merge. In the merged file, both cases one and two have the same value for mean_propvalue because they're both in the 85718 zip code.

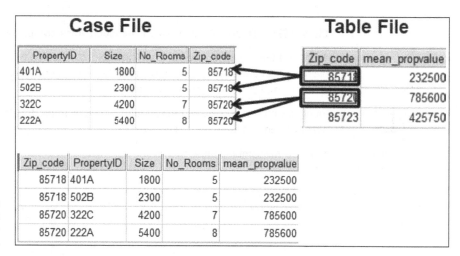

FIGURE 11-8:
Adding variables using a one-to-many match.

The following example of a one-to-one merge uses the data files electronics_company_info and electronics_complete. Before starting any merge example, close all other data files. Merges can be confusing if you have a lot of unrelated files open.

Follow these steps to perform a one-to-one merge:

1. Choose File ⇨ Open ⇨ Data and load the electronics_company_info file.

Download this file and the electronics_complete file from the book's companion website at www.dummies.com/go/spss4e. The data file, which has 5 variables and 5,003 cases, is shown in Figure 11-9. This file contains information on each customer's company.

Input files must be sorted on key variables. In this example, the data has already been sorted on the ID key variable.

WARNING

FIGURE 11-9:
The electronics_company_info data file.

2. **Choose File ⇨ Open ⇨ Data and load the electronics_complete file.**

As mentioned, download the file from the book's companion website. The data file has 12 variables and 5,003 cases and is shown in Figure 11-10. This file contains each customer's purchase history.

WARNING

Input files must be sorted on key variables. In this example, the data has already been sorted on the ID key variable.

Now you will combine these two files.

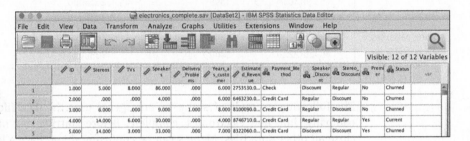

FIGURE 11-10: The electronics_ complete data file.

3. **Choose Data ⇨ Merge Files ⇨ Add Variables.**

The Add Variables dialog appears.

At this point, you can combine the active dataset (electronics_complete) with any files open in IBM SPSS Statistics or saved as an IBM SPSS Statistics data file.

REMEMBER

If you want to combine files in a format other than a .sav file, you must first read the files into IBM SPSS Statistics.

4. **Select the electronics_company_info file, as shown in Figure 11-11, and then click Continue.**

The dialog shown in Figure 11-12 appears.

5. **Make sure that One-to-One Merge Based on Key Values is selected.**

Note that the Sort Files on Key Values before Merging option has also been selected, so technically SPSS will sort both files again. If you have previously sorted your files (as we have done), this option does not need to be selected. Also note that SPSS has identified the ID variable as the key variable.

WARNING

The One-to-One Based on File Order option combines files based on order. The first record in the first dataset is joined with the first record in the second dataset, and so on. When a dataset runs out of records, no further output records are produced. The order method can be dangerous if cases are missing from a file or if files have been sorted differently.

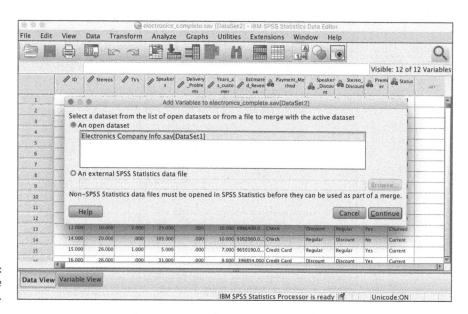

FIGURE 11-11:
Identifying the
files to merge.

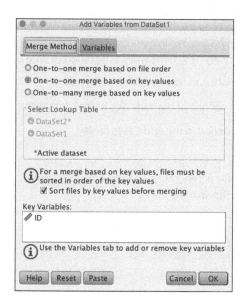

FIGURE 11-12:
The Merge
method dialog.

6. **Click the Variables tab of the dialog, as shown in Figure 11-13.**

Before running the merge, make sure there are no problems with the variables.

Variables that have unique names are listed in the Included Variables box. If the same variable name is used in both files, only one set of data values can be retained — these variables will appear in the Excluded Variables box. Although a renaming facility is available in the Add Variables dialog, it's safer to use unique names from the beginning.

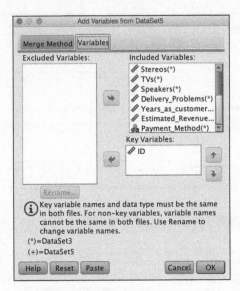

FIGURE 11-13:
The Variables
dialog.

If you're merging two files from two time periods, some of the variables may
have the same name because they measure the same concept. In this case,
each variable should be given a unique name — perhaps numbered or based
on the date of the survey — to differentiate the different time periods.

You can rename variables in two ways:

- Change the name of one of the variables before adding the files together.

- Use the rename option in the Add Cases facility.

7. **Click OK.**

The new combined file is generated. The result is a new file with 16 variables
and 5,003 cases, as shown in Figure 11-14.

FIGURE 11-14:
The combined
data file.

8. **Choose File ⇨ Save As.**

9. **Name the file** combined_electronics **and click Save.**

Now you can perform analyses on the combined data file and investigate relationships that wouldn't have been possible without first performing the merge.

Only two data files can be combined simultaneously when using dialogs. However, you can merge an unlimited number of files using Syntax.

Following is an example of a one-to-many match:

1. Choose File ⇨ Open ⇨ Data and load the rfm_aggregated file.

Download this file and the rfm_transactions1 file from the book's companion website at www.dummies.com/go/spss4e. The rfm_aggregated data file, which has 4 variables and 995 cases, is shown in Figure 11-15. This file contains customers' purchase history, where each row represents a customer.

Input files must be sorted on key variables. In this example, the data has already been sorted on the ID key variable.

FIGURE 11-15: The rfm_ aggregated data file.

	ID	Most_Recent_Date	Amount_Spent	Number_of_Purchases	var	var	var	var
1	1	04-Sep-2006	485.00	5				
2	2	10-Nov-2005	350.00	4				
3	3	04-Jun-2005	233.00	2				
4	4	18-Aug-2006	936.00	7				
5	5	07-Jul-2006	359.00	3				

2. Choose File ⇨ Open ⇨ Data and load the rfm_transactions1 file.

As mentioned, download the file from the book's companion website. The data file, which has 5 variables and 4,906 cases, is shown in Figure 11-16. This file contains customer transactional data, where each row represents a transaction.

Input files must be sorted on key variables. In this example, the data has already been sorted on the ID key variable.

FIGURE 11-16: The rfm_ transactions1 data file.

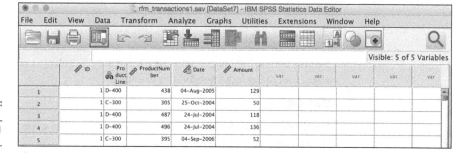

	ID	Product Line	ProductNumber	Date	Amount	var	var	var	var	var
1	1	D-400	438	04-Aug-2005	129					
2	1	C-300	305	25-Oct-2004	50					
3	1	D-400	487	24-Jul-2004	118					
4	1	D-400	496	24-Jul-2004	136					
5	1	C-300	395	04-Sep-2006	52					

3. **Choose Data ⇨ Merge Files ⇨ Add Variables.**

4. **Select the rfm_aggregated file and then click Continue.**

5. **Make sure that the One-to-Many Merge Based on Key Values option is selected.**

   When doing a one-to-many merge, you must identify which file is the aggregated file, or *lookup table* (the file that will have a case merge with several cases in the other file). In our case, the non-active dataset (rfm_aggregated) is the aggregated file.

6. **Make sure that the non-active dataset (the dataset without the asterisk) is chosen as the Select Lookup table.**

   As in the preceding example, note that the Sort Files on Key Values before Merging option has also been selected, and that SPSS has identified the ID variable as the key variable. Figure 11-17 shows the completed dialog.

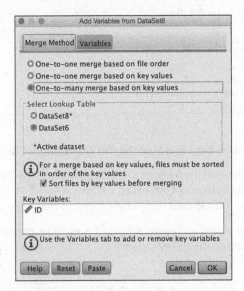

7. **Click the Variables tab of the dialog.**

   Before running the merge, make sure there are no problems with the variables. Everything looks good in this example.

8. **Click OK.**

   The new combined file is generated, with 8 variables and 4,906 cases, as shown in Figure 11-18.

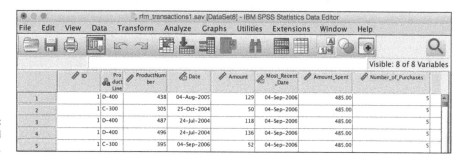

FIGURE 11-18:
The combined
data file.

9. Choose File ⇨ Save As.

10. Name the file combined_rfm and click Save.

Now you can perform analyses on the combined data file and investigate relation-ships that wouldn't have been possible without first performing the merge.

4

Graphing Data

IN THIS PART . . .

Explore all the graphing options in SPSS.

Use Chart Builder to make dozens of different charts.

Chapter **12**

On the Menu: Graphing Choices in SPSS

S PSS can display your data in a bar chart, a line graph, an area graph, a pie chart, a scatterplot, a histogram, a collection of high-low indicators, a box plot, or a dual-axis graph. Adding to this flexibility, each of these basic forms can have multiple appearances. For example, a bar chart can have a two- or three-dimensional appearance, represent data in different colors, or contain simple lines or I-beams for bars. The choice of layouts is almost endless.

TIP

In the world of SPSS, the terms *chart* and *graph* mean the same thing and are used interchangeably.

The Graphs menu in the SPSS Data Editor window has three main options: Chart Builder, Graphboard Template Chooser, and Legacy Dialogs (the other options you see are Python plug-ins). These options are different ways of doing the same job. Legacy dialogs are the original graphs in SPSS and are the choice mainly of people who have been using them for years and who find changing to another option too much trouble. In this chapter, we work only with the other two alternatives.

TECHNICAL STUFF

Chapter 16 has an example of how to use legacy dialogs to create a graph that can't be created using the other graphing options.

Graphboard Template Chooser and Chart Builder go about creating graphs in different ways. In Graphboard Template Chooser, you first select the variables you want to display. Based on this information, different chart options are suggested. Chart Builder begins by presenting various chart types. After you select a chart, you specify which variables you will use.

Both graphing methods are popular, but if you build a lot of graphs, you may find advantages and uses for all of them. For the most part, you can get the same graphs from both options; only the process is different.

Building Graphs the Chart Builder Way

SPSS contains Chart Builder, which uses a graphic display to guide you through the steps of constructing graphs. It checks what you're doing as you proceed and doesn't allow you to use things that won't work. Chart Builder has seven tabs, and we describe them all in this section.

The Gallery tab

The Gallery tab is the most common way to use Chart Builder. The following example takes you through the process of creating a bar chart, but you can use the same fundamental procedure to build any type of chart. Follow this tutorial once to see how it all works. Later, you can use your own data and choices.

TIP

You can't hurt your data by generating a graphic display. Even if you thoroughly mess up the graph, you can always redo it without fear.

Follow these steps to create a bar chart:

1. **Choose File ⇨ Open ⇨ Data and load the GSS2012 Abbreviated.sav file.**

   To find the file, go to www.dummies.com/go/spss4e.

2. **Choose Graphs ⇨ Chart Builder.**

   A warning appears, informing you that before you use this dialog, the measurement level should be set properly for each variable in your chart. (We've set the correct measurement level, so you can proceed.)

3. **Click OK.**

   The Chart Builder dialog appears.

4. If you generated a graph previously, click the Reset button to clear the Chart Builder display.

5. Make sure the Gallery tab is selected.

6. In the Choose From list, select Bar as the graph type.

Various types of bar charts appear in the gallery to the right of the list, as shown in Figure 12-1.

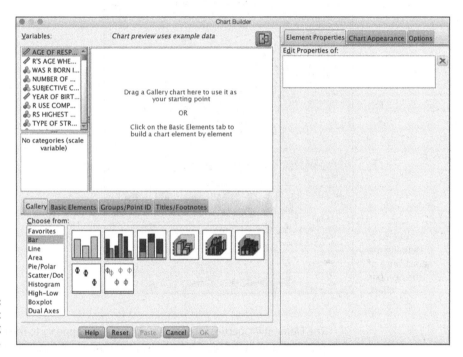

FIGURE 12-1:
The initial Chart Builder dialog with Bar chosen.

7. Define the general shape of the bar graph to be drawn.

You can do this in two ways:

• The simplest way is to choose one of the prefabricated bar graphs to the right of the list. For this exercise, select the graph in the upper-left corner and drag it to the large chart preview panel at the top.

• Alternatively, you can click the Basic Elements tab and create a graph from scratch. You'd choose the number of axes and the elements you want to display, and drag each of these properties to the panel on top, which constructs the same diagram as the bar graph.

Figure 12-2 shows the appearance of the window after you've finished dragging, regardless of which method you followed.

TIP

You can always back up and start over anytime during the design of a graph. Simply click the Reset button. Anything you dragged to the display panel will be removed.

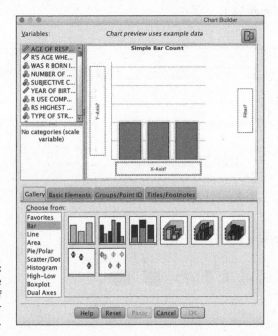

FIGURE 12-2:
Defining the appearance of the new bar chart.

The Element Properties tab (see Figure 12-3) now appears to the right of the preview panel at the top. This tab lets you know which features of the element you can change. For example, you can change the statistic to display or the style of the bars. In this example, you don't use the Element Properties tab.

8. **In the variable list in Chart Builder, select the** `Highest Year of School Completed (Educ)` **variable and drag it to the Y-Axis label in the diagram.**

9. **In similar fashion, select the** `Region of Interview (region)` **variable and drag it to the X-Axis label in the diagram.**

The chart preview now looks like the one shown in Figure 12-4.

REMEMBER

The graphic display inside the Chart Builder preview window *never* represents your actual data, even after you insert variable names. This preview window simply displays a diagram that demonstrates the composition and appearance of the graph that will be produced.

FIGURE 12-3:
Use the Element Properties tab to modify chart elements.

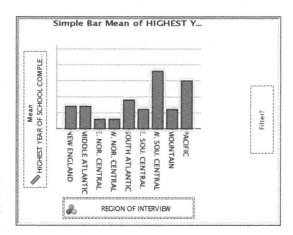

FIGURE 12-4:
The chart preview after assigning the x- and y-axes.

10. **Click the OK button to produce the graph.**

The SPSS Statistics Viewer window appears, containing the graph shown in Figure 12-5. This graph is based on the actual data. It shows that the average number of years of education varied little from one part of the country to the other in this survey.

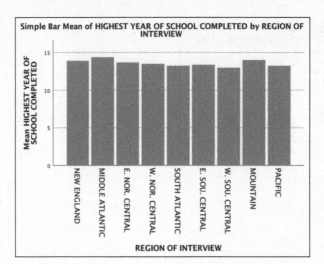

FIGURE 12-5:
A bar chart
produced from a
data file and
displayed by SPSS
Statistics Viewer.

These steps demonstrate the simplest way of generating a chart. We left out most of the options so we could demonstrate the simplicity of the basic process. (The result could also use a little editing to the y-axis; for details on editing, see Chapter 24.) The following sections describe the additional tabs available in Chart Builder.

The Basic Elements tab

The example in the preceding section used the Gallery tab to select the type and appearance of the chart. Alternatively, as mentioned, you can click the Basic Elements tab in the Chart Builder dialog and select the number of axes and elements you would like to include in the graph, as shown in Figure 12-6.

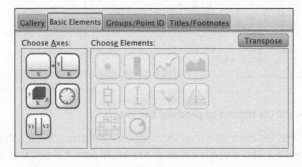

FIGURE 12-6:
Choose the axes
and elements to
construct the
graph you want.

In the Basic Elements tab, you drag one element from the Choose Axes area to the panel on the top. Then drag another element from the Choose Elements area to the top. These elements combine to construct a diagram of the graph you want.

The result is the same as using the Gallery tab. The only difference is that you use the Basic Elements tab to build the graph from its components. Whether you use this technique or the Gallery tab depends on your conception of the graph you want to produce.

The Groups/Point ID tab

You've selected the type and appearance of your chart through either the Gallery tab or the Basic Elements tab. Next, click the Groups/Point ID tab in the Chart Builder dialog, which provides you with a group of options you can use to add more variables to your graphs.

In the example in Figure 12-7, we selected the Rows Panel Variable option, which generates a more complex graph. The new dimension adds a separate graph for whether the respondent uses a computer. A separate set of bars is drawn: one for those who use a computer, and one for those who do not.

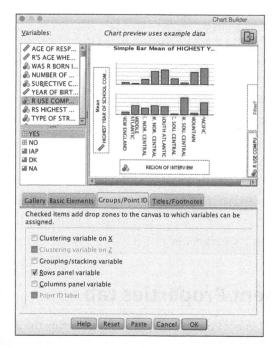

FIGURE 12-7:
You can add dimensions to your graph.

The Columns Panel Variable option enables you to add a variable along the other axis, thus adding another dimension. Adding variables and new dimensions in this way is known as *paneling*, or *faceting*.

Whereas paneling involves creating separate graphs for each value of the paneling variable, *clustering* (gathering data into groups) can be done along the x- or y-axis and the variables you're clustering by are added to the original graph so that either colors or patterns distinguish groups.

The Titles/Footnotes tab

Figure 12-8 shows the window that appears when you click the Titles/Footnotes tab in the Chart Builder dialog. Each option in the bottom panel places text at a different location on the graph. When you select an option, the Element Properties tab appears so you can enter the text for the specified location.

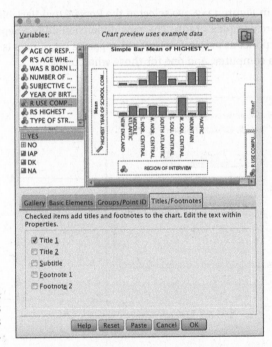

FIGURE 12-8: Select the chart's text and its location.

The Element Properties tab

You can use the Element Properties tab at any time during the design of a chart to set the properties of individual elements in the chart. For example, we displayed the count in Figure 12-3 but the mean in Figure 12-9. The Element Properties tab changes every time you choose a different member from the list at the top.

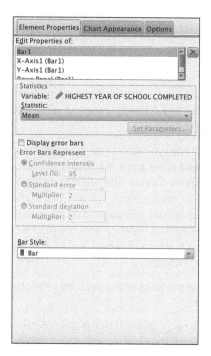

FIGURE 12-9:
The options for an axis variable.

Okay, the upcoming list of options is long, but four facts make the options simple to use:

>> **All options have reasonable defaults.** You don't have to change any of them unless you want to.

>> **You can always back up and change a setting.** Nothing is permanent, so you can make changes until you have finished or run out of time and decide, "That's good enough."

>> **Not all options appear at once.** Only a few show up at a time.

>> **All options become obvious when you see what they do.** You don't have to memorize any of them, but you'll find they're easy to remember.

The following is a simple explanation of all possible options that can appear in the Element Properties tab:

>> **Edit Properties Of:** This list, which appears at the top of the tab, is used for selecting which element in the chart you want to edit. Each element has a type, and the type of element you select determines the other options available in the tab. The selected element is also highlighted in the diagram of the graph.

- **X:** When an element is selected, the X button to the right of the list becomes enabled, clicking the button removes the element from the list and from the graph.

- **Arrow:** For charts with dual y-axis variables, the arrow to the right in the list indicates which of the variables will be drawn on top of the other. You can click the arrows to change the order.

- **Statistics:** For certain elements, you can specify the statistics (that is, the type of value) to be displayed in the graph. For example, you can select Count and use simple numeric values. You can also select Sum, Median, Variance, Percentile, or any of up to 32 statistic types. Not all types of charts have that many options; the available options also depend on the type of variable. For certain statistics options — such as Number in Range and Percentage Less Than — the Set Parameters button is activated; you have to click it to set the parameters controlling your choice.

- **Axis Label:** You can change the text used to describe a variable. By default, the variable's label is used.

- **Automatic:** If selected, the range of the selected axis is determined automatically to include all the values of the scale variable being displayed along that axis. This is the default.

- **Minimum/Maximum:** You can replace the Automatic default values and choose the extreme values that determine the start and end points of an axis.

- **Origin:** Specify a point from which chart information is graphed, and has different effects for different types of charts. For example, choosing an origin value for a bar chart can cause bars to extend both up and down from a center line.

- **Major Increment:** You can specify the spacing that determines the placing of tick marks, along with numeric or textual labels, on an axis. The value of this option determines the interval of spacing when you also specify minimum and maximum values.

- **Scale Type:** You can use four different types of scale along an axis:

  - **Linear:** This simple, rulerlike scale is the default.

  - **Logarithmic (standard):** This type transforms the values into logarithmic values for display. You can also select a base for the logarithms.

  - **Logarithmic (safe):** This type is the same as standard logarithms, except the formulas that calculate values can handle 0 and negative numbers.

  - **Power:** This type raises the values to an exponential power. You can select an exponent other than the default value of 0.5 (which is the square root).

- » **Sort By:** You can select which characteristic of a variable will be used as the sort key:

  - **Label:** Nominal variables are sorted by the names assigned to the values; you can choose whether to sort in ascending or descending order.

  - **Value:** This option uses numeric values for sorting. You can choose whether to sort in ascending or descending order.

  - **Custom:** This option uses the order specified in the Order list.

- » **Order:** The list of possible values is flanked by up and down arrows. You can change the sorting order by selecting a value and clicking an arrow to move the selection up or down. To remove a value from the produced chart, select its name in the list and click the X button; the value moves to the Excluded list. When you change the Order list, Sort By switches automatically to Custom.

- » **Excluded:** Any value you want to exclude from the Order list appears in this list. To move a value back to the Order list (which also causes the value to reappear on the chart), select its name and click the arrow to the right of the list.

TIP

  If a value (or a margin annotation representing a value) is unexpectedly missing from a graph based your selections, look in the Excluded list. You may have excluded too much.

- » **Collapse:** If you have a number of values that seldom occur, you can select this option to have them gathered into an Other category. You specify the percentage of the total number of occurrences to make it an Other value.

- » **Error Bars:** This option displays confidence intervals for Mean, Median, and Count. For Mean, you must choose whether the error bars will represent the confidence interval, a multiple of the standard error, or a multiple of the standard deviation.

- » **Bar Style:** You can choose one of three possible appearances of the bars on a bar graph.

- » **Categories:** You can choose the order in which the values appear when they're placed along an axis. You can select ascending or descending order. If the variable is nominal, you can select the individual order and even specify values to be left out.

- » **Small/Empty Categories:** You can choose to include or exclude missing value information.

- » **Display Normal Curve:** For a histogram, you can choose to have a normal curve superimposed over the chart. The curve will use the same mean and standard deviation values as the histogram.

» **Stack Identical Values:** For a chart that will appear as a *dot plot* (a pattern of plotted points), you can choose whether points at the same location should appear next to one another or one on top of one another (that is, with one point blocking out the one below it).

» **Display Vertical Drop Lines between Points:** For a chart that will appear as a dot plot, any points with the same x-axis values are joined with a vertical line.

» **Plot Shape:** For a dot plot, you can choose

- **Asymmetric:** Stacks the points on the *x*-axis. This is the default.

- **Symmetric:** Stacks the points centered around a line drawn horizontally across the center of the screen.

- **Flat:** The same as Symmetric, except no line is drawn.

» **Interpolation:** For line and area charts, choose the algorithm used to calculate how the line should be drawn between points:

- **Straight:** Draws a line directly from one point to the next.

- **Step:** Draws a horizontal line through each point; the ends of the horizontal lines are connected with vertical lines.

- **Jump:** Draws a horizontal line through each point, but the ends of the lines are not connected.

- **Location:** For Step and Jump interpolation; using this option adds an indicator at the actual point.

- **Interpolation through Missing Values:** For Straight, Step, or Jump, this option draws lines through missing values. Otherwise, the line shows a gap.

» **Anchor Bin:** This option is the starting value of the first bin. This option is available for histograms.

» **Bin Sizes:** You can set the sizes of the bins when you're producing a histogram.

» **Angle:** Rotate a pie chart by selecting the clock position at which the first value starts. You can also specify whether the values should be included clockwise or counterclockwise.

» **Display Axis:** For a pie chart, you can choose to display the axis points on the outer rim.

FINDING GRAPHS IN UNEXPECTED PLACES

The Graphs menu isn't the only place where you'll find powerful graphing options. (For example, most analysis methods have a Plots tab.) However, you may not find these graphing options in the same form or with the same features as in the Graphs menu. They also tend to be turned off by default, so if you don't request them, you usually won't get them.

Here is a quick list of places where you'll find graphs options:

- On the Analyze menu, many statistical techniques have a Plots tab or a Charts tab that creates graphs.

- Some menus are dedicated to specialty modules. For instance, the best graphs for time series data are in the Forecasting menu (see the following figure).

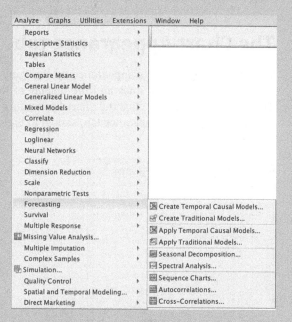

- The primary purpose of some analysis techniques is the production of a graph, such as correspondence analysis, clustering models, spatial and temporal modeling, and decision trees. (The following figure shows an example of a Decision Tree model in the Classify menu.)

(continued)

(continued)

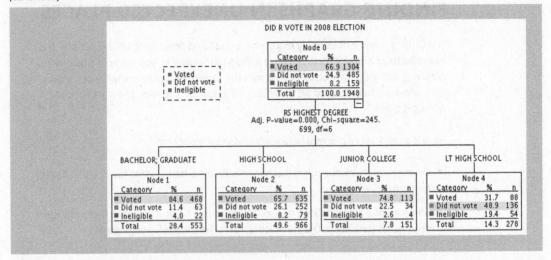

The Chart Appearance tab

You can edit your chart's appearance by changing the colors used in the graphs and by controlling grid lines and the display of inner and outer border frames. To make these changes, click the Chart Appearance tab in the Chart Builder dialog to display the Chart Appearance tab, shown in Figure 12-10.

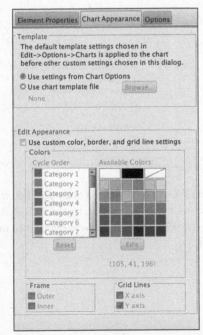

FIGURE 12-10: Changing your chart's appearance.

The first section of this tab controls the colors in the graph and their order. You can also specify border and grid line settings.

Templates are files that contain all or part of a chart definition, such as the layouts, fonts, margins, styles, and colors. You can specify which template files you want to use by clicking the Browse button in the Template section and then navigating to and selecting a template. SPSS will apply the template definitions as the default starting points for all charts you build. SPSS comes with various templates, and you can also create a template file from any finished chart displayed in SPSS Statistics Viewer.

Templates come in handy only when you want to build several similar charts.

The Options tab

Click the Options tab in the Chart Builder dialog to open the Options tab, shown in Figure 12-11. In the Options tab, you specify how you want to handle *missing data* — that is, when an individual's response is not available.

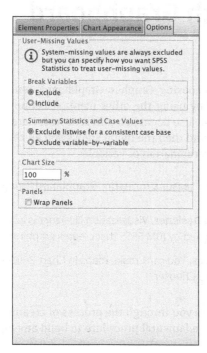

FIGURE 12-11:
The options you can apply to a chart.

If the variables used to define categories or subgroups in your graph have missing values, the Break Variables area allows you to decide whether you want to include or exclude missing categories from your chart.

In the Summary Statistics and Case Values section, the Exclude Listwise for a Consistent Case Basis option includes only cases that have complete data for all variables in a graph, and the Exclude Variable-by-Variable option includes individuals that are missing information on some but not all variables in a graph. (Missing values are discussed in Chapter 4, and the different types of summary data are described in Chapter 14.)

Use the Chart Size option to make the generated charts smaller or larger, as needed. The Wrap Panels option determines how the panels are displayed when you have a number of them in a chart. SPSS is using the word *panel* to refer to the rectangular area in which a chart is placed in SPSS Statistics Viewer. Normally, panels shrink automatically to fit; if you select this option, they remain full size and wrap to the next line.

Building Graphs with Graphboard Template Chooser

The charts you build by choosing Graphs ⇨ Graphboard Template Chooser are similar to those you build by using the other menu selections, but you get less guidance along the way. You also begin in a different way. Here you specify which variables you want to use, and then the menu shows you all the graphing choices that are available for that combination of variables.

Following are the two major reasons for using Graphboard Template Chooser:

>> **You own Visualization Designer.** Visualization Designer is a separate software program designed by IBM SPSS that creates graphing templates.

>> **You want to make maps.** You can't make maps in Chart Builder, but you can in Graphboard Template Chooser.

The following example takes you through the process of creating a 3-D bar chart, but you can use the same fundamental procedure to build any type of chart:

1. **Choose File ⇨ Open ⇨ Data and load the Bank.sav file.**

   You have to download the file from www.dummies.com/go/spss4e.

2. **Choose Graphs ⇨ Graphboard Template Chooser.**

3. **Make sure the Basic tab is selected.**

   As with Chart Builder, Graphboard Template Chooser has both a gallery approach (Basic tab) or an elements approach (Detailed tab).

4. **Select the variables you want to include.**

   To select multiple variables, Ctrl-click. To follow along with the example, select Sex of Employee, Employment Category, and Current Salary.

   The displayed graphs change with each selection. Finally, you see several graphs that allow you to display the relationship between two categorical variables and one continuous variable.

5. **Select 3-D Bar Chart as the graph type.**

6. **In the Summary drop-down menu, choose Mean, as shown in Figure 12-12.**

   At this point, you're ready to create a 3-D bar chart. Before you do, however, you'll take a brief look at the other tabs in Graphboard Template Chooser.

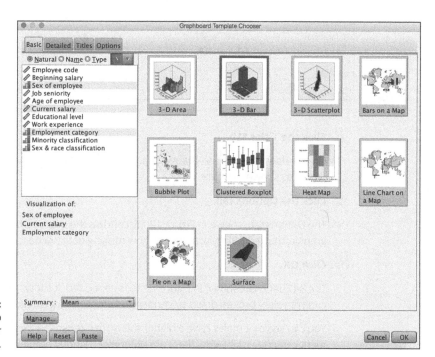

FIGURE 12-12:
The Basic tab with a 3-D bar chart defined.

7. Click the Detailed tab.

On the Detailed tab, shown in Figure 12-13, you can specify the same information as on the Basic tab. However, on the Basic tab, variable placement is determined by the order in which you select variables. On the Detailed tab, you can specify where you want each variable to go.

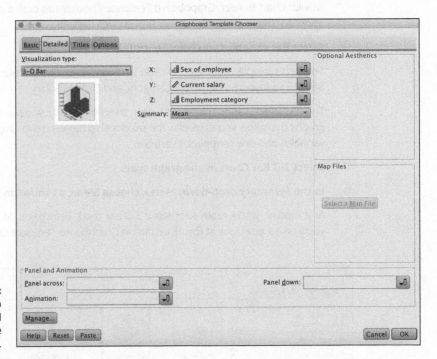

FIGURE 12-13:
The Detailed tab of Graphboard Template Chooser.

8. Click the Titles tab.

On the Titles tab, you can change or add titles, subtitles, and footnotes for your graph, as shown in Figure 12-14.

9. Click the Options tab.

The Options tab, shown in Figure 12-15, controls the output label of the graphic, the general style, as well as how missing data will be handled.

10. Click OK.

The 3-D bar chart shown in Figure 12-16 is generated. It shows employee current salary broken down by gender and employment category.

You can see that males have a higher salary than females across all employment categories. Likewise, there are differences among employment categories; for example, employees in the technical category have a much higher current salary than employees in the clerical category.

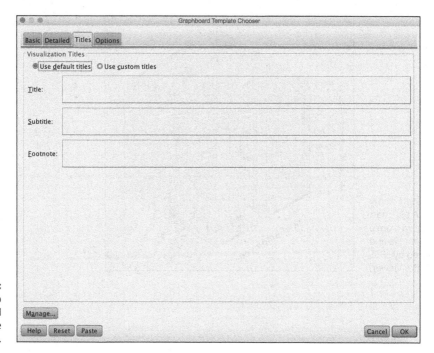

FIGURE 12-14:
The Titles tab
of Graphboard
Template
Chooser.

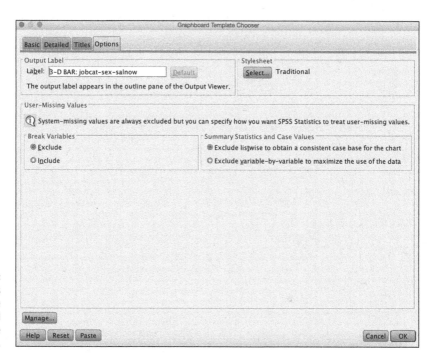

FIGURE 12-15:
The Options
tab of the
Graphboard
Template
Chooser.

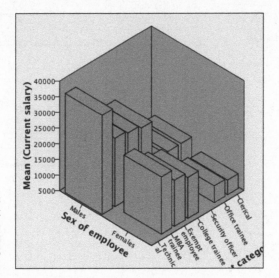

FIGURE 12-16:
A bar chart produced from a data file and displayed by SPSS Statistics Viewer.

Chapter **13**

Building Graphs Using Chart Builder

In this chapter, you discover how to create all the different graph types by following simple, step-by step procedures. Although we don't cover every combination of chart features, you can use the steps here to produce some neat graphs. When you get the basic idea of how to build graphs using Chart Builder, you can explore making some graphs on your own.

The first part of the chapter provides examples of simple graphs and charts and shows you how to build the graphs that you're already familiar with. Next, you see examples of graph types that may be less familiar and are more complex. The last part of the chapter focuses on creating maps.

You can work through the examples to get an overview of building graphs using SPSS — not a bad idea for a beginner — or simply choose the look you want for your data and follow the steps here to construct the chart that does the job. Either way, when you get a handle on the basics, you can step through the process again and again, using your data and trying variations until you get charts that appear the way you want them to.

TIP

When you use Chart Builder, you can drag and drop any variables you want to see into your graph. If the variable doesn't make sense there, the drop will fail. Chart Builder in SPSS will tell you what will and won't work.

REMEMBER

No matter what you try to do while building a graph, your data won't change.

Simple Graphs

The graphs in this section are a great way to use Chart Builder to show the distribution of a single variable or to display relationships between two variables. We cover the following types of graphs: scatterplot, dot plot, bar graph, error bar, histogram, population pyramid, and stacked area chart.

Simple scatterplots

A *scatterplot* is simply an xy plot where you don't care about interpolating the values — that is, the points aren't joined with lines. Instead, a disconnected dot appears for each data point. The overall pattern of these scattered dots often exposes a pattern or trend.

Follow these steps to construct a simple scatterplot:

1. **Choose File ⇨ Open ⇨ Data and open the Cars.sav file.**

    The file is not in the SPSS installation directory. You have to download it from the book's companion website at www.dummies.com/go/spss4e.

2. **Choose Graphs ⇨ Chart Builder.**

3. **In the Choose From list, select Scatter/Dot.**

4. **Select the first scatterplot diagram (the one with the Simple Scatter tooltip), and drag it to the panel at the top.**

5. **In the Variables list, select Horsepower and drag it to the rectangle labeled X-Axis in the diagram.**

    In a scatterplot, both the x-axis and y-axis variables are scale. Look for the ruler icon when dragging your variable over.

    REMEMBER

6. **In the Variables list, select Miles Per Gallon (MPG) and drag it to the rectangle labeled Y-Axis in the diagram.**

7. **Click OK.**

    The chart in Figure 13-1 appears, where each dot in the scatterplot represents both the horsepower and miles per gallon for each car. As you can see, miles per gallon depends largely on horsepower. The pattern of the dots clearly shows a linear trend from the upper left to the lower right. The relationship between horsepower and miles per gallon is inverse: As the horsepower of a car increases, there is a decrease in the miles per gallon that the car gets.

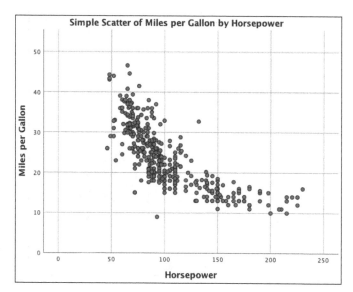

FIGURE 13-1:
A simple
scatterplot
showing the
effect of
horsepower on
miles per gallon.

Simple dot plots

No plot is simpler to produce than the *dot plot*. It has only one dimension. Although SPSS groups it among the scatterplots, it displays data more like a bar chart. As you build this type of chart, you'll notice that you won't need a y-axis.

It's easy to create a dot plot. You select the dot plot as the type of graph you want and then select one variable. SPSS does the rest. The following steps guide you through the process of creating a simple dot plot:

1. Choose File ⇨ Open ⇨ Data and open the Employee data.sav file.

The file is in the SPSS installation directory.

2. Choose Graphs ⇨ Chart Builder.

3. In the Choose From list, select Scatter/Dot.

4. Select the seventh graph image (the one with the Simple Dot Plot tooltip) and drag it to the panel at the top.

5. In the Variables list, select Date of Birth and drag it to the X-Axis rectangle.

6. Click OK.

The chart shown in Figure 13-2 appears, displaying the number of people born each year. As you can see, more people were born between 1960 and 1970 than any other time periods.

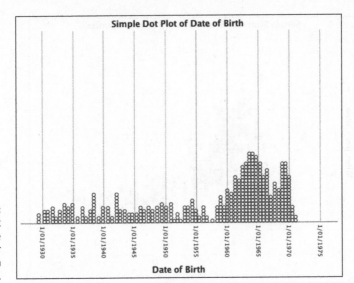

FIGURE 13-2:
A dot plot showing the relative number of people born each year.

Simple bar graphs

A *bar graph* is a comparison of relative magnitudes. Simple bar graphs and simple line graphs are the most common ways of charting statistics. It would make an interesting statistical study to determine which is more common. The results could be displayed as either a bar graph or a line graph, whichever is more popular.

A fundamental bar graph is simple enough that the decisions you need to make when preparing one are almost intuitive. Follow these steps to generate a simple bar graph:

1. **Select File ⇨ Open ⇨ Data and open the Employee data.sav file.**

   The file is in the SPSS installation directory.

2. **Choose Graphs ⇨ Chart Builder.**

3. **In the Choose From list, select Bar.**

4. **Select the first graph image (the one with the Simple Bar tooltip) and drag it to the panel at the top of the window.**

5. **In the Variables list, select Employment Category and drag it to the X-Axis rectangle.**

6. **In the Variables list, select Current Salary and drag it to the Count rectangle.**

   The label changes from Y-Axis to Mean to indicate the type of variable that will now be applied to that axis.

7. Click OK.

The simple bar graph in Figure 13-3 appears. You can see that the average current salary for the manager employment category is much higher than the average current salary for the clerical and custodial employment categories.

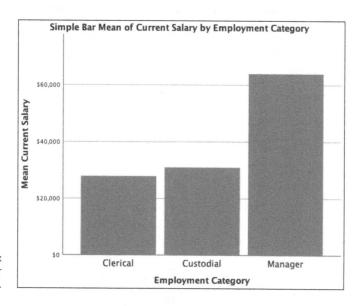

TIP

The display of data in a line chart and a bar chart is similar. If you decide to display data as a bar chart, you should probably try the same data as a line graph to see which you prefer.

Simple error bars

Some errors come from flat-out mistakes — but those aren't the errors we're talking about when we describe error bars. Statistical sampling can help you arrive at a conclusion, but that conclusion has a *margin of error.* This margin can be calculated and quantified according to the size of the sample and the distribution of the data. For example, suppose you want to know how typical a result is when you calculate the mean of all values for a particular variable — for any one case, the mean could be as big as the largest value or as small as the smallest value. The maximum and minimum are the extremes of the possible error. You can choose values and mark the points that contain, say, 90 percent of all values. Marking these points on a graph creates *error bars.*

You can add error bars to the display of most types of graphs. For example, you could add error bars to the simple bar graph presented earlier (refer to Figure 13-3) by making selections in the Element Properties dialog.

For an example of how to add error bars to a bar chart, follow the same procedure described previously in the "Simple bar graphs" section — but just before the final step (clicking OK to produce the chart), do the following:

1. **In the Element Properties window, make sure that a check mark appears in the Display Error Bars option and that Bar1 is selected.**

2. **Select Display Error Bars and make sure the Confidence Intervals value is 95% (the default).**

3. **Click OK.**

   The chart shown in Figure 13-4 appears.

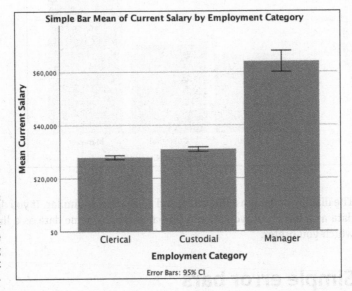

FIGURE 13-4: A bar chart with error bars that show a range containing 95 percent of all values.

Another way to present the same data is to display the range of errors without displaying the full range of all values. To do so, follow these steps:

1. **Choose File ⇨ Open ⇨ Data and open the Employee data.sav file.**
   The file is in the SPSS installation directory.

2. **Choose Graphs ⇨ Chart Builder.**

3. **In the Choose From list, select Bar.**

4. **Select the seventh graph image (the one with the Simple Error Bar tooltip) and drag it to the panel at the top of the window.**

5. **In the Element Properties window, make sure the Point1 and Display Error Bars options are selected and that Confidence Intervals Level is set to 95%.**

188   PART 4 **Graphing Data**

6. **In the Variables list, select Employment Category and drag it to the X-Axis rectangle.**

7. **In the Variables list, select Current Salary and drag it to the Mean rectangle.**

   The label changes from Y-Axis to Mean to indicate the type of data that will be displayed on that axis.

8. **Click OK.**

   The bar graph in Figure 13-5 appears.

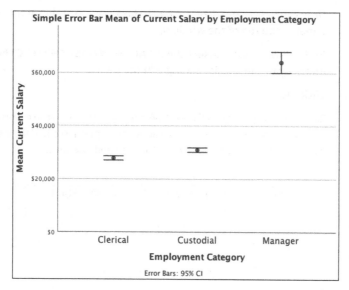

FIGURE 13-5: An error bar graph showing the mean values as dots and the upper and lower bounds of the error.

This example shows one way to make error calculations: The magnitude of the error is based on 95 percent of all values being within the upper and lower error bounds. If you prefer, you can base the error on the bell curve and mark the upper and lower errors at some multiple of the standard error or standard deviation.

Simple histograms

A *histogram* represents the number of items that appear within a range of values. You can use a histogram to look at a graphic representation of the frequency distribution of a variable's values. Histograms are useful for demonstrating the patterns in your data when you want to display information to others rather than discover data patterns for yourself.

You can use the following steps to create a simple histogram that displays the frequency of the ages at which the respondent's first child was born:

1. Choose File ⇨ Open ⇨ Data and open the GSS2012 Abbreviated.sav file.

The file is not in the SPSS Statistics installation directory. Download it at www.dummies.com/go/spss4e.

2. Choose Graphs ⇨ Chart Builder.

The Chart Builder dialog appears.

3. In the Choose From list, select Histogram.

4. Drag the first graph diagram (with the Simple Histogram tooltip) to the panel at the top of the window.

5. In the Variables list, select the R'S AGE WHEN 1ST CHILD BORN variable and drag to the X-Axis rectangle in the panel.

6. Click OK.

The histogram shown in Figure 13-6 appears. (Although the graph looks like a bar chart, it's a histogram.) The majority of respondents had their first child when they were in their late teens through mid-twenties.

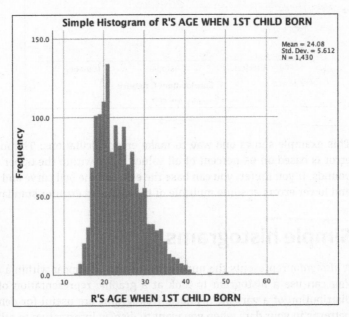

FIGURE 13-6:
A histogram displaying frequency of the age at which the respondent's first kid was born.

Population pyramids

A *population pyramid* provides an immediate comparison of the number of items that fall into different categories. It's called a pyramid because it often takes a triangular shape — wide at the bottom and tapering to a point at the top.

Follow these steps to build a pyramid histogram chart:

1. **Choose File ⇨ Open ⇨ Data and open the GSS2012 Abbreviated.sav file.**

Download the file at www.dummies.com/go/spss4e.

2. **Choose Graphs ⇨ Chart Builder.**

3. **In the Choose From list, select Histogram.**

4. **Drag the fourth graph diagram (with the Population Pyramid tooltip) to the panel at the top of the window.**

5. **In the Variables list, do the following:**

a. Select the Respondent's Sex variable and drag it to the Split Variable rectangle. This variable a categorical variable with two possible values, so one category will be placed on each side of the center line.

b. Select R'S AGE WHEN 1ST CHILD BORN and drag it to the Distribution Variable rectangle.

6. **Click OK.**

The chart shown in Figure 13-7 appears. You can see that males tended to be slightly older than females when they had their first child.

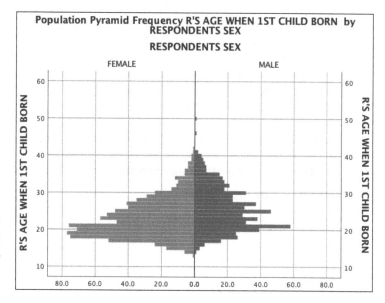

FIGURE 13-7:
A population pyramid shows the occurrence of values within categories.

You can create pyramid histograms based on categorical variables with three, four, or more values. The plot produced will consist of as many pairs as needed (and even a single-sided pyramid for one category, if necessary) to display bars that show the relative number of occurrences of different values in the categories.

Stacked area charts

An *area graph* is really a line graph, or a collection of line graphs, with the areas below the lines filled in to represent the mean of one or more values at the various points.

In a *stacked area chart*, more than one variable is displayed along the x-axis. The values are stacked in such a way that the ups and downs of the lower value in the chart affect the upper values in the chart. That is, the chart is not a group of independent lines; instead, it represents a cumulative total — to which each variable displayed adds a value.

To include two or more variables in your chart, simply repeat Step 5c in the following procedure. They will all appear in the legend at the upper right, and each variable will provide the value for one layer of the stack.

If you include more than one variable, make sure that the variables you select for stacking have similar ranges of values so that the scale on the left will make sense for all of them. If, for example, one variable ranges in the thousands and the other doesn't go over a hundred, the smaller one will compress itself visually and appear in the final graph as a line.

REMEMBER

When you select multiple variables for stacking, be sure to select them in the order in which you want them stacked. The first one you select remains on top, the second one is placed under it, and so on.

TIP

The two types of area charts — simple and stacked — act the same when you construct them. You can select the stacked chart and produce a simple area chart, or you can start with the simple area chart and stack your variables.

Follow these steps to produce a stacked area chart with two stacked variables:

1. **Choose File ⇨ Open ⇨ Data and open the Employee data.sav file.**

   The file is in the SPSS installation directory.

2. **Choose Graphs ⇨ Chart Builder.**

3. In the Choose From list, select Area.

4. Drag the second graph diagram (with the Stacked Area tooltip) to the panel at the top of the window.

5. In the Variables list, do the following:

   a. Select the Educational Level variable, right-click it and change its measurement level to Nominal, and then drag it to the X-Axis rectangle.

   b. Select Current Salary and drag it to the Y-Axis rectangle (now renamed Count).

   c. Select Beginning Salary and drag it to the Current Salary rectangle. A plus sign appears when you drag Beginning Salary over Current Salary. Be sure to drag Beginning Salary to the plus sign and not simply to the rectangle in general. (The plus sign appears at the top of the rectangle when you drag the new variable's name across it.)

   The Create Summary Group dialog appears. After dragging in Beginning Salary, the Stacked: Set Color rectangle is relabeled Index.

6. Click OK.

   The area chart shown in Figure 13-8 appears. Employees with at least a bachelor's degree (16 or more years of education) had a higher initial salary and their current salary increased at a much faster rate.

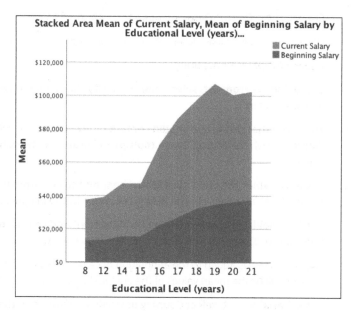

FIGURE 13-8: A stacked area chart showing one variable added to another in the display.

Fancy Graphs

Fancy graphs are just like they sound: fancy. Whether you're trying to show relationships with lines, bars, dots, or more, you can use Chart Builder to create these graphs to show relationships between more than two variables.

Charts with multiple lines

A *line chart* works well as a visual summary of categorical values. They're useful also for displaying timelines because they demonstrate up and down trends so well. Line graphs are popular because they're easy to read. If they're not *the* most common type of statistical chart, they're a contender for the title.

You can have more than one line appear on a chart by adding more than one variable name to an axis. But the variables must contain a similar range of values so they can be properly represented by the same axis. For example, if one variable ranges from 0 to 1,000 pounds and another variable ranges from 1 to 2 pounds, the values of the second variable will show up as a straight line, regardless of how much the values fluctuate.

The following steps generate a basic multiline graph:

1. **Choose File ⇨ Open ⇨ Data and open the Cars.sav file.**

   Download the file at www.dummies.com/go/spss4e.

2. **Choose Graphs ⇨ Chart Builder.**

3. **In the Choose From list, select Line to specify the general type of graph to be constructed.**

4. **To specify that this graph should contain multiple lines, select the second diagram (with the Multiple Line tooltip) and drag it to the panel at the top.**

5. **In the Variables list, right-click Model Year and select Ordinal. Then select Model Year and drag it to the X-Axis rectangle in the diagram.**

6. **In the Variables list, select Engine Displacement and drag it to the Y-Axis rectangle in the panel at the top where it says Count.**

   The word *Mean* is added to the annotation because the values displayed on this axis will be the mean values of the engine displacement.

7. **In the Variables list, select Country of Origin and drag it to the Set Color rectangle in the panel at the top.**

8. Click OK.

The chart shown in Figure 13-9 appears. The mean engine displacement for European and Japanese cars is similar across the years, whereas the values for American cars are different, especially in earlier years.

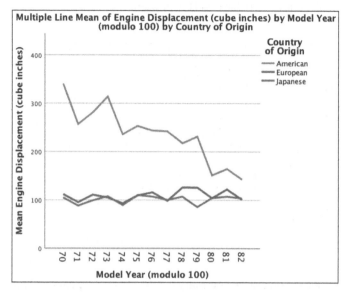

FIGURE 13-9:
A line graph charting Engine Displacement against Model Year according to Country of Origin.

The following steps generate a multiline graph with two variables in the Y-axis:

1. Choose File ⇨ Open ⇨ Data and open the Cars.sav file.

You can download the file at www.dummies.com/go/spss4e.

2. Choose Graphs ⇨ Chart Builder.

3. In the Choose From list, select Line to specify the general type of graph to be constructed.

4. To specify that this graph should contain multiple lines, select the second diagram (with the Multiple Line tooltip) and drag it to the panel at the top.

5. In the Variables list, right-click Model Year and select Ordinal. Then select Model Year and drag it to the rectangle named X-Axis in the diagram.

6. In the Variables list, select Engine Displacement and drag it to the Y-Axis rectangle in the panel at the top where it says Count.

The word *Mean* is added to the annotation because the values displayed on this axis will be the mean values of the engine displacement.

7. **In the Variables list, select Horsepower and drag it to the Y-axis rectangle in the panel at the top.**

Be careful how you drop Horsepower. To add Horsepower as a new variable, you want to drop it on the little box containing the plus sign, as shown in Figure 13-10. If you drop the new name on top of the one that's already there, the original variable could be replaced.

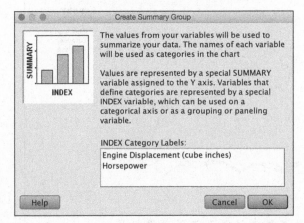

FIGURE 13-10:
Adding another
variable to
the y-axis.

8. **When the Create Summary Group window appears, telling you that SPSS is combining the two variables along the y-axis, click OK.**

9. **Click OK.**

The chart shown in Figure 13-11 appears.

The variables you choose as members of the y-axis must have a similar range of values to make sense. For example, if you were to choose Vehicle Weight and Engine Displacement to be charted together, the result wouldn't be all that interesting; the Vehicle Weight values would be in the thousands and the Engine displacement, regardless of their variation, would all appear in a single line at the bottom. In Chapter 24, we discuss how to edit these graphs to display information in a better way.

Colored scatterplots

Colored scatterplots can be dramatic in appearance, but clarity is not their strongest point. Because the scatterplot is drawn on a two-dimensional surface, you may find it difficult to envision where each point is supposed to appear in space. On the other hand, if your data distributes appropriately on the display, the resulting chart may demonstrate the concept you're trying to get across.

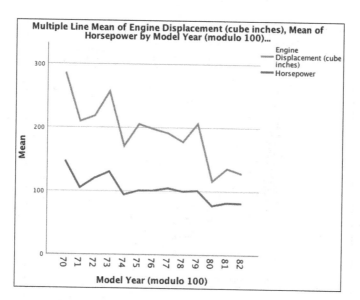

FIGURE 13-11:
A line graph with
two variables in
the y-axis.

The following example uses the same data as in the preceding example but displays it as a three-dimensional plot:

1. **Choose File ⇨ Open ⇨ Data and open the Cars.sav file.**

   Download the file at www.dummies.com/go/spss4e.

2. **Choose Graphs ⇨ Chart Builder.**

3. **In the Choose From list, select Scatter/Dot.**

4. **Select the third scatterplot diagram (with the Grouped Scatter tooltip) and drag it to the panel at the top.**

5. **In the Variables list, do the following:**

   a. Select Engine Displacement and drag it to the X-Axis rectangle.

   b. Select Miles Per Gallon and drag it to the Y-Axis rectangle.

   c. Select Country of Origin and drag it to the Set Color rectangle.

6. **Click OK.**

   The graph shown in Figure 13-12 appears. In general, you can see that there is an inverse relationship between horsepower and miles per gallon: As the horsepower of a car increases, its miles per gallon decreases. Also, note how many of the Japanese and European cars are in the same area of the graph, whereas American cars tend to have much larger engine displacement values, which correspond to fewer miles per gallon.

   We recommend using a bubble chart rather than a 3D scatterplot when displaying three-scale variables because graphs are often not printed in color.

TIP

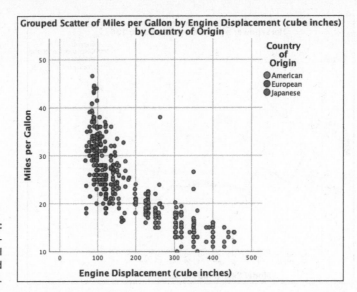

Grouped Scatter of Miles per Gallon by Engine Displacement (cube inches) by Country of Origin

FIGURE 13-12:
A two-dimensional colored scatterplot.

Scatterplot matrices

A *scatterplot matrix* is a group of scatterplots combined into a single graphic image. You choose a number of scale variables and include them as a member of your matrix, and SPSS creates a scatterplot for each possible pair of variables. You can make the matrix as large as you like — its size is controlled by the number of variables you include.

The following steps walk you through the creation of a matrix:

1. **Choose File ➪ Open ➪ Data and open the Cars.sav file.**

   You can download the file at www.dummies.com/go/spss4e.

2. **Choose Graphs ➪ Chart Builder.**

3. **In the Choose From list, select Scatter/Dot.**

4. **Select the eighth graph image (with the Scatterplot Matrix tooltip) and drag it to the panel at the top.**

5. **In the Variables list, drag Engine Displacement to the Scattermatrix rectangle in the panel.**

   The selected name replaces the label in the rectangle.

6. **Drag the variable names Miles Per Gallon, Horsepower, and Vehicle Weight to the plus sign on the x-axis.**

   The labels may or may not change with each variable you add, depending on their length and the amount of space available. All your labels appear in the list at the bottom of the Element Properties dialog.

7. Click OK.

The chart in Figure 13-13 appears. Each variable is plotted against each of the others. Note that the scatterplots along the diagonal from the upper left to the lower right are blank —because it's useless to plot a variable against itself.

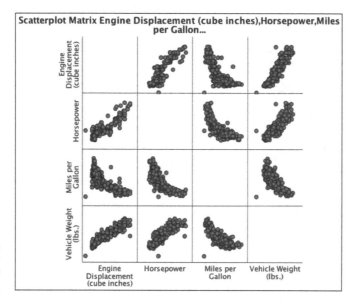

FIGURE 13-13:
A four-by-four matrix of scatterplots.

Stacked bar charts

A *stacked bar chart* is similar to the clustered bar chart in that it displays multiple values of a variable for each value of a categorical variable. But the stacked bar chart does so by stacking them instead of placing them side by side. The following chart displays the same data as the preceding example, but it emphasizes different aspects of the data.

Follow these steps to create a stacked bar chart:

1. Choose File ⇨ Open ⇨ Data and open the Cars.sav file.

Download the file from this book's companion website at www.dummies.com/go/spss4e.

2. Choose Graphs ⇨ Chart Builder.

3. In the Choose From list, select Bar.

4. Select the third graph image (with the Stacked Bar tooltip) and drag it to the panel at the top of the window.

5. In the Variables list, do the following:

a. *Right-click Model Year and select Ordinal.*

b. *Drag Model Year to the X-Axis rectangle.*

c. *Drag Miles Per Gallon to the Count rectangle.* The rectangle was originally labeled Y-Axis. The label changed to help you understand the type of variable that needs to be placed there.

d. *Drag Country of Origin to the rectangle in the upper-right corner, the one now labeled Stack Set Color.*

6. Click OK.

The graph in Figure 13-14 appears.

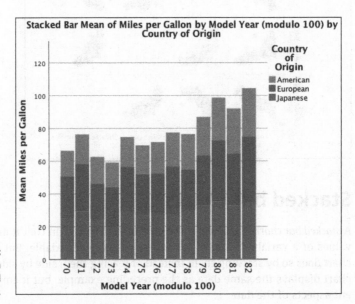

FIGURE 13-14: A bar graph with values displayed in stacks.

Pie charts

Pie charts are the easiest graphs to spot — they're the only chart that shows up as a circle. The purpose of a *pie chart* is simply to show how something (the "whole") is divided into pieces — whether two, ten, or any other number. Each slice in the pie chart represents its percentage of the whole. For example, if a slice takes up 40 percent of the total pie, that slice represents 40 percent of the total number. A pie chart is also called a *polar chart*, so SPSS calls this option Pie/Polar.

In the following steps, you construct a pie chart:

1. **Choose File ⇨ Open ⇨ Data and open the Bank.sav file.**

   Download the file at www.dummies.com/go/spss4e.

2. **Choose Graphs ⇨ Chart Builder.**

3. **In the Choose From list, select Pie/Polar.**

4. **Drag the pie diagram to the panel at the top of the window.**

5. **Click the Groups/Point ID tab, and then click the Columns Panel variable.**

   A rectangle with Panel should appear in the summary area.

6. **Click the Options tab, and then select Wrap Panels at the bottom.**

7. **In the Variables list, drag Sex of Employee to the Slice By rectangle at the bottom of the panel.**

8. **In the Variables list, drag Employment Category to the Panel rectangle at the top of the panel.**

9. **Click OK.**

   The pie chart shown in Figure 13-15 appears, displaying the gender breakdown for each employment category.

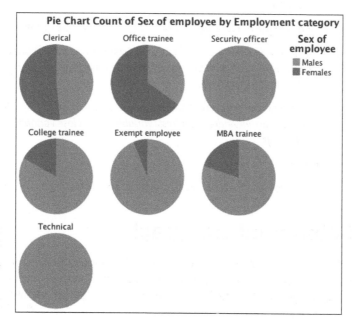

FIGURE 13-15: A pie chart displaying the number of employees in each employment category.

Clustered range bar graphs

The *clustered range bar graph* displays the relationship among five variables. No other chart can be used to so clearly display so many variables. This example demonstrates the relationships among five employee variables: years of employment, income ranges, years with employer, ages, and the years they've lived at their current addresses.

Do the following to build a clustered range bar graph:

1. **Choose File ⇨ Open ⇨ Data and open the Customer_dbase.sav file.**

   The file is in the SPSS installation directory.

2. **Choose Graphs ⇨ Chart Builder.**

3. **In the Choose From list, select High-Low.**

4. **Drag the third graph diagram (with the Clustered Range Bar tooltip) to the panel at the top of the window.**

5. **In the Variables list, do the following:**

   a. *Drag the Years With Current Employer [empcat] variable to the Cluster on X rectangle in the upper-right corner.*

   b. *Drag the Income Category in Thousands [inccat] variable to the X-Axis rectangle at bottom.*

   c. *Drag the Age In Years [age] variable to the High Variable rectangle at the top left.*

   d. *Right-click Years with Current Employer [employ] and make it Scale. Then drag the measure Years with Current Employer [employ] variable to the Low Variable rectangle at the center left.*

   e. *Right-click Years at Current Address [address] and make it Scale. Then drag the Years at Current Address [address] variable to the Close Variable rectangle at the bottom left.*

6. **Click OK.**

   The high-low graph shown in Figure 13-16 appears.

Differenced area graphs

A *differenced area graph* provides a pair of line graphs that emphasize the difference between two variables, filling the area between them with a solid color. The two graphs are plotted against the points of a categorical variable.

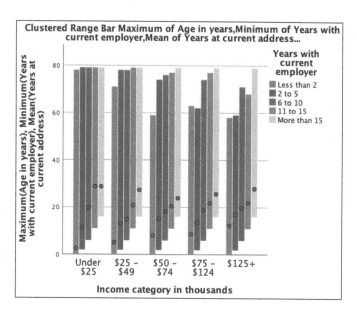

FIGURE 13-16:
A clustered range bar graph, displaying relationships among five variables.

The following steps produce a differenced area graph:

1. **Choose File ⇨ Open ⇨ Data and open the property_assess.sav file.**

The file is in the SPSS installation directory.

2. **Choose Graphs ⇨ Chart Builder.**

3. **In the Choose From list, select High-Low.**

4. **Drag the fourth graph diagram (with the Differenced Area tooltip) to the panel at the top of the window.**

5. **In the Variables list, do the following:**

a. Drag the Township variable to the X-Axis rectangle.

b. Drag the Sale Value of House variable to either Y-Axis rectangle.

c. Drag the Value at Last Appraisal variable to the other Y-Axis rectangle.

Note that the color of the differenced area of the graph may be blue instead of red, depending on which variable is placed in which Y-Axis rectangle.

6. **Click OK.**

The differenced area chart shown in Figure 13-17 appears. You can see the difference between the mean values for the sale and appraisal of homes broken down by region. In each region, the sale value was larger than the appraisal value, which is why the differenced area appears in the color associated with the larger value (red).

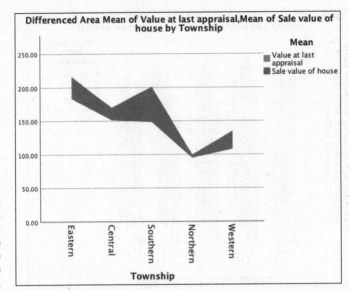

Differenced Area Mean of Value at last appraisal,Mean of Sale value of house by Township

FIGURE 13-17:
In a differenced area chart, the filled region emphasizes the difference between two values.

Dual-axis graph

Many types of graphs allow you to plot two or more variables on the same chart, but they must always be plotted against the same scale. In the *dual-axis graph*, two variables are plotted and two different scales are used to plot them. As a result, the values don't require the same ranges (as they do in the other plots). The curves and trends of the two variables can be easily compared, even though they're on different scales.

Two variables with different ranges that vary across the same set of categories can be plotted together, as shown in the following example:

1. Choose File ⇨ Open ⇨ Data and open the property_assess.sav file.

   The file is in the SPSS installation directory.

2. Choose Graphs ⇨ Chart Builder.

3. In the Choose From list, select Dual Axes.

4. Drag the first diagram (the Dual Y Axes with Categorical X Axis tooltip) to the panel at the top of the window.

5. **In the Variables list, do the following:**

   a. *Drag the Value at Last Appraisal variable to the Y-Axis rectangle on the left.*

   b. *Drag the Sale Value of House variable to the Y-Axis rectangle on the right, which is now named Count.*

   c. *Drag the Township variable to the X-Axis rectangle.*

6. **Click OK.**

   The dual-axis graph shown in Figure 13-18 appears.

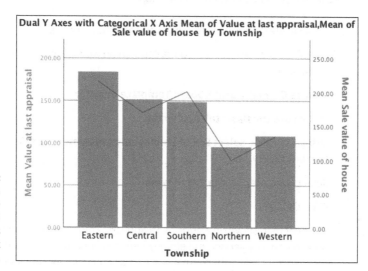

FIGURE 13-18:
A dual-axis graph displaying the curves inscribed by two variables with different ranges.

Fancy Maps Using Graphboard Template Chooser

In this section, we describe fancy maps that you can create only with Graphboard Template Chooser. When data has a geographical component, maps allow you to see patterns in the data that might not be evident in traditional charts, such as clusters or regions with a higher concentration of values.

The three types of maps we describe are the heat map, the choropleth of values map, and the coordinates on a reference map.

Heat map

A *heat map* calculates a summary statistic for a continuous field for the joint distribution of two categorical fields. A heat map is like a table that uses colors instead of numbers to represent cell values. Furthermore, color saturation is used to represent values that correspond to the variables depicted on the map (here, darker values represent higher values). Bright deep red indicates the highest value, and gray indicates a low value. The value of each cell, in this instance, will be the mean of Current Salary by Gender and Employment Category.

The following steps generate a heat map:

1. **Choose File ⇨ Open ⇨ Data and load the Bank.sav file.**

   Download the file from the book's companion website at www.dummies.com/go/spss4e.

2. **Choose Graphs ⇨ Graphboard Template Chooser.**

3. **Make sure the Basic tab is selected.**

4. **Using Ctrl-click, select Sex of Employee, Employment Category, and Current Salary.**

5. **Select Heat Map as the graph type.**

6. **Click OK.**

   The heat map shown in Figure 13-19 appears. Employee current salary is broken down by gender and employment category. You can see that males have a higher salary than females across all employment categories. Likewise, differences exist among employment categories. For example, males employees in the technical category have the highest current salary, while female employees in the technical and security categories have the lowest salary (because there are no people with this combination).

Choropleth of values

Maps can be used in a wide variety of settings to help answer many important questions. For example, organizations may want to know the location of certain client characteristics to determine where to send salespeople, where to hire additional employees, where to create new stores, or which marketing campaigns to use.

Investigators can also use maps to determine the spread of disease, fluctuations in temperature, population growth, distance traveled, where to send school buses, or how to create new districts. One of the nice features of maps is that they give meaningful context and can allow you to see patterns in data that might not be evident in traditional charts.

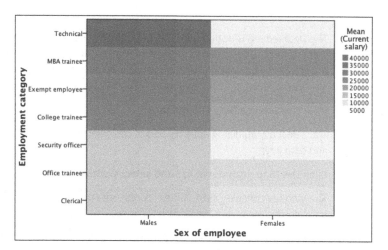

FIGURE 13-19:
A heat map charting current salary against gender and employment.

Maps can be created from a single variable or multiple variables. Maps can use categorical variables, continuous variables, and combinations of categorical and continuous variables.

The *choropleth of values map* shows relationships between two categorical variables and the mode for each location is depicted on the map in a different color.

Let's go through some examples on how to create maps:

1. **Choose File ⇨ Open ⇨ Data and load the Worldsales.sav file.**

   Download the file at www.dummies.com/go/spss4e.

2. **Choose Graphs ⇨ Graphboard Template Chooser.**

3. **Make sure the Basic tab is selected. Then select Continent, hold down the Ctrl key, and click Product Variable.**

   When you selected Continent, you could create only one type of map. When you then selected Product Variable, you selected a second categorical variable and can now create six types of maps.

4. **Select Choropleth of Values as the graph type.**

5. **Click the Detailed tab.**

   The Detailed tab is an alternative to the Basic tab where you can specify all required variables, summary statistics, and aesthetics. You select the graph type, specify the type of data, and then specify details that are not available on the Basic tab.

The Detailed tab is optional for most visualizations but is required when you're creating a map. You need to make sure that the right template and data key are selected. For example, if you have data for Africa, the map template must also be for Africa.

6. **Click the Select a Map File button.**

   The Select a Map dialog appears so you can select the appropriate map key and data key.

7. **Click the Map drop-down list and select Continents.**

   The *map key* consists of the values represented on the map template, which is basically the areas represented on the map.

8. **Click the Data Key drop-down list and select Continent.**

   A *data key* is a variable that contains the values in your dataset. It ties the data to the map, so that the data can be displayed on the map correctly. It's important to make sure that the map and data key values match.

9. **Click the Compare button.**

   The screen shown in Figure 13-20 appears. Now you can see which keys in the map key and data key match. Ideally, you want all the values to match. Make sure that all values for the data key match the values on the map. It's okay if your data does not have some of the values on the map key.

10. **Click OK, and then click OK again.**

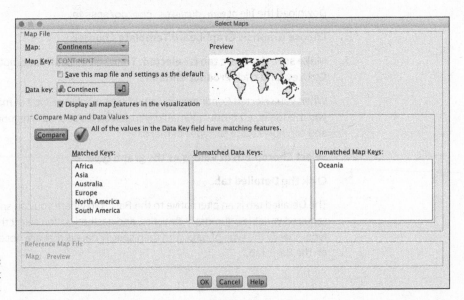

FIGURE 13-20:
The Select
Maps dialog.

208   PART 4 Graphing Data

Graphboard Template Chooser comes with several map files, which you can see by clicking the Manage button. The Manage button allows you to import or export map files. However, if you want to create your own map files, you need to use the map conversion utility, which is in the Utility menu.

The choropleth of values map shows relationships between two categorical variables. Note that the mode, or most common value, is depicted on the map in a different color. Figure 13-21 illustrates the relationship between the Continent and Product variables. The map shows that the continents of North America, Europe, and Australia prefer Product B, the biggest seller in South America and Africa is Product A, and Asia prefers Product C.

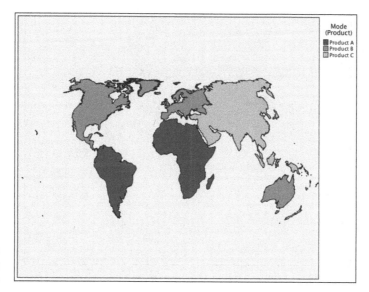

FIGURE 13-21:
A choropleth
of values.

Coordinates on a reference map

The *coordinates on a reference map* uses two continuous variables, one representing longitude and one representing latitude. A map is drawn that displays points using longitude and latitude coordinates. This type of map can be used, for example, to show the location of different crimes, customers, or the spread of disease.

Follow these steps to create a coordinates on a reference map:

1. **Choose File ⇨ Open ⇨ Data and load the Coordinates.sav file.**

   Download the file at www.dummies.com/go/spss4e.

2. **Choose Graphs ⇨ Graphboard Template Chooser.**

3. **Make sure the Basic tab is selected, and then select Longitude.**

4. **Hold the Ctrl key down and click the Latitude variable.**

5. **Select Coordinates on a Reference Map as the graph type.**

6. **Click the Detailed tab, and then click the Select a Map File button.**

7. **Click the Map drop-down list and select Continents.**

8. **Click OK, and then click OK again.**

On the reference map that appears, as shown in Figure 13-22, you can see that most customers are located in the eastern United States and western Europe.

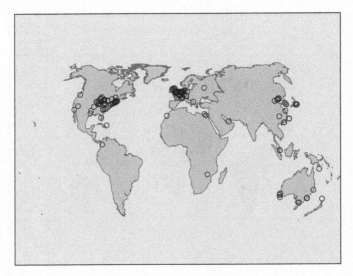

FIGURE 13-22:
Coordinates on a reference map.

REMEMBER

We have presented just a few of the many graphs that you can create in SPSS. Play around with different options to see what you can come up with. After all, a good graph can easily help you convey a great deal of important information to your audience.

5
Analyzing Data

Summarize variables.

Perform hypothesis testing.

Compare one group to the norm.

Create crosstabulations.

Get comfortable comparing groups.

Assess relationships.

Chapter **14**

Using Descriptive Statistics

S ummaries of individual variables provide the basis for more complex analyses (as you see in the next few chapters). They also help establish base rates, answer important questions (for example, the percent of satisfied customers), allow users to check sample size and the data for unusual cases or errors, and provide insights into ways in which you may combine different groups. Ideally, you want to obtain as much information as possible from your data. In practice, given the measurement level of the variables, only some summary statistics are meaningful.

In this chapter, we begin by discussing level of measurement. Next, you run the frequencies procedure to obtain summary statistics for both categorical and continuous variables. Finally, you use the descriptives procedure to summarize continuous variables.

Looking at Levels of Measurement

The level of measurement of a variable determines the appropriate summary statistics and graphs that can be used to describe the data. For example, if you have a variable such as marital status, it wouldn't make sense to ask for the mean of the variable; instead, you might ask for the percentages associated with the different categories. In addition, level of measurement determines the kind of research questions you can answer, so determining the level of measurement is a critical step in the research process.

REMEMBER

Choosing the appropriate summary statistic for each level of measurement is not the same as setting up the metadata in variable view.

The term *levels of measurement* refers to the coding scheme or the meaning of the numbers associated with each variable. Many statistical techniques are appropriate only for data measured at particular levels or combinations of levels of measurement. Different statistical measures are appropriate for different types of variables, and the statistical summaries depend on the level of measurement.

Defining the four levels of measurement

Introductory statistics textbooks present four levels of measurement, each defined by certain properties. Each successive level contains the properties of the preceding types as well as additional characteristics. The four levels of measurement are as follows:

>> **Nominal:** For nominal data, each value represents a category, but the categories have no inherent order. For example, the variable eye color may be coded as 0 (blue), 1 (brown), 2 (black), and 3 (green), but these values tell you only that you have distinct categories, *not* that one category has more or less, or is better or worse than the other.

>> **Ordinal:** For ordinal data, each value is a category and the categories have a meaningful order or rank, but there is no measurable distance between categories. For example, if you're measuring the outcome of a foot race, you can determine which contestant came in first, second, third, and so on. However, based on the ranking, you can't tell how much faster each competitor was compared to the others, nor can you say that the difference between first and second place is the same as the difference between second and third place. Other examples of ordinal variables are attitudinal questions with categories, such as strongly disagree (1), disagree (2), neutral (3), agree (4), and strongly agree (5), or variables such as income coded into categories representing ranges of values.

>> **Interval:** Interval data has all the properties of ordinal variables, and in addition, a one-unit change in the numeric value represents the same change in quantity regardless of where it occurs on the scale. For example, for a variable such as

temperature measured in Fahrenheit, the difference between 20 degrees and 21 degrees (1 unit) is equal to the difference between 50 degrees and 51 degrees. In other words, these variables have equal intervals between points on the scale.

>> **Ratio:** Ratio data has all the properties of interval variables with the addition of a true zero point, representing the absence of the property being measured. For example, temperature measured in Fahrenheit is measured on an interval scale because zero degrees does not represent the absence of temperature. However, a variable such as number of purchases is a ratio variable because a value of zero indicates no purchases. Ratios can then be calculated (for example, eight purchases represents twice as many purchases as four purchases).

These four levels of measurement are often combined into two main types:

>> **Categorical:** Nominal and ordinal measurement levels where different values represent qualitative differences

>> **Continuous (or scale):** Interval and ratio measurement levels where different values represent quantitative differences

SPSS uses three levels of measurement: nominal, ordinal, and scale. *Scale variables* are interval- or ratio-level variables. SPSS does not differentiate between interval- and ratio-level variables because, from a statistical standpoint, no difference exists in the summary statistics you can obtain and in the statistical procedures you can perform for either variable.

Defining summary statistics

The most common way to summarize variables is to use measures of central tendency and variability:

>> **Central tendency:** One number that is often used to summarize the distribution of a variable. Typically, we think of *central tendency* as referring to the average value. The three main measures of central tendency follow:

- **Mode:** The category or value that contains the most cases — in other words, the most common value. This measure is typically used on nominal or ordinal data and can easily be determined by examining a frequency table.

- **Median:** The midpoint of a distribution — in other words, the 50th percentile. If all the cases for a variable are arranged in order according to their value from lowest to highest, the median is the value that splits the data into two equally sized groups. The median is most useful when there are extreme values, such as when analyzing home sales prices.

- **Mean:** The mathematical average of all the values in the distribution — that is, the sum of the values of all cases divided by the total number of cases. The mean is the most common measure of central tendency in statistical tests.

- **5% Trimmed Mean:** The mathematical average of all the values in the distribution after the upper 5 percent and the lower 5 percent of data has been removed. Thus, the 5% trimmed mean is calculated on the middle 90 percent of the distribution. The 5% trimmed mean is most useful for continuous data with outliers.

» **Variability:** The amount of spread or dispersion around the measure of central tendency. Several measures of variability are available:

- **Maximum:** The highest value for a variable.

- **Minimum:** The lowest value in the distribution.

- **Range:** The difference between the maximum and minimum values. It provides a broad sense of the distribution, but it is affected by outliers.

- **Interquartile Range:** The difference between the 75th and 25th percentile values. It is the range for the middle 50 percent of the sample and it is not affected by outliers.

- **Variance:** Provides information about the amount of spread around the mean value. It's an overall measure of how clustered data values are around the mean. The variance is calculated by summing the square of the difference between each value and the mean and dividing this quantity by the number of cases minus one. In general terms, the larger the variance, the more spread there is in the data; the smaller the variance, the more the data values are clustered around the mean.

- **Standard deviation:** The square root of the variance. The variance is expressed in the units of the variable squared. Thus, if you were looking at the variability of the number of apples sold at a supermarket from day to day, the units of the variation would be apples^2. This squared unit is difficult to interpret, so the standard deviation restores the unit of variability to the units of measurement of the original variable.

In conclusion, we care about level of measurement because it determines which summary statistics and graphs we should use to describe the data. Table 14-1 summarizes the most common summary statistics and graphs for each of the measurement levels used by SPSS.

TABLE 14-1   **Level of Measurement and Descriptive Statistics**

	Nominal	Ordinal	Scale
Definition	Unordered categories	Ordered categories	Numeric values
Examples	Gender, geographic location, job category	Satisfaction ratings, income groups, ranking of preferences	Number of purchases, cholesterol level, age
Measures of central tendency	Mode, count, percentages	Mode, count, percentages, median	Mode, median, mean, trimmed mean
Measures of dispersion	None	Minimum, maximum, range, interquartile range	Minimum, maximum, range, standard deviation, variance
Graph	Pie or bar	Pie or bar	Histogram, box and whisker plot

Focusing on Frequencies for Categorical Variables

The most common technique for describing categorical data — nominal and ordinal levels of measurement — is to request a *frequency table,* which provides a summary showing the number and percentage of cases falling into each category of a variable. Users can also request additional summary statistics such as the mode or median, among others.

Here's how to run the *frequencies procedure* so you can create a frequency table that will allow you to obtain summary statistics for categorical variables:

1. **From the main menu, choose File ⇨ Open ⇨ Data and load the Merchandise.sav data file.**

    The file is not in the SPSS installation directory. You have to download it from this book's companion website at www.dummies.com/go/spss4e. The file contains customer purchase history and has 16 variables and 3,338 cases.

2. **Choose Analyze ⇨ Descriptive Statistics ⇨ Frequencies.**

    The Frequencies dialog appears.

    In this example, you want to study the distribution of the variables Payment_Method (Auto Pay, Check, or Credit Card), Premier (Yes or No), and Status (Current or Churned). You can place these variables in the Variable(s) box and each will be analyzed separately.

3. **Select the Payment_Method, Premier, and Status variables, and place them in the Variable(s) box, as shown in Figure 14-1.**

   If you were to run the frequencies procedure now, you would get three tables, each showing the distribution of one variable. It's customary, though, to request additional summary statistics.

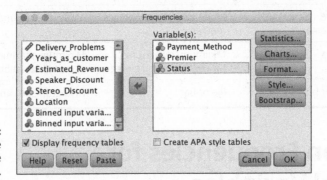

FIGURE 14-1:
Place the
variables in the
Variable(s) box.

4. **Click the Statistics button.**

   The Frequencies: Statistics dialog appears.

5. **In the Central Tendency section, select the Mode check box, as shown in Figure 14-2.**

WARNING

   This dialog provides many statistics, but it's critical that you request only those appropriate for the level of measurement of the variables you placed in the Variable(s) box. For nominal variables, the only suitable statistic is mode.

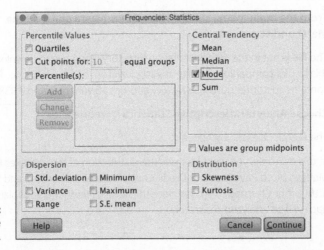

FIGURE 14-2:
The Select the
Mode check box.

6. **Click Continue.**

Requesting a graph can be useful, so you can have a visual display of the data. That's what you'll do now.

7. **Click the Charts button.**

The Frequencies: Charts dialog appears.

8. **In the Chart Type section, select the Bar Charts radio button; in the Chart Values section, select the Percentages radio button (see Figure 14-3).**

This dialog has options for pie charts and bar charts. Either type of chart is acceptable for a nominal variable. Charts can be built using either counts or percentages, but normally percentages are a better choice.

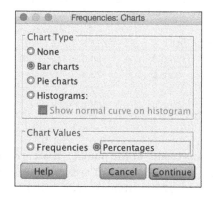

FIGURE 14-3:
Select Bar Charts
and Percentages.

9. **Click Continue, and then click OK.**

SPSS runs the frequencies procedure and calculates the summary statistics, frequency table, and bar chart you requested.

The statistics table shown in Figure 14-4 displays the number of valid and missing cases for each variable requested in the frequencies procedure.

REMEMBER

Be sure to review this table to check the number of missing cases. In this example, you have 3,338 valid cases and no missing data.

The statistics table also displays any additional statistics that were requested. You asked only for the mode, the category that has the highest frequency, so only the mode is shown for each of the variables. In this example, the mode is represented by values of 3, 1, and 2, respectively, and denotes the category of Credit Card for Payment_Method, No for Premier, and Current group for Status.

Statistics

		Payment_Method	Premier	Status
N	Valid	3338	3338	3338
	Missing	0	0	0
Mode		3	1	2

FIGURE 14-4:
The Statistics
table for three
variables.

The frequency table, which is shown in Figure 14-5, displays the distribution of the Payment_Method variable. (In this case, you focus on the Payment_Method variable because all other frequency tables will have similar information.) The information in the frequency table is comprised of counts and percentages.

Payment_Method

		Frequency	Percent	Valid Percent	Cumulative Percent
Valid	Auto Pay	669	20.0	20.0	20.0
	Check	743	22.3	22.3	42.3
	Credit Card	1926	57.7	57.7	100.0
	Total	3338	100.0	100.0	

FIGURE 14-5:
The frequency
table for the
Payment_Method
variable.

The Frequency column contains *counts*, or the number of occurrences of each data value. So, for the Payment_Method variable, it's easy to see why the category Credit Card was the mode — 1,926 customers made purchases this way. The Percent column shows the percentage of cases in each category relative to the number of cases in the entire dataset, including those with missing values. In the example, those 1,926 customers who paid via credit card account for 57.7 percent of all customers. The Valid Percent column contains the percentage of cases in each category relative to the number of valid (nonmissing) cases. Because there is no missing data, the percentages in the Percent column and in the Valid Percent column are identical. The Cumulative Percent column contains the percentage of cases whose values are less than or equal to the indicated value. Cumulative percent is useful only for variables that are ordinal or scale.

TIP

Depending on your research question, the Percent column or the Valid Percent column may be useful when you have a lot of missing data or a variable was not applicable to a large percentage of people.

Bar charts, like the one in Figure 14-6, summarize the distribution that was observed in the frequency table and allow you to see the distribution. For the Payment_Method variable, more than half of the people are in the Credit Card category.

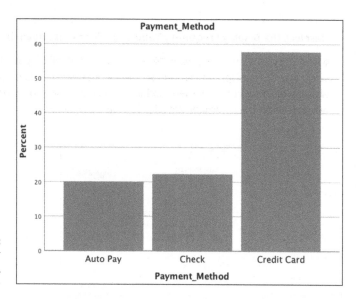

FIGURE 14-6:
A bar chart for
the Payment_
Method variable.

Understanding Frequencies for Continuous Variables

As you have seen, frequency tables show counts and percentages, which are extremely useful when working with categorical variables. However, for continuous variables, which can have many values, frequency tables become less useful. For example, if you were working with a variable such as income, it wouldn't be very useful to know that only one person in the dataset made $22,222 last year. It's likely that each response would have a different value, so the frequency table would be very, very large and not useful as a summary of the variable.

Instead, if the variables of interest are continuous, the frequencies procedure can be useful because of the summary statistics it can produce. To run frequencies for continuous variables, follow these steps:

1. **From the main menu, choose File ⇨ Open ⇨ Data and load the Merchandise.sav data file.**

Download the file from this book's companion website, at www.dummies.com/go/spss4e.

2. **Choose Analyze ⇨ Descriptive Statistics ⇨ Frequencies.**

3. **Select the Stereos, TVs, Speakers, Delivery_Problems, Years_as_customer, and Estimated_Revenue variables, and place them in the Variable(s) box.**

4. Deselect the Display Frequency Tables check box, as shown in Figure 14-7.

A warning dialog appears saying, "You have turned off all output. Unless you select any Output Options this procedure will not be run." You receive this warning because at the moment nothing is selected. This is okay because you will now select the summary statistics you want to display.

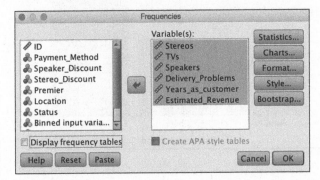

FIGURE 14-7:
The Frequencies
dialog.

5. Click the Statistics button.

The Frequencies: Statistics dialog appears.

All these summary statistics are appropriate for scale variables. The statistics can be divided into those summarizing the central tendency, those measuring the amount of variation (dispersion) in the data, different percentile values you can request, and statistics assessing the shape of the distribution.

6. In the Central Tendency section, select the Mean, Median, and Mode check boxes. In the Dispersion section, select the Std. Deviation, Minimum, and Maximum check boxes.

These selections are shown in Figure 14-8.

7. Click Continue.

8. Click the Charts button.

The Frequencies: Charts dialog appears.

9. Select the Histograms radio button and select the Show Normal Curve on Histogram check box, as shown in Figure 14-9.

10. Click Continue, and then click OK.

SPSS runs the frequencies procedure and calculates the summary statistics and the histogram you requested.

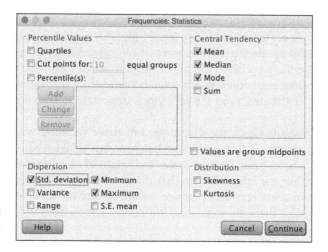

FIGURE 14-8:
The Frequencies:
Statistics dialog.

FIGURE 14-9:
The Frequencies:
Charts dialog.

The statistics table in Figure 14-10 shows that you have 3,338 valid cases and don't have any missing data. The statistics table contains the requested statistics. For example, for the Speakers variable, the minimum value is 0 and the maximum value is 451. This range of values seems to be very large, so it would be useful to double-check the data to make sure there are no errors.

		Stereos	TVs	Speakers	Delivery_Pro blems	Years_as_cus tomer	Estimated_R evenue
Statistics							
N	Valid	3338	3338	3338	3338	3338	3338
	Missing	0	0	0	0	0	0
Mean		13.71	.83	51.30	.13	6.38	5034510.94
Median		14.00	.00	36.00	.00	6.00	5029070.00
Mode		0	0	4	0	7	5029070
Std. Deviation		9.417	2.228	54.104	.434	2.565	2828800.41
Minimum		0	0	0	0	2	11028
Maximum		30	10	451	4	11	9983290

FIGURE 14-10:
The Statistics
table for six
variables.

Likewise, in an ideal world, you would like the mean, median, and mode to be similar, because they're all measures of central tendency. In this case, note that for the Speakers variable, the mean (51.3), median (36), and mode (4) are very different from each other, which is an indication that this variable is probably not normally distributed. (You see why this is important in later chapters.)

You can visually check the distribution of these variables with a histogram, as shown in Figure 14-11. A histogram has bars, but unlike a bar chart, the bars are plotted along an equal interval scale. The height of each bar is the count of values falling within the interval. Note that the lower range of values is truncated at 0 and the number of speakers is greatest down toward the lower end of the distribution, although there are some extreme values. The distribution is not normal.

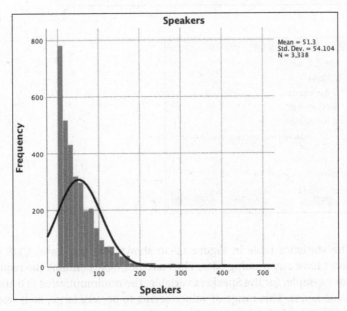

FIGURE 14-11: A histogram for the Speakers variable.

Summarizing Continuous Variables with the Descriptives Procedure

The *descriptive procedure* is an alternative to the frequencies procedure (see the preceding section) when the objective is to summarize continuous variables. The descriptives procedure provides a succinct summary of various statistics and the number of cases with valid values for each variable included in the table.

To use the descriptives procedure, follow these steps:

1. **From the main menu, choose File ⇨ Open ⇨ Data and load the Merchandise.sav data file.**

   Download the file at www.dummies.com/go/spss4e.

2. **Choose Analyze ⇨ Descriptive Statistics ⇨ Descriptives.**

   The Descriptives dialog appears.

3. **Select the Stereos, TVs, Speakers, Delivery_Problems, Years_as_customer, and Estimated_Revenue variables, and place them in the Variable(s) box, as shown in Figure 14-12.**

4. **Click OK.**

   SPSS runs the descriptives procedure and calculates the summary statistics.

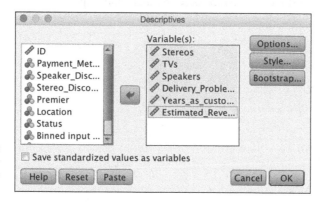

FIGURE 14-12:
Place the variables in the Variable(s) box.

The minimum and maximum values provide an efficient way to check for values outside the expected range (see Figure 14-13). If you see a value that is too low or too high, you might have data errors or potential outliers. Likewise, it's always important to investigate the mean and determine whether the value makes sense. Ask yourself, "Is this what I was expecting?" Sometimes a mean may be lower or higher than expected, which can indicate a problem related to how the data was coded or collected.

It is important also to check the standard deviation. For example, if you have a standard deviation of zero, every person in the dataset provided the same value. This information might be useful from a business perspective if everyone loved your product. From a statistical perspective, however, a variable that doesn't vary isn't useful.

Descriptive Statistics					
	N	Minimum	Maximum	Mean	Std. Deviation
Stereos	3338	0	30	13.71	9.417
TVs	3338	0	10	.83	2.228
Speakers	3338	0	451	51.30	54.104
Delivery_Problems	3338	0	4	.13	.434
Years_as_customer	3338	2	11	6.38	2.565
Estimated_Revenue	3338	11028	9983290	5034510.94	2828800.41
Valid N (listwise)	3338				

FIGURE 14-13:
The Descriptive
Statistics table.

Finally, the last row in the table, Valid N (listwise), is the number of cases that have a valid value for all the variables appearing in the table. In this example, you have no missing data, so this number is at least partially useful because it shows that all the data entries are in a sense complete. Valid N (listwise) is useful for a set of variables that you intended to use for a *multivariate analysis* (an analysis looking at the relationships between many variables).

Chapter **15**

Knowing When Not to Trust Your Data

W hat is inferential statistics and who uses it? *Inferential statistics* is the practice of collecting and analyzing numerical data for the purpose of making scientific inferences from a representative sample to a population. Government agencies, business analysts, market researchers, health researchers, survey companies, education researchers, and many others use inference.

In this chapter, you discover the benefits and potential limitations of sampling. You then find out about hypothesis testing so you can learn the logic behind performing statistical tests. From there, we describe distributions, which provide insight into statistical theory and will lead you to calculating z-scores, so that you can identify the position of any data point on a distribution.

Sampling

Descriptive statistics, which we introduce in Chapter 14, describe the data in a sample through a number of summary procedures and statistics. For example, you can calculate the mean or standard deviation of a group of people so that you can better describe them. Descriptive statistics are mostly useful if you just want to describe a specific sample. Most of the time, however, researchers are concerned not about a sample but about a population. They use the results from a sample to make inferences about the true values in a population.

In an ideal world, you'd collect data from every single person you're interested in. Because that is not realistic, you use samples. *Sampling* is the process of collecting data on a portion of all the elements of interest as an alternative to looking at the entire set of elements. Sampling allows us to describe and draw conclusions about the population, and is performed for feasibility, accessibility, and efficiency in terms of both time and money. If you follow some rules when sampling, you can get answers that are close to the population values, with high probability.

Following are the characteristics of an effective sample:

>> **Probabilistic sampling:** One in which each element of the population has a known, nonzero chance of being included in the sample. A probability sample allows you to do statistical tests, place confidence intervals around statistics (so that you know the probable range of values), and make inferences about the total population.

>> **Sufficiently large:** Small samples will not provide the appropriate statistical power to discover true differences between groups or to determine the effect of one variable on another.

>> **Unbiased:** *Bias* occurs because some units are overselected or underselected for the sample. Some types of bias include selection bias in how the sampling itself is done, and nonresponse bias, which occurs when those who decline to participate are different than those who do respond.

WARNING

With nonprobability samples (such as snowball, convenience, quota, or focus groups), calculating the probability of selection for all elements in the population is impossible. Therefore, statistical theory does not apply to a nonprobability sample, which tells us only about the elements in the sample, not about any greater population.

Understanding Sample Size

An important aspect of statistics is that they *vary* from one sample to another. Due to the effects of random variability, it is unlikely that any two samples drawn from the same population will produce the same statistics.

By plotting the values of a particular statistic, such as the mean, from a large number of samples, you can obtain a *sampling distribution* of the statistic. For small numbers of samples, the mean of the sampling distribution may not closely resemble that of the population. However, as the number of samples taken increases, the closer the mean of the sampling distribution (the mean of all the means) gets to the population mean. For an infinitely large number of samples, the mean will be exactly the same as the population mean.

Additionally, as sample size increases, the amount of variability in the distribution of sample means decreases. If you think of variability in terms of the error made in estimating the mean, it should be clear that the more evidence you have — that is, the more cases in the sample — the smaller the error in estimating the mean.

Sample size strongly influences *precision*, that is, how close estimates from different samples are to each other. As an example, the precision of a sample proportion is approximately equal to one divided by the square root of the sample size. Table 15-1 displays the precision for various sample sizes.

TABLE 15-1 **Sample Size and Precision**

Sample Size	Precision
100	$1/\sqrt{100} = 10\%$
400	$1/\sqrt{400} = 5\%$
1,600	$1/\sqrt{1600} = 2.5\%$

Testing Hypotheses

Suppose you collected customer satisfaction data on a subset of your customers and determine that the average customer satisfaction is 3.5 on a 5-point scale. You want to take this information a step further, though, and determine whether a difference in satisfaction exists between customers who bought Product A (3.6) and customers who bought Product B (3.3). The numbers aren't exactly the same, but are the differences due to random variation? Inferential statistics can answer this type of question.

Inferential statistics enables you to infer the results from the sample on which you have data and apply it to the population that the sample represents. Understanding how to make inferences from a sample to a population is the basis of inferential statistics. You can reach conclusions about the population without studying every single individual, which can be costly and time consuming.

Whenever you want to make an inference about a population from a sample, you must test a specific hypothesis. Typically, you state two hypotheses:

>> **Null hypothesis:** The *null hypothesis* is the one in which no effect is present. For example, you may be looking for differences in mean income between males and females, but the (null) hypothesis you're testing is that there is no difference between the groups. Or the null hypothesis may be that there are no differences in satisfaction between customers who bought Product A (3.6) and customers who bought Product B (3.3). In other words, the differences are due to random variation.

>> **Alternative hypothesis:** The *alternative hypothesis* (also known as the *research hypothesis*) is generally (although not exclusively) the one researchers are really interested in. For example, you may hypothesize that the mean incomes of males and females are different. Or for the customer satisfaction example, the alternative hypothesis may be that there is a difference in satisfaction between customers who bought Product A (3.6) and customers who bought Product B (3.3). In other words, the differences are real.

When making an inference, you never know anything for certain because you're dealing with samples rather than populations. Therefore, you always have to work with probabilities. You assess a hypothesis by calculating the probability, or the likelihood, of finding your result. A probability value can range from 0 to 1 (corresponding to 0 percent to 100 percent, in terms of percentages). You can use these values to assess whether the likelihood that any differences you've found are the result of random chance.

So, how do hypotheses and probabilities interact? Suppose you want to know who will win the Super Bowl. You ask your fellow statisticians, and one of them says that he has built a predictive model and he knows Team A will win. Your next question should be, "How confident are you in your prediction?" Your friend says, "I'm 50 percent confident." Are you going to trust this prediction? Of course not, because there are only two outcomes and 50 percent means the prediction is random.

So, you ask another fellow statistician, and he tells you that he has built a predictive model. He knows that Team A will win, and he's 75 percent confident in his prediction. Are you going to trust his prediction? Well, now you start to think about it a little. You have a 75 percent chance of being right and a 25 percent chance of being wrong, and decide that a 25 percent chance of being wrong is too high.

So, you ask another fellow statistician, and she tells you that she has built a predictive model and knows Team A will win, and she's 90 percent confident in her prediction. Are you going to trust her prediction? Now you have a 90 percent chance of being right, and only a 10 percent chance of being wrong.

This is the way statistics work. You have two hypotheses — the null hypothesis and the alternative hypothesis — and you want to be sure of your conclusions. So, having formally stated the hypotheses, you must then select a criterion for acceptance or rejection of the null hypothesis. With probability tests, such as the chi-square test of independence or the independent samples t-test, you're testing the likelihood that a statistic of the magnitude obtained (or greater) would have occurred by chance, assuming that the null hypothesis is true.

Remember, you always assess the null hypothesis, which is the hypothesis that states there is no difference or no relationship. In other words, you reject the null hypothesis only when you can say that the result would have been extremely unlikely under the conditions set by the null hypothesis; if this is the case, the alternative hypothesis should be accepted.

TIP

But what criterion (or alpha level, as it is often known) should you use? Traditionally, a 5 percent level is chosen, indicating that a statistic of the size obtained would be likely to occur on only 5 percent of occasions (or once in 20 occasions) should the null hypothesis be true. By choosing a 5 percent criterion, you're accepting that you'll make a mistake in rejecting the null hypothesis 5 percent of the time (should the null hypothesis be true).

TECHNICAL
STUFF

Hypothesis testing has been frustrating students and instructors of statistics for years! Don't be surprised if you have to reread this chapter several times — hypothesis testing is confusing stuff!

Calculating Confidence Intervals

Consider the example in Figure 15-1, in which a treatment group has a mean of 14.43 and a control group has a mean of 12.37. You need to detect whether the means are significantly different or due to chance.

FIGURE 15-1:
The Group
Statistics table.

Group Statistics					
	Group	N	Mean	Std. Deviation	Std. Error Mean
Score	Treatment	258	14.43	2.979	.185
	Control	216	12.37	2.319	.158

A *95 percent confidence interval* provides a measure of the precision with which the true population difference is estimated. In the example (see Figure 15-2), the 95 percent confidence interval for the mean difference between groups ranges from 1.571 to 2.549; the actual mean difference is 2.06. So the 95 percent confidence interval indicates the likely range of the population mean difference.

FIGURE 15-2:
The Independent
Samples test.

Independent Samples Test				
	Mean Difference	Std. Error Difference	95% Confidence Interval of the Difference	
			Lower	Upper
Score	2.060	.249	1.571	2.549

Although the actual value is 2.06, you are 95 percent confident that the difference value will fall anywhere between 1.571 to 2.549 (basically the mean difference +/– the standard error of the difference (.249) multiplied by 1.96).

TECHNICAL STUFF

The only value that you're getting directly from the data is the mean, 2.06. Statistics students often memorize the number 1.96, which is the 5 percent cutoff from the normal distribution — but not from this specific dataset. So the lower value (1.571) and upper value (2.549) of the confidence interval are derived using the value 1.96, which assumes a normal distribution. If the distribution is not normal, the confidence interval numbers will be wrong.

Note that the confidence interval does not include zero because there is a statistically significant difference between groups. If zero had been included within the range, it would indicate that there are no differences between the groups — that is, you're saying that the probability value is greater than 0.05. In essence, the 95 percent confidence interval is another way of testing the null hypothesis. So, if the value of zero does not fall within the 95 percent confidence interval, you're saying that the probability of the null hypothesis (that is, no difference or a difference of zero) is less than 0.05.

Conducting In-Depth Hypothesis Testing

We just introduced inferential statistics, which allows us to infer the results from your sample to the population. This concept is important because you want to do research that applies to a larger audience than just the specific group of people you test.

As mentioned, hypothesis testing allows researchers to develop hypotheses, which are then assessed to determine the probability, or likelihood, of the findings. Two hypotheses are typically created: The null hypothesis states that no effect is present, and the alternative hypothesis states that an effect is present.

For example, suppose you want to assess whether differences in mean income exist between males and females. The null hypothesis states that there is no difference in income between the groups, and the alternative hypothesis states that there is a difference in income between the groups. You then assess the null hypothesis by calculating the probability that it is true. At this point, you investigate the probability value, and if it's less than 0.05, you say that you've found support for the alternative hypothesis because the probability that the null hypothesis is true is low (less than 5 percent). If it's greater than 0.05, you say that you've found support for the null hypothesis because there is a decent chance that it's true (greater than 5 percent).

However, too often people immediately jump to the conclusion that the finding is statistically significant or is not statistically significant. Although that's literally true, because you use those words to describe probability values below 0.05 and above 0.05, statistical significance doesn't imply that only two conclusions can be drawn about your finding. Table 15-2 is a more realistic scenario.

TABLE 15-2   **Types of Statistical Outcome**

In the Real World	Statistical Test Outcome	
	Not Significant	Significant
No difference (null is true)	Correct decision	False positive; Type I error
True difference (alternative is true)	False negative; Type II error	Correct decision, power

Note that several outcomes are possible. Let's take a look at the first row. It could be that, in the real world, there is no relationship between the variables, which is what your test found. In this scenario, you would be making a correct decision. However, what if in the real world there was no relationship between the variables and your test found that there was a significant relationship? In this case, you would be making *a Type 1 error*. This type of error is known also as a *false positive* because the researcher falsely concludes a positive result (thinks it does occur when it does not).

A Type I error is explicitly taken into account when performing statistical tests. When testing for statistical significance using a 0.05 criterion, you acknowledge that if there is no effect in the population, the sample statistic will exceed the criterion on average 5 times out of 100 (or 0.05). So this type of error could occur strictly by chance — or if the researcher used the wrong test. (An *inappropriate test* is used when you don't meet the assumptions of a test, which is why knowing and testing assumptions is important.)

TECHNICAL STUFF

How could SPSS let you do the wrong test? The calculations will always be correct, but you have to know which menu to work in. For instance, the T-test is a parametric test, and it assumes that your data is shaped like a bell curve. In fact (and this is even more technical), it assumes that the errors are shaped like a bell curve. And there is a separate menu with tests that you can use when this isn't true. You may be surprised by how many SPSS users get confused about these issues. What happens is this: A parametric test might yield a probability of 0.047 and a nonparametric test might yield a probability of 0.053. You can see the problem now. If you declare a result is significant, an expert might say the same result is not significant.

REMEMBER

For now, the main message is this — assumptions are not just a bunch of arbitrary rules. They sometimes affect which conclusions you draw.

Now let's take a look at the second row of Table 15-2. It could be that in the real world there is a relationship between the variables, and this is what your test found. In this scenario, you would be making a correct decision. *Power* is defined as the ability to detect true differences if they exist.

However, what if in the real world there was a relationship between the variables and your test found that there was no significant relationship? In this case, you would be making a Type II error. This type of error is known also as a *false negative* because the researcher falsely concludes a negative result (thinks it does not occur when in fact it does). This type of error typically happens when you use small samples, so your test is not powerful enough to detect true differences. (When sample sizes are small, precision tends to be poor.) The error could occur also if the researcher used the wrong test.

You know that larger samples are more precise, thus power analysis was developed to help researchers determine the minimum sample size required to have a specified chance of detecting a true difference or relationship.

Power analysis can be useful when planning a study but you must know the magnitude of the hypothesized effect and an estimate of the variance.

A related issue involves drawing a distinction between statistical significance and practical importance. When an effect is found to be statistically significant, you conclude that the population effect (difference or relation) is not zero. However, this conclusion allows for a statistically significant effect that is not quite zero yet so small as to be insignificant from a practical or policy perspective.

As mentioned, very large samples yield increased precision, and in such samples very small effects may be found to be statistically significant but the question is whether the effects make any practical difference. For example, suppose a company is interested in customer ratings of one of its products and obtains scores from several thousand customers. Furthermore, suppose the mean ratings on a 1 to 5 satisfaction scale are 3.25 for male customers and 3.15 for female customers, and this difference is found to be statistically significant. Would such a small difference be of any practical interest or use?

When sample sizes are small (say under 30), precision tends to be poor and so only relatively large effects are found to be statistically significant. With moderate samples (say 50 to 200), small effects tend to show modest significance while large effects are highly significant. For very large samples (several hundred or thousand), small effects can be highly significant. Thus, an important aspect of an analysis is to examine the effect size and determine if it is important from a practical or policy perspective.

Using the Normal Distribution

The *distribution* of a variable refers to the numbers of times each outcome occurs. Many statistical distributions exists, such as binomial, uniform, and Poisson, but one of the most common distributions is the normal distribution. Many naturally occurring phenomena, such as height, weight, and blood pressure, follow a normal distribution (curve).

The *normal distribution* (often referred to as the *normal bell-shaped curve*) is a frequency distribution in which the mean, median, and mode exactly coincide and are symmetrical, so that 50 percent of cases lie to either side of the mean. In addition, the proportion of cases contained within any portion of the normal curve can be calculated mathematically, which is why the normal distribution is used in many inferential statistical procedures. Figure 15-3 illustrates a normal distribution.

Random errors tend to conform to a normal distribution, which is why many statistical techniques have the assumption of normality, which says that errors follow a normal distribution. In fact, every statistical technique that we describe that has a continuous dependent variable has the assumption of normality. In Chapter 21, we talk about situations and tests you can use when you don't have a normal distribution.

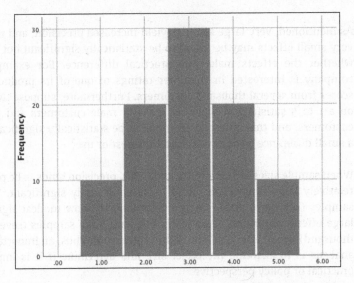

FIGURE 15-3:
A normal
distribution.

Normal distributions are frequently used in statistics also because the *Central Limit Theorem* suggests that as sample size increases, the sampling distribution of the sample's means approaches normality, regardless of the shape of the population distribution. This extremely useful statistical axiom doesn't require that the original population distribution be normal; it states that the sample mean is distributed normally, regardless of the distribution of the variable itself.

Working with Z-Scores

After you know the characteristics of the distribution of a variable, that is, the mean and standard deviation, you can calculate standardized scores, more commonly referred to as z-scores. *Z-scores* indicate the number of standard deviations a score is above or below the sample mean. You can use standardized scores to calculate the relative position of each value in a normal distribution because the mean of a standardized distribution is 0 and the standard deviation is 1. Z-scores are most often used in statistics to standardize variables of unequal scale units for statistical comparisons or for use in multivariate procedures.

Z-scores are calculated by subtracting the mean from the value of the observation in question and then dividing by the standard deviation for the sample:

Z = (score − mean) / standard deviation

For example, if you have a score of 75 out of 100 on a test of math ability, this information alone is not enough to tell how well you did in relation to others taking the test. However, if you know that the mean score and the standard deviation, you can calculate the proportion of people who achieved a score at least as high as you. For example, if the mean is 50 and the standard deviation is 10, you can calculate the following:

$$(75 - 50) / 10 = 2.5$$

You scored 2.5 standard deviations above the mean.

In Chapter 14, we show you how to use the descriptives procedure as an alternative to the frequencies procedure. Now you use the descriptives procedure to calculate z-scores.

To use the descriptives procedure, follow these steps:

1. **From the main menu, choose File ⇨ Open ⇨ Data, and load the Merchandise.sav data file.**

   The file is not in the SPSS installation directory. Download it from the book's companion website at www.dummies.com/go/spss4e.

2. **Choose Analyze ⇨ Descriptive Statistics ⇨ Descriptives.**

3. **Select the Stereos, TVs, and Speakers variables and place them in the Variable(s) box.**

4. **Select the Save Standardized Values as Variables option, as shown in Figure 15-4.**

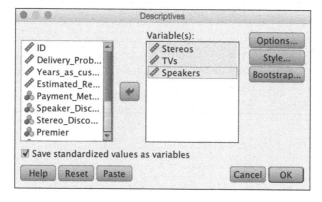

FIGURE 15-4: The Descriptives dialog used to calculate z-scores.

5. **Click OK.**

   SPSS runs the descriptives procedure and calculates the z-scores.

6. **Switch over to the Data Editor window.**

Figure 15-5 shows the three new standardized variables created at the end of the data file. Note that the screen was split to better illustrate the creation of the new variables. By default, the new variable names are the old variable names prefixed with the letter Z. You can save these variables in the file and use them in any statistical procedure.

Stereos	TVs	Speakers	Delivery_Problems	Years_as_customer	ZStereos	ZTVs	ZSpeakers
5	8	86	0	6	-.92448	3.21911	.64131
0	0	4	0	6	-1.45542	-.37136	-.87429
6	0	9	1	8	-.81829	-.37136	-.78188
14	6	30	0	4	.03121	2.32149	-.39373
14	3	33	0	7	.03121	.97506	-.33829
0	0	1	0	9	-1.45542	-.37136	-.92974
0	0	9	0	3	-1.45542	-.37136	-.78188
2	0	20	0	6	-1.24305	-.37136	-.57856
11	0	34	0	10	-.28736	-.37136	-.31980
0	0	73	0	10	-1.45542	-.37136	.40103

FIGURE 15-5:
The Stereos, TVs, and Speakers variables have been standardized.

Focusing on the first row, note that the first person purchased 5 stereos, 8 TVs, and 86 speakers. Typically, you'd think that 86 is a large number, but when you look at the z-scores, the only value above average is for the number of TVs purchased, not stereos purchased. Figure 15-6 shows the respective mean and standard deviation for each variable. Given that the mean number of TVs purchased is .83 with a standard deviation of 2.23, someone buying 8 TVs is unusual.

Descriptive Statistics

	N	Minimum	Maximum	Mean	Std. Deviation
Stereos	3338	0	30	13.71	9.417
TVs	3338	0	10	.83	2.228
Speakers	3338	0	451	51.30	54.104
Valid N (listwise)	3338				

FIGURE 15-6:
The Descriptive Statistics table of stereos, TVs, and speakers.

Chapter **16**

Testing One Group

I n Chapter 14, we discuss the concept of level of measurement and how to obtain summary statistics for both categorical and continuous variables. In Chapter 15, we talk about the notions of sampling and hypothesis testing. In this chapter, we tie together these ideas and cover two simple inferential tests that can be performed on a single variable: the chi-square goodness of fit test, which is used on categorical variables, and the one-sample t-test, which is used on continuous variables.

Conducting Inferential Tests

As we mention in Chapter 14, obtaining descriptive statistics can be important for various reasons. For example, descriptive statistics forms the basis for more complex analyses. When you run a chi-square test of independence (see Chapter 17), an independent samples t-test (see Chapter 18), or a simple linear regression (see Chapter 19), you're simply plugging descriptive statistics into a fancy formula and adding the inference that you learned in the previous chapter, which then provides useful information.

Inferential tests are available for all levels of measurement. In practice, the statistical method you choose depends on the questions you're asking and the level of measurement of the variables. The simplest case involves assessing only a single variable; in this situation you would compare that single variable to the population norm. As you can see in Table 16-1, level of measurement determines the test you can use; incidentally, these are the two tests we cover in this chapter.

TABLE 16-1   **Level of Measurement and Statistical Tests for One Variable**

Variable	Test
Categorical	Chi-square goodness of fit
Continuous	One-sample t-test

Running the Chi-Square Goodness of Fit Test

The *chi-square goodness of fit test* studies the distribution of one categorical variable to determine if the categories of that variable appear more or less often than they should when compared to the population norm. For example, suppose you want to look at the distribution of the variable gender, as shown Figure 16-1. In this example, you can see that 474 people are in the sample, 273 males and 201 females.

Gender

	Observed N	Expected N	Residual
Male	273	237.0	36.0
Female	201	237.0	-36.0
Total	474		

FIGURE 16-1: The distribution of gender.

Now suppose that in the population there was a 50-50 split between the genders. This suggests that if the sample were representative of the population, you would expect 50 percent of the sample to be female and 50 percent of the sample to be male, so there should be 237 males and 237 females. However, males are slightly overrepresented and females are slightly underrepresented, each by a count of 36.

Are you surprised that the numbers for each gender group are not exactly the same? No, not really, because someone might have been sick or in a meeting when the sample was conducted, or not counted for various other reasons. However, you still expect the numbers for each group to be relatively similar. So how do you know if these differences between what you observed and what you expect are real differences or differences due to random fluctuation (chance)?

To answer this question, you need to perform the chi-square goodness of fit test. Going back to the idea of hypothesis testing, you set up two hypotheses:

» **Null hypothesis:** All categories are appropriately represented, thus reflecting the population values.

» **Alternative hypothesis:** All categories are not appropriately represented, thus not reflecting the population values.

For this example, you'll work with the Employment category variable, which has the distribution shown in Figure 16-2. Ideally, based on the population, you expect 60 percent of the sample to be clerical, 10 percent to be custodial, and 30 percent to be managers.

Employment Category

		Frequency	Percent	Valid Percent	Cumulative Percent
Valid	Clerical	363	76.6	76.6	76.6
	Custodial	27	5.7	5.7	82.3
	Manager	84	17.7	17.7	100.0
	Total	474	100.0	100.0	

FIGURE 16-2: The frequency table of the Employment Category variable.

Here's how to perform a chi-square goodness of fit test:

1. **From the main menu, choose File ⇨ Open ⇨ Data and load the Employee data.sav data file.**

   The file is not in the IBM SPSS Statistics directory. Go to the book's website, at www.dummies.com/go/spss4e, to download the file.

2. **Choose Analyze ⇨ Nonparametric Tests ⇨ Legacy Dialogs ⇨ Chi-Square.**

   The Chi-Square Tests dialog appears.

TIP

   You can run the chi-square goodness of fit test also by choosing Analyze ⇨ Nonparametric Tests ⇨ One Sample, but the commands in Step 2 make it easier to understand the logic behind the test.

   In this example, you want to study the distribution of the Employment category variable with the following categories: Clerical, Custodial, and Manager.

3. Select the Employment category variable, and place it in the Test Variable List box.

If you expect the percentage of cases in each category to be equal, you can run the analysis at this point. However, if you need to specify a different percentage of cases for each category, you need to select the Values option in the Expected Values area.

4. In the Expected Values area, click Values and then type the following in the Values field:

   a. Type 60 and click the Add button.

   b. Type 10 and click Add.

   c. Type 30 and click Add.

Be sure to assign values in the order of the categories of the variable so that the appropriate comparisons are made. The completed dialog is shown in Figure 16-3.

5. Click OK.

The Employment Category table, shown in Figure 16-4, displays the number of people in the clerical (363), custodial (27), and manager (84) categories. This table also displays the number of people who were expected in each of the employment categories — clerical (284.4), custodial (87.4), and manager (142.2) — based on the population percentages you specified in the chi-square procedure.

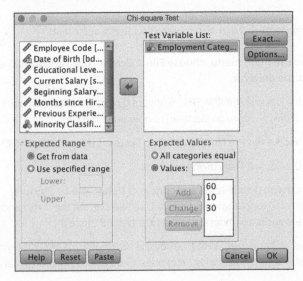

FIGURE 16-3: The completed Chi-Square Test dialog.

FIGURE 16-4:
The Employment
Category table.

Employment Category			
	Observed N	Expected N	Residual
Clerical	363	284.4	78.6
Custodial	27	47.4	-20.4
Manager	84	142.2	-58.2
Total	474		

Finally, the Residual column presents the difference between observed and expected counts for each employment category: clerical (78.6), custodial (–20.4), and manager (–58.2). People in the clerical group are overrepresented and people in the custodial and manager groups are underrepresented.

Going back to the gender example (refer to Figure 16-1), you can easily calculate the amount of misfit between what was observed and what was expected by using the chi-square formula:

$$X^2 = \Sigma \left(O_i - E_i \right)^2 / E_i$$

For each cell, you take the observed count (O) minus the expected count (E), then square the difference and divide by the expected count, and then add the values across all the cells.

Now if there were no differences between the observed and expected counts (that is, they are the same), subtracting one from the other will yield a chi-square statistic of 0. However, if the observed and expected counts are not the same, the chi-square statistic would not be zero. In fact, larger chi-square statistic values would indicate larger discrepancies between the observed and expected counts.

The chi-square value is used to test for a relationship. As mentioned, the chi-square statistic is calculated by testing the difference between the *observed counts* (the number of cases you actually observed in each category) and the *expected counts* (the number of cases you should have observed in each category based on the population percentages). So, the chi-square statistic is an indication of misfit between observed minus expected counts.

The actual chi-square value (here, 10.937) is used with the number of degrees of freedom (df), which is related to the number of cells in the table, to calculate the significance for the chi-square statistic. This can be found in the row labeled *Asymp. Sig.* (see Figure 16-5).

The *significance value* provides the probability of the null hypothesis being true. It assesses the difference between the population and the sample, so the lower the significance value, the less likely the observed values (based on the sample) and expected values (based on the population) are the same.

Test Statistics

	Gender
Chi-Square	10.937[a]
df	1
Asymp. Sig.	.001

a. 0 cells (0.0%) have expected frequencies less than 5. The minimum expected cell frequency is 237.0.

FIGURE 16-5:
The Test Statistics table for gender.

Analysts often use a cutoff value of 0.05 or lower to determine whether the results are statistically significant. For example, with a cutoff value of 0.05, if the significance value is smaller than 0.05, the null hypothesis is rejected. In this case, you can see that the probability of the null hypothesis being true is very small — less than 0.05 — so you can reject the null hypothesis and have no choice but to say you found support for the alternative hypothesis. Therefore, you can conclude that the distribution of gender in the sample does not match the distribution of gender in the population.

With regard to the employment category example (see Figure 16-6), the chi-square value (54.323) results in a significance value smaller than 0.05, so the null hypothesis is rejected. You can conclude that the distribution of the employment category in the sample does not match the distribution of the employment category in the population. Specifically, people in the clerical group are overrepresented and people in the custodial and manager groups are underrepresented.

Test Statistics

	Employment Category
Chi-Square	54.323[a]
df	2
Asymp. Sig.	.000

a. 0 cells (0.0%) have expected frequencies less than 5. The minimum expected cell frequency is 47.4.

FIGURE 16-6:
The Test Statistics table for the employment category.

TECHNICAL STUFF

Every statistical test has assumptions. The better you meet these assumptions, the more you can trust the results of the test. The chi-square goodness of fit test assumes the following:

>> The variables are categorical (that is, nominal or ordinal).

>> Each case is assessed only once (hence, this test is not used in a test-retest scenario).

>> The levels of the variables are mutually exclusive (each person can be in only one category of a variable).

>> You have a large enough sample.

In the example, you meet all these assumptions. The last assumption is assessed by the footnote on the Test Statistics table (refer to Figure 16-6), which notes the number of cells with expected counts less than 5. In the example, zero cells (0%) have expected counts less than 5. Ideally, that is what you want to see because the chi-square test is not as reliable when sample sizes are very small (expected counts less than 5).

If you ever have a situation where more than 20 percent of the cells have expected counts less than 5, increase your sample size if possible or reduce the number of categories in the table (by combining or removing categories). Otherwise, you do not have enough data to trust the results of the analysis.

For presentations, providing a graph of the distribution of a categorical variable, such as a simple bar chart, is often useful. Follow these steps to create a simple bar chart of the employment category:

1. **From the main menu, choose File ⇨ Open ⇨ Data, and then load the Employee data.sav data file.**

   Download the file from the book's website, at www.dummies.com/go/spss4e.

2. **Choose Graphs ⇨ Chart Builder.**

3. **In the Choose From list, select Bar.**

4. **Select the first graph image (the one with the Simple Bar tooltip) and drag it to the panel at the top of the window.**

5. **Select the Employment Category variable, and place it in the X-axis box.**

6. **In the Element Properties box, change Statistic to Percentage().**

7. **Click OK.**

   The graph shown in Figure 16-7 appears. This graph with percentages shows that most of the people in the sample worked in the clerical sector.

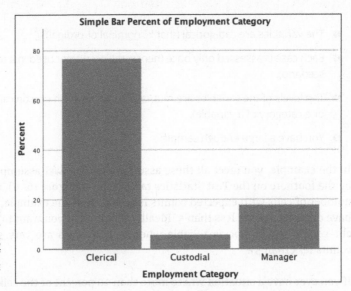

FIGURE 16-7:
A simple bar graph displaying the distribution of employment category.

Running the One-Sample T-Test Procedure

In this section, you focus on the *one-sample t-test,* which assesses whether the mean of one group differs from the population norm. For example, you can use this test to help determine if your sample is representative of a population on a continuous variable. Suppose you know that your population has a mean age 32. With the one-sample t-test, you can determine if the age of the sample you collected is similar to or different from the population.

You can use this test to determine also if an intervention has had an effect on a characteristic of interest. For example, suppose the average IQ score for your students is 100, and you've implemented a program designed to affect IQ. After the intervention period ends, you can assess the students to determine whether IQ scores have changed from the norm. Going back to the idea of hypothesis testing, you set up two hypotheses:

» **Null hypothesis:** The mean of the group will be the same as the population norm.

» **Alternative hypothesis:** The mean of the group will not be the same as the population norm.

You look at the number of years of education in the sample and determine whether the sample education is similar to the education in the population (12 years).

Follow these steps to perform a one-sample t-test:

1. **From the main menu, choose File ⇨ Open ⇨ Data, and then load the Employee_data.sav file.**

   Download the file at www.dummies.com/go/spss4e.

2. **Choose Analyze ⇨ Compare Means ⇨ One-Sample T Test.**

   The One-Sample T Test dialog appears.

3. **Select the Education Level variable and place it in the Test Variable(s) box.**

   Continuous variables are placed in the Test Variable(s) box.

4. **In the Test Value box, type 12, as shown in Figure16-8.**

   In the Test Value box, you specify the value you're using as the population norm. You can also click the Options button and decide how to treat missing values and confidence intervals.

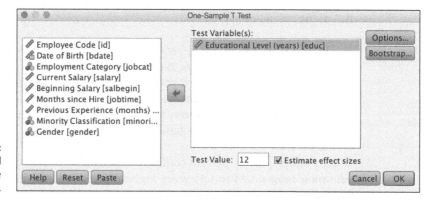

FIGURE 16-8:
The completed One-Sample T-Test dialog.

5. **Click OK.**

   You see the table shown in Figure 16-9. The One-Sample Statistics table provides the sample size, mean, standard deviation, and standard error for the group. You can see that the mean years of education for this sample is 13.49, which is about a year and a half more than the population norm of 12.

FIGURE 16-9:
The One-Sample Statistics table.

One-Sample Statistics				
	N	Mean	Std. Deviation	Std. Error Mean
Educational Level (years)	474	13.49	2.885	.133

The One-Sample Test table (shown in Figure 16-10) displays the result of the one-sample t-test. The t column displays the result of the t-test and the df column tells SPSS Statistics how to determine the probability of the t statistic. The Sig. (2-tailed) column tells you the probability of the null hypothesis being correct. If the probability value is very low (less than 0.05), you can conclude that the mean is significantly different from the norm.

One-Sample Test					
Test Value = 12					
	t	df	Sig. (2-tailed)	Mean Difference	95% Confidence Interval of the Difference	
					Lower	Upper
Educational Level (years)	11.257	473	.000	1.492	1.23	1.75

FIGURE 16-10:
The One-Sample
Test table.

In Figure 16-10, there are significant differences between the group mean and the norm because the significance value is less than 0.05. For your sample, years of education was significantly higher than the population norm of 12 years, so you can conclude that the education of respondents for the sample is not representative of the U.S. adult population.

An additional piece of useful information is the 95 percent confidence interval for the population mean difference. Technically, this value tells you that if you were to continually repeat this study, you would expect the true population difference to fall within the confidence intervals 95 percent of the time. From a more practical standpoint, the 95 percent confidence interval provides a measure of the precision with which the true population difference is estimated.

In the example, the 95 percent confidence interval for the group mean of years of education ranges 1.23 to 1.75 years higher than the norm; the mean difference from the norm is 1.492 years of education. So the 95 percent confidence interval indicates the likely range within which you should expect the population mean difference to fall. In this case, the actual value is 1.492, but you are 95 percent confident that the education difference value will fall anywhere between 1.23 to 1.75 years of education — basically, the mean difference +/– the standard error of the difference (.133) multiplied by 1.96).

Note that the confidence interval does not include 0 because there is a statistically significant difference between the group and the population mean (or norm). If 0 had been included within the range, it would indicate that there is no difference between the sample and the population. In essence, the 95 percent confidence interval is another way of testing the null hypothesis. So, if the value of 0 does not fall within the 95 percent confidence, you're saying that the probability of the null hypothesis being true (that is, no difference or a difference of zero) is less than 0.05.

TECHNICAL
STUFF

Every statistical test has assumptions. The better you meet these assumptions, the more you can trust the results of the test. The one-sample t-test has two assumptions:

>> Only one sample is compared on a continuous dependent variable.

>> The dependent variable is normally distributed within the group (normality).

A simple error bar chart is the most effective way to show the results of the one-sample t-test. The *error bar chart* focuses more on the precision of the estimated mean for the group than the mean itself.

Follow these steps to create an error bar chart corresponding to the one-sample t-test displaying the number of years of education:

1. **From the main menu, choose File ⇨ Open ⇨ Data, and load the Employee_ data.sav data file.**

Download the file at www.dummies.com/go/spss4e.

2. **Choose Graphs ⇨ Legacy Dialogs ⇨ Error Bar.**

3. **Click Simple, and then select the Summaries of Separate Variables option, as shown in Figure 16-11.**

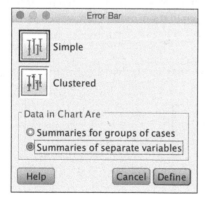

FIGURE 16-11:
The Error
Bar dialog.

4. **Click Define.**

5. **Select the Education Level variable, and place it in the Error Bars box, as shown in Figure 16-12.**

6. **Click OK.**

The graph in Figure 16-13 appears.

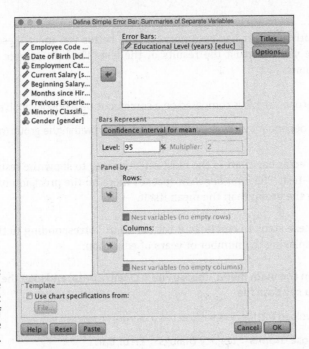

FIGURE 16-12:
The Define
Simple Error Bar:
Summaries of
Separate
Variables dialog.

The error bar chart generates a graph depicting the distribution of a scale variable. The mean number of years of education along with 95 percent confidence intervals are represented in this chart. Note that the confidence intervals for the sample doesn't encompass the population mean (12), which is consistent with the result from the t-test.

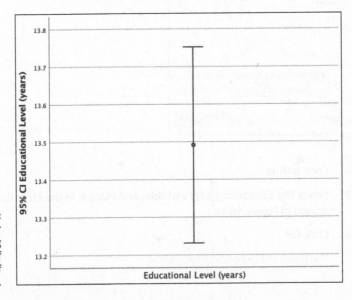

FIGURE 16-13:
The error bar
chart depicting
the distribution
of years of
education.

Chapter **17**

Showing Relationships between Categorical Variables

Many data analysts consider *crosstabulations*, which display the joint distribution of two or more categorical variables, to be part of the core of data analysis. In this chapter, we provide examples and advice on how best to construct and interpret crosstabulations.

After crosstabulations have been performed, you'll want to use the chi-square test of independence to see whether a statistically significant relationship exists between two categorical variables. If a statistically significant relationship exists, you'll then want to use the compare column proportions test to determine which groups differ from each other. You can extend the crosstabs procedure by including a control variable. We cover all these topics in this chapter. Finally, to support your analysis, we show how to display crosstabulations graphically.

Running the Crosstabs Procedure

One of the most common ways to analyze data is to use crosstabulations. As mentioned, you use a crosstabulation when you want to study the relationship between two or more categorical variables. For example, you may want to look at the relationship between gender and handedness (whether you're right- or left-handed). This way, you can determine if handedness is equally distributed between the genders. Figure 17-1 shows a hypothetical example of a crosstabulation depicting the relationship between gender and handedness.

FIGURE 17-1:
The
crosstabulation
between gender
and handedness.

Handedness * Gender Crosstabulation			Gender		
			Male	Female	Total
Handedness	Right Handed	Count	32	32	64
		% within Gender	66.7%	66.7%	66.7%
	Left Handed	Count	16	16	32
		% within Gender	33.3%	33.3%	33.3%
Total		Count	48	48	96
		% within Gender	100.0%	100.0%	100.0%

The sample consists of 96 people, 48 males and 48 females. Of the 48 males, 32 (67 percent) are right-handed and 16 (33 percent) are left-handed. The numbers are the same for females. Therefore, you can say that although there are more right-handers than left-handers, the proportions are equally distributed between the genders.

Now you'll go through an example in which the numbers are not the same. Here's how to perform a crosstabulation using the Merchandise.sav data file:

1. **Choose File ⇨ Open ⇨ Data, and load the Merchandise.sav data file.**

   You can download the file at www.dummies.com/go/spss4e. The file contains customer purchase history and has 16 variables and 3,338 cases.

2. **Choose Analyze ⇨ Descriptive Statistics ⇨ Crosstabs.**

   The Crosstabs dialog appears.

   In this example, you are studying whether the number (Small, Medium, or Large) of TVs (Binned input variable TVs [TVs_bin]) purchased this year is related to the customer's status (Current or *Churned,* which means you lost the customer).

TIP

Although you can place the variables in either the Rows or Columns boxes, it's customary to place the independent variable in the column of the crosstabulation table.

3. **Select the Status variable, and place it in the Row(s) box.**

4. **Select Binned Input Variable TVs, and place it in the Column(s) box, as shown in Figure 17-2.**

As mentioned, crosstabulations are used when looking at the relationship between categorical variables, which is what you have in this situation.

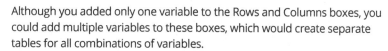

TECHNICAL STUFF

Although you added only one variable to the Rows and Columns boxes, you could add multiple variables to these boxes, which would create separate tables for all combinations of variables.

At this point, you could run the crosstabulation procedure, but you normally want to request additional statistics, typically percentages, to better understand the relationship.

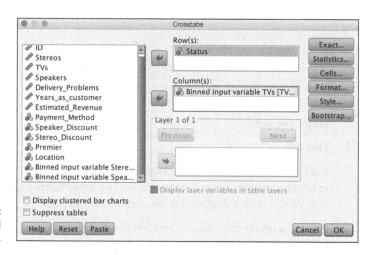

FIGURE 17-2: The completed Crosstabs dialog.

5. **Click the Cells button.**

The Cell Display dialog appears. By default, you see *observed counts,* which are the number of cases in each cell combination. Various other statistics are available in this dialog, including *expected counts,* which are the number of cases you would expect in each cell combination if there was no relationship between the variables (that is, if the null hypothesis is true). You can also request *unstandardized residuals,* which are the differences between observed and expected counts. Typically, you would select row percents, or column percents, or both.

6. Select the Column check box in the Percentages area, as shown in Figure 17-3.

Although you can request row and column percentages, most researchers request percentages based on the independent variable, which as mentioned is typically placed in the column dimension.

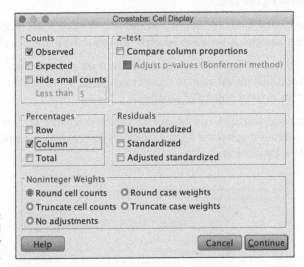

FIGURE 17-3:
The completed
Cell Display
dialog.

7. Click Continue.

8. Click OK.

The Case Processing Summary table shown in Figure 17-4 displays the number of valid and missing cases for the variables requested in the crosstabulation. Only valid cases are displayed in the crosstabulation table.

Be sure to review this table to check the number of missing cases. If the amount of missing data is substantial, you may want to question why this is the case and how your analysis will be affected. In this example, you don't have any missing data.

FIGURE 17-4:
The Case
Processing
Summary table.

Case Processing Summary						
	Cases					
	Valid		Missing		Total	
	N	Percent	N	Percent	N	Percent
Status * Binned input variable TVs	3338	100.0%	0	0.0%	3338	100.0%

The crosstabulation table (shown in Figure 17-5) shows the relationship between the variables. Each cell in the table represents a unique combination of the variables values. For example, the first cell in the crosstabulation table shows the number of customers who purchased a small number of TVs and also churned (1,093).

Status * Binned input variable TVs Crosstabulation

| | | | Binned input variable TVs | | | |
			Small	Medium	Large	Total
Status	Churned	Count	1093	98	258	1449
		% within Binned input variable TVs	37.8%	96.1%	74.4%	43.4%
	Current	Count	1796	4	89	1889
		% within Binned input variable TVs	62.2%	3.9%	25.6%	56.6%
Total		Count	2889	102	347	3338
		% within Binned input variable TVs	100.0%	100.0%	100.0%	100.0%

FIGURE 17-5: The crosstabulation table.

TIP

Although looking at counts is useful, it's usually much easier to detect patterns by examining percentages. This is why you selected the Column check box in the Cell Display dialog.

Looking at the first column in the crosstabulation table, you can see that 37.8 percent of customers who purchased a small number of TVs churned, while 62.2 percent of customers who purchased a small number of TVs stayed as customers. It seems as though purchasing a few TVs is associated with staying as a customer. However, the opposite seems to be true when more TVs are purchased — in other words, purchasing more TVs seems to be associated with losing customers, because you lost 96.1 percent and 74.4 percent of customers, respectively, who purchased a medium and large number of TVs.

These differences in percentages would certainly lead you to conclude that the number of TVs purchased is related to customer status. But how do you know if these differences in percentages are real differences or if they are due to chance? To answer this question, you need to perform the chi-square test of independence.

Running the Chi-Square Test of Independence

The purpose of the *chi-square test of independence* is to study the relationship between two or more categorical variables to determine whether one category of a variable is more likely to be associated with a category of another variable. Going back to the idea of hypothesis testing, you can set up two hypotheses:

>> **Null hypothesis:** Variables are not related to each other (variables are independent).

>> **Alternative hypothesis:** Variables are related to each other (variables are associated).

With the gender and handedness example (refer to Figure 17-1), you can easily see that females and males are equally likely to be right-handed because they have the same numeric values and, conversely, equally likely to left-handed, again because the numbers are the same.

You can use the chi-square test of independence to quantify the relationship between gender and handedness. The formula is

$$X^2 = \Sigma \left(O_i - E_i \right)^2 / E_i$$

For each cell, you take the observed count (O) minus the expected count (E); square the difference and divide by the expected count; and then add the values across all the cells. Figure 17-6 displays the observed and expected counts for the gender and handedness example.

FIGURE 17-6:
The crosstabulation between gender and handedness displaying observed and expected counts.

Handedness * Gender Crosstabulation

			Gender Male	Female	Total
Handedness	Right Handed	Count	32	32	64
		Expected Count	32.0	32.0	64.0
	Left Handed	Count	16	16	32
		Expected Count	16.0	16.0	32.0
Total		Count	48	48	96
		Expected Count	48.0	48.0	96.0

Because you know that there were no differences between the genders with regard to handedness, it is no surprise that the observed and expected counts are the same. By the same token, if the observed and expected counts are the same, subtracting one from the other will yield a chi-square statistic of 0, as shown by the Pearson Chi-Square value in Figure 17-7.

Chi-Square Tests					
	Value	df	Asymptotic Significance (2-sided)	Exact Sig. (2-sided)	Exact Sig. (1-sided)
Pearson Chi-Square	.000[a]	1	1.000		
Continuity Correction[b]	.000	1	1.000		
Likelihood Ratio	.000	1	1.000		
Fisher's Exact Test				1.000	.586
Linear-by-Linear Association	.000	1	1.000		
N of Valid Cases	96				
a. 0 cells (0.0%) have expected count less than 5. The minimum expected count is 16.00.					
b. Computed only for a 2x2 table					

FIGURE 17-7:
The Chi-Square Tests table.

The chi-square statistic is then translated into a probability value of the null hypothesis being true. Viewing the Asymptotic Significance (2-sided) column, you can see that probability of the null hypothesis being true is 100 percent, which means there are no differences between the groups (because the observed and expected counts are the same).

Next, you go through an example of how to perform the chi-square test of independence to determine whether a relationship exists between number of TVs purchased and customer status. To run the chi-square test of independence, follow these steps:

1. **Choose Analyze ⇨ Descriptive Statistics ⇨ Crosstabs.**

   Remember that you should have the Status variable in the Row(s) box and the TVs_bin variable in the Column(s) box.

2. **Click the Statistics button.**

   The Statistics dialog appears. The dialog contains many association measures, which characterize the relationship between the variables in the table. The measures are grouped by the measurement level of the variables (nominal or ordinal) and show the strength of the relationship between the variables, whereas the chi-square test of independence determines whether there is a statistically significant relationship between two categorical variables, which is the statistic you want.

3. **Select the Chi-Square check box, as shown in Figure 17-8.**

4. **Click Continue.**

5. **Click OK.**

In addition to the Case Processing Summary and Crosstabulation tables shown previously (refer to Figure 17-4 and 17-5, respectively), the Chi-Square Tests table also appears, as shown in Figure 17-9.

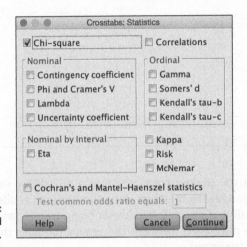

FIGURE 17-8:
The completed
Statistics dialog.

Chi-Square Tests

	Value	df	Asymptotic Significance (2–sided)
Pearson Chi-Square	286.989[a]	2	.000
Likelihood Ratio	308.196	2	.000
Linear-by-Linear Association	225.583	1	.000
N of Valid Cases	3338		

a. 0 cells (0.0%) have expected count less than 5. The minimum expected count is 44.28.

FIGURE 17-9:
A statistically
significant
Chi-Square Tests
table.

Three chi-square values are listed. The first two are used to test for a relationship. Concentrate on the Pearson Chi-Square statistic, which is adequate for almost all purposes. As mentioned, the Pearson Chi-Square statistic is calculated by testing the difference between the *observed counts* (the number of cases that were observed in each crosstabulation cell) and the *expected counts* (the number of cases that should have been observed in each crosstabulation cell if no relationship existed between the variables). So, the chi-square statistic is an indication of misfit between observed minus expected counts.

The actual chi-square value (here, 286.989) is used with the number of degrees of freedom (df), which is determined by the number of cells in the table, to calculate the significance for the chi-square statistic. You can see the probability value for the chi-square statistic in the Asymptotic Significance (2-sided) column.

The significance value provides the probability of the null hypothesis being true; the lower the number, the less likely that the variables are unrelated. Analysts often use a cutoff value of 0.05 or lower to determine whether the results are statistically significant. For example, with a cutoff value of 0.05, if the significance value is smaller than 0.05, the null hypothesis is rejected. In this case, you can see that the probability of the null hypothesis being true is very small — in fact, it's less than 0.05, so you can reject the null hypothesis and have no choice but to say that you found support for the research hypothesis. Therefore, you can conclude that a relationship exists between the number of TVs purchased and customer status.

TECHNICAL
STUFF

Every statistical test has assumptions. The better you meet these assumptions, the more you can trust the results of the test. The chi-square test of independence assumes the following:

>> The variables are categorical (nominal or ordinal).

>> Each case is assessed only once (hence, this test is not used in a test-retest scenario).

>> The levels of the variables are mutually exclusive (each person can be in only one category of a variable).

>> The sample is large enough.

In the example, you meet all these assumptions. However, the last assumption is assessed by the footnote to the Chi-Square Tests table (refer to Figure 17-9), which notes the number of cells with expected counts less than 5. In the example, you have zero cells (0 percent) with expected counts less than 5. Ideally, this is what you want to see because the chi-square is not as reliable when sample sizes are very small (expected counts less than 5).

If more than 20 percent of the cells have expected counts less than 5, consider increasing your sample size if you can or reducing the number of cells in your crosstabulation table (by combining or removing categories). Otherwise, you don't have enough data to trust the result of the analysis.

Comparing Column Proportions

After determining that a relationship exists between two variables, the next step is to determine the nature of the relationship — that is, which groups differ from each other. You can determine which groups differ from each other by comparing column proportions as follows:

1. **Choose Analyze ⇨ Descriptive Statistics ⇨ Crosstabs.**

   Remember that you should have the Status variable in the Row(s) box and the TVs_bin variable in the Column(s) box.

2. **Click the Cells button.**

3. **Select the Compare Column Proportions check box.**

4. **Select the Adjust P-Values (Bonferroni Method) check box.**

   Figure 17-10 shows the completed Cell Display dialog. The *compare column proportions test* (also called the *z-test*) determines which groups differ from each other. The adjust p-values (Bonferroni method) option is a technical adjustment that controls for Type I error rates (see Chapter 14).

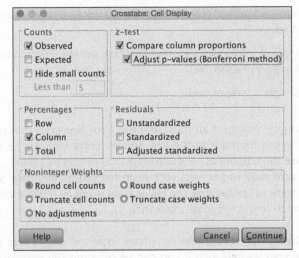

FIGURE 17-10:
The completed
Cell Display
dialog.

5. **Click Continue.**

6. **Click OK.**

   The same Case Processing Summary and Chi-Square Tests tables appear as shown previously (refer to Figure 17-4 and 17-9, respectively), but a modified version of the crosstabulation table now appears as well, as shown in Figure 17-11.

The crosstabulation table now includes the column proportions test notations. Subscript letters are assigned to the categories of the column variable. For each pair of columns, the column proportions are compared using a z-test. If a pair of values is significantly different, different subscript letters are displayed in each cell.

As you can see in Figure 17-11, the different subscript letters indicate that the proportion of customers who purchased a small number of TVs and churned (37.8 percent) is smaller and significantly different, according to the z-test, than the proportion of customers who purchased a medium number of TVs and churned (96.1 percent). In addition, the proportion of customers who purchased a small number of TVs and churned (37.8 percent) is significantly smaller than the proportion of customers who purchased a large number of TVs and churned (74.4 percent). Finally, you can see that the proportion of customers who purchased a large number of TVs and churned (74.4 percent) is significantly smaller than the proportion of customers who purchased a medium number of TVs and churned (96.1 percent). In other words, because all groups have different subscripts, all the groups are significantly different from each other.

Status * Binned input variable TVs Crosstabulation						
			Binned input variable TVs			
			Small	Medium	Large	Total
Status	Churned	Count	1093a	98b	258c	1449
		% within Binned input variable TVs	37.8%	96.1%	74.4%	43.4%
	Current	Count	1796a	4b	89c	1889
		% within Binned input variable TVs	62.2%	3.9%	25.6%	56.6%
Total		Count	2889	102	347	3338
		% within Binned input variable TVs	100.0%	100.0%	100.0%	100.0%

Each subscript letter denotes a subset of Binned input variable TVs categories whose column proportions do not differ significantly from each other at the .05 level.

FIGURE 17-11: The crosstabulation table with the compare column proportions test.

Adding Control Variables

Tables can be made more complex by adding additional variables to the layer dimension. This way, you can create layered tables displaying relationship among three or more variables. A *layered variable* further subdivides a crosstabulation table by the categories of the layer variable(s).

Layer variables are often referred to as *control variables* because they show the relationship between the row and column variables when you control for the effects of the third variable. Layer variables are usually added to a table after the two-variable crosstabulation table has been examined.

To add a layer variable, follow these steps:

1. **Choose Analyze ⇨ Descriptive Statistics ⇨ Crosstabs.**

    You should have the Status variable in the Row(s) box and the TVs_bin variable in the Column(s) box.

2. **Select the Location variable, and place it in the Layer 1 of 1 box, as shown in Figure 17-12.**

3. **Click OK.**

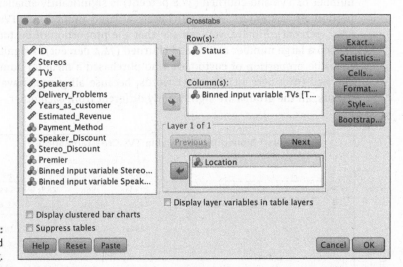

FIGURE 17-12:
The completed
Crosstabs dialog.

TECHNICAL
STUFF

You can add more than one control variable to a table by clicking the Next button in the Layer 1 of 1 box, but you'll need to have a large sample size. Otherwise, you may quickly create tables with only a few cases, or even no cases, in several cells.

As shown in Figure 17-13, adding a layer variable creates subtables for each category of the layer variable (in this case, you now have a table for international and national customers). In this example, there is a difference in the relationship between the number of TVs purchased and customer status based on customer location. For international customers, the Medium and Large TV Orders columns do not differ from each other at the 0.05 level because they have the same subscript (b). However, for national customers, the Medium and Large TV Orders columns have two separate subscripts (b and c) and thus differ.

Figure 17-14 simply shows that a relationship exists between the TV Orders and Customer Status variables at the international, national, and total levels of analysis. Layer variables often help qualify a relationship, so that a relationship holds only in certain conditions and not others.

Status * Binned input variable TVs * Location Crosstabulation

Location				Small	Medium	Large	Total
				Binned input variable TVs			
International	Status	Churned	Count	463a	27b	109b	599
			% within Binned input variable TVs	39.1%	87.1%	73.2%	43.9%
		Current	Count	721a	4b	40b	765
			% within Binned input variable TVs	60.9%	12.9%	26.8%	56.1%
	Total		Count	1184	31	149	1364
			% within Binned input variable TVs	100.0%	100.0%	100.0%	100.0%
National	Status	Churned	Count	630a	71b	149c	850
			% within Binned input variable TVs	37.0%	100.0%	75.3%	43.1%
		Current	Count	1075a	0b	49c	1124
			% within Binned input variable TVs	63.0%	0.0%	24.7%	56.9%
	Total		Count	1705	71	198	1974
			% within Binned input variable TVs	100.0%	100.0%	100.0%	100.0%
Total	Status	Churned	Count	1093a	98b	258c	1449
			% within Binned input variable TVs	37.8%	96.1%	74.4%	43.4%
		Current	Count	1796a	4b	89c	1889
			% within Binned input variable TVs	62.2%	3.9%	25.6%	56.6%
	Total		Count	2889	102	347	3338
			% within Binned input variable TVs	100.0%	100.0%	100.0%	100.0%

Each subscript letter denotes a subset of Binned input variable TVs categories whose column proportions do not differ significantly from each other at the .05 level.

FIGURE 17-13: The crosstabulation table with a layer variable.

Chi-Square Tests

Location		Value	df	Asymptotic Significance (2-sided)
International	Pearson Chi-Square	86.313[b]	2	.000
	Likelihood Ratio	88.760	2	.000
	Linear-by-Linear Association	74.856	1	.000
	N of Valid Cases	1364		
National	Pearson Chi-Square	203.538[c]	2	.000
	Likelihood Ratio	230.678	2	.000
	Linear-by-Linear Association	152.732	1	.000
	N of Valid Cases	1974		
Total	Pearson Chi-Square	286.989[a]	2	.000
	Likelihood Ratio	308.196	2	.000
	Linear-by-Linear Association	225.583	1	.000
	N of Valid Cases	3338		

a. 0 cells (0.0%) have expected count less than 5. The minimum expected count is 44.28.

b. 0 cells (0.0%) have expected count less than 5. The minimum expected count is 13.61.

c. 0 cells (0.0%) have expected count less than 5. The minimum expected count is 30.57.

FIGURE 17-14: The Chi-Square Tests table with a layer variable.

Creating a Clustered Bar Chart

For presentations, a graph showing the relationship between two categorical variables is often useful, and a *clustered bar chart* is the most effective graph for a crosstabulation.

In this section, you create a clustered bar chart of the crosstabulation table of status and TVs purchased. You want to see how TVs purchased varies across categories of status, so you use status as the clustering variable. This setup is equivalent to the percentage you requested in the crosstabulation table.

Follow these steps to create a clustered bar chart:

1. **From the main menu, choose File ⇨ Open ⇨ Data, and then load the Merchandise.sav data file.**

   Download the file on the book's companion website, at www.dummies.com/ go/spss4e.

2. **Choose Graphs ⇨ Chart Builder.**

3. **In the Choose From list, select Bar.**

4. **Select the second graph image (with the Clustered Bar tooltip) and drag it to the panel at the top of the window.**

5. **Select the Status variable, and place it in the Cluster on X: Set Color box.**

6. **Select the Binned Input Variable TVs, and place it in the X-Axis box.**

7. **In the Statistics Area of the Property Elements tab, change Statistic to Percentage().**

8. **Click the Set Parameters button and choose Total for Each Legend Variable Category (same fill color).**

9. **Click Continue.**

10. **Click OK.**

    The graph in Figure 17-15 appears.

A crosstabulation table with percentages based on status lets you compare percentages of that variable within categories of TVs purchased, which is mirrored in the clustered bar chart. Note in the example that you're more likely to keep customers who purchased a small number of TVs and to lose customers who purchased a medium or large number of TVs. It sure looks like you'll need to improve the quality of your TVs if you expect to run a successful business!

TIP

If you would like to incorporate a control variable in a clustered bar chart, simply click the Groups/Point ID tab in Chart Builder and select the Row Panel variable.

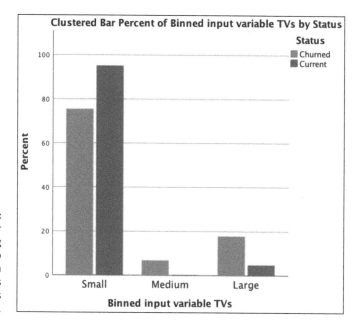

FIGURE 17-15:
A cluster bar graph displaying the relationship between customer status and TVs purchased.

IN THIS CHAPTER

» **Running an inferential test**

» **Comparing means**

» **Comparing independent-samples**

» **Graphing means**

» **Comparing independent-samples summary statistics**

» **Comparing paired-samples**

Chapter **18**

Showing Relationships between Continuous Dependent and Categorical Independent Variables

n this chapter, we explain how to compare different groups on a continuous outcome variable. For example, you can compare the money spent on rent by residents of two cities to determine if significant differences exists. You also learn how to compare the same group of people that have been assessed at two different time points or conditions, such as before and after an intervention.

Conducting Inferential Tests

In Chapter 16, we discuss how to conduct inferential tests for one variable. However, most statistical tests involve at least two variables: the dependent (effect) and independent (cause) variables.

The *independent variable* is the variable that the researcher controls or that is assumed to have a direct effect on the dependent variable. The *dependent variable* is the variable measured in research, that is, affected by the independent variable. For example, if you are testing the effect of a drug on depression, drug type is the independent variable and depression symptom is the dependent variable. Table 18-1 shows some appropriate statistical techniques based on the measurement level of the dependent and independent variables.

TABLE 18-1 **Level of Measurement and Statistical Tests for Two or More Variables**

Dependent Variables	Independent Variables	
	Categorical	Continuous
Categorical	Crosstabs, nonparametric tests	Logistic regression, discriminant analysis
Continuous	T-test, analysis of variance (ANOVA)	Correlation, linear regression

In Chapter 17, we discuss the crosstabs procedure, which is used when both the independent and dependent variables are categorical. In this chapter, we discuss t-tests, which are used when the independent variable is categorical and the dependent variable is continuous. In Chapter 19, we discuss correlation and simple linear regression, which are used when both the independent and dependent variables are continuous. In Part 6, we briefly discuss some additional advanced statistical techniques.

Using the Compare Means Dialog

Often, you encounter situations where you have a continuous dependent variable and a categorical independent variable. For example, you may want to determine if differences in SAT scores exist according to sex. Or you may want to see if there was a change in behavior by assessing someone before and after an intervention. In both examples, you're comparing groups on some continuous outcome measure, and the statistic you're using to make comparisons between groups is the mean. For this type of analysis, you use the procedures in the Compare Means dialog, shown in Figure 18-1. The Compare Means dialog (which is accessed by choosing Analyze ⇨ Compare Means) contains six statistical techniques that allow users to compare sample means:

>> **Means:** Calculates subgroup means and related statistics for dependent variables within categories of one or more independent variables.

>> **One-sample t-test:** Tests whether the mean of a single variable differs from a specified value (for example, a group using a new learning method compared to the school average). See Chapter 16 for an example.

>> **Independent-samples t-test:** Tests whether the means for two different groups differ on a continuous dependent variable (for example, females versus males on income).

>> **Summary independent-samples t-test:** Uses summary statistics to test whether the means for two different groups differ on a continuous dependent variable (for example, females versus males on income).

>> **Paired-samples t-test:** Tests whether the means of the same group differ under two conditions or time points (for example, assessing the same group of people before versus after an intervention or under two distinct conditions, such as standing versus sitting).

>> **One-way ANOVA:** Tests whether the means for two or more different groups differ on a continuous dependent variable (for example, drug1 versus drug2 versus drug3 on depression). See Chapter 20 for an example.

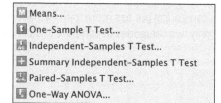

FIGURE 18-1:
The Compare
Means dialog.

Running the Independent-Samples T-Test Procedure

In this section, you focus on the *independent-samples t-test*, which allows you to compare two different groups on a continuous dependent variable. For example, you might be comparing two different learning methods to determine their effect on math skills.

Here's how to perform an independent-samples t-test:

1. **On the main menu, choose File ⇨ Open ⇨ Data and load the Employee_data.sav file.**

You can download the file from the book's companion website at www.dummies.com/go/spss4e. The file contains employee information from a bank in the 1960s and has 10 variables and 474 cases.

2. **Choose Analyze ⇨ Compare Means ⇨ Independent-Samples T Test.**

The Independent-Samples T Test dialog appears.

3. **Select the Current Salary, Beginning Salary, Months since Hire, Educational Level, and Previous Experience variables, and place them in the Test Variable(s) box.**

Continuous variables are placed in the Test Variable(s) box.

4. **Select the gender variable and place it in the Grouping Variable box.**

Categorical independent variable are placed in the Grouping Variable box. Note that you can have only one independent variable and that the program requires you to indicate which groups are to be compared.

5. **Click the Define Groups button.**

The Define Groups dialog appears.

6. **In the Group 1 box, type 0; in the Group 2 box, type 1 (see Figure 18-2).**

TIP

If the independent variable is continuous, you can specify a cut point value to define the two groups. Cases less than or equal to the cut point go into the first group, and cases greater than the cut point are in the second group. Also, if the independent variable is categorical but has more than two categories, you can still use it by specifying only two categories to compare in an analysis.

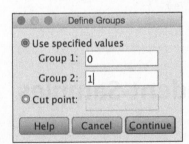

FIGURE 18-2:
The Define Groups dialog.

7. Click Continue.

You're returned to the Independent-Samples T Test dialog (shown in Figure 18-3).

You can also click the Options button and decide how to treat missing values and confidence intervals.

8. Click OK.

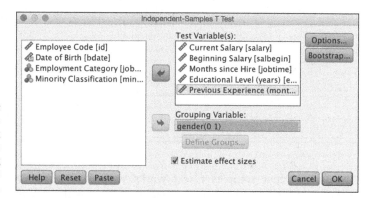

FIGURE 18-3: The Independent-Samples T Test dialog, with the Grouping Variable box completed.

TECHNICAL STUFF

Every statistical test has assumptions. The better you meet these assumptions, the more you can trust the results of the test. The independent-samples t-test has four assumptions:

>> The dependent variable is continuous.

>> Only two different groups are compared.

>> The dependent variable is normally distributed within each category of the independent variable (normality).

>> Similar variation exists within each category of the independent variable (homogeneity of variance).

The purpose of the independent samples t-test is to test whether the means of two separate groups differ on a continuous dependent variable and, if so, whether the difference is significant. Going back to the idea of hypothesis testing, you can set up two hypotheses:

>> **Null hypothesis:** The means of the two groups will be the same.

>> **Alternative hypothesis:** The means of the two groups will differ from each other.

The Group Statistics table shown in Figure 18-4 provides sample sizes, means, standard deviations, and standard errors for the two groups on each of the dependent variables. You can see that the sample has a few more males (258) than females (216), but you're certainly not dealing with small sizes.

Group Statistics					
	Gender	N	Mean	Std. Deviation	Std. Error Mean
Current Salary	Male	258	$41,441.78	$19499.214	$1,213.968
	Female	216	$26,031.92	$7,558.021	$514.258
Beginning Salary	Male	258	$20,301.40	$9,111.781	$567.275
	Female	216	$13,091.97	$2,935.599	$199.742
Months since Hire	Male	258	81.72	10.351	.644
	Female	216	80.38	9.676	.658
Educational Level (years)	Male	258	14.43	2.979	.185
	Female	216	12.37	2.319	.158
Previous Experience (months)	Male	258	111.62	109.692	6.829
	Female	216	77.04	95.012	6.465

FIGURE 18-4: The Group Statistics table.

TECHNICAL STUFF

The independent-samples t-test works well even when you have moderate violations of the assumption of normality as long as the sample sizes are at least moderate (more than 50 cases per group), which is what you have in this situation. When we describe tests in which you can get away with moderate violations, we often use the term *robust.* Some tests can be more robust than others, and some assumptions can be more robust than others. There is even a category of tests called collectively robust tests.

In this example, you can see that males have higher means than females on all dependent variables. This is precisely what the independent-samples t-test assesses — whether the differences between the means are significantly different or if the differences are due to chance.

The Independent Samples Test table shown in Figure 18-5 displays the result of the independent-samples t-test. Before you look at this test, you must determine if you met the assumption of homogeneity of variance.

REMEMBER

The *assumption of homogeneity of variance* says that similar variation exists within each category of the independent variable — in other words, the standard deviation of each group is similar. Violating the assumption of homogeneity of variance is more critical than violating the assumption of normality, because when the former occurs, the significance or probability value reported by SPSS is incorrect and the test statistics must be adjusted.

		Levene's Test for Equality of Variances		t-test for Equality of Means						
		F	Sig.	t	df	Sig. (2–tailed)	Mean Difference	Std. Error Difference	95% Confidence Interval of the Difference Lower	Upper
Current Salary	Equal variances assumed	119.669	.000	10.945	472	.000	$15409.862	$1,407.906	$12643.322	$18176.401
	Equal variances not assumed			11.688	344.262	.000	$15409.862	$1,318.400	$12816.728	$18002.996
Beginning Salary	Equal variances assumed	105.969	.000	11.152	472	.000	$7,209.428	$646.447	$5,939.158	$8,479.698
	Equal variances not assumed			11.987	318.818	.000	$7,209.428	$601.413	$6,026.188	$8,392.667
Months since Hire	Equal variances assumed	2.168	.142	1.447	472	.148	1.341	.927	−.480	3.162
	Equal variances not assumed			1.456	466.269	.146	1.341	.921	−.469	3.152
Educational Level (years)	Equal variances assumed	17.884	.000	8.276	472	.000	2.060	.249	1.571	2.549
	Equal variances not assumed			8.458	469.595	.000	2.060	.244	1.581	2.538
Previous Experience (months)	Equal variances assumed	2.582	.109	3.631	472	.000	34.583	9.524	15.869	53.297
	Equal variances not assumed			3.678	471.444	.000	34.583	9.404	16.105	53.062

FIGURE 18-5: The Independent Samples Test table.

Levene's test for equality of variances assesses the assumption of homogeneity of variance. This test determines if the variation is similar or different between the groups. When Levene's test is not statistically significant (that is, the assumption of equal variance was met), you can continue with the regular independent-samples t-test and use the results from the Equal Variances Are Assumed row.

When Levene's test is statistically significant (that is, the assumption of equal variance was not met), differences in variation exist between the groups, so you have to make an adjustment to the independent-samples t-test. In this situation, you would use the results from the Equal Variances Are Not Assumed row. Note that if the assumption of homogeneity of variance is not met, you can still do the test but must apply a correction.

In the left section of the Independent Samples Test table, Levene's test for equality of variances is displayed. The F column displays the actual test result, which is used to calculate the significance level (the Sig. column).

In the example, the assumption of homogeneity of variance was met for the Months Since Hire and Previous Experience variables because the value in the Sig. column is greater than 0.05 (no difference exists in the variation of the groups). Therefore, you can look at the row that specifies that equal variances are assumed. However, the assumption of homogeneity of variance was not met for the Educational Level, Current Salary, and Beginning Salary variables because the value in the Sig. column is less than 0.05 (a difference exists in the variation of the groups). Therefore, you have to look at the row that specifies that equal variances are not assumed.

Now that you've determined whether the assumption of homogeneity of variance was met, you're ready to see if the differences between the means are significantly different or are due to random variation. The t column displays the result of the t-test and the df column tells SPSS Statistics how to determine the probability of the t-statistic. The Sig. (2-tailed) column tells you the probability of the null hypothesis being correct. If the probability value is very low (less than 0.05), you can conclude that the means are significantly different.

In Figure 18-5, you can see that significant differences exist between males and females on all variables except Months Since Hire. Thus, you can conclude that for the sample, males had significant higher beginning and current salary than females. Males also had more years of education and previous work experience than females. However, no difference exists in the amount of time that females and males had worked at the bank.

An additional piece of useful information is the 95 percent confidence interval for the population mean difference. Technically, this tells you that if you were to continually repeat this study, you would expect the true population difference to fall within the confidence intervals 95 percent of the time. From a more practical standpoint, the 95 percent confidence interval provides a measure of the precision with which the true population difference is estimated.

In the example, the 95 percent confidence interval for the mean difference between groups on years of education ranges from 1.581 to 2.538 years; the actual mean difference is 2.06 years of education. So the 95 percent confidence interval indicates the likely range within which you expect the population mean difference to fall. In this case, the value is 2.06, but you are 95 percent confident that the education difference value will fall anywhere between 1.581 to 2.538 years — basically the mean difference +/- the standard error of the difference (.249) multiplied by 1.96.

Note that the confidence interval does not include zero because a statistically significant difference exists between groups. If zero had been included within the range, it would indicate no differences between the groups — that is, the probability value is greater than 0.05.

In essence, the 95 percent confidence interval is another way of testing the null hypothesis. If the value of zero does not fall within the 95 percent confidence, the probability of the null hypothesis being true (that is, no difference or a difference of zero) is less than 0.05.

For each t-test, Figure 18-6 shows the *effect sizes*, which indicate the strength of the relationship between variables or the magnitude of the difference between groups. *Cohen's d* is one of the most popular effect size measures; other measures of effect size are also available.

Cohen's d was just added to version 27 of SPSS. If you have an earlier version of the software, you will not have this output.

	Independent Samples Effect Size				
		Standardizer[a]	Point Estimate	95% Confidence Interval	
				Lower	Upper
Current Salary	Cohen's d	$15265.862	1.009	.817	1.201
	Hedges' correction	$15290.172	1.008	.816	1.199
	Glass' delta	$7,558.021	2.039	1.774	2.302
Beginning Salary	Cohen's d	$7,009.395	1.029	.836	1.220
	Hedges' correction	$7,020.558	1.027	.834	1.218
	Glass' delta	$2,935.599	2.456	2.161	2.749
Months since Hire	Cohen's d	10.049	.133	-.048	.314
	Hedges' correction	10.065	.133	-.047	.314
	Glass' delta	9.676	.139	-.043	.320
Educational Level (years)	Cohen's d	2.699	.763	.576	.950
	Hedges' correction	2.703	.762	.575	.949
	Glass' delta	2.319	.888	.688	1.087
Previous Experience (months)	Cohen's d	103.264	.335	.153	.517
	Hedges' correction	103.429	.334	.152	.516
	Glass' delta	95.012	.364	.180	.548

a. The denominator used in estimating the effect size.
   Cohen's d uses the pooled standard deviation.
   Hedges' correction uses the pooled standard deviation, plus a correction factor.
   Glass's delta uses the sample standard deviation of the control group.

FIGURE 18-6: The Independent Samples Effect Size table.

Effect sizes do vary by research field. To get a general sense of effect sizes, you can use Table 18-2 as a guideline. In the example, you can see that the effect sizes for both beginning and current salary are quite large because the values are bigger than 0.8.

TABLE 18-2

Cohen's d Effect Size Measure

Effect	Value
Small	0.2
Medium	0.5
Large	0.8

Comparing the Means Graphically

For presentations, it's often useful to show a graph of the results of an independent samples t-test. The most effective way to do this when comparing means is to use a *simple error bar chart,* which focuses more on the precision of the estimated mean for each group than the mean itself.

Next, you create an error bar chart corresponding to the independent-samples t-test of gender and number of years of education. To see how the number of years of education varies across categories of gender, you'll use education as the Y-axis variable.

Follow these steps to create a simple error bar chart:

1. **From the main menu, choose File ⇨ Open ⇨ Data and load the Employee_data.sav data file.**

   You can download the file at www.dummies.com/go/spss4e.

2. **Choose Graphs ⇨ Chart Builder.**

3. **In the Choose From list, select Bar.**

4. **Select the seventh graph image (the one with the Simple Error Bar tooltip) and drag it to the panel at the top of the window.**

5. **Select the Educational Level variable, and place it in the Y-axis box.**

6. **Select the Gender variable, and place it in the X-axis box.**

7. **Click OK.**

   The graph in Figure 18-7 appears.

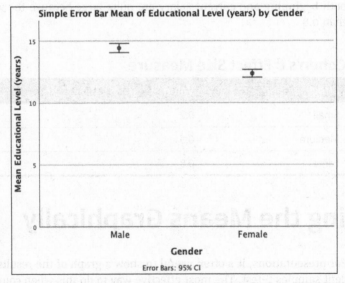

FIGURE 18-7:
A simple error bar graph displaying the relationship between years of education and gender.

The error bar chart generates a graph depicting the relationship between a scale and a categorical variable. It provides a visual sense of how far the groups are separated.

The mean number of years of education for each gender along with 95 percent confidence intervals is represented in this chart. The confidence intervals for the two genders don't quite overlap, which is consistent with the result from the t-test and indicates that the groups are significantly different from each other. Also, the error bars have a small range compared to the range of years of education, which indicates that you're fairly precisely estimating the mean number of years of education for each gender (because of large sample sizes).

Running the Summary Independent-Samples T-Test Procedure

The summary independent-samples t-test procedure, like the independent-samples t-test procedure, performs an independent-samples t-test. However, the independent-samples t-test procedure requires you to have all your data to run the analysis (SPSS is reading your data directly from Data Editor). In the summary independent-samples t-test procedure, however, you specify only the number of cases, the means, and the standard deviations for each group to run the analysis.

REMEMBER

The summary independent-samples t-test procedure is a Python extension and is available only if you allow Python extensions to be installed either during the SPSS installation process or at a later point.

The summary independent-samples t-test procedure is useful when it's too time-consuming to enter all the data in the SPSS Data Editor window. With this technique, you can quickly obtain means and standard deviations using a calculator and then run a t-test. Or you can use this procedure to replicate the results of a published study for which you don't have the data.

To perform the summary independent-samples t-test procedure, follow these steps:

1. **From the main menu, choose File ⇨ Open ⇨ Data and load the Employee_data.sav file.**

   You can download the file at www.dummies.com/go/spss4e.

2. **Choose Analyze ⇨ Compare Means ⇨ Summary Independent-Samples T Test.**

   The T Test Computed from Summary Data dialog appears. You want to study whether there are differences between two samples. You need to specify the number of cases in each group, along with the respective means and standard deviations.

3. **In the Number of Cases boxes under both Sample 1 and Sample 2, type 50.**

4. **In the Mean box for Sample 1, type** 4.2; **in the Mean box for Sample 2, type** 3.5.

5. **In the Standard Deviation box for Sample 1, type** 1.6; **in the Standard Deviation box for Sample 2, type** 1.5.

The completed dialog is shown in Figure 18-8.

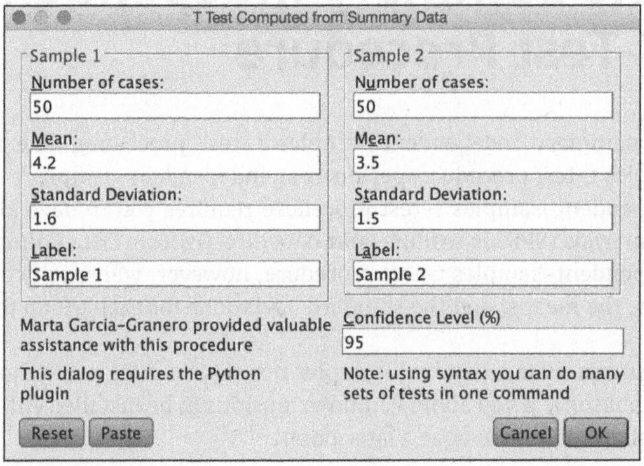

FIGURE 18-8:
The completed T
Test Computed
from Summary
Data dialog.

```
●  ●  ●                T Test Computed from Summary Data

┌ Sample 1 ──────────────────────┐  ┌ Sample 2 ──────────────────────┐
│  Number of cases:              │  │  Number of cases:              │
│  [50                        ]  │  │  [50                        ]  │
│                                │  │                                │
│  Mean:                         │  │  Mean:                         │
│  [4.2                       ]  │  │  [3.5                       ]  │
│                                │  │                                │
│  Standard Deviation:           │  │  Standard Deviation:           │
│  [1.6                       ]  │  │  [1.5                       ]  │
│                                │  │                                │
│  Label:                        │  │  Label:                        │
│  [Sample 1                  ]  │  │  [Sample 2                  ]  │
└────────────────────────────────┘  └────────────────────────────────┘

 Marta Garcia–Granero provided valuable   Confidence Level (%)
 assistance with this procedure           [95                          ]

 This dialog requires the Python          Note: using syntax you can do many
 plugin                                   sets of tests in one command

 ( Reset )  ( Paste )                            ( Cancel )  ( OK )
```

6. **Click OK.**

SPSS calculates the summary independent-samples t-test.

The Summary Data table shown in Figure 18-9 provides sample sizes, means, standard deviations, and standard errors for the two groups. You provided this summary information to perform the analysis.

FIGURE 18-9:
The Summary
Data table.

Summary Data

	N	Mean	Std. Deviation	Std. Error Mean
Sample 1	50.000	4.200	1.600	.226
Sample 2	50.000	3.500	1.500	.212

The Independent Samples Test table shown in Figure 18-10 displays the result of the independent-samples t-test, along with the *Hartley test of equal variance* (which, like Levene's test, assesses the assumption of homogeneity of variance). In the example, the assumption of homogeneity of variance was met because the Sig. value for Hartley's test is greater than 0.05. Therefore, use the Equal Variances Are Assumed row. At this point, you're ready to see if the differences between the means are significantly different or due to chance.

As before, the t column displays the result of the t-test and the df column tells SPSS how to determine the probability of the t-statistic. The Sig. (2-tailed) column tells you the probability of the null hypothesis being correct. If the probability value is very low (less than 0.05), you can conclude that the means are significantly different. In Figure 18-10, you can see that significant differences exist between the samples.

Independent Samples Test					
	Mean Difference	Std. Error Difference	t	df	Sig. (2–tailed)
Equal variances assumed	.700	.310	2.257	98.000	.026
Equal variances not assumed	.700	.310	2.257	97.595	.026
Hartley test for equal variance: F = 1.138, Sig. = 0.3249					

FIGURE 18-10: The Independent Samples Test table.

The final table, 95.0% Confidence Intervals for Difference (shown in Figure 18-11), displays the 95 percent confidence intervals for the population mean difference. As mentioned, confidence intervals tell you that if you were to continually repeat this study, you would expect the true population difference to fall within the confidence intervals 95 percent of the time.

95.0% Confidence Intervals for Difference		
	Lower Limit	Upper Limit
Asymptotic (equal variance)	.092	1.308
Asymptotic (unequal variance)	.092	1.308
Exact (equal variance)	.084	1.316
Exact (unequal variance)	.084	1.316

FIGURE 18-11: The 95.0% Confidence Intervals for Difference table.

Similar to the preceding example, you have confidence intervals for when the assumption of homogeneity of variance is met and not met. However, now you have the option to use asymptotic (an approximation) or exact (the exact value) confidence intervals, whereas in the preceding example you had to use asymptotic confidence intervals. The exact 95 percent confidence interval for the mean difference between groups is from 0.84 to 1.316. Because the difference values don't include zero, there is a difference between groups.

Running the Paired-Samples T-Test Procedure

In this section, you focus on the *paired-samples t-test*, which tests whether the means of the same group differ on a continuous dependent variable under two different conditions or time points. For example, a paired-samples t-test could be used in medical research to compare means on a measure administered both before and after some type of treatment. In market research, if participants rated on some attribute a product they usually purchase and a competing product, a paired-samples t-test could compare the mean ratings. In customer satisfaction studies, if a special customer care program were implemented, you could test the level of satisfaction before and after the program was in place.

The goal of the paired-samples t-test is to determine if a significant difference or change from one time point or condition to another exists. To the extent that an individual's outcomes across the two conditions are related, the paired-samples t-test provides a more powerful statistical analysis (greater probability of finding true effects) than the independent-samples t-test because each person serves as his or her own control.

Going back to the idea of hypothesis testing, you can set up two hypotheses:

>> **Null hypothesis:** The mean of the difference or change variable will be zero.

>> **Alternative hypothesis:** The mean of the difference or change variable will not be zero.

Follow these steps to perform a paired-samples t-test:

1. **From the main menu, choose File ⇨ Open ⇨ Data and load the Employee_ data.sav file.**

   Download the file at www.dummies.com/go/spss4e. This file contains employee information from a bank in the 1960s and has 10 variables and 474 cases.

2. **Choose Analyze ⇨ Compare Means ⇨ Paired-Samples T Test.**

   The Paired-Samples T Test dialog appears.

3. **Select the Current Salary and Beginning Salary variables, and place them in the Paired Variables box (see Figure 18-12).**

   These variables are now in the same row, so they will be compared.

REMEMBER

Technically, the order in which you select the pair of variables does not matter. The calculations will be the same. However, SPSS subtracts the second variable from the first. So in terms of presentation, you might want to be careful how SPSS displays the results so as to facilitate reader understanding.

4. **Click OK.**

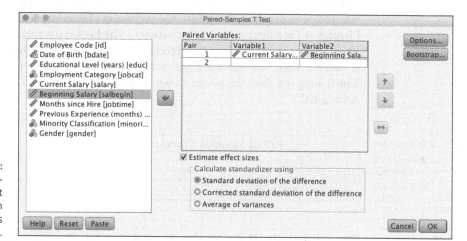

FIGURE 18-12:
The Paired-Samples T Test dialog, with variables selected.

TECHNICAL STUFF

Every statistical test has assumptions. The better you meet these assumptions, the more you can trust the results of the test. The paired-samples t-test has three assumptions:

>> The dependent variable is continuous.

>> The two time points or conditions that are compared are on the same continuous dependent variable. In other words, the dependent variable should be measured in a consistent format: not, for example, on a seven-point scale the first time and then on a ten-point scale the second time.

>> The difference scores are normally distributed (normality).

The Paired Samples Statistics table shown in Figure 18-13 provides sample sizes, means, standard deviations, and standard errors for the two time points. You can see that 474 people were in this analysis, with an average beginning salary of about $17,016 and average current salary of about $34,419.

TECHNICAL STUFF

As with the independent-samples t-test, the paired-samples t-test also works well even when you have moderate violations of the assumption of normality as long as sample sizes are at least moderate (more than 50 cases per group), which is what you have in this situation.

FIGURE 18-13:
The Paired
Samples
Statistics table.

Paired Samples Statistics					
		Mean	N	Std. Deviation	Std. Error Mean
Pair 1	Current Salary	$34,419.57	474	$17075.661	$784.311
	Beginning Salary	$17,016.09	474	$7,870.638	$361.510

The Paired Samples Correlations table shown in Figure 18-14 displays the sample size (number of pairs) along with the correlation between the two variables. (See Chapter 19 for a discussion of correlations.) The higher the correlations, the more likely you are to detect a mean difference if differences exist. The correlation (.88) is positive, high, and statistically significant (differs from zero in the population), which suggests that the power to detect a difference between the two means is substantial.

FIGURE 18-14:
The Paired
Samples
Correlations
table.

Paired Samples Correlations				
		N	Correlation	Sig.
Pair 1	Current Salary & Beginning Salary	474	.880	.000

The null hypothesis is that the two means are equal. The mean difference in current salary compared to beginning salary is about $17,403. The Paired Samples Test table in Figure 18-15 reports this along with the sample standard deviation and standard error.

FIGURE 18-15:
The Paired
Samples Test
table.

Paired Samples Test									
		Paired Differences							
					95% Confidence Interval of the Difference				Sig. (2-tailed)
		Mean	Std. Deviation	Std. Error Mean	Lower	Upper	t	df	
Pair 1	Current Salary – Beginning Salary	$17403.481	$10814.620	$496.732	$16427.407	$18379.555	35.036	473	.000

The t column displays the result of the t-test and the df column tells SPSS Statistics how to determine the probability of the t-statistic. The Sig. (2-tailed) column tells you the probability of the null hypothesis being correct. If the probability value is very low (less than 0.05), you can conclude that the means are significantly different. You can see that there are significant differences between the means. Thus, you can conclude that current salary is significantly higher than beginning salary.

As with the independent-samples t-test, the 95 percent confidence interval provides a measure of the precision with which the true population difference is estimated. In the example, the 95 percent confidence interval indicates the likely range within which you expect the population mean difference to fall. In this case, the mean difference value is about $17,403, but you are 95 percent confident that the true difference in change in salary will fall anywhere between $16,427 to $18,379, which is basically the mean difference +/- the standard error of the difference ($497) multiplied by 1.96. Again, note that the confidence interval does not include zero because a statistically significant difference between the time point exists.

Figure 18-16 shows the effect sizes for the t-test. As mentioned, effect sizes indicate the strength of the relationship between variables or the magnitude of the difference between groups. The value of the effect size is found in the Point Estimate column. (As mentioned, you can get a sense of effect sizes by using Table 18-1.) In the example, you can see that the effect size is very large because the value is larger than 0.8.

FIGURE 18-16:
The Paired
Samples Effect
Size table.

Paired Samples Effect Size			Standardizer[a]	Point Estimate	95% Confidence Interval	
					Lower	Upper
Pair 1	Current Salary – Beginning Salary	Cohen's d	$10814.620	1.609	1.472	1.745
		Hedges' correction	$10823.203	1.608	1.471	1.744

a. The denominator used in estimating the effect size.
  Cohen's d uses the sample standard deviation of the mean difference.
  Hedges' correction uses the sample standard deviation of the mean difference, plus a correction factor.

Chapter **19**

Showing Relationships between Continuous Variables

The two most commonly used statistical techniques to analyze relationships between continuous variables are the Pearson correlation and linear regression.

Many people use the term *correlation* to refer to the idea of a relationship between variables or a pattern. This view of the term *correlation* is correct, but correlation also refers to a specific statistical technique. Pearson correlations are used to study the relationship between two continuous variables. For example, you may want to look at the relationship between height and weight, and you may find that as height increases, so does weight. In other words, the variables are correlated with each other because changes in one variable affects the other.

Whereas correlation just tries to determine if two variables are related, linear regression takes this one step further and tries to predict the values of one variable based on another variable. (If you know someone's height, you can make an intelligent prediction for that person's weight.) Most of the time you wouldn't make a prediction based on just one independent variable (height); instead, you would typically use several variables that you deemed important (age, gender, BMI, and so on).

In this chapter, you use a scatterplot to visually display the relationship between two continuous variables. You then use correlation to quantify the relationship. Finally, you use linear regression to predict the dependent variable from an independent variable.

Viewing Relationships

Correlation and linear regression procedures are appropriate only when you have a linear relationship between the variables. Therefore, before running one of these procedures, you must create a scatterplot, which will show the relationship between the variables. (For more on creating scatterplots, see Chapter 13.)

The following steps show you how to construct a simple scatterplot:

1. **Choose File ⇨ Open ⇨ Data and open the Employee_data.sav file.**

   To download the file, go to the book's companion website at www.dummies. com/go/spss4e. This file contains employee information from a bank in the 1960s and has 10 variables and 474 cases.

2. **Choose Graphs ⇨ Chart Builder.**

3. **In the Choose From list, select Scatter/Dot.**

4. **Select the first scatterplot diagram (with the Simple Scatter tooltip), and drag it to the panel at the top.**

5. **In the Variables list, select Beginning Salary and drag it to the rectangle labeled X-Axis in the diagram.**

6. **In the Variables list, select Current Salary and drag it to the rectangle labeled Y-Axis in the diagram.**

7. **Click OK.**

   The chart in Figure 19-1 appears.

REMEMBER

A correlation, unlike linear regression, does not require that variables be defined as dependent or dependent. However, when creating a scatterplot, the dependent variable should go on the y-axis and the independent variable should go on the x-axis.

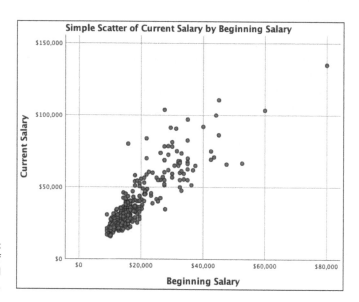

FIGURE 19-1:
The scatterplot of current and beginning salary.

Note that, for the most part, low beginning salaries are associated with low current salaries, and that high beginning salaries are associated with high current salaries — this is called a *positive relationship.* Positive relationships indicate that as you increase in one variable, you increase in the other variable, so that low numbers in one variable go with low numbers in another variable and high numbers in one variable go with high numbers in another variable.

Using the example mentioned earlier, you may find that as height increases, so does weight — this would be an example of a positive relationship. In the current example, you can see that the individual with the highest beginning salary (about $80,000) is also the person with the largest current salary (approximately $135,000).

Negative relationships indicate that as you increase in one variable, you decrease in the other variable, so low numbers on one variable go with high numbers on the other variable. An example of a negative relationship may be that the more depressed you are, the less exercise you do.

WARNING

You can use the bivariate procedure, which we demonstrate here, whenever you have a positive or negative linear relationship. However, you shouldn't use the bivariate procedure when you have a nonlinear relationship because the results will be misleading.

Figure 19-2 shows a scatterplot of a nonlinear relationship. As an example of a nonlinear relationship, consider the test anxiety variable (on the x-axis) and test performance variable (on the y-axis). People with very little test anxiety may not take a test seriously (they don't study), so they don't perform well. Likewise, people with a lot of test anxiety may not perform well because the test anxiety didn't allow them to concentrate or even read the test questions correctly. However, people with a moderate level of test anxiety should be motivated enough to study and don't suffer the crippling effects of test anxiety.

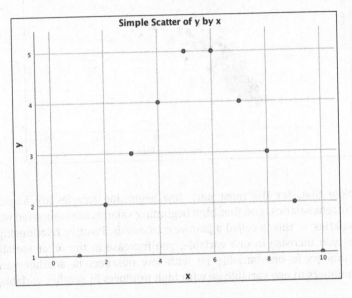

FIGURE 19-2:
A scatterplot of a nonlinear relationship.

In this example, as you increase in one variable, you increase in the other variable up to a certain point. Then as you continue to increase in one variable, you decrease in the other variable. Clearly, a relationship exists between these two variables, but the bivariate procedure would indicate (incorrectly) that there is no relationship between these two variables. For this reason, it's important to always create a scatterplot of any variables you want to correlate so that you don't reach incorrect conclusions.

Running the Bivariate Procedure

Although a scatterplot visually shows the relationship between two continuous variables, the *Pearson correlation coefficient* is used to quantify the strength and direction of the relationship between continuous variables. The Pearson correlation coefficient is a measure of the extent to which there is a linear (straight line) relationship between two variables. It has values between –1 and +1, so that the larger the absolute value, the stronger the correlation.

For example, a correlation of +1 indicates that the data falls on a perfect straight line sloping upward (positive relationship), and a correlation of –1 represents data forming a perfect straight line sloping downward (negative relationship). A correlation of 0 indicates that no straight-line relationship exists.

Bivariate correlation studies the relationship between two continuous variables, such as SAT scores and first-year-college GPA. Its goal is to determine if one variable increases or decreases in relation to another variable. Returning to the idea of hypothesis testing, you can set up two hypotheses:

>> **Null hypothesis:** The variables are not linearly related to each other. That is, the variables are independent.

>> **Alternative hypothesis:** The variables are linearly related to each other. That is, the variables are associated.

To perform a correlation, follow these steps:

1. **From the main menu, choose File ⇨ Open ⇨ Data and load the Employee_ data.sav data file.**

   Download the file at www.dummies.com/go/spss4e.

2. **Choose Analyze ⇨ Correlate ⇨ Bivariate.**

   The Bivariate Correlations dialog appears.

   In this example, you will study whether current salary is related to beginning salary, months on the job, education level, and previous job experience. Note that there is no designation of dependent and independent variables. Correlations will be calculated on all pairs of variables listed.

3. **Select the Current Salary, Beginning Salary, Months Since Hire, Educational Level, and Previous Experience variables and place them in the Variables box, as shown in Figure 19-3.**

   You can choose up to three different types of correlations. The most common form is the Pearson correlation, which is the default. Pearson is used for continuous variables, while Spearman rho and Kendall's tau-b are less common and are used for non-normal data or ordinal data, as relationships are evaluated after the original data has been transformed into ranks.

4. **(Optional) Click the Options button and do the following:**

   a. Decide what should be done about missing values.

   b. Tell SPSS Statistics whether you want to calculate standard deviations.

5. **Click OK.**

   SPSS calculates the correlations between the variables.

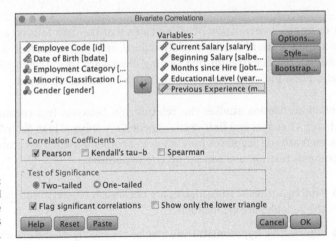

FIGURE 19-3:
The completed
Bivariate
Correlations
dialog.

Statistical tests are used to determine whether a relationship between two variables is statistically significant. In the case of correlations, you test whether the correlation differs from zero. (Zero indicates no linear association.) Figure 19-4 is a standard Correlations table.

Correlations

		Current Salary	Beginning Salary	Months since Hire	Educational Level (years)	Previous Experience (months)
Current Salary	Pearson Correlation	1	.880**	.084	.661**	-.097*
	Sig. (2-tailed)		.000	.067	.000	.034
	N	474	474	474	474	474
Beginning Salary	Pearson Correlation	.880**	1	-.020	.633**	.045
	Sig. (2-tailed)	.000		.668	.000	.327
	N	474	474	474	474	474
Months since Hire	Pearson Correlation	.084	-.020	1	.047	.003
	Sig. (2-tailed)	.067	.668		.303	.948
	N	474	474	474	474	474
Educational Level (years)	Pearson Correlation	.661**	.633**	.047	1	-.252**
	Sig. (2-tailed)	.000	.000	.303		.000
	N	474	474	474	474	474
Previous Experience (months)	Pearson Correlation	-.097*	.045	.003	-.252**	1
	Sig. (2-tailed)	.034	.327	.948	.000	
	N	474	474	474	474	474

**. Correlation is significant at the 0.01 level (2-tailed).
*. Correlation is significant at the 0.05 level (2-tailed).

FIGURE 19-4:
The Correlations
table.

Note that the table is symmetric, so the same information is represented above and below the major diagonal. Also, the correlations in the major diagonal are 1, because these are the correlations of each variable with itself.

If you want to remove the redundancy in the table, along with the correlation of a variable with itself in the major diagonal, select the Show Only the Lower Triangle option in the Bivariate Correlations dialog.

The Correlations table provides three pieces of information:

>> **Pearson correlation:** The Pearson correlation ranges from +1 to –1. The further away from 0, the stronger the relationship.

>> **Two-tailed significance level:** All correlations with a significance level less than 0.05 will have an asterisk next to the coefficient, indicating that there is a statistically significant correlation. In other words, the correlation is not zero.

>> **N:** N is the sample size.

In the example, you have a very strong positive correlation (0.880) that is statistically significant between current and beginning salary. Note that the probability of the null hypothesis being true for this relationship is extremely small (less than 0.01). Therefore you can reject the null hypothesis and conclude that a positive, linear relationship exists between these variables. The next strongest correlation, between current salary and educational level, is also a positive relationship (0.661).

The correlations between months on the job and all other variables were not statistically significant. Surprisingly, a statistically significant negative correlation, although weak (−0.097), exists between current salary and previous job experience.

Every statistical test has assumptions. The better you meet these assumptions, the more you can trust the results of the test. The Pearson correlation coefficient has the following assumptions:

>> The variables are continuous.

>> The variables are linearly related (linearity).

>> The variables are normally distributed (normality).

>> There are no influential outliers.

>> Similar variation exists throughout the regression line (homoscedasticity).

Earlier in this chapter, we discuss how scatterplots allow you to determine if a linear relationship exists. In the next section, we discuss how to use a scatterplot to look for influential outliers.

Running the Simple Linear Regression Procedure

Correlations allow you to determine if two continuous variables are linearly related to each other. So, for example, current and beginning salaries are positively related for employees. *Regression analysis* is about predicting the future (the unknown) based on data collected from the past (the known). Regression allows you to further quantify relationships by developing an equation so you can predict, for example, current salary based on beginning salary. *Linear regression* is a statistical technique used to predict a continuous dependent variable from one or more continuous independent variables.

Returning to the idea of hypothesis testing, you can set up two hypotheses:

>> **Null hypothesis:** The variables are not linearly related to each other. That is, the variables are independent.

>> **Alternative hypothesis:** The variables are linearly related to each other. That is, the variables are associated.

When there is a single independent variable, the relationship between the independent variable and dependent variable can be visualized in a scatterplot.

The following steps show you how to construct a scatterplot:

1. **Choose File ⇨ Open ⇨ Data and open the Employee_data.sav file.**

   Download the file from the book's companion website at www.dummies.com/go/spss4e.

2. **Choose Graphs ⇨ Chart Builder.**

3. **In the Choose From list, select Scatter/Dot.**

4. **Select the second scatterplot diagram (with the Simple Scatter with Fit Line tooltip), and drag it to the panel at the top.**

5. **In the Variables list, select Beginning Salary and drag it to the rectangle labeled X-Axis in the diagram.**

6. **In the Variables list, select Current Salary and drag it to the rectangle labeled Y-Axis in the diagram.**

7. **Click OK.**

   The chart in Figure 19-5 appears.

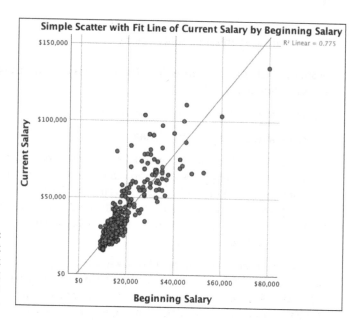

FIGURE 19-5:
A scatterplot
of current
and beginning
salary with a
regression line.

The line superimposed on the scatterplot is the best straight line that describes the relationship. The line has the equation, $y = mx + b$, where m is the slope (the change in y for a one-unit change in x) and b is the y-intercept (the value of y when x is zero or where the regression line crosses the y axis). You will develop this linear regression equation shortly.

In the scatterplot, note that many points fall near the line, but some are quite a distance from it. For each point, the difference between the value of the dependent variable and the value predicted by the equation (the value on the line) is called the *residual* (also known as the *error*). Points above the line have positive residuals (they were underpredicted), and points below the line have negative residuals (they were overpredicted). A point falling on the line has a residual of zero (a perfect prediction). The regression equation is built so that if you were to add up all the residuals (some will be positive and some will be negative), the result would be zero.

TECHNICAL
STUFF

Overpredictions and underpredictions constitute noise in the model, and noise is normal. All models have some error. A way of thinking about R Square (discussed and defined in the next section) is that noise, or error, is unexplained variance. R Square, or the signal in the model, is a measure of explained variance. If you add the signal and noise (R Square and error), you get the total variance, which we just call *variance* — the same variance that we use for measures such as standard deviation. Conceptually, it makes a lot of sense.

To perform a linear regression, follow these steps:

1. **From the main menu, choose File ⇨ Open ⇨ Data and load the Employee_data.sav data file.**

   Download the file at www.dummies.com/go/spss4e.

2. **Choose Analyze ⇨ Regression ⇨ Linear.**

   The Linear Regression dialog appears. In this example, you want to predict current salary from beginning salary. You can place the dependent variable, Current Salary, in the Dependent box; this is the variable for which you want to set up a prediction equation. You can place the predictor variable Beginning Salary in the Independent(s) box; this is the variable you'll use to predict the dependent variable.

   REMEMBER

   When only one independent variable is taken into account, the procedure is a *simple regression*. If you use more than one independent variable, it's a *multiple regression*. All dialogs in SPSS are designed to accommodate for multiple regression. You perform multiple linear regression in the next chapter.

3. **Select the Current Salary variable, and place it in the Dependent box.**

4. **Select the Beginning Salary variable, and place it in the Independent(s) box, as shown in Figure 19-6.**

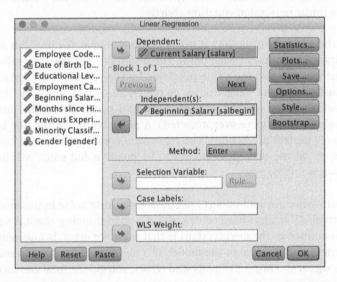

FIGURE 19-6:
The completed Linear Regression dialog.

5. In the Method drop-down list, specify the method to use.

By default, the enter regression method is used, which means that all independent variables will be entered into the regression equation simultaneously. This method works well when you have a limited number of independent variables or you have a strong rationale for including all your independent variables. However, at times, you may want to select predictors from a larger set of independent variables. In this case, request the stepwise method so that the best predictors from a statistical sense are used.

At this point, you can run the linear regression procedure, but we want to briefly point out the general uses of some of the other dialogs (which you can access by clicking the buttons on the right side of the dialog):

- The Statistics dialog has many additional descriptive statistics, as well as statistics that determine variable overlap.

- The Plots dialog is used to create graphs that allow you to better assess assumptions.

- The Save dialog adds new variables (predictions, errors) to the data file.

- The Options dialog controls the criteria when running stepwise regression and choices in handling missing data.

6. Click OK.

SPSS performs the linear regression.

REMEMBER

Performing regression analysis is the process of looking for predictors and determining how well they predict a future outcome.

The Model Summary table shown in Figure 19-7 provides several measures of how well the model fits the data. R (which can range from 0 to 1) is the correlation between the dependent measure and the independent variable, so the closer R is to 1, the better the fit. In this example, you have an R of 0.880, which is huge. R is the correlation between the dependent variable and the independent variable you're using. You can also think of R as the correlation between the dependent variable and the predicted values.

FIGURE 19-7:
The Model
Summary table.

Model Summary				
Model	R	R Square	Adjusted R Square	Std. Error of the Estimate
1	.880[a]	.775	.774	$8,115.356
a. Predictors: (Constant), Beginning Salary				

You may notice that most stats books use a lowercase *r* for correlation but an uppercase *R* for R Square. Make note of this when you're deciding how to write your work.

Remember that the ultimate goal of linear regression is to create a prediction equation so you can predict future values. The value of the equation is linked to how well it actually describes or fits the data, so part of the regression output includes fit measures.

To quantify the extent to which the straight-line equation fits the data, the fit measure, R Square was developed. *R Square* (which can range from 0 to 1) is the correlation coefficient squared. It can be interpreted as the proportion of variance of the dependent measure that can be predicted from the combination of independent variable(s). In this example, you have an R Square of 0.775, which is huge. This value tells you that the predictor can explain about 78 percent of the variation in the dependent variable, Current Salary. See Table 19-1 for more context of the relative size of an R Square of 78 percent.

TABLE 19-1 **Some R Value Ranges and Their Equivalent R Square Value Ranges**

	r	R Square
Noteworthy	Greater than 0.3	Greater than 9% to 10%
Large	Greater than 0.5	Greater than 25%
Very large	Greater than 0.7	Greater than 49% to 50%

It's reasonable for people to disagree about what constitutes a big correlation. For instance, if you're a chemist or physicist, correlations in those research areas would be expected to be very high because physical objects follow natural laws consistently. When human behavior is involved, however, even correlations in the 0.3 to 0.5 range, which would correspond to an R Square of 10 percent to 25 percent, are quite high. Some research would report correlations in the 0.1 range, but when you square that, you realize that a pretty low percentage of variance is explained.

Adjusted R Square represents a technical improvement over R Square in that it explicitly adjusts for the number of predictor variables relative to the sample size. If adjusted R Square and R Square differ dramatically, you have too many predictors or your sample size is too small. In the example, adjusted R Square has a value of 0.774, which is very similar to the R Square value of 0.775. Therefore, you aren't capitalizing on chance by having too many predictors relative to the sample size.

The Standard Error of the Est. column provides an estimate (in the scale of the dependent variable) of how much variation remains to be accounted for after the prediction equation has been fit to the data. In the example, your predictions are off on average by about $8,115.

While the fit measures in the Model Summary table indicate how well you can expect to predict the dependent variable, they don't tell you whether a statistically significant relationship exists between the dependent and independent variables. That is, the fit measures don't tell you if the correlation between dependent and independent variable differs from zero (zero indicates no linear association). For that information, you use the ANOVA table.

The Sig. column provides the probability that the null hypothesis is true — that is, no relationship exists between the independent and dependent variables. As shown in Figure 19-8, the probability of the null hypothesis being correct is extremely small (less than 0.05), so the null hypothesis has to be rejected and the conclusion is that a linear relationship exists between these variables. In other words, you have a statistically significant relationship between current salary and beginning salary.

		Sum of Squares	df	Mean Square	F	Sig.
Model						
1	Regression	1.068E+11	1	1.068E+11	1622.118	.000[b]
	Residual	3.109E+10	472	65858997.2		
	Total	1.379E+11	473			

ANOVA[a]

a. Dependent Variable: Current Salary
b. Predictors: (Constant), Beginning Salary

FIGURE 19-8:
The ANOVA table.

If the results from the ANOVA table were not statistically significant, you would conclude that there was no relationship between the dependent variable and the predictor, so there would be no reason to continue investigating the results. However, you do have a statistically significant model, so you now want to determine which predictor is statistically significant. (Because you have only one predicator in a simple linear regression, when the overall model is significant you know that the predictor will be statistically significant.) You also want to see your prediction equation, as well as determine which predictor is the most important. To answer these questions, turn to the Coefficients table, which is shown in Figure 19-9.

FIGURE 19-9:
The Coefficients
table.

Coefficients[a]					
	Unstandardized Coefficients		Standardized Coefficients		
Model	B	Std. Error	Beta	t	Sig.
1 (Constant)	1928.206	888.680		2.170	.031
Beginning Salary	1.909	.047	.880	40.276	.000
a. Dependent Variable: Current Salary					

Linear regression takes into consideration the effect each independent variable has on the dependent variable. The B coefficients are important for both prediction and interpretive purposes; however, analysts usually look first to the t-test at the end of each row to determine which independent variable(s) are significantly related to the outcome variable. Looking at the significance value, you see that your predictor is statistically significant, so you need to retain this predictor.

The first column of the Coefficients table contains a list of the independent variables plus the *constant*, which is the intercept where the regression line crosses the y-axis. The intercept is the value of the dependent variable when the independent variable is 0.

The B column shows you how a one-unit change in an independent variable affects the dependent variable. For example, the Beginning Salary variable has a B coefficient of $1.9, so each additional dollar for beginning salary increases current salary by $1.9.

The B column also contains the regression coefficients you would use in a prediction equation. In this example, current salary can be predicted with the following equation:

Current Salary = 1928 + (1.9)(Beginning Salary)

As an example of how to use a prediction equation, suppose you have someone with a beginning salary of $30,000. Based on the preceding equation, you would estimate that this person's current salary would be: 1928 + (1.9) (30,000) = $58,928.

The Std. Error column contains standard errors of the regression coefficients. The standard errors can be used to create a 95 percent confidence interval around the B coefficients.

Betas are standardized regression coefficients and are used to judge the relative importance of each of the independent variables. The values range between −1 and +1, so that the larger the value, the greater the importance of the variable. In the example, the most important predictor is beginning salary. Note that in the case of simple linear regression, beta is the correlation between beginning salary and current salary.

TECHNICAL STUFF

Every statistical test has assumptions. The better you meet these assumptions, the more you can trust the results of the test. Linear regression assumes the following:

>> The variables are continuous.

>> The variables are linearly related (linearity).

>> The variables are normally distributed (normality).

>> There are no influential outliers.

>> A similar variation exists throughout the regression line (homoscedasticity).

>> Multicollinearity is absent. That is, predictors are not highly correlated with each other.

Scatterplots not only enable you to determine if you have a linear relationship but also help you look for influential outliers. *Outliers* are data points that are different from the norm. For example, Figure 19-10 is the same scatterplot as Figure 19-5 except the data for the outlier has been modified.

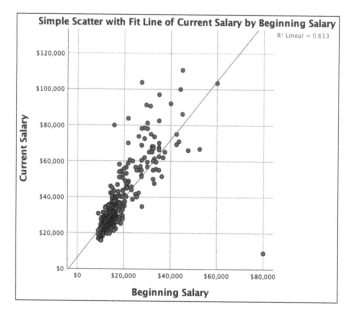

FIGURE 19-10:
A scatterplot with an influential outlier.

In Figure 19-5, the individual with the highest beginning salary, about $80,000, is also the person with the largest current salary, approximately $135,000. This person's data is an outlier but it falls close to the regression line and therefore is in sync with the rest of the data. The R Square for this regression line is .78.

In Figure 19-10, the individual with the highest beginning salary, about $80,000, now has a current salary of approximately $9,000. This person's data falls nowhere near the regression line, and as a consequence the R Square is .61. This person's data is not only an outlier but an influential outlier, which affects the quality of the prediction. An *influential outlier* is a data point that pulls the regression equation in its direction, thereby affecting predictive accuracy. (As mentioned, overpredictions and underpredictions must add up to zero.)

In the next chapter, you learn how to assess some of the other linear regression assumptions.

6

Getting More Advanced with Analyzing Data

Go beyond the basics.

Analyze nonparametric data.

Identify which test you need and why.

Chapter **20**

Doing More Advanced Analyses

This chapter is a direct extension of Chapters 18 and 19. In Chapter 18, we discuss t-tests, which are used when the dependent variable is continuous and the independent variable has two categories. In this chapter, we will talk about the one-way ANOVA procedure, which is an extension of the independent samples t-test and is used when you have a continuous dependent variable and the independent variable has two or more categories.

In Chapter 19, we talk about simple linear regression, which is used when the dependent variable is continuous and there is one continuous independent variable. In this chapter, we talk about how to perform multiple linear regression, which is used when the dependent variable is continuous and there are various continuous independent variables.

Running the One-Way ANOVA Procedure

The purpose of the one-way ANOVA is to test whether the means of two or more separate groups differ from each other on a continuous dependent variable. Its goal is to determine if a significant difference exists among the groups. Analysis of variance (ANOVA) is a general method of drawing conclusions regarding differences in population means when two or more comparison groups are involved. The independent-samples t-test applies only to the simplest instance (two groups), whereas the one-way ANOVA procedure can accommodate more complex situations (three or more groups).

You might be wondering why this procedure is called analysis of variance instead of analysis of means (because you are comparing the means of several groups). The general idea behind ANOVA is that you have a population of interest and then draw random samples from this population, as shown in Figure 20-1.

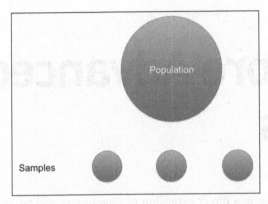

FIGURE 20-1:
Population and
samples.

Variation will occur within each sample because people differ from each other. This variation, shown in Figure 20-2, is called *within-group variation*. Likewise, because each sample is random, you would not be surprised if the mean of each sample is not exactly the same. This variation, which is shown in Figure 20-3, is called *between-group variation*. In essence, you now have two estimates of the population mean, one based on the variation within a sample and one based on the variation between the samples.

If the null hypotheses is correct and the amount of variation among group means (between-group variation) is compared to the amount of variation among observations within each group (within-group variation), the only source of variation among sample means would be the fact that the groups are composed of different individual observations. Thus, a ratio of the two sources of variation (between group/within group) should be about 1, as shown in Figure 20-4. The statistical distribution of this ratio is known as the *F distribution*. The ratio of 1 would indicate that no differences exist among the groups. However, if the variation between groups is much larger than the variation within the groups, the ratio, or F statistic, will be much larger than 1, indicating that differences exist among the groups.

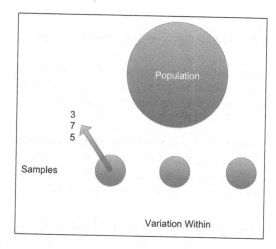

FIGURE 20-2:
Within-groups
variation.

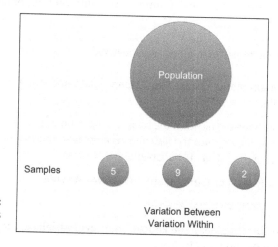

FIGURE 20-3:
Between-groups
variation.

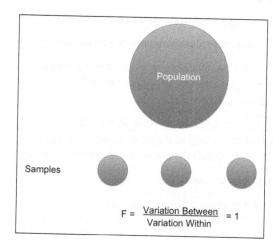

FIGURE 20-4:
The F ratio.

Going back to the idea of hypothesis testing, you can set up two hypotheses:

>> **Null hypothesis:** The means of the groups will be the same. Stating the null hypothesis as an equation, we can say that the null hypothesis is true when there is similar variation between and within, which results in an F statistic of 1.

>> **Alternative hypothesis:** The means of the groups will differ from each other. Stating the alternative hypothesis as an equation, we can say that the null hypothesis is not true when the variation between is much larger than the variation within, which results in an F statistic larger than 1.

In this example you investigate the relationship between employment category and years of education and current salary. You want to determine whether educational or salary differences exist among the different employment category groups.

Follow these steps to perform a one-way ANOVA:

1. **From the main menu, choose File ⇨ Open ⇨ Data and load the employee_data.sav file.**

   You can download the file from the book's companion website at www.dummies.com/go/spss4e. The file contains employee information from a bank in the 1960s and has 10 variables and 474 cases.

2. **Choose Analyze ⇨ Compare Means ⇨ One-Way ANOVA.**

   The One-Way ANOVA dialog appears.

3. **Select the Current Salary and Educational Level variables, then place them in the Dependent List box.**

   Continuous variables are placed in the Dependent List box.

4. **Select the Employment Category variable and place it in the Factor box.**

   Categorical independent variables are placed in the Factor box. Because you are performing a one-way ANOVA, you can have only one independent variable, as shown in Figure 20-5.

   A two-way ANOVA (two independent variables), three-way ANOVA (three independent variables), and so on are possible, but these need to be performed by choosing Choose Analyze ⇨ General Linear Model ⇨ Dialogs.

5. **Select the Options button.**

   The Options dialog appears.

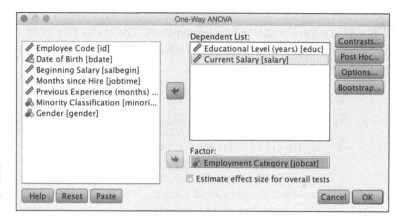

FIGURE 20-5:
The completed
One-Way ANOVA
dialog.

6. **Select the Descriptive, Homogeneity of Variance Test, Brown-Forsythe Test, and Welch Test options, as shown in Figure 20-6.**

Descriptive provides group means and standard deviations. The homogeneity of variance test assesses the assumption of homogeneity of variance. Brown-Forsythe and Welch are robust tests that do not assume homogeneity of variance and thus can be used when this assumption is not met.

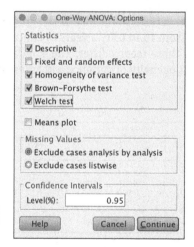

FIGURE 20-6:
The completed
Options dialog.

7. **Click Continue.**

8. **Click OK.**

TECHNICAL STUFF

Every statistical test has assumptions. The better you meet these assumptions, the more you can trust the results of the test. The one-way ANOVA has four assumptions:

» The dependent variable is continuous.

» Two or more different groups are compared.

» The dependent variable is normally distributed within each category of the independent variable (normality). One-way ANOVA is robust to moderate violations of the normality assumption as long as the sample sizes are moderate to large (over 50 cases per group) and the dependent measure has the same distribution (for example, skewed to the right) within each comparison group.

» Similar variation exists within each category of the independent variable (homogeneity of variance). One-way ANOVA is robust to moderate violations of the homogeneity assumption as long as the sample sizes of the groups are similar.

As with all analyses, first look to see how many cases are in each group, along with the means and standard deviations. The Descriptives table shown in Figure 20-7 provides sample sizes, means, standard deviations, and standard errors for the groups on each of the dependent variables. The size of the groups ranges from 27 to 363 people. The means vary from 10.19 to 17.2 years of education; the one-way ANOVA procedure will assess if these means differ. The standard deviations vary from 1.61 to 2.33; the test of homogeneity of variance will assess if these standard deviations differ.

Descriptives						95% Confidence Interval for Mean			
		N	Mean	Std. Deviation	Std. Error	Lower Bound	Upper Bound	Minimum	Maximum
Educational Level (years)	Clerical	363	12.87	2.333	.122	12.63	13.11	8	19
	Custodial	27	10.19	2.219	.427	9.31	11.06	8	15
	Manager	84	17.25	1.612	.176	16.90	17.60	12	21
	Total	474	13.49	2.885	.133	13.23	13.75	8	21
Current Salary	Clerical	363	$27,838.54	$7,567.995	$397.217	$27,057.40	$28,619.68	$15,750	$80,000
	Custodial	27	$30,938.89	$2,114.616	$406.958	$30,102.37	$31,775.40	$24,300	$35,250
	Manager	84	$63,977.80	18244.776	$1,990.668	$60,018.44	$67,937.16	$34,410	$135,000
	Total	474	$34,419.57	17075.661	$784.311	$32,878.40	$35,960.73	$15,750	$135,000

FIGURE 20-7: The Descriptives table.

You can see that managers have higher means than the other groups on the dependent variables. This mean comparison is precisely what the one-way ANOVA assesses — whether the differences between the means are significantly different from each other or if the differences you are seeing are just due to chance.

The next table of output is the test of homogeneity of variances, shown in Figure 20-8. The null hypothesis here is that the variances are equal, so if the significance level is low enough (as it is in the figure), you reject the null hypothesis and conclude the variances are not equal.

Test of Homogeneity of Variances		Levene Statistic	df1	df2	Sig.
Educational Level (years)	Based on Mean	6.159	2	471	.002
	Based on Median	2.158	2	471	.117
	Based on Median and with adjusted df	2.158	2	418.818	.117
	Based on trimmed mean	6.519	2	471	.002
Current Salary	Based on Mean	59.733	2	471	.000
	Based on Median	51.189	2	471	.000
	Based on Median and with adjusted df	51.189	2	240.176	.000
	Based on trimmed mean	56.201	2	471	.000

FIGURE 20-8: The Test of Homogeneity of Variances table.

In the one-way ANOVA, similar to in the independent-samples t-test, violation of the assumption of homogeneity of variances is more serious than violation of the assumption of normality. And like the independent-samples t-test, the one-way ANOVA applies a two-step strategy for testing:

» Test the homogeneity of variance assumption.

» If the assumption holds, proceed with the standard test (the ANOVA F-test) to test equality of means. If the null hypothesis of equal variances is rejected, use an adjusted F-test to test equality of means.

In the Test of Homogeneity of Variances table, Levene's test for equality of variances is displayed. The test result is used to calculate the significance level (the Sig. column). The test of homogeneity of variance can be calculated using various criteria (mean, median, and so on), as shown in the table. However, most people look at the mean row, because they are comparing means.

The example did not meet the assumption of homogeneity of variance for the variables because the value in the Sig. column is less than 0.05 (a difference exists in the variation of the groups), so you need to look at the Robust Tests of Equality of Means table. However, before you do that, let's take a look at the standard ANOVA table, which is the table you would inspect if the assumption of homogeneity of variance was met.

Most of the information in the ANOVA table (see Figure 20-9) is technical and not directly interpreted. Rather, the summaries are used to obtain the F statistic and, more importantly, the probability value you use in evaluating the population differences.

ANOVA						
		Sum of Squares	df	Mean Square	F	Sig.
Educational Level (years)	Between Groups	1622.989	2	811.495	165.212	.000
	Within Groups	2313.477	471	4.912		
	Total	3936.466	473			
Current Salary	Between Groups	8.944E+10	2	4.472E+10	434.481	.000
	Within Groups	4.848E+10	471	102925714		
	Total	1.379E+11	473			

FIGURE 20-9:
The ANOVA table.

The standard ANOVA table will provide the following information:

>> The first column has a row for the between-group variation and a row for within-group variation.

>> Sums of squares are intermediate summary numbers used in calculating the between-group variances (deviations of individual group means around the total sample mean) and within-group variances (deviations of individual observations around their respective sample group mean).

>> The df column contains information about *degrees of freedom,* related to the number of groups and the number of individual observations within each group.

>> *Mean squares* are measures of the between-group and within-group variation. (Sum of squares divided by their respective degrees of freedom.)

>> The F statistic is the ratio of between-group to within-group variation and will be about 1 if the null hypothesis is true.

>> The Sig. column provides the probability of obtaining the sample F ratio (taking into account the number of groups and sample size), if the null hypothesis is true.

In practice, most researchers move directly to the significance value because the columns containing the sums of squares, degrees of freedom, mean squares, and F statistic are all necessary for the probability calculation but are rarely interpreted in their own right. In the table, the low significance value will lead you to reject the null hypothesis of equal means. You can see that significant differences exist among the employment categories on education and salary.

When the condition of equal variances is not met, an adjusted F-test has to be used. SPSS Statistics provides two such tests, Welch and Brown-Forsythe. You selected both but you can use either test. The Robust Tests of Equality of Means table provides the details (see Figure 20-10). Again, the columns containing test statistic and degrees of freedom are technical details to compute the significance.

FIGURE 20-10:
The Robust Tests
of Equality of
Means table.

Robust Tests of Equality of Means					
		Statistic[a]	df1	df2	Sig.
Educational Level (years)	Welch	250.414	2	65.611	.000
	Brown–Forsythe	201.407	2	72.997	.000
Current Salary	Welch	162.200	2	117.312	.000
	Brown–Forsythe	306.810	2	93.906	.000
a. Asymptotically F distributed.					

Both tests mathematically attempt to adjust for the lack of homogeneity of variance. And both tests indicate that highly significant differences exist in education and current salary among employment categories, which is consistent with the conclusions drawn from the standard ANOVA. Having concluded that differences exist among the employment categories, you'll need to probe to find specifically which groups differ from which others.

Conducting Post Hoc Tests

Post hoc tests are typically performed only after the overall F-test indicates that population differences exist. At this point, there is usually interest in discovering just which group means differ from which others. In one aspect, the procedure is straightforward: Every possible pair of group means is tested for population differences and a summary table is produced.

As more tests are performed, however, the probability of obtaining at least one false-positive result increases. As an extreme example, if there are ten groups, 45 pairwise group comparisons (n*(n–1)/2) can be made. If testing at the .05 level, you would expect to obtain on average about two (.05 * 45) false-positive tests.

Statisticians have developed a number of methods to reduce the false-positive rate when multiple tests of this type are performed. Often, more than one post hoc test is used and the results are compared to provide more evidence about potential mean differences.

Follow these steps to perform post hoc tests for a one-way ANOVA:

1. **From the main menu, choose File ➪ Open ➪ Data and load the employee_ data.sav file.**

   Download the file at www.dummies.com/go/spss4e.

2. **Choose Analyze ➪ Compare Means ➪ One-Way ANOVA.**

3. **Select the Current Salary and Educational Level variables, and place them in the Dependent List box.**

4. Select the Employment Category variable and place it in the Factor box.

5. Click the Options button.

6. Select the Descriptive, Homogeneity of Variance Test, Brown-Forsythe Test, and Welch Test options.

7. Click Continue.

8. Select the Post Hoc button.

The Post Hoc Multiple Comparisons dialog appears. Post hoc analyses are accessed from the One-Way ANOVA dialog. Select the appropriate method of multiple comparisons, which depends on whether the assumption of homogeneity of variance has been met.

9. Select Bonferroni and Games-Howell, as shown in Figure 20-11.

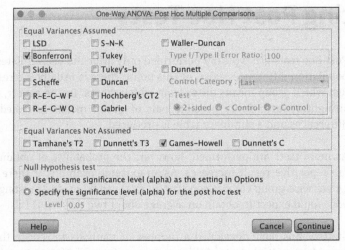

FIGURE 20-11:
The completed
Post Hoc Multiple
Comparisons
dialog.

10. Click Continue.

11. Click OK.

The one-way ANOVA is now rerun, along with the post hoc tests.

Why so many tests in the dialog shown in Figure 20-11? The ideal post hoc test would demonstrate tight control of Type I (false-positive) errors, have good statistical power (probability of detecting true population differences), and be robust over assumption violations (failure of homogeneity of variance, non-normal error distributions). Unfortunately, there are implicit tradeoffs involving some of these desired features (Type I error and power) and no current post hoc procedure is best in all these areas.

In addition, pairwise tests can be based on different statistical distributions (t, F, studentized range, and others) and Type I errors can be controlled at different levels (per individual test, per family of tests, and variations in between), and you have a large collection of post hoc tests.

Statisticians don't agree on a single test that is optimal in all situations. However, the Bonferroni test is currently the most popular procedure. This procedure is based on an additive inequality, so the criterion level for each pairwise test is obtained by dividing the original criterion level (say .05) by the number of pairwise comparisons made. Thus, with five means, and therefore ten pairwise comparisons, each Bonferroni test will be performed at the .05/10 or .005 level.

Most post hoc procedures were derived assuming homogeneity of variance and normality of error. Post hoc tests in the Equal Variances Not Assumed section of the dialog adjust for unequal variances and sample sizes in the groups. Simulation studies suggest that Games-Howell can be more powerful than the other tests in this section, which is why you chose this test.

Back to the results of the post hoc tests, the Multiple Comparisons table shown in Figure 20-12 provides all pairwise comparisons. The rows are formed by every possible combination of groups. The Mean Difference (I-J) column contains the sample mean difference between each pairing of groups. If this difference is statistically significant at the specified level after applying the post hoc adjustments, an asterisk (*) appears beside the mean difference.

Multiple Comparisons

Dependent Variable		(I) Employment Category	(J) Employment Category	Mean Difference (I–J)	Std. Error	Sig.	95% Confidence Interval	
							Lower Bound	Upper Bound
Educational Level (years)	Bonferroni	Clerical	Custodial	2.683*	.442	.000	1.62	3.74
			Manager	-4.382*	.268	.000	-5.03	-3.74
		Custodial	Clerical	-2.683*	.442	.000	-3.74	-1.62
			Manager	-7.065*	.490	.000	-8.24	-5.89
		Manager	Clerical	4.382*	.268	.000	3.74	5.03
			Custodial	7.065*	.490	.000	5.89	8.24
	Games-Howell	Clerical	Custodial	2.683*	.444	.000	1.59	3.78
			Manager	-4.382*	.214	.000	-4.89	-3.88
		Custodial	Clerical	-2.683*	.444	.000	-3.78	-1.59
			Manager	-7.065*	.462	.000	-8.19	-5.93
		Manager	Clerical	4.382*	.214	.000	3.88	4.89
			Custodial	7.065*	.462	.000	5.93	8.19
Current Salary	Bonferroni	Clerical	Custodial	-3100.349	$2,023.760	.379	-$7,962.56	$1,761.86
			Manager	-36139.26*	$1,228.352	.000	-$39090.45	-33188.07
		Custodial	Clerical	$3,100.349	$2,023.760	.379	-$1,761.86	$7,962.56
			Manager	-33038.91*	$2,244.409	.000	-38431.24	-27646.58
		Manager	Clerical	36139.258*	$1,228.352	.000	$33,188.07	$39,090.45
			Custodial	33038.909*	$2,244.409	.000	$27,646.58	$38,431.24
	Games-Howell	Clerical	Custodial	-3100.349*	$568.679	.000	-$4,454.82	-$1,745.88
			Manager	-36139.26*	$2,029.912	.000	-$40977.01	-31301.51
		Custodial	Clerical	$3,100.349*	$568.679	.000	$1,745.88	$4,454.82
			Manager	-33038.91*	$2,031.840	.000	-37881.37	-28196.45
		Manager	Clerical	36139.258*	$2,029.912	.000	$31,301.51	$40,977.01
			Custodial	33038.909*	$2,031.840	.000	$28,196.45	$37,881.37

*. The mean difference is significant at the 0.05 level.

FIGURE 20-12: The Multiple Comparisons table.

The actual significance value for the test appears in the Sig. column. In addition, the standard errors and 95 percent confidence intervals for each mean difference provide information on the precision with which you've estimated the mean differences. As you would expect, if a mean difference is not significant, the confidence interval includes 0.

Also note that each pairwise comparison appears twice. For each such duplicate pair, the significance value is the same, but the signs are reversed for the mean difference and confidence interval values.

The clerical and custodial groups have a mean difference of 2.68 years of education. This difference is statistically significant at the specified level after applying the post hoc adjustments. The interval [1.62, 3.74] contains the difference between these two population means with 95 percent confidence.

Summarizing the entire table, you would say that regardless of the post hoc test used, all groups differed significantly from each other in the amount of education such that the manager group was the most educated, followed by the clerical group, and then the custodial group. Regarding current salary, regardless of the post hoc test used, the manager group had a higher current salary than either the clerical or custodial group. Interestingly, the Bonferroni procedure did not find a significant difference in current salary between the clerical and custodial groups, but the Games-Howell procedure did find a statistically significant difference such that the clerical group had a lower salary than the custodial group.

Comparing Means Graphically

As with t-tests, a simple error bar chart is the most effective way of comparing means. You will create an error bar chart corresponding to the one-way ANOVA of employment category and number of years of education. To see how the number of years of education varies across categories of employment, you'll use education as the Y-axis variable. Follow these steps to create a simple error bar chart:

1. **From the main menu, choose File ⇨ Open ⇨ Data and load the employee_data.sav data file.**

   Download the file at www.dummies.com/go/spss4e.

2. **Choose Graphs ⇨ Chart Builder.**

3. **In the Choose From list, select Bar.**

4. **Select the seventh graph image (the Simple Error Bar tooltip) and drag it to the panel at the top of the window.**

5. **Select the Educational Level variable, and place it in the Y-axis box.**

6. **Select the Employment Category variable, and place it in the X-axis box.**

7. **Click OK.**

The graph in Figure 20-13 appears.

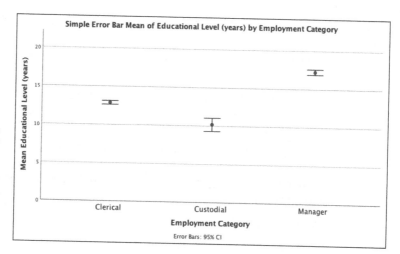

FIGURE 20-13: A simple error bar graph displaying the relationship between years of education and employment category.

The error bar chart generates a graph depicting the relationship between a scale and categorical variable. It provides a visual sense of how far the groups are separated. The mean number of years of education for each employment category along with 95 percent confidence intervals is represented in the chart.

The confidence intervals for the employment categories don't overlap, which is consistent with the result from the one-way ANOVA. Because the confidence intervals do not overlap, the groups are significantly different from each other.

Running the Multiple Linear Regression Procedure

In Chapter 19, we discuss *simple linear regression*, where one continuous independent variable is used to predict a continuous dependent variable. In this section, we talk about *multiple linear regression*, where several continuous independent variables are used to predict or understand a continuous dependent variable.

When running a multiple regression, you will again be concerned with how well the equation fits the data, whether a linear model is the best fit to the data, whether any of the variables are significant predictors, and estimating the coefficients for the best-fitting prediction equation. In addition, you'll be interested in the relative importance of each of the independent variables in predicting the dependent measure.

Returning to the idea of hypothesis testing, you can set up two hypotheses:

>> **Null hypothesis:** The variables are not linearly related to each other. That is, the variables are independent.

>> **Alternative hypothesis:** The variables are linearly related to each other. That is, the variables are associated.

To perform a multiple linear regression, follow these steps:

1. **From the main menu, choose File ⇨ Open ⇨ Data and load the employee_ data.sav data file.**

   Download the file at www.dummies.com/go/spss4e.

2. **Choose Analyze ⇨ Regression ⇨ Linear.**

   In this example, you want to predict current salary from beginning salary, months on the job, number of years of education, gender, and previous job experience. You can place the predictor variables in the Independent(s) box.

3. **Select the Beginning Salary variable, and place it in the Dependent box.**

   This is the variable for which you want to set up a prediction equation.

4. **Select the Beginning Salary, Months Since Hire, Educational Level, Gender, and Previous Experience variables, and place them in the Independent(s) box, as shown in Figure 20-14.**

   These are the variables you'll use to predict the dependent variable.

TECHNICAL STUFF

   Gender is a dichotomous variable coded 0 for males and 1 for females, but it was added to the regression model because a variable coded as a dichotomy can be considered a continuous variable. Why? Because technically a continuous variable assumes that a one-unit change has the same meaning throughout the range of the scale. If a variable's only possible codes are 0 and 1 (or 1 and 2), a one-unit change means the same thing throughout the scale. Thus, dichotomous variables can be used as predictor variables in regression. Regression also allows the use of nominal predictor variables if they're converted into a series of dichotomous variables; this technique is called *dummy coding*.

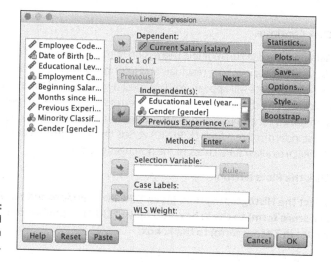

FIGURE 20-14:
The completed
Linear Regression
dialog.

5. **Click the Statistics button.**

6. **Select Casewise Diagnostics, and then select Collinearity Diagnostics (see Figure 20-15).**

The Casewise Diagnostics check box requests information about all cases whose standardized residuals are more than three standard deviations from the fit line. *Collinearity diagnostics* displays a number of criteria that provide information on the amount of redundancy among the predictors. The Estimates and Model Fit options are selected by default.

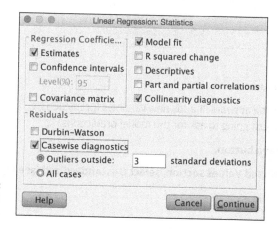

FIGURE 20-15:
The completed
Statistics dialog.

7. Click Continue.

Although you can run multiple regression at this point, you will request some diagnostic plots involving residuals and information about outliers. By default, no residual plots will appear. You'll request a histogram of the standardized residuals for a check of the normality of errors. Regression can produce summaries concerning various types of residuals. You'll request a scatterplot of the standardized residuals (*ZRESID) versus the standardized predicted values (*ZPRED) to allow for a check of the homogeneity of errors.

8. Click the Plots button.

9. Select the Histogram option. Move *ZRESID (standardized residual values in Z score form) to the Y: box, and move *ZPRED (standardized predicted values in Z score form) to the X: box.

The dialog now looks like Figure 20-16.

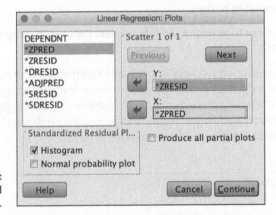

FIGURE 20-16:
The completed
Plots dialog.

10. Click Continue.

The Save dialog appears. It adds new variables (predictions, errors) to the data file. You are just going to ask for the model predictions.

11. Click the Save button.

12. In the Predicted Values section, select Unstandardized (see Figure 20-17).

13. Click Continue.

14. Click OK.

SPSS performs the linear regression.

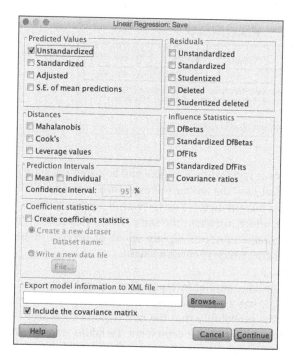

FIGURE 20-17:
The completed Save dialog.

TECHNICAL
STUFF

Every statistical test has assumptions. The better you meet these assumptions, the more you can trust the results of the test. Linear regression assumes the following:

>> The variables are continuous.

>> The variables are linearly related (linearity).

>> The variables are normally distributed (normality).

>> No influential outliers exist.

>> Similar variation exists throughout the regression line (homoscedasticity).

>> Multicollinearity is absent. That is, the predictors are not highly correlated with each other.

The Model Summary table of multiple linear regression, like the table with simple linear regression, provides several measures of how well the model fits the data, as shown in Figure 20-18.

R is the correlation between the dependent measure and the combination of the independent variables, so the closer R is to 1, the better the fit. You have an R of 0.902, which is huge. R is the correlation between the dependent variable and the combination of the five independent variables you're using. You can also think of R as the correlation between the dependent variable and the predicted values.

Model Summary[b]				
Model	R	R Square	Adjusted R Square	Std. Error of the Estimate
1	.902[a]	.814	.812	$7,410.457

a. Predictors: (Constant), Previous Experience (months), Months since Hire, Beginning Salary, Gender, Educational Level (years)

b. Dependent Variable: Current Salary

FIGURE 20-18: The Model Summary table.

As in simple linear regression, R square and adjusted R square are interpreted the same, except that now the amount of explained variance is from a group of predictors, not just one predictor. You have an R square of 0.814 and an adjusted R square of 0.812, which are about the same. These values tell you that your combination of five predictions can explain about 81 percent of the variation in the dependent variable, which is current salary.

The ANOVA table has a similar interpretation, except that now it tests whether any predictor variable has a significant effect on the dependent variable. The Sig. column provides the probability that the null hypothesis is true — that is, no relationship exists between the independent variables and dependent variable. As shown in Figure 20-19, the probability of the null hypothesis being correct is extremely small (less than 0.05), so the null hypothesis has to be rejected and a linear relationship exists between the dependent variable and the combination of independent variables.

ANOVA[a]						
Model		Sum of Squares	df	Mean Square	F	Sig.
1	Regression	1.122E+11	5	2.244E+10	408.692	.000[b]
	Residual	2.570E+10	468	54914875.0		
	Total	1.379E+11	473			

a. Dependent Variable: Current Salary

FIGURE 20-19: The ANOVA table.

Because the results from the ANOVA table were statistically significant, turn next to the Coefficients table. If the results from the ANOVA table were not statistically significant, you would conclude that no relationship exists between the dependent variable and the combination of the predictors, so there would be no reason to continue investigating the results.

Because you do have a statistically significant model, however, you want to determine which predictors are statistically significant. You also want to see your prediction equation, as well as determine which predictors are the most important. To answer these questions, you turn to the Coefficients table shown in Figure 20-20.

Coefficients[a]								
		Unstandardized Coefficients		Standardized Coefficients			Collinearity Statistics	
Model		B	Std. Error	Beta	t	Sig.	Tolerance	VIF
1	(Constant)	–12550.032	3474.744		–3.612	.000		
	Beginning Salary	1.723	.061	.794	28.472	.000	.512	1.953
	Months since Hire	154.536	34.085	.091	4.534	.000	.987	1.013
	Educational Level (years)	593.031	166.630	.100	3.559	.000	.502	1.990
	Gender	–2232.917	792.078	–.065	–2.819	.005	.744	1.343
	Previous Experience (months)	–19.436	3.583	–.119	–5.424	.000	.827	1.210
a. Dependent Variable: Current Salary								

FIGURE 20-20: The Coefficients table.

Linear regression takes into consideration the effect each independent variable has on the dependent variable. In the Coefficients table, the independent variables appear in the order in which they were listed in the Linear Regression dialog, not in order of importance.

The B coefficients are important for both prediction and interpretive purposes. However, analysts usually look first to the t-test at the end of each row to determine which independent variables are significantly related to the outcome variable. Because five variables are in the equation, you're testing whether a linear relationship exists between each independent variable and the dependent variable after adjusting for the effects of the four other independent variables. Looking at the significance values, you see that all five predictors are statistically significant, so you need to retain all five predictors. (Often researchers will remove predictors that are not statistically significant because they are not contributing to the equation.)

The first column of the Coefficients table contains a list of the independent variables plus the *constant* (the intercept where the regression line crosses the y-axis). The *intercept* is the value of the dependent variable when the independent variable is 0.

The B column shows you how a one-unit change in an independent variable affects the dependent variable after controlling for all other variables in the model. For example, for each additional year of education completed, the expected increase in current salary is $593.03. The Months Since Hire variable has a B coefficient of $154.54, so each additional month increases current salary by $154.54. The Previous Experience variable has a B coefficient of –$19.44, so each additional month decreases current salary by –$19.44.

The Gender variable has a B coefficient of about –$2,232.92. This means that a one-unit change in gender (moving from male to female, or being female) is associated with a drop in current salary of –$2,232.92. Finally, the Beginning Salary variable has a B coefficient of $1.72, so each additional dollar increases current salary by $1.72. This coefficient is similar but not identical to the coefficient found in the simple regression using beginning salary alone (1.9).

In the simple regression, the B coefficient for beginning salary was estimated ignoring any other effects, because none were included in the model. Here the effect of beginning salary was evaluated after controlling (statistically adjusting) education level, sex, previous work experience, and months on the job. If the independent variables are correlated, the change in the B coefficient from simple to multiple regression can be substantial.

The B column also contains the regression coefficients you would use in a prediction equation. In this example, current salary can be predicted with the following equation:

Current Salary = −12550 + (1.7)(Beginning Salary) + (154.5)(Months Hired) + (−19.4)(Previous Experience) + (593)(Years of Education) + (−2232.9) (Gender)

The Std. Error column contains standard errors of the regression coefficients. The standard errors can be used to create a 95 percent confidence interval around the B coefficients.

If you simply look at the B coefficients, you might think that gender is the most important variable. However, the magnitude of the B coefficient is influenced by the amount of variation of the independent variable. The Beta coefficients explicitly adjust for such variation differences in the independent variables. Linear regression takes into account which independent variables have more effect than others.

Betas are standardized regression coefficients and are used to judge the relative importance of each of the independent variables. The values range between −1 and +1, so that the larger the value, the greater the importance of the variable. (If any Betas are above 1 in absolute value, it suggests a problem with the data, potentially multicollinearity.) In the example, the most important predictor is beginning salary, followed by previous experience, and then education level.

Regarding assumptions, multicollinearity, which is the common problem, occurs when the independent variables in a regression model are highly intercorrelated. This happens often in market research when ratings on many attributes of a product are analyzed, or in economics when many economic measures are used in an equation. The more variables you have, the greater the likelihood of multicollinearity occurring, although in principle only two variables are necessary for multicollinearity to occur.

The problem of multicollinearity is easy to understand. When you interpret a variable's coefficient, you state what the effect of a variable is after *controlling for the other variables* in the equation. But if two or more variables vary together, you can't hold one constant while varying the others.

Multicollinearity in typical data is a matter of degree, not an absolute condition. All survey data, for example, will have some multicollinearity. The question to ask is, "When is there too much?" SPSS provides a number of indicators of multicol-linearity that are worthwhile to examine as standard checks in regression analysis.

You can begin your formal assessment of multicollinearity by examining the tolerance and VIF values in the Coefficients table. *Tolerance* is the proportion of variation in a predictor variable independent of any other predictor variables. Tolerance values will range from 0 to 1, where higher numbers are better. A toler-ance of .10 means that an independent variable shares 90 percent of its variance with the one or more of the other independent variables and is largely redundant.

VIF values indicate how much larger the standard errors are (how much less pre-cise the coefficient estimates are) due to correlation among the predictors. The VIF is equal to the inverse of the tolerance. It's a direct measure of the cost of multicollinearity in loss of precision, and is directly relevant when performing statistical tests and calculating confidence intervals. These values range from 1 to positive infinity. VIF values greater than the cutoff value of 5 indicate the possible presence of multicollinearity. In the example, you do not have a problem with multicollinearity.

TECHNICAL
STUFF

If multicollinearity is detected in your dataset, you should attempt to adjust for it because it will make your regression coefficients unstable. The two most common ways to fix multicollinearity are to exclude redundant variables or combine redun-dant variables.

The Casewise Diagnostics table (see Figure 20-21) lists cases that are more than three standard deviations (in error) from the regression fit line. Assuming a nor-mal distribution, errors of three standard deviations or more would happen less than 1 percent of the time by chance alone. In this data file, errors of three stan-dard deviations or more would be about five outliers (.01*474), so the nine cases you have does not seem too excessive.

Casewise Diagnostics[a]				
Case Number	Std. Residual	Current Salary	Predicted Value	Residual
18	6.179	$103,750	$57,961.66	45788.344
103	3.404	$97,000	$71,773.26	25226.738
106	3.794	$91,250	$63,138.14	28111.862
160	-3.121	$66,000	$89,128.03	-23128.030
205	-3.839	$66,750	$95,196.45	-28446.450
218	6.006	$80,000	$35,490.38	44509.621
274	5.042	$83,750	$46,384.08	37365.918
449	3.497	$70,000	$44,084.52	25915.478
454	3.829	$90,625	$62,249.47	28375.529
a. Dependent Variable: Current Salary				

FIGURE 20-21:
The Casewise
Diagnostics table.

Residuals should normally be balanced between positive and negative values; when they are not, investigate the data further. In this data, seven residuals are positive, indicating that some additional investigation is required. It seems that the model is not predicting as well for higher current salaries, so you could see if these observations have anything in common. Because their case numbers (an ID variable can be substituted) are known, you could find them easily in the dataset to look at them more closely.

You also do not want to see very large prediction errors, but here two residuals are very, very high, over six standard deviations above the fit line, which indicates instances where the regression equation is very far off the mark.

To test the assumptions of regression, turn to the histogram of residuals shown in Figure 20-22. The residuals should be approximately normally distributed, which is basically true for the histogram. Note the distribution of the residuals with a normal bell-shaped curve superimposed. The residuals are fairly normal, although they are a bit too concentrated in the center and are somewhat positively skewed. However, just as with ANOVA, larger sample sizes protect against moderate departures from normality.

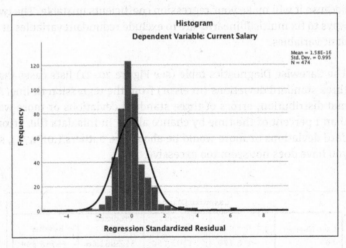

FIGURE 20-22:
The histogram of
residuals.

In the scatterplot of residuals shown in Figure 20-23, you hope to see a horizontally oriented blob of points with the residuals showing the same spread across different predicted values. Unfortunately, note the hint of a curving pattern: The residuals seem to slowly decrease, and then swing up at higher salaries. This type of pattern can mean the relationship is curvilinear.

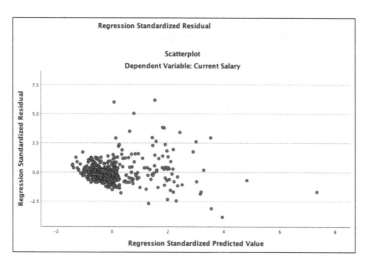

FIGURE 20-23:
The scatterplot of residuals.

Also, the spread of the residuals is much more pronounced at higher predicted salaries, which suggests lack of homogeneity of variance. Does this mean that the model you built is problematic? Not necessarily. But it does point out that you are doing a better job at predicting lower salaries, so you might trust the predictions of this model more for lowered salaried individuals. Alternatively, you can take this result and try to determine if you can use additional variables (for example, job category) to better understand higher salaried individuals and improve the model that way.

Viewing Relationships

You will use a scatterplot to visualize the relationship between the dependent variable and your predictions from the multiple linear regression model. Now that the unstandardized predicted value is in Data Editor, follow these steps to construct a scatterplot:

1. **Choose Graphs ⇨ Chart Builder.**

2. **In the Choose From list, select Scatter/Dot.**

3. **Select the second scatterplot diagram (the Simple Scatter with Fit Line tooltip), and drag it to the panel at the top.**

4. **In the Variables list, select Unstandardized Predicted Value and drag it to the rectangle labeled X-Axis in the diagram.**

5. In the Variables list, select Current Salary and drag it to the rectangle labeled Y-Axis in the diagram.

6. Click OK.

The chart in Figure 20-24 appears.

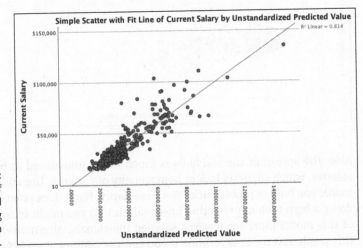

FIGURE 20-24:
The scatterplot of current and beginning salary with a regression line.

The line superimposed on the scatterplot is the best straight line that describes the relationship. This line is the linear regression equation you developed. In the scatterplot, many points fall near the line, but as you found in the regression output, more spread (less concentration of data points) exists for higher current salary values.

Chapter **21**

What Is Normal Anyway?

arametric tests — such as the t-tests, ANOVA, Pearson correlations, and linear regression — make several assumptions about the data. They typically assume that the variables have a normal distribution for continuous variables, and that the variance is equal within categories of a grouping or factor variable (homogeneity of variance). If these assumptions are violated, the results of the tests are in doubt. Starting with Chapter 16, we've been discussing how to check statistical assumptions, but we haven't provided a path forward if you fail to meet them.

Fortunately, there are alternatives. An entire family of various tests and methods called nonparametric statistics make fewer assumptions about the data. Nonparametric tests allow you to determine if relationships exist in the data when important distributional assumptions are not met.

In this chapter, we begin by introducing nonparametric tests. Then we discuss various distributions. Finally, you go through examples of running and interpreting both nonparametric independent and nonparametric related samples tests.

Understanding Nonparametric Tests

Nonparametric tests have the following characteristics:

>> Don't assume normality or homogeneity of variance.

>> Are generally less powerful than parametric tests, which means they have a lower chance of finding true differences.

>> Are most useful with questions using a short response scale of 3, 4, or 5 points. These scales are not truly interval in measurement.

>> Are useful also when variables have very skewed distributions or have very unusual distributions.

>> Are commonly used when the sample size is small.

>> Are more difficult to interpret than, say, means differences.

SPSS Statistics includes submenus to guide users through selecting the appropriate nonparametric test for a particular set of variables. You'll need to know whether the general situation is:

>> **One sample:** A dependent variable with no grouping variable

>> **Independent samples:** A dependent variable with a grouping (factor) variable

>> **Related samples:** Two (or more) dependent variables whose association you want to test (such as experiments with pre-test and post-test measurements)

REMEMBER

By default, nonparametric tests procedures use the defined level of measurement of the variables to determine how they will be used. It's critical that the measurement level be set correctly for each variable in the analysis.

TECHNICAL
STUFF

In this chapter, we address only basic inferential nonparametric tests. But in the add-on modules, it's possible to perform elaborate nonparametric statistical models, such as ordinal regression and categorical regression. Both techniques are discussed in our book, *SPSS Statistics for Data Analysis and Visualization* (Wiley).

Understanding Distributions

As mentioned in Chapter 15, the *distribution* of a variable refers to the frequency with which each outcome occurs. Many different statistical distributions are available, and the most common is the normal distribution. The *normal distribution* is a frequency distribution in which the mean, median, and mode coincide and is symmetrical, so that 50 percent of cases lie to either side of the mean. Figure 21-1 illustrates a normal distribution.

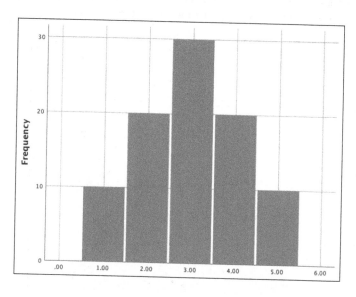

FIGURE 21-1:
A normal distribution.

Skewed or asymmetrical distributions are also common. Figure 21-2 shows a *positively skewed distribution*, which is characterized by having a much longer tail on the right side of the distribution. Positively skewed distributions are common in the social sciences. For example, income is often a positively skewed variable because many people have lower incomes while few individuals have high incomes.

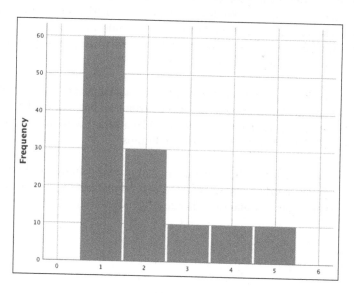

FIGURE 21-2:
A positively skewed distribution.

On the other hand, a *negatively skewed distribution* is characterized by having a much longer tail on the left side of the distribution, as shown in Figure 21-3. For example, age of onset for Alzheimer's is very rare among 40- and 50-year-olds and much more prevalent for those in their 80s or 90s.

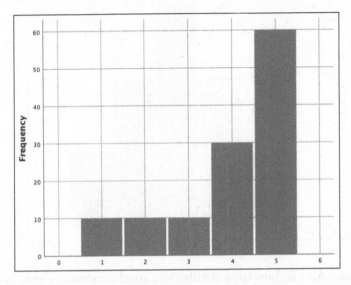

FIGURE 21-3:
A negatively skewed distribution.

Skewed distributions tend to have means that are affected by outlying scores, therefore it's appropriate to use tests based on medians because they provide a better measure of central tendency. *Bimodal distributions* have two modes — the most common category or value in the distribution. In the following example, values 1 and 5 are the modes (see Figure 21-4). The mean in this situation is not representative of the sample because it would be somewhere between the two modes. You tend to see bimodal distributions when people love or hate a product or have extreme positions on an issue.

REMEMBER

The mode is the most common value in a distribution. A normal distribution has only one mode, whereas a bimodal distribution has two modes. A popular metaphor is that a normal distribution is like a camel with one hump and a bimodal distribution is like a camel with two humps.

When you have distributions that are not normal, oftentimes researchers will turn to nonparametric tests. We present two nonparametric tests in this chapter: the Kruskal Wallis test and the Wilcoxon signed-rank test.

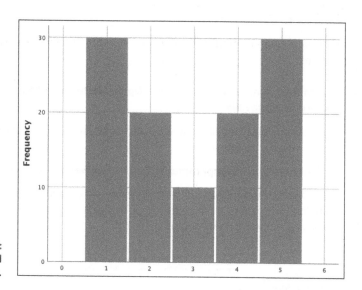

FIGURE 21-4:
A bimodal
distribution.

Running a Nonparametric Independent Samples Test

In previous chapters, when the dependent variable was continuous and you wanted to compare the means for either two groups or three or more groups, you used the independent-samples t-test and one-way ANOVA, respectively. Certain assumptions (normality, homogeneity of variances) had to be satisfied to use these procedures.

If the assumptions are violated, or if the variable is ordinal in nature, these tests can't be used and an alternative is needed. Nonparametric independent samples tests provide this alternative. The nonparametric independent samples procedure selects the appropriate test, depending on whether there are two groups or three or more groups. If there are more than two groups, you can run a post hoc analysis to determine which groups differ significantly, analogous to the post hoc pairwise comparisons in the one-way ANOVA procedure.

In this example, you use the GSS2012 Abbreviated.sav file. The objective is to see how one's political position (from liberal to conservative; the polviews variable) is related to age group. For example, are retired people more conservative than other age groups? The polviews variable is measured on a seven-point scale that is ordinal, not interval. Therefore, testing for differences by age group is best done with a nonparametric method.

To request a nonparametric test for two or more independent samples, follow these steps:

1. **From the main menu, choose File ⇨ Open ⇨ Data and load the GSS2012 Abbreviated.sav file.**

   You can download the file from the book's companion website at www.dummies.com/go/spss4e.

2. **Choose Analyze ⇨ Nonparametric Tests ⇨ Independent Samples.**

   The Objective tab appears, as shown in Figure 21-5, allowing you to specify whether you want to compare the shape of the distributions, compare the medians, or customize the analysis.

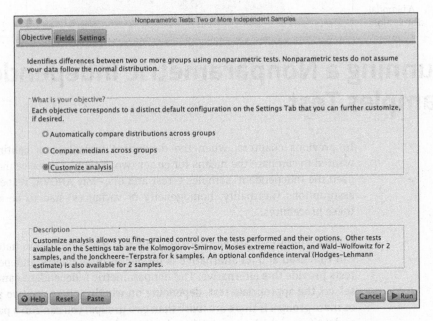

3. **Select Customize Analysis.**

   This choice allows you to control the tests performed and their options.

4. **Click the Fields tab.**

   On the Fields tab, you specify the dependent variable (Test Fields box) and the independent variable (Group box) that will be used in the analysis.

5. **Place the Think of Self as Liberal or Conservative variable in the Test Fields box.**

6. Place the Age of Respondent (Binned) variable in the Groups box, as shown in Figure 21-6.

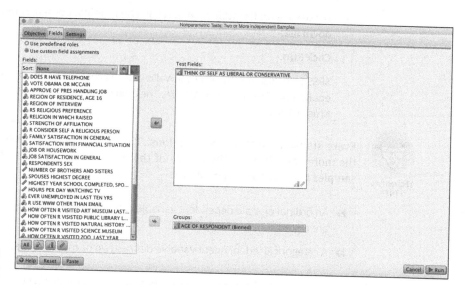

FIGURE 21-6:
The Fields tab.

7. Click the Settings tab.

On the Settings tab, shown in Figure 21-7, you specify the desired test and, if applicable, any multiple comparisons option.

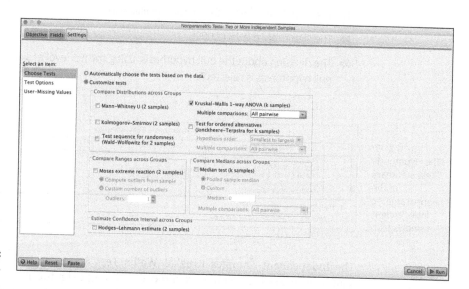

FIGURE 21-7:
The Settings tab.

8. Select **Customize Tests.**

9. Select **Kruskal-Wallis 1-Way ANOVA (k Samples).**

10. Make sure **All Pairwise** is selected in the **Multiple Comparisons** drop-down list.

11. Click **Run.**

SPSS Statistics runs the Kruskal-Wallis test, which is the nonparametric equivalent of the one-way ANOVA. The following figures are produced by the Kruskal-Wallis test.

Every statistical test has assumptions. The better you meet these assumptions, the more you can trust the results of the test. The nonparametric independent-samples test has two assumptions:

» An ordinal or scale dependent variable exists on which group differences are tested.

» A categorical independent variable defines two or more groups.

The output from the nonparametric independent samples test begins by displaying the Hypothesis Test Summary table shown in Figure 21-8, which provides the following:

» The null hypothesis being tested

» The specific test used (the Kruskal-Wallis test)

» The significance level (0.000)

» The decision about the null hypothesis, using the .05 level of significance (the null hypothesis is rejected)

FIGURE 21-8:
The Hypothesis Test Summary of the nonparametric independent samples test.

Hypothesis Test Summary				
	Null Hypothesis	Test	Sig.^{a,b}	Decision
1	The distribution of THINK OF SELF AS LIBERAL OR CONSERVATIVE is the same across categories of AGE OF RESPONDENT (Binned).	Independent-Samples Kruskal-Wallis Test	.000	Reject the null hypothesis.

a. The significance level is .050.
b. Asymptotic significance is displayed.

The Independent-Samples Kruskal-Wallis Test Summary table in Figure 21-9 shows the overall test statistics and corresponding significance level, which was also reported in the Hypothesis Test Summary table. The significance of the

Kruskal-Wallis test is .000. This test uses the ranks of cases on the dependent variable to determine whether differences exist between categories. You can conclude that significant differences exist.

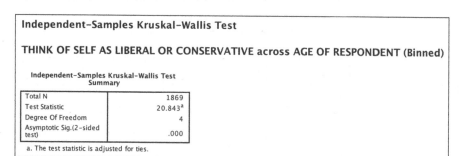

Independent-Samples Kruskal-Wallis Test

THINK OF SELF AS LIBERAL OR CONSERVATIVE across AGE OF RESPONDENT (Binned)

Independent-Samples Kruskal-Wallis Test
Summary

Total N	1869
Test Statistic	20.843[a]
Degree Of Freedom	4
Asymptotic Sig.(2-sided test)	.000

a. The test statistic is adjusted for ties.

FIGURE 21-9:
The Independent-Samples
Kruskal-Wallis
Test Summary.

The distribution of the dependent variable, broken down for each category of the grouping variable, is displayed using a boxplot (see Figure 21-10). The graph lists the average rank (the dark horizontal marks on the graph), which you can see is close to the value of 4 for each category. The rank is used because this is a nonparametric test, and data can be ranked without making many assumptions about the dependent variable. The main purpose of this graph is to give a sense of the distribution as well as to identify outliers, which are represented as circles.

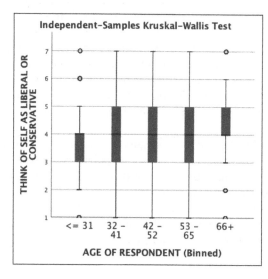

FIGURE 21-10:
The boxplot of
political views by
age group.

To decide which categories differ from others, you need to look at the Pairwise Comparisons table shown in Figure 21-11, which lists all pairwise comparisons (with no redundancies). You are making multiple comparisons (10 tests), so the tests are adjusted by using the Bonferroni correction (see Chapter 19).

Pairwise Comparisons of AGE OF RESPONDENT (Binned)					
Sample 1-Sample 2	Test Statistic	Std. Error	Std. Test Statistic	Sig.	Adj. Sig.[a]
<= 31-32 – 41	–86.364	38.104	–2.267	.023	.234
<= 31–42 – 52	–95.580	37.703	–2.535	.011	.112
<= 31–53 – 65	–137.207	36.847	–3.724	.000	.002
<= 31–66+	–159.201	38.842	–4.099	.000	.000
32 – 41–42 – 52	–9.215	38.540	–.239	.811	1.000
32 – 41–53 – 65	–50.842	37.702	–1.349	.177	1.000
32 – 41–66+	–72.837	39.654	–1.837	.066	.662
42 – 52–53 – 65	–41.627	37.297	–1.116	.264	1.000
42 – 52–66+	–63.622	39.269	–1.620	.105	1.000
53 – 65–66+	–21.994	38.447	–.572	.567	1.000

Each row tests the null hypothesis that the Sample 1 and Sample 2 distributions are the same.
Asymptotic significances (2-sided tests) are displayed. The significance level is .050.
a. Significance values have been adjusted by the Bonferroni correction for multiple tests.

FIGURE 21-11:
Pairwise
comparisons.

Many possible comparisons can be made, and here it was found that those 31 years or younger were significantly more liberal than those between the ages of 53 and 65. The group 31 years or younger was also significantly more liberal than those 66 years and older. No other pairs are significantly different.

The distance network graph shown in Figure 21-12 lists the average rank for each category of the grouping variable. In this graphical representation of the pairwise comparisons table, the distances between nodes in the network correspond to differences between samples. Purple lines correspond to statistically significant differences; blue lines correspond to non-significant differences.

The average rank for the under 31 category is 840.74. This rank is lower than the rank of any other category; lower values on polviews indicate more liberal attitudes. There are purple lines between the 31 years or younger group and the 53–65 group and the 66 years and older group.

The final two graphs show the distribution of the dependent variable (see Figure 21-13) and independent variable (see Figure 21-14).

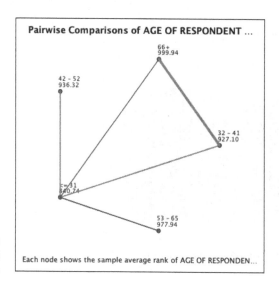

FIGURE 21-12:
The distance
network graph.

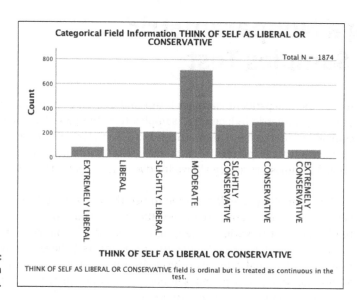

FIGURE 21-13:
The distribution
of political views.

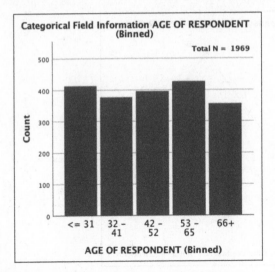

FIGURE 21-14:
The distribution
of age groups.

Running a Nonparametric Related Samples Test

Just as the independent-samples t-test and one-way ANOVA have their analog in the nonparametric independent samples test, the paired-samples t-test has its equivalent in the nonparametric related samples test. (Actually, the paired-samples t-test is performed with two paired variables, but the nonparametric related samples procedure allows for two or more paired variables.)

In this example, you will continue to use the GSS2012 Abbreviated.sav data file. Several questions were asked about the respondents' perception of government funds allocated to various areas, on a three-point scale from Too Little to Too Much. You want to see whether the respondents believe a difference exists in funding for national defense or the environment. These variables are measured on an ordinal scale, so a paired-sample t-test is not justified. You will use a test based on the median of the distribution.

To request a nonparametric test for two or more related samples, do the following:

1. **From the main menu, choose File ⇨ Open ⇨ Data and load the GSS2012 Abbreviated.sav file.**

You can download the file from www.dummies.com/go/spss4e.

2. **Choose Analyze ⇨ Nonparametric Tests ⇨ Related Samples.**

The Objective tab, shown in Figure 21-15, appears.

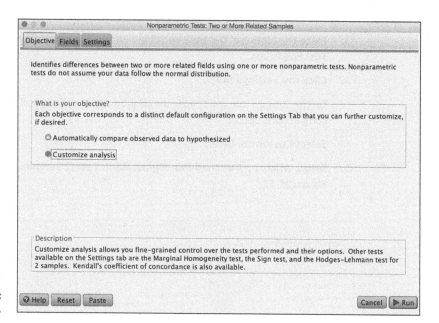

FIGURE 21-15:
The Objective tab.

3. **Select Customize Analysis.**

4. **Click the Fields tab.**

   On the Fields tab, shown in Figure 21-16, you specify the variables to use in the analysis.

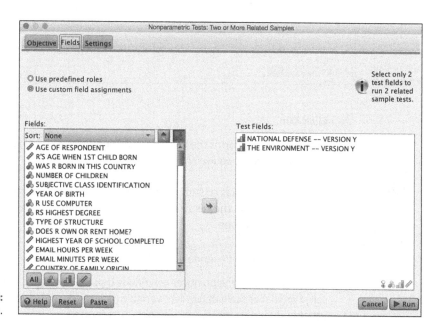

FIGURE 21-16:
The Fields tab.

5. **Place the National Defense variable and the Environment variable in the Test Fields box.**

6. **Click the Settings tab.**

   On the Settings tab, you specify the desired test and, if applicable, any multiple comparisons option.

7. **Select Customize tests.**

8. **Select Wilcoxon Matched-Pair Signed-Rank Test (2 Samples), as shown in Figure 21-17.**

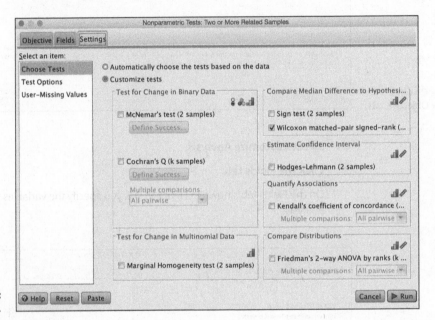

FIGURE 21-17: The Settings tab.

9. **Click Run.**

   SPSS Statistics performs the Wilcoxon matched-pair signed-rank test, which is the nonparametric equivalent of the paired samples t-test.

TECHNICAL STUFF

Every statistical test has assumptions. The better you meet these assumptions, the more you can trust the results of the test. The nonparametric related-samples test has two assumptions:

>> An ordinal or scale dependent variable exists.

>> The two or more time points or conditions that are compared are on the same ordinal or scale dependent variable (which means the dependent variable should be measured in a consistent format).

The output from the nonparametric related samples test begins by displaying the Hypothesis Test Summary table shown in Figure 21-18. The table describes the following:

>> The null hypothesis being tested

>> The specific test used (the Wilcoxon signed-rank test)

>> The significance level (0.000)

>> The decision about the null hypothesis, using the .05 level of significance (the null hypothesis is rejected)

Hypothesis Test Summary

	Null Hypothesis	Test	Sig. a,b	Decision
1	The median of differences between NATIONAL DEFENSE -- VERSION Y and THE ENVIRONMENT -- VERSION Y equals 0.	Related-Samples Wilcoxon Signed Rank Test	.000	Reject the null hypothesis.

a. The significance level is .050.
b. Asymptotic significance is displayed.

The Related-Samples Wilcoxon Signed Rank Test Summary table in Figure 21-19 shows the overall test statistics and corresponding significance level, which was also reported in the Hypothesis Test Summary table. You can see that the significance of the Wilcoxon signed-rank test is .000. This test uses the ranks of cases on the variables to determine whether differences between them exist. You can conclude that differences exists.

Related-Samples Wilcoxon Signed Rank Test

NATIONAL DEFENSE -- VERSION Y, THE ENVIRONMENT -- VERSION Y

Related-Samples Wilcoxon Signed Rank Test Summary	
Total N	898
Test Statistic	46052.000
Standard Error	4299.680
Standardized Test Statistic	-11.748
Asymptotic Sig.(2-sided test)	.000

The bar chart of differences in Figure 21-20 shows the distributions of the differences between these two variables, which varies from –2 to 2 because the variables are coded from 1 to 3.

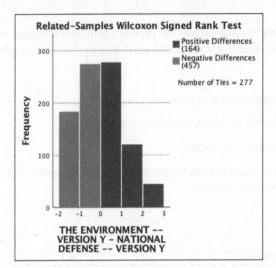

FIGURE 21-20:
The bar chart of
differences.

Clearly, more differences exist in one direction than another (the actual direction depends on how the variables are coded and the order of variables in the dialog). The number of positive and negative differences is used to calculate the test statistic. The output doesn't tell you which variable has a higher level of interest, which is why you'll view the frequency tables next.

The final two graphs show the distribution of the variables. You can see that respondents believe more is spent on national defense (see Figure 21-21) or conversely less is spent on the environment (see Figure 21-22).

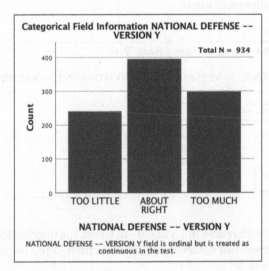

FIGURE 21-21:
The distribution
of national
defense.

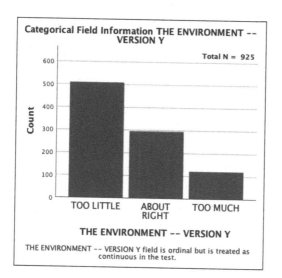

FIGURE 21-22:
The distribution of the environment.

This information now allows you to determine that, as you have seen, significant differences exist in the perception of respondents regarding government funding and respondents tend to believe that more was spent on national defense than on the environment.

These are just a few of the many nonparametric tests available in SPSS. Play around with different options to see what you can come up with. The general setup and interpretation will be similar.

This information now allows you to determine that, as you have seen, significant differences exist in the perception of respondents regarding government ranking and respondents tend to believe that more was spent on national defense than on the environment.

These are just a few of the many nonparametric tests available in SPSS. Play around with different options to see what you can come up with. The setup and interpretation will be similar.

Chapter **22**

When to Do What

The previous eight chapters cover a broad range of statistical techniques for exploring and summarizing data, as well as investigating and testing underlying relationships. You discover when to use several statistical techniques, the assumptions each method makes, how to set up the analysis, and how to interpret the results.

The goals of this chapter are twofold. First, we present a general flowchart for analyzing data to provide a larger context of where in the research process the statistical techniques presented in the previous chapters are typically used. Second, we briefly introduce you to additional, more advanced data analytic techniques that you can use to further investigate data analytical queries.

REMEMBER

SPSS has a vast array of statistical techniques. In this book, we have examples of only the statistical techniques available in SPSS base, but that doesn't define the limits of what SPSS can do. To more thoroughly help you find a technique that you might need, in this chapter we mention some techniques that do require an add-on module.

Determining Which Statistical Test to Perform

All research projects — whether analyzing a survey, evaluating programs, assessing marketing campaigns, conducting pharmaceutical research, and so on — begin by specifying the aims and objectives of the research. Research projects must begin with a set of well-defined objectives. As shown in the flowchart in Figure 22-1, you need to know which questions you're asking of the data, along with the level of measurement of the variables. These two characteristics determine the types of statistical analyses that you can perform.

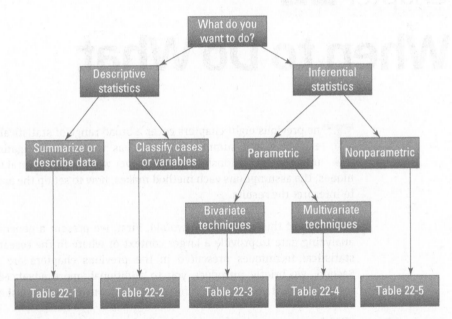

FIGURE 22-1: Taxonomy of statistical methods.

For example, are you simply describing data (see Chapter 14) or drawing some inference from the sample about the population (see Chapter 15). If you will be using inferential statistics, you also have to ask yourself if the data is normal (see Chapter 21).

Typically, most research projects begin by requesting descriptive statistics. Table 22-1 shows three common statistical techniques you can use to obtain descriptive statistics. Descriptive statistics do not require the calculation of probability values or statistical significance testing. Instead, the focus is on summarizing individual variables to help establish base rates, answer important questions (for example, the percent of satisfied customers), allow users to check sample size and the data for unusual cases or errors, and provide insights into ways in which you may combine different groups.

TABLE 22-1   ## Summarize or Describe Data

Statistical Technique	General Use	Covered
Frequencies	Provides statistics and graphical displays that are useful for describing many types of variables.	Chapter 14
Descriptives	Displays summary statistics for several variables in a single table and calculates z scores.	Chapter 14
Explore	Produces summary statistics and graphical displays, either for all of your cases or separately for groups of cases.	

Summaries of individual variables provide the basis for more complex analyses. Therefore, after conducting this initial step, researchers often create new variables from the original variables. For example, it's common to create total scores by combining various variables that measure the same general characteristic. Or researchers might create difference variables, whereby the difference between two time points is calculated.

Along this same vein, researchers might begin to use techniques associated with classifying variables or cases, as shown in Table 22-2. Here researchers can use a technique such as factor analysis to create new variables that simplify a set of variables by identifying a smaller number of underlying constructs. Or researchers can use cluster analysis, which is an exploratory data analysis technique designed to reveal natural groupings within a collection of data.

TABLE 22-2   ## Classify Cases or Variables

Statistical Technique	General Use
Factor	Used in data reduction to identify a small number of factors that explain most of the variance observed in a much larger number of variables.
Hierarchical cluster	Identifies homogeneous groups of cases, using an algorithm that starts with each case in a separate cluster and combines clusters until only one is left. This procedure works best with a relatively small number of cases.
K-means cluster	Identifies homogeneous groups of cases, using an algorithm that can handle large numbers of cases. However, the algorithm requires that you specify the number of clusters.
Two-step cluster	An exploratory tool designed to reveal natural groupings within a dataset that would otherwise not be apparent. This algorithm can handle large numbers of cases and assesses a range of possible solutions.

Having created the final versions of each variable and obtained summary statistics, at this point you would know if your dependent or outcome variables meet the assumptions for parametric tests (normality, homogeneity of variance, and so on). If you do not meet the assumptions or your dependent variables are nominal or ordinal, you'll need to perform nonparametric tests, as outlined in Table 22-3. We cover all these tests in various chapters in the book.

TABLE 22-3   ## Nonparametric Tests

Statistical Technique	General Use	Covered
Crosstabs	Uses counts and percentages to create two-way and multiway tables and provides a variety of tests and measures of association for the tables	Chapter 17
One sample	Compares the distribution of a categorical dependent variable to population norms	Chapter 16
Independent samples	Tests whether the means or medians for two or more different groups differ on a dependent variable	Chapter 21
Related samples	Tests whether the means or medians of the same group differ under two conditions or time points	Chapter 21

If your dependent variables are continuous and you do meet assumptions, you can perform parametric tests. Researchers will often begin by using bivariate techniques, which require only one dependent variable and one independent variable. Table 22-4 outlines these tests, most of which are covered in this book.

If, on the other hand, you have more than one independent variable, you can use some of the commonly used multivariate techniques outlined in Table 22-5.

Logistic regression and discriminant analysis are both nonparametric multivariate techniques since they use categorical dependent variables.

REMEMBER

TABLE 22-4 **Bivariate Techniques**

Statistical Technique	General Use	Covered
Means	Calculates subgroup means and related statistics for dependent variables within categories of one or more independent variables	
One-sample t-test	Tests whether the mean of a single variable differs from a specified value	Chapter 16
Independent-samples t-test	Tests whether the means for two different groups differ on a continuous dependent variable	Chapter 18
Summary independent-samples t-test	Uses summary statistics to test whether the means for two different groups differ on a continuous dependent variable	Chapter 18
Paired-samples t-test	Tests whether the means of the same group differ under two conditions or time points	Chapter 18
One-way ANOVA	Tests whether the means for two or more different groups differ on a continuous dependent variable	Chapter 20
Bivariate correlation	Used when you want to quantify the relationship between two continuous variables	Chapter 19

TABLE 22-5 **Multivariate Techniques**

Statistical Technique	General Use	Covered
Multiway ANOVA	An extension of one-way ANOVA where there is more than one independent variable	
MANOVA	An extension of one-way ANOVA where there is more than one dependent variable	
Repeated measures ANOVA	An extension of the paired-samples t-test where the same group is assessed under two or more conditions or time points.	
Linear regression	Used when you have a continuous dependent variable that is linearly related to one or more independent variables	Chapters 19 and 20
Binary logistic regression	Used in situations similar to linear regression, but the dependent variable is dichotomous	
Multinomial logistic regression	An extension of binary logistic regression where the dependent variable is not restricted to two categories	
Discriminant analysis	Builds a predictive model for group membership based on the linear combinations of predictors that best separate the groups	

Using Advanced Techniques

The preceding section outlines some of the most commonly used statistical procedures, which are used in a large percentage of data analytic projects. However, many other techniques are highly specialized and used in specific situations. Table 22-6 highlights some of the advanced techniques you can find in SPSS.

TABLE 22-6 **Advanced Techniques**

Statistical Technique	General Use
Simulation	A computerized mathematical technique that allows researchers to account for risk in data analysis and decision-making
Ordinal regression	Used when you are predicting an ordinal-level dependent variable from one or more independent variables
Categorical regression	Quantifies categorical data by assigning numerical values to the categories, resulting in an optimal linear regression equation for the transformed variables
Hierarchical linear modeling	Takes into account the hierarchical nature of data, such as when students are nested within classrooms or schools or both
Neural network	Data-mining technique developed for hard-to-predict situations that involve nonlinear relationships and interactions
Decision tree	Splits data into subgroups based on the relationship between predictors and the outcome variable, allowing you to create rules that describe a segment of the data in relation to the output

TIP

Visit Chapter 28 to learn more about some of the additional modules in SPSS.

Finally, for those of you who would like to learn more about some of the many advanced statistical options in SPSS, be sure to check out our book, *SPSS Statistics for Data Analysis and Visualization* (Wiley), which covers various advanced statistical procedures in detail!

7

Making SPSS
Your Own

IN THIS PART . . .

Make SPSS your own with customized features and appearance.

Learn all about graph editing and how to save your customizations for the future.

Discover how to edit tables and where to find TableLooks in SPSS.

Chapter **23**

Changing Settings

O ver time, you'll find that you want to configure your system to work in ways that are different from the defaults. SPSS has lots of options that you can set to do just that. If you're new to this and you've just started looking at the software, you probably don't want to change any options just yet, but you need some idea of the possibilities it offers. Later, when you absolutely, positively have to make some sort of change, you'll know where to go to do it.

With the Data Editor window on the screen, choose Edit⇨Options to display the Options window. You can set any and all possible options in this window. At the top of the window are some tabs; each tab contains a different collection of options. In this chapter, we walk you through changing these options.

REMEMBER

Sometimes a change in configuration has an immediate effect, and sometimes it doesn't. For example, if you change the way values are labeled in a report that's already onscreen, nothing happens because the report has already been constructed. You have to run the report-generating software again — so it builds a new report — to have the changes take effect.

TIP

If you're not familiar with the kinds of options that are available under Edit⇨ Options, check out some of the settings we frequently change:

» Modifying variable lists in dialogs to make it easier to find variables in large data files

» Changing the TableLook to meet presentation requirements (the APA TableLook is especially useful)

» Changing the chart templates to meet organizational requirements

» Removing decimals if they're unnecessary

» Adjusting a table's width when trying to fit it on the screen

General Options

The first tab in the Options window, the General tab (shown in Figure 23-1), displays options that don't fit into any of the other categories. The options displayed on the General tab are as follows:

» **Variable Lists:** Displays lists of variables in your output by label or by name. (Think of *names* as short titles and *labels* as long titles.) By default, your variables can be displayed in variable lists by name or label. Also, you can have your data appear in alphabetical order by the titles you use for individual items, or simply by the order in which the data appears in the file. File order usually makes more sense.

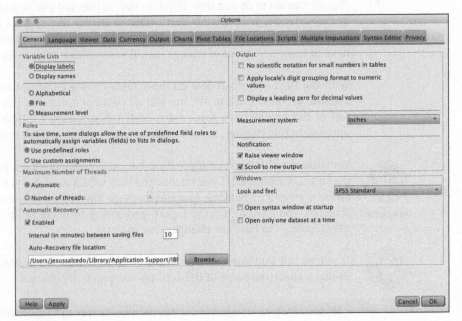

FIGURE 23-1:
The General tab.

>> **Roles:** For some actions, the Roles section determines whether variables that play certain roles in the procedure can be preselected for you when you select the first option, Use Predefined Roles. If you select the other option, Use Custom Assignments, you must choose all the variables.

>> **Maximum Number of Threads:** Controls the number of threads that procedures use when calculating results. Automatic uses all available processing cores. Number of Threads allows you to specify a lower value if you want to make more processing resources available to other applications.

>> **Automatic Recovery:** Controls computer failures and attempts to recover files.

>> **Output:** Controls the appearance of tables and graphs:

- **No Scientific Notation for Small Numbers:** Suppresses scientific notation for small numbers. For example, 12 appears as 12 instead of 1.2e1, which is a little harder to read. SPSS doesn't say exactly what it considers to be a small number.

- **Apply Locale's Digit Grouping Format to Numeric Values:** Applies the current locale's digit grouping format to numeric values in pivot tables and charts as well as in Data Editor.

- **Display a leading zero for decimal values:** Allows for a zero to appear before decimal values.

- **Measurement System:** Specifies the margins between table cells, the width of cells, and the spacing between printed characters. You can use inches, centimeters, or points. (A point is $\frac{1}{72}$ inch.)

>> **Notification:** Specifies the software method used to notify you when the results of a calculation are available. With the Raise Viewer Window option, the display window opens automatically. With the Scroll to New Output option, the window scrolls and exposes the location of the new data. The Notification section also allows you to receive notifications when updates are available.

>> **Windows:** Determines the appearance of SPSS dialogs. These options are cosmetic:

- **Look and Feel:** Controls the display of the SPSS user interface. Your choices are SPSS Standard, SPSS Classic, Windows, and Macintosh if you're using a Mac.

- **Open Syntax Window at Startup:** Displays the Syntax window instead of the Data Editor window when SPSS launches. Choose this option if you use the scripting language more often than the window interface to enter data and run your predefined procedures.

- **Open Only One Dataset at a Time:** Controls how many datasets can be opened at a time. With this option selected, an already opened dataset is closed when a new one is opened. By the way, this option does not apply to datasets opened inside a Syntax language process.

Language Options

The Language tab (shown in Figure 23-2) displays options for changing language and character encoding. The options displayed on the Language tab are as follows:

>> **Language:** Determines the language used for the user interface as well as output files. You have about a dozen choices. Note that you may have to use Unicode mode to handle all the characters in some languages.

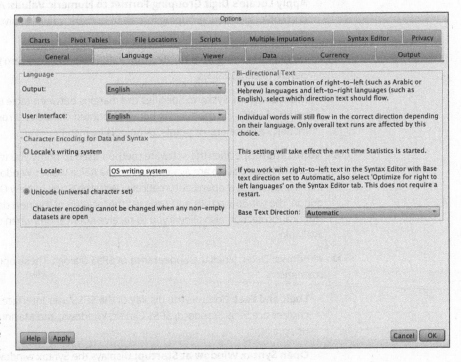

FIGURE 23-2:
The Language tab.

>> **Character Encoding for Data and Syntax:** Reads and writes files in Unicode or Locale (UTF-8 format) mode. The default is UTF-8 format. You shouldn't choose Unicode unless you have a good reason to do so (such as when you

TIP

receive data in multiple languages). If you write a Unicode file, you need to be sure that the software that reads it understands that format. When you read a file in Unicode mode, it's much larger in memory than it would be otherwise.

You can change character encoding only before you open a data file.

>> **Bi-Directional Text:** Selects which direction text should flow in the software. You can use left-to-right languages (such as English) or right-to-left languages (such as Arabic or Hebrew). Make sure to restart SPSS to see your selected changes.

Viewer Options

Output from SPSS is formatted for viewing with either the draft viewer or the regular viewer. SPSS thinks in terms of a printed page, but the same layouts are used for displaying data onscreen. The options you can set for the regular viewer can be accessed with the Viewer tab, shown in Figure 23-3. The options in the Viewer tab are as follows:

>> **Initial Output State:** Determines which items are displayed each time you run a procedure. You choose an item either by selecting its name (Log, Warnings, Notes, Title, and so on) from the drop-down list or by selecting its icon. Then you can select whether you want the item to appear or remain hidden, how you want its text justified (Align Left, Center, or Align Right), and whether the information occurrence should be included as part of the log (Display Commands in the Log).

>> **Title:** Chooses the font used for the main output title, which appears at the top of the first page of a report.

>> **Page Title:** Chooses the font used for the title appearing at the top of subsequent pages of a report.

>> **Text Output:** Determines the font used for the text of your report and the labels on graphs and tables. The font size also affects the page width and length because the sizes are measured by counting characters.

TIP

Some fonts have variable-width characters, which throws off the alignment of your columns. If you want everything to align in neat columns all the time, use the monospaced font.

>> **Default Page Setup:** Determines the default settings for the orientation and margins. You can choose Portrait or Landscape for the Orientation setting, as well as set your own margins.

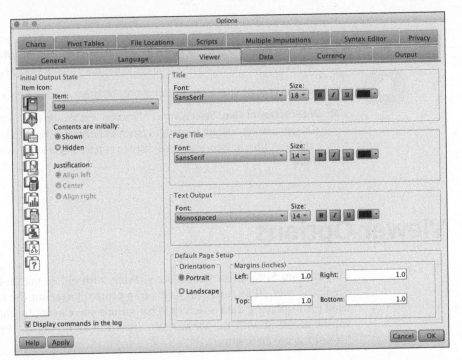

FIGURE 23-3:
The Viewer tab.

Data Options

You use the Data tab, shown in Figure 23-4, to specify how SPSS handles a few special numeric situations. The options in the Data tab are as follows:

>> **Transformation and Merge Options:** Determines when — not how — results are calculated. You can have SPSS perform calculations immediately, or you can have it wait until it needs the number for something (either another calculation or a displayed value).

>> **Display Format for New Numeric Variables:** Determines how many digits are used in the display of values and how many digits are to the right of the decimal. Width is the total number of characters, including the decimal point. The Decimal Places setting determines the number of digits that appear to the right of the decimal point. If the number of places to the right is too small, values are rounded to fit. If the number of places is too large, values are put in scientific notation.

>> **Random Number Generator:** Generates random numbers using one of two methods. Long period Mersenne Twister is considered the better option. But if you need to replicate your random values from older versions of SPSS, use the Compatible with SPSS 12 and Earlier option.

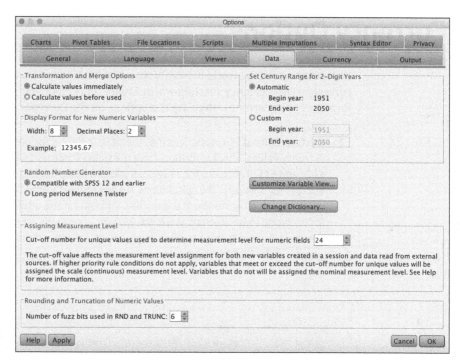

FIGURE 23-4:
The Data tab.

» **Set Century Range for 2-Digit Years:** Provides a solution to the Y2K problem. You thought that was all over, right? It is, but the solutions are still with us. You put in two four-digit years here, and any two-digit value that you supply to identify a year is assumed to be between the two years you specify. This option is mostly for old data. If you always use four digits for years in your data, you'll never need this setting.

» **Customize Variable View:** Determines which variable attributes are displayed and in what order in the Variable View tab of the Data Editor window.

» **Change Dictionary:** Determines which dictionary is used to check the spelling on the Variable View tab.

» **Assigning Measurement Level:** Determines the level of measurement for variables. When SPSS reads numeric data, it counts the number of unique values assigned to a variable and uses the count (24 is the default) to determine whether the variable is nominal or scalar.

» **Rounding and Truncation of Numeric Values:** Determines the threshold for rounding numbers. SPSS does the calculation in base two, so the count is a number of bits. *Fuzz bits* refers to a count of the number of bits to be considered. The setting is specified to 6 at install time, which should be sufficient for most applications.

Currency Options

Different parts of the world use different symbols and formats when writing about currency. The Currency tab (shown in Figure 23-5) lets you specify the display format of your currency. Here are the options on the Currency tab:

>> **Custom Output Formats:** Specifies the default format for presenting currency values. The five formats have the unlikely names CCA, CCB, CCC, CCD, and CCE. Those are the only ones you can have, but that has to be enough for anybody. The calculations are always performed the same way — the differences are in the display. You can set the display configuration for each one to be anything you'd like (dollars, euros, yen, and so on), and then switch among them as often as you want. To view a format's options, select it in the list.

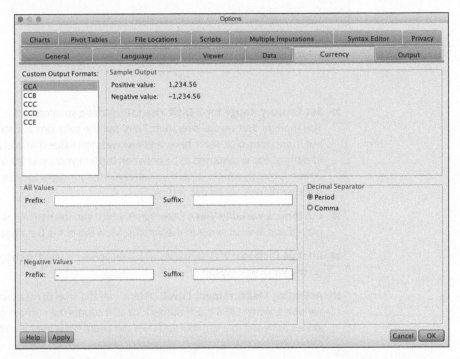

FIGURE 23-5:
The Currency tab.

>> **Sample Output:** Displays the printed format of positive and negative currency values. As you switch from one currency selection to another, and as you change the formatting of any of them, the sample displays examples of the format.

- **All Values:** Specifies the characters that appear onscreen to identify the currency, at the front or back of all values. Such characters include the British pound sign and the cent mark.

- **Decimal Separator:** Specifies the use of commas or periods to denote the fractional portion of an amount.

- **Negative Values:** Specifies the characters placed before and after negative values. For example, some folks like to use < and > to surround negative monetary values.

Output Options

Every variable can be identified in two ways: by a label and by a name. In your output, you can specify to have variables identified by one or the other or both. You configure output labeling on the Output tab, shown in Figure 23-6. Following are the options in the Output tab:

- **Outline Labeling:** Determines the text used to identify the parts of charts and graphs

- **One Click Descriptives:** Suppresses or limits the columns in a table's output

- **Output Display:** Determines whether the output is viewed using the Model Viewer or pivot tables and charts

- **Pivot Table Labeling:** Specifies the text used to identify the rows and columns of tables

- **Screen Reader Accessibility:** Changes the accessibility of rows and columns in the output

TIP

It can be useful to modify Pivot Table Labeling so that the results are presented using Labels, or Names, or Labels and Names, depending on your audience.

TIP

Longer labels can be descriptive and make your data easier to determine, but they can also screw up some formats.

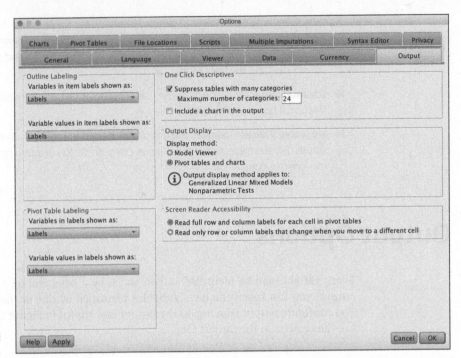

FIGURE 23-6:
The Output tab.

Chart Options

The default appearance of charts is determined by the settings on the Charts tab, shown in Figure 23-7. The options in the Charts tab are as follows:

>> **Chart Template:** Uses the settings in the default chart template or any specified chart template file when creating a new chart. You can select any file to be your default starting template. It's easy to create a chart template: Simply create a chart that has all the configuration settings you like — and save it so you can use it as the template file.

>> **Chart Aspect Ratio:** Changes the ratio of the width to the height of the produced charts, initially set to 1.25. Which ratio looks better is a matter of opinion; you'll have to experiment.

>> **Current Settings:** Controls two drop-down menus:

  • **Font:** Specifies the default font for the text in any chart you design.

- **Style Cycle Preference:** Determines the styles and colors when laying out data items in a chart. You can have SPSS cycle through only the colors so each item included in the graph is identified by only its color. If you're using a black-and-white printer or display, choose Cycle Through Patterns Only; each data item is identified by a graphic pattern of line styles and marker symbols.

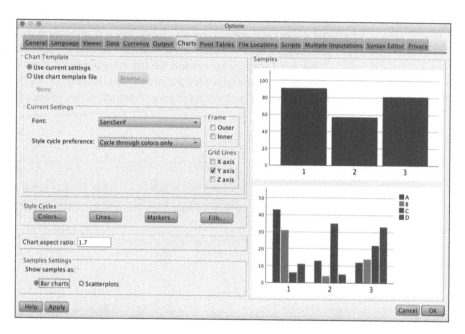

>> **Frame:** Determines whether charts display an inner frame, an outer frame, both, or neither.

>> **Grid Lines:** Displays dividing lines on the x, y, and/or z axes.

>> **Style Cycles:** Customizes the sequence of colors and patterns to be cycled through.

>> **Sample Settings:** Provides an example of how bar charts or scatterplots will look depending on the selected settings.

Pivot Tables Options

The tabular output format of SPSS is the *pivot table*. The Pivot Tables tab (shown in Figure 23-8) is used to set display options for the tables. The options on the Pivot Tables tab are as follows:

>> **TableLook:** Contains in a file your standard pivot table and determines the initial appearance of any new tables you create. Several such files come with the system and are listed in the dialog. You can also create your own file by choosing TableLook from the menu in the Pivot Table Editor window. The Set TableLook Directory button sets the currently displayed directory as the one in which your new table files are stored. You can choose any directory you like; clicking this button causes your chosen directory to appear in this window by default.

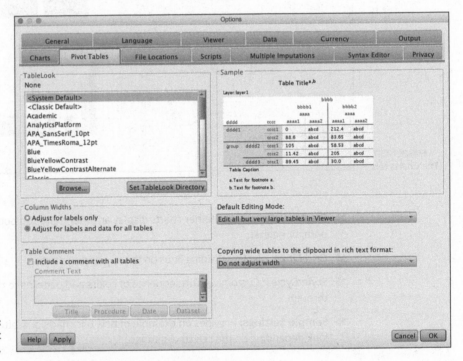

FIGURE 23-8:
The Pivot
Tables tab.

>> **Column Widths:** Controls the way SPSS adjusts column widths in pivot tables. You can adjust them according to the width of the labels or according to the width of the data and labels, whichever is wider.

>> **Table Comment:** Automatically includes comments for each table.

>> **Sample:** Shows an example of how each TableLook will render.

>> **Default Editing Mode:** Determines what happens when you double-click a pivot table. You can edit the table in an output window or a newly opened edit window.

>> **Copying Wide Tables to the Clipboard in Rich Text Format:** Determines what happens when a table copied to the Microsoft Word format or Rich Text Format is too wide for the document. The table is wrapped to fit, scaled to fit, or left as is.

File Locations Options

The options on the File Locations tab (shown in Figure 23-9) specify the locations of the files opened for input and output. The options for the file locations are as follows:

>> **Startup Folders for Open and Save Dialogs:** Determines the directories that initially appear in the Save and Open dialogs when you read or write data files. Optionally, you can select to simply use the last directory used to read or write a file.

TIP

If you're taking a class, reading this book, or generally have your files in one directory, specifying your startup folders can be a timesaver.

>> **Session Journal:** Configures a journal file to receive a copy of every Syntax language command, whether it comes from a script or a user entering instructions through a dialog.

>> **Temporary Folder:** Specifies the name of the directory where SPSS creates its temporary working files.

>> **Number of Recently Used Files to List:** Specifies how many of the most recently read or written files are listed in the File menu.

>> **Python Location:** Specifies the name of the directory where you have a version of Python installed. If you installed Python during the installation of SPSS Statistics 27, you don't need to worry about this option.

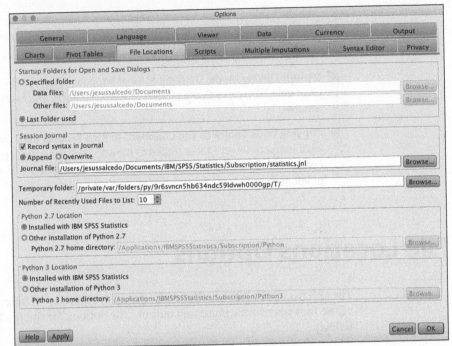

FIGURE 23-9:
The File
Locations tab.

Scripts Options

The Scripts tab (shown in Figure 23-10) is used to determine some fundamental defaults about scripts.

WARNING

Don't mess with any of these options until you've been writing scripts for a bit and know what you're doing — a single change here can affect the execution of a number of scripts.

Here are the options on the Scripts tab:

>> **Default Script Language:** Determines which script editor is launched when new scripts are created. The default script language is Basic. No other choice is available unless you have installed the Python add-on.

>> **Autoscripts:** Scripts are used to automate many functions, including customizing pivot tables.

• **Enable Autoscripting:** Enables the autoscripting feature.

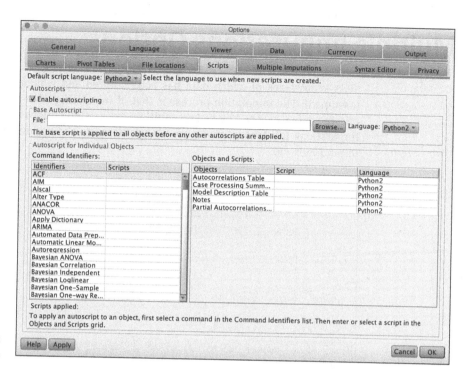

FIGURE 23-10:
The Scripts tab.

- **Base Autoscript:** Defines a global procedure that runs automatically when you create an object. It always runs before any other autoscript for that object. The choice of languages for it are Basic or Python (but only if the Python add-on is installed).

- **Autoscript for Individual Objects:** Associates a type of object with an autoscript to make an autoscript execute when an object of that specific type is created. To associate an autoscript with an object type, first select the command that generates an object of the desired type (these commands appear in the Identifiers column on the left). On the right, the Objects column displays the types of objects that your chosen identifier command will generate. In the script cell to the right of the object type you want to tag, enter the path name of the file containing the autoscript. Alternatively, you can click the ellipsis button that appears in the cell and browse for a script file. When you've chosen the file you want, click OK or Apply to make the association.

To delete an autoscript association, in the Script column on the right, select the name of the script file you want to disassociate, and then delete it. Select some other cell to make sure your deletion has been accepted, and then click OK or Apply.

Multiple Imputations Options

SPSS keeps track of which data has been entered and which has been *imputed* (assumed). The imputation process is that of calculating what the values of your missing data *would be.* You can set multiple imputation options using the Multiple Imputations tab (shown in Figure 23-11). Here are the options on the Multiple Imputations tab.

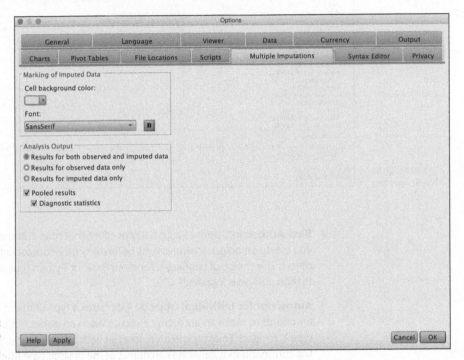

FIGURE 23-11:
The Multiple
Imputations tab.

>> **Marking of Imputed Data:** Changes the appearance of imputed data on the Data View tab of the Data Editor window. You can highlight the imputed data by changing the background color of the cell in which it's displayed and by using a different font to write its values.

>> **Analysis Output:** Performs analytical calculations using imputed data, without using it, or both ways. Also, you can set the imputation process to pool previously imputed data for further imputation. We suggest leaving this setting alone for now — it takes a mathematician to figure it all out. Some analysis procedures can produce separate analysis results using only imputed data — you can choose to generate output from such pooled data.

Syntax Editor Options

The editor of the Syntax Command language is capable of recognizing and highlighting various parts of the syntax language. The Syntax Editor tab (shown in Figure 23-12) has the following options:

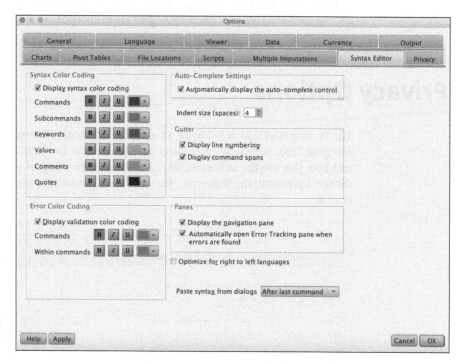

FIGURE 23-12:
The Syntax
Editor tab.

>> **Syntax Color Coding:** Specifies different colors for commands, subcommands, keywords, values, and even comments. You can also specify each one as bold, italic, or underlined. A single switch turns on all coloring and highlighting.

>> **Error Color Coding:** Specifies the font style and color coding of error information. A single switch turns on all coloring and highlighting.

>> **Auto-Complete Settings:** Suppresses or allows the display, in the Syntax Editor window, of the option button that turns auto-complete on or off.

>> **Indent Size (Spaces):** Specifies the number of spaces in an indent.

>> **Gutter:** Determines what appears in the *gutter,* which is the space to the left of the commands. You can use the gutter to display the line numbers or the span of a command (the beginning and ending of a single command).

» **Panes:** Displays or hides the navigation pane, which contains a list of all Syntax commands, and determines whether the error-tracking pane automatically appears when SPSS encounters an error.

» **Optimize for Right to Left Languages:** Manages languages that reads right to left (such as Hebrew or Arabic).

» **Paste Syntax from Dialogs:** Specifies the position at which syntax is inserted in the Syntax window when pasting syntax from a dialog.

Privacy Options

The Privacy tab (shown in Figure 23-13) improves your SPSS experience. Here you can give SPSS permission to collect information on the program's performance and how you use the software. You can also control whether you want to receive content updates in the Welcome dialog box and to automatically send error reports to IBM.

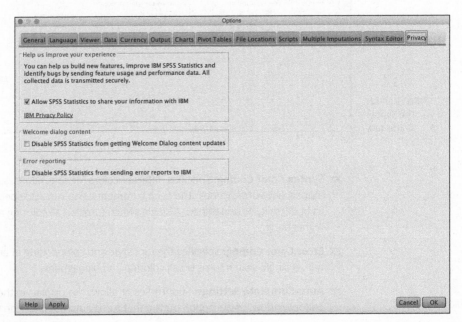

FIGURE 23-13:
The Privacy tab.

Chapter **24**

Editing Charts and Chart Templates

In Chapter 13, you see how to make simple graphs and fancy graphs. This chapter explains how to edit those graphs to create a better visual representation of the information in the chart. This chapter also helps you learn how to showcase the most important information to your audience.

Although this chapter doesn't cover every type of edit you can make to a chart, you can use the steps here as a baseline to explore additional editing options. When you get the basic idea of how to edit graphs using Chart Builder, you can continue to explore making edits on your own.

Chart Editor provides an easy-to-use environment for customizing charts and exploring data. You can quickly select and edit parts of a chart using toolbar menus, context menus, and toolbar options, and you can enter text directly into a chart.

To use Chart Editor, you select the element you want to modify and then use the Properties dialog to change the properties for the selected element. The tabs you see in the Properties dialog are based on your current selection, so they change depending on what you've selected.

TIP

Chart Editor works in a drill-down fashion, so you might need to click a specific element multiple times to arrive at the element level you want to modify.

Changing and Editing Axes

An *axis* on a chart or graph acts as a reference that gives information on how variables are related. In this section, we explain how to edit an axis to help better represent the information in a graph.

Changing the axis range

In Chapter 13, you create a differenced area graph that has empty space between the bottom of the graph and where the information begins along the y-axis. (Refer to Chapter 13 if you need to re-create the graph.) In the following steps, you edit the y-axis so that the range of the axis begins at 50:

1. **In the SPSS Statistics Viewer window, navigate to the differenced area graph and double-click the chart.**

   The Chart Editor window appears (see Figure 24-1).

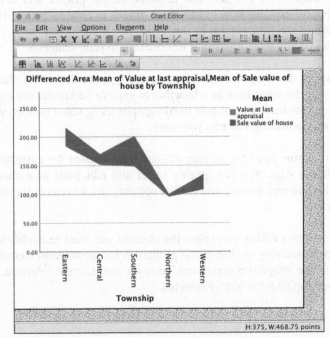

FIGURE 24-1:
The Chart Editor window.

2. **Click the Y button at the top of the menu bar.**

   The Properties dialog appears.

3. **Click the Scale tab (see Figure 24-2).**

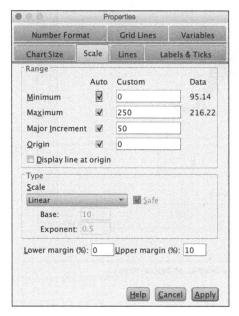

FIGURE 24-2:
The Scale tab of
the Properties
dialog.

4. **In the Range section, deselect the Auto check box next to Minimum, and change the number in the Custom box to 50.**

5. **Click Apply.**

   The chart in Figure 24-3 appears. As you can see, the y-axis has changed to eliminate unnecessary space in the graph.

Editing graphs like this allows you to create clearer graphs and improve how the information is visualized.

Scaling the axis range

No plot is simpler to produce than the *dot plot* because it has only one dimension. Although SPSS does an excellent job of grouping information, it doesn't create a visually scaled chart like the one we presented in Chapter 13 and reproduced in Figure 24-4. (Refer to Chapter 13 if you need to re-create the graph.)

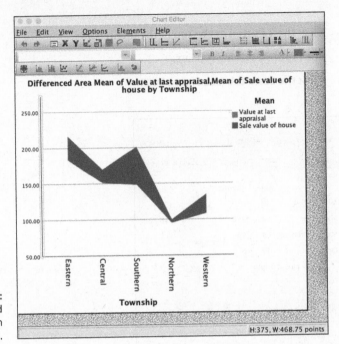

FIGURE 24-3:
The differenced area graph with the edited y-axis.

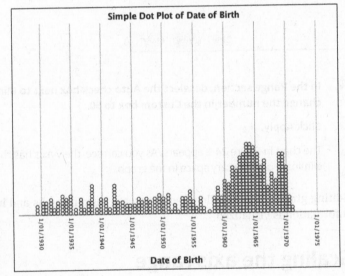

FIGURE 24-4:
A dot plot showing the relative number of people born in each year.

Without scaling, your chart may fail to convey your information with the effect that you want. For example, when you built the dot plot in Chapter 13, the information was scrunched, with too much white space at the top of the graph.

To be able to make this chart more readable, follow these steps to change how SPSS scales the graph:

1. **In the SPSS Statistics Viewer window, navigate to the dot plot and double-click the chart.**

   The Chart Editor window appears.

2. **Double-click the graph.**

   The Properties dialog appears.

3. **Click the Chart Size tab (see Figure 24-5).**

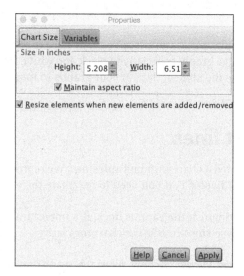

4. **Deselect the Maintain Aspect Ratio check box and change the Height to 2.5.**

5. **Click Apply.**

   The chart shown in Figure 24-6 appears.

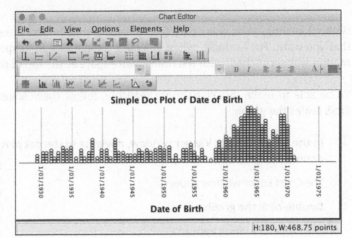

FIGURE 24-6:
A dot plot
showing the
relative numbers
of persons born
in each year with
an edited axis.

Changing Style: Lines and Symbols

When creating line graphs and scatterplots, it can be hard to differentiate between lines and data points on a graph, especially in black and white. In this section, you discover how to change the style of data in your graphs to make it easier to visualize the information.

Editing chart lines

In Chapter 13, you created a chart with multiple lines. We reproduced that chart in Figure 24-7. (Refer to Chapter 13 if you need to re-create the chart.)

To help the viewer distinguish the various lines, it's important to modify the way they appear. Follow these steps to edit the chart for clarity:

1. **In the SPSS Statistics Viewer window, navigate to and double-click the multiple line chart.**

The Chart Editor window appears.

2. **Double-click one of the lines in the graph.**

Make sure that only one line is selected. The Properties dialog appears.

3. **Click the Lines tab.**

4. **In the Style drop-down list (see Figure 24-8), choose a new line style.**

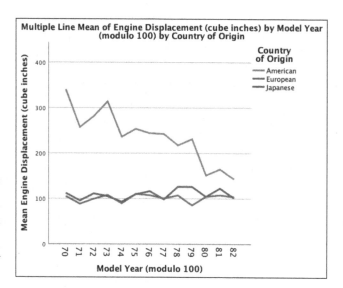

FIGURE 24-7:
A line graph charting engine displacement against model year according to the country of origin.

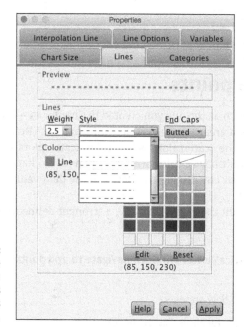

FIGURE 24-8:
The Style drop-down list in the Properties window's Lines tab.

5. **Click Apply.**

The style you chose is applied to the line.

6. **Repeat the process for the other lines.**

When you finish, a line chart similar to Figure 24-9 will appear.

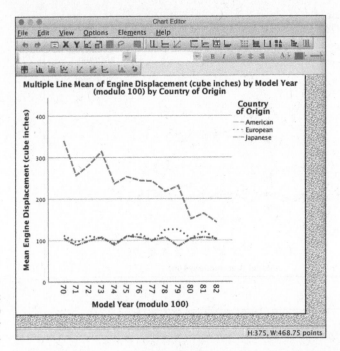

FIGURE 24-9:
A line chart with
the edited line
style.

Editing data points

Colored scatterplots such as the one you created in Chapter 13 — and shown again in Figure 24-10 — are a great way to visualize information. (Refer to Chapter 13 if you need to re-create the scatterplot.) When color scatterplots are not an option (for example, if you don't have a color printer), you need to change the style of the data points so the viewer can distinguish between the data values.

Follow these steps to edit the chart and allow a stronger delineation between data values in a chart:

1. **In the SPSS Statistics Viewer window, navigate to and double-click the scatterplot.**

   The Chart Editor window appears.

2. **Double-click one of the circles in the graph.**

   Make sure that only one set of data is selected. The Properties dialog appears.

3. **Click the Marker tab.**

4. **In the Type drop-down list, choose a new marker type (see Figure 24-11).**

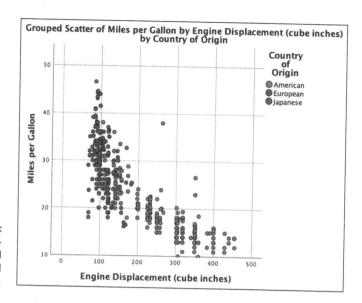

FIGURE 24-10:
A two-
dimensional
colored
scatterplot.

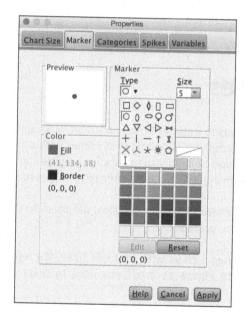

FIGURE 24-11:
The Type
drop-down list in
the Properties
window's
Marker tab.

5. **Click Apply.**

   The style you selected is applied to the graph.

6. **Repeat the process for the other values.**

   When you've finished, the chart will appear similar to Figure 24-12.

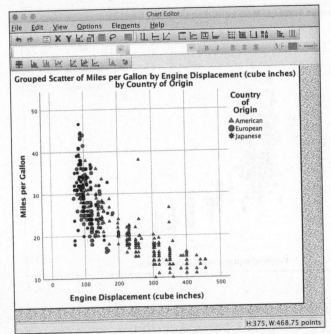

FIGURE 24-12:
A scatterplot with the edited data point style.

Applying Templates

Templates are a great way to improve how your graph looks and feels. To save you from having to create templates yourself, SPSS comes with a set of templates for charts and graphs that you can apply to make your graphic stand out. In this section, you find out how to apply these templates to your graph.

TIP

You can also create your own templates and then use them so that you can have a standard look for all your graphs.

In Chapter 13, you created a chart with multiple lines. We reproduced the chart in this chapter; refer to Figure 24-7. (If you need to re-create the chart, see Chapter 13.)

In the following steps, you apply a grayscale template to change the look of a chart:

1. **In the SPSS Statistics Viewer window, navigate to and double-click the line chart.**

The Chart Editor window appears.

2. **Choose File ➪ Apply Chart Template.**

The Apply Template dialog appears.

3. **Click APA_Styles.sgt.**

4. **Click Open.**

The chart shown in Figure 24-13 appears.

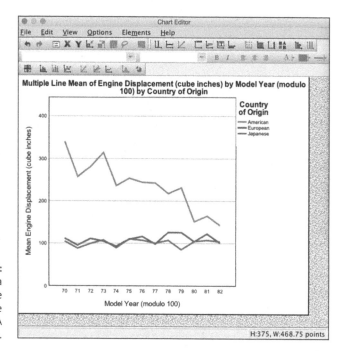

You've modified this chart by applying a template with a different style than the SPSS default. As mentioned, SPSS comes with a variety of templates that you can apply to any graph. You can also create your own templates, which is handy if, for example, you want to standardize the look of all graphs in your organization.

TIP

To change the default chart template in SPSS, specify the template you want to use in the Edit ➪ Options menu on the Chart Options tab.

IN THIS CHAPTER

» Changing the appearance of tables
with TableLooks

» Using the Style Output feature to
highlight certain cells in your output

» Transforming tables using pivoting
trays

Chapter **25**

Editing Tables

S PSS pivot tables are pretty cool. In fact, in 1997, two years after they came out, SPSS pivot tables were added to the Smithsonian Institutes Permanent Research Collection of Information Technology. Virtually all SPSS tabular output comes in the form of a pivot table. It isn't the product of a special menu. FREQUENCIES tables, DESCRIPTIVES tables, and just about every other command make them.

In this chapter, you discover how to edit pivot tables. Many more options than we can cover in this one short chapter are available, but we get you off to a good start. The menus that we describe have many additional options, which we suggest you explore.

SPSS pivot tables are comprised of objects and elements that can be rearranged and edited using Pivot Table Editor. You can *pivot* the table (change rows to columns and columns to rows, or move individual elements, such as a variable or a set of statistics); change cell properties such as fonts, colors, and data alignment in individual cells; and change table properties associated with areas of the table, such as border lines and style. Changing the layout of the table does not affect the results.

You can edit pivot tables also by modifying cell properties or table properties or both. You use cell properties to edit specific cells or multiple cells, such as a table column. You can adjust attributes such as number format, font, and background color. You use table properties to edit designated areas of a table. For example, you can change a table's appearance by adding a border and background color and changing the format of an entire area.

Working with TableLooks

If users find a table difficult to read, they may not understand the information it contains. The look and feel of your tables are a critical part of providing clear, concise, and meaningful results. The TableLooks feature allows you to customize the look and feel of the tables you create.

TableLooks are templates with predefined layouts, fonts, margins, styles, and so on that you can apply to any pivot table. Although you can change the format of a table after you've created it, changing the default TableLook is often more efficient, especially if you have several tables that should have the same style.

By default, SPSS uses a system default TableLook. You can also choose from one of the several predefined TableLooks or create a customized TableLook.

In this section, you create a similar table three times, applying various TableLooks and edits. The goal is to focus on editing, not on creating the table. The table itself is pretty standard. Follow these steps:

1. **Open the cars.sav file.**

    The file is not in the SPSS installation directory. You have to download it at www.dummies.com/go/spss4e.

2. **Choose Analyze ⇨ Descriptive Statistics ⇨ Crosstabs.**

3. **Choose Number of Cylinders as the Row and Country of Origin as the Column, as shown in Figure 25-1.**

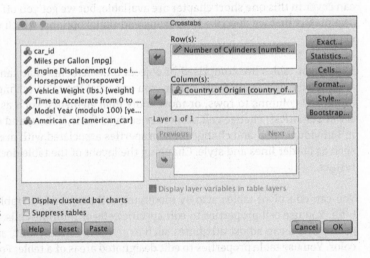

FIGURE 25-1:
The Crosstabs dialog after selection.

4. Click the Cells button.

The Crosstabs: Cell Display dialog appears.

5. In the Counts section, deselect the Observed check box; in the Percentages section, select the Row check box (see Figure 25-2).

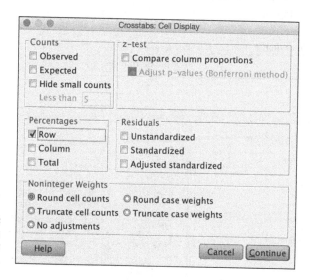

FIGURE 25-2:
The Crosstabs:
Cell Display
dialog.

6. Click Continue.

7. Click OK.

A crosstabulation table of number of cylinders and country of origin is created.

8. Right-click the crosstabulation table of Number of Cylinders and Country of Origin, and choose Edit Content ⇨ In Separate Window, as shown in Figure 25-3.

You're in editing mode and ready to go.

TIP

When working on a pivot table, such as this crosstabulation table, you can enter editing mode also by double-clicking anywhere in the table. The same editing features are available, but editing happens in the main Output Viewer window, not a new Pivot Table Editor window.

9. Choose Format ⇨ TableLooks.

The TableLooks dialog appears, as shown in Figure 25-4.

WARNING

If you can't find the TableLooks option, make sure you're looking in the menu for the new window you've opened. Data Editor, Output Viewer, Syntax Editor, and Pivot Table Editor windows have slightly different menu choices.

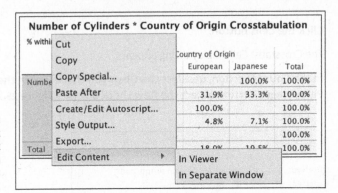

FIGURE 25-3:
The context
menu that
appears when
you right-click a
pivot table.

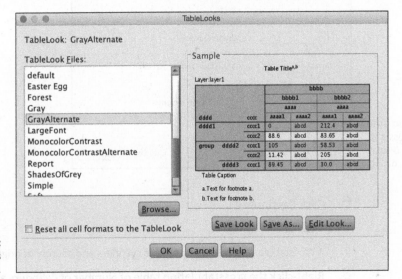

FIGURE 25-4:
The TableLooks
dialog.

10. From the TableLook Files list, select GrayAlternate.

You can try other choices. Note that when you make a selection in the left column, a sample appears on the right.

11. Click OK.

You've now changed the TableLook and the result appears in the Pivot Table Editor window, as shown in Figure 25-5. When you close the editing window, the changes are saved automatically and will now appear as part of your output window.

Editing tables is difficult and tedious, which is why we love the Custom Tables module. You can use the module to create a table exactly the way you want, so you don't have to edit it.

TIP

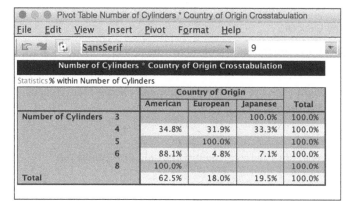

Number of Cylinders * Country of Origin Crosstabulation

Statistics % within Number of Cylinders

		Country of Origin			
		American	European	Japanese	Total
Number of Cylinders	3			100.0%	100.0%
	4	34.8%	31.9%	33.3%	100.0%
	5		100.0%		100.0%
	6	88.1%	4.8%	7.1%	100.0%
	8	100.0%			100.0%
Total		62.5%	18.0%	19.5%	100.0%

FIGURE 25-5:
The crosstab table with a new appearance.

Style Output

The Style Output feature is powerful. You can specify the changes to various aspects of a pivot table, such as titles, fonts, and order. In this example, you specify conditions for automatically changing properties of the pivot table. The following example shows how to highlight certain cells in your output and leave the rest unchanged.

TIP

Menus in SPSS are sticky, meaning they stay the same unless you click the Reset button in a dialog. So, if you're working through this section immediately after the preceding section, you have already completed most of these steps and will just need to run the crosstab procedure to create the table; then you can start editing.

1. **Open the cars.sav file.**

   If necessary, download the file at www.dummies.com/go/spss4e.

2. **Choose Analyze ⇨ Descriptive Statistics ⇨ Crosstabs.**

3. **Choose Number of Cylinders as the Row and Country of Origin as the Column.**

   Refer to Figure 25-1.

4. **Click the Cells button.**

   The Crosstabs: Cell Display dialog appears.

5. **In the Counts section, deselect the Observed check box; in the Percentages section, select the Row check box (refer to Figure 25-2).**

6. **Click Continue.**

7. Click OK.

The crosstabulation table between number of cylinders and country of origin is created.

8. Right-click the resulting output and choose Style Output, as shown in Figure 25-6.

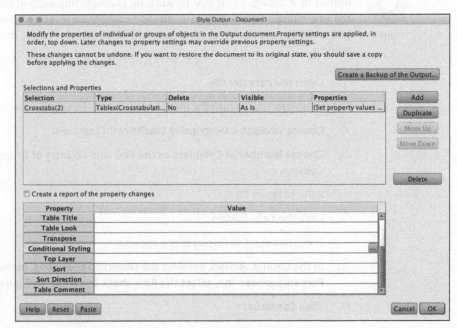

Number of Cylinders * Country of Origin Crosstabulation

% within	Cut		ountry of Origin		
	Copy		European	Japanese	Total
	Copy Special...			100.0%	100.0%
Number	Paste After		31.9%	33.3%	100.0%
	Create/Edit Autoscript...		100.0%		100.0%
	Style Output...		4.8%	7.1%	100.0%
	Export...				100.0%
Total	Edit Content ▶		18.0%	19.5%	100.0%

FIGURE 25-6:
Accessing the
Style Output
option.

9. When the dialog appears, click Continue.

10. Scroll down to the Conditional Styling row (see Figure 25-7) and click the small square button with three dots.

Style Output - Document1

Modify the properties of individual or groups of objects in the Output document.Property settings are applied, in order, top down. Later changes to property settings may override previous property settings.

These changes cannot be undone. If you want to restore the document to its original state, you should save a copy before applying the changes.

Create a Backup of the Output...

Selections and Properties

Selection	Type	Delete	Visible	Properties	
Crosstabs(2)	Tables(Crosstabulati...	No	As Is	(Set property values ...	Add
					Duplicate
					Move Up
					Move Down
					Delete

☐ Create a report of the property changes

Property	Value
Table Title	
Table Look	
Transpose	
Conditional Styling	...
Top Layer	
Sort	
Sort Direction	
Table Comment	

Help   Reset   Paste   Cancel   OK

FIGURE 25-7:
The Style Output
main dialog.

11. **In the Table Style dialog (see Figure 25-8), choose Percent in the Value column, and then click OK.**

This dialog has a lot of interesting options, but the defaults are pretty good. Because the chart is all percentages, we chose Percent. The default is to highlight above 50 percent, and that works well for this example.

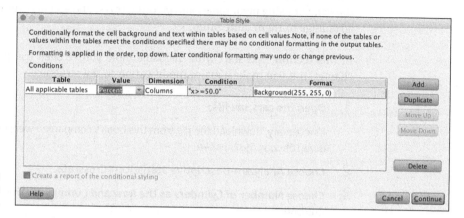

FIGURE 25-8:
The Table Style
dialog.

12. **Click Continue.**

TIP

Instead of applying a style to your pivot table after it has been created, you could click the Style button in the Crosstabs dialog (refer to Figure 25-1) to achieve the same result.

13. **Click OK.**

The chart now highlights the percent above 50 percent, as shown in Figure 25-9.

Number of Cylinders * Country of Origin Crosstabulation

% within Number of Cylinders

		Country of Origin			
		American	European	Japanese	Total
Number of Cylinders	3			100.0%	100.0%
	4	34.8%	31.9%	33.3%	100.0%
	5		100.0%		100.0%
	6	88.1%	4.8%	7.1%	100.0%
	8	100.0%			100.0%
Total		62.5%	18.0%	19.5%	100.0%

FIGURE 25-9:
The table with
highlighted
percentages.

Pivoting Trays

Pivot tables allow you to rearrange your output in all kinds of ways. For example, you can transpose rows and columns (flip the table) or adjust the order of data in a table. One of the first features added to SPSS pivot tables was the pivoting tray, which allows you to move data between columns, rows, and layers. After you get the hang of using pivot tables and pivoting trays, and you may find yourself taking advantage of them quite often.

In this section, you start with the same table you've been using throughout the chapter, but you make a major modification to the structure:

1. **Open the cars.sav file.**

   If necessary, download the file from this book's companion website at www.dummies.com/go/spss4e.

2. **Choose Analyze ⇨ Descriptive Statistics ⇨ Crosstabs.**

3. **Choose Number of Cylinders as the Row and Country of Origin as the Column.**

   Refer to Figure 25-1.

4. **Click the Cells button.**

   The Crosstabs: Cell Display dialog appears.

5. **In the Percentages section, select the Row and Column check boxes; in the Counts section, select the Observed check box.**

   Note that you're selecting the Observed check box, not deselecting it as in the other sections.

6. **Click Continue.**

7. **Click OK.**

   The result is a larger and more detailed table, as shown in Figure 25-10.

8. **Right-click the pivot table and choose Edit Content ⇨ In a Separate Window.**

9. **Choose the Pivot menu, and then select the Pivoting Trays option.**

   The Pivoting Trays dialog visualizes each data element in the table, as shown in Figure 25-11:

   • The Column area at the top of the pivoting tray contains Country of Origin, which is displayed in the column dimension in the table.

Number of Cylinders * Country of Origin Crosstabulation						
			Country of Origin			
			American	European	Japanese	Total
Number of Cylinders	3	Count	0	0	4	4
		% within Number of Cylinders	0.0%	0.0%	100.0%	100.0%
		% within Country of Origin	0.0%	0.0%	5.1%	1.0%
	4	Count	72	66	69	207
		% within Number of Cylinders	34.8%	31.9%	33.3%	100.0%
		% within Country of Origin	28.5%	90.4%	87.3%	51.1%
	5	Count	0	3	0	3
		% within Number of Cylinders	0.0%	100.0%	0.0%	100.0%
		% within Country of Origin	0.0%	4.1%	0.0%	0.7%
	6	Count	74	4	6	84
		% within Number of Cylinders	88.1%	4.8%	7.1%	100.0%
		% within Country of Origin	29.2%	5.5%	7.6%	20.7%
	8	Count	107	0	0	107
		% within Number of Cylinders	100.0%	0.0%	0.0%	100.0%
		% within Country of Origin	42.3%	0.0%	0.0%	26.4%
Total		Count	253	73	79	405
		% within Number of Cylinders	62.5%	18.0%	19.5%	100.0%
		% within Country of Origin	100.0%	100.0%	100.0%	100.0%

FIGURE 25-10: The crosstab table with three statistics.

- The Row area at the left contains the elements displayed across the rows of the table, in this case Number of Cylinders and Statistics.

- The Layer area in the Pivoting Trays window is shown in the upper left of the pivoting tray (empty here).

TIP

Layers can be useful for large tables with nested categories of information. By creating layers, you simplify the look of the table, making it easier to read. Layers work best when the table has at least three variables.

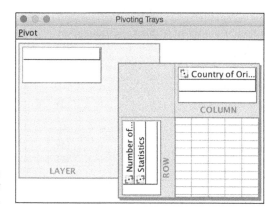

FIGURE 25-11: The pivoting tray as it first appears.

CHAPTER 25 **Editing Tables** 391

10. Click the Statistics label in the Pivoting Tray and drag it to a new position in the Layer area, as shown in Figure 25-12.

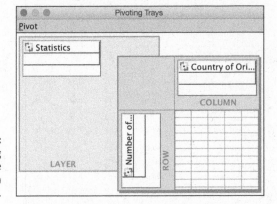

FIGURE 25-12:
The pivoting tray appearance after making a modification.

11. Close the Pivoting Trays window.

12. Click the new Statistics menu directly on the pivot table, as shown in Figure 25-13.

The three versions are stacked like a small stack of paper. You can choose whichever layer you want to display.

TIP

You can also print all layers of a table. This features comes in handy, for example, if you want to show your boss or coworker all three versions. You can print to paper or to a PDF file.

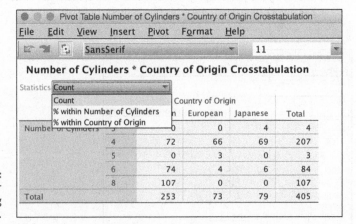

FIGURE 25-13:
Choosing a layer in the Pivoting Trays window.

8

Programming SPSS with Command Syntax

Chapter **26**

Getting Acquainted with Syntax

You've probably encountered folks who perform statistical calculations and build statistical models by coding in R and Python, two open-source languages. Well, SPSS has a programming language, and for decades this language was the only way to work in SPSS.

Frankly, you might be glad that you can work in menus because they provide a lot of help. However, almost everything that happens in SPSS is the result of Syntax running behind the scenes. For example, when you use a dialog to specify a set of options and then click OK, Syntax commands are generated and executed. In fact, you've already seen examples of Syntax at the top of the SPSS Statistics Viewer window every time a command runs.

If you take a look at the Help menu, you will find the Command Syntax Reference, which is a real door stopper at more than 2,000 pages. (Don't try reading that until you read this chapter and the next one.) This chapter describes some Syntax language fundamentals and explains why Syntax is helpful. The next chapter gets into more of the details on using Syntax.

TECHNICAL
STUFF

You can use R and Python in SPSS. Through a set of features called programmability, you can customize SPSS so that you can add almost anything to SPSS, including the capability to program in R and Python.

Why use Syntax? First, it's a lot easier than you might think, but no tip or trick in SPSS is worthwhile unless it improves your results or makes your life easier. Syntax may both improve your results and make your life easier. Second, Syntax might be a better option than menus in the following four situations:

>> Pasting

>> Performing repetitive calculations

>> Labeling

>> Requesting repetitive output

In this chapter, you explore how to use Syntax in these situations through the use of a simple web survey as a case study. Many researchers check survey results daily, as new data arrives. Here you'll see how to deal with daily routines like this more efficiently.

Pasting

Here's the secret to learning Syntax, but this is a secret you can tell all your friends: *You usually don't have to type anything.* This also means you usually don't have to look up commands.

How can this be? It all looks so complicated at first. The secret is the Paste button. Almost every dialog in SPSS has a Paste button that writes Syntax code for you. You just have to save the code for the next time you need it.

REMEMBER

The Paste button translates mouse clicks into code.

A super-easy example is recoding variables, such as the example demonstrated in Chapter 8. (Refer to Chapter 8 for the specifics on how to recode variables.) In this example, we created a new attending variable using the existing response variable, as shown in Figure 26-1.

The following steps create the recoded values and store them in a new variable:

1. **From the main menu, choose File ⇨ Open ⇨ Data and load the rsvp.sav file.**

   This file can be downloaded from the book's companion website at www. dummies.com/go/spss.

2. **Choose Transform ⇨ Recode into Different Variables.**

3. In the left panel, move the `response` **variable, which holds the values you want to change, to the center panel.**

4. In the Output Variable area, enter a name (attending) and label (Attending or not) **for the new variable.**

5. Click the Change button.

The output variable is defined, as shown in Figure 26-1.

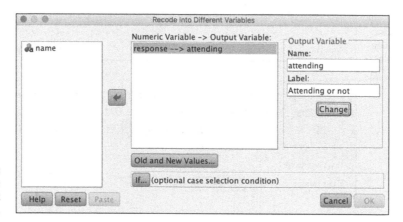

FIGURE 26-1:
The Recode
into Different
Variables dialog.

6. Click the Old and New Values button.

7. Define the recoding:

  a. In the Old Value text box, enter an existing value.

  b. In the New Value text box, enter the new recoded value.

  c. Click the Add button for the Old ⇨ New list (see Figure 26-2).

We created the `attending` variable by assigning a new value of 1 to all the scores of 1 on the `response` variable, and assigning a value of 0 to all the scores of 0 and –1, as shown in Figure 26-2.

8. Click Continue.

9. Click Paste.

Normally you would click OK to run the command. Now, however, you click the Paste button in the bottom left of the dialog. *Voilà!* — the result shown in Figure 26-3 appears in the Syntax editor window.

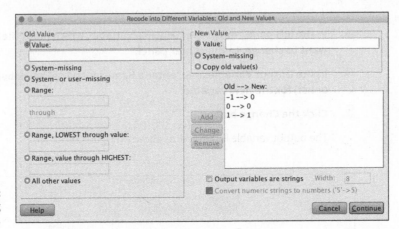

FIGURE 26-2:
Recoding
variables.

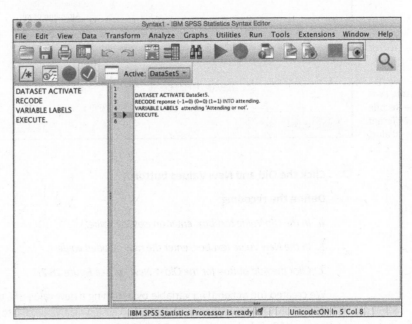

FIGURE 26-3:
The Syntax Editor
window.

When you click OK in the Recode into Different Variables dialog, the recode command is run automatically behind the scenes. Working with Syntax, you construct the recode command in the Syntax Editor window and then run the command from there. But in both cases, the same recode command is run.

REMEMBER

Most commands are available from the dialogs. However, some commands and options are available only by using the command language, which is another motivation to learn Syntax.

Whenever you want to run Syntax, you can simply choose Run⇨All from the Syntax Editor window, or you can highlight just a portion of Syntax and choose Data⇨Select. It's that simple.

Now, there's more to Syntax than that. We have an entire second chapter on Syntax (and entire books are dedicated to it), but that's about all you need to know about pasting.

WARNING

Make sure you don't confuse the Paste button with the Ctrl+V operation in SPSS Statistics and Microsoft Excel. The Paste button doesn't perform a copy and paste; it generates Syntax code for you. However, after the code is in the Syntax window, you'll frequently reuse and repurpose that code by copying and pasting it.

TECHNICAL STUFF

The EXECUTE command (refer to Figure 26-3) looks so official that you'd probably guess that you need it. The truth is, you usually don't. In this case, we need it because nothing generates output after EXECUTE. If you had any kind of table- or graph-generating command after EXECUTE — and you almost always do — you could (and should) delete it. More on this in the next chapter.

Performing a Series of Related Compute Statements

Here's what makes pasting so powerful. After you have pasted the Syntax code, you can easily modify it and reuse it. With practice, doing so is faster than the using the menus for many tasks.

Consider the following line of code you just pasted:

```
RECODE Sat1 (4 thru 5=1) (ELSE=0) INTO HighSat1.
```

Now assume that you want to do this calculation for all five variables (Sat1 through Sat5), as follows:

```
RECODE Sat1 (4 thru 5=1) (ELSE=0) INTO HighSat1.
RECODE Sat2 (4 thru 5=1) (ELSE=0) INTO HighSat2.
RECODE Sat3 (4 thru 5=1) (ELSE=0) INTO HighSat3.
RECODE Sat4 (4 thru 5=1) (ELSE=0) INTO HighSat4.
RECODE Sat5 (4 thru 5=1) (ELSE=0) INTO HighSat5.
```

Using a copy-and-paste maneuver in the Syntax window and changing the number in the original and new names is easier than using the Recode dialog five times.

Labeling

Adding variable and value labels in Data Editor can be time consuming because it involves clicking in many cells. However, typing Syntax commands in the Syntax editor is easy. For example, open the Syntax window, and enter the following commands:

```
VARIABLE LABELS
Sat1 "Product Selection"
Sat2 "Pricing"
Sat3 "Product Quality"
Sat4 "Website"
Sat5 "Customer Service".
VALUE LABELS Sat1 TO Sat5
1 'Very Dissatisfied'
2 'Dissatisfied'
3 'Neither Satisfied nor Dissatisfied'
4 'Satisfied'
5 'Very Satisfied'.
```

Using Syntax to create variable and value labels is considerably faster, especially if you use this data repeatedly. And because you can save your Syntax, your coworkers will love it because they can borrow your code.

Repeatedly Generating the Same Report

Imagine that every morning your boss wants a quick rundown on the web survey activity that's taken place since the previous report. She's busy, so she wants it organized as follows:

>> At the top, she wants to know which aspects of the business people are the most happy with.

>> She wants to read comments left by survey takers, but she doesn't want blank comments getting in the way.

>> She wants the comments from happy folks at the beginning.

In other words, your boss wants a Descriptive Statistics report like the one in Figure 26-4 and another report like the one in Figure 26-5.

FIGURE 26-4:
Satisfaction
variables
reported in order
of satisfaction.

Descriptive Statistics

	N	Minimum	Maximum	Mean
Product Selection	10	1	5	4.50
Customer Service	9	1	5	4.44
Product Quality	9	1	5	4.22
Pricing	10	1	5	4.20
Website	9	1	5	4.11
Valid N (listwise)	9			

FIGURE 26-4:
Satisfaction
variables
reported in order
of satisfaction.

Report[a]

			Name	Comment	Mean_Sat
Any_Ones	.00	1	Ann	None	5.00
		2	Erin	Your company is great!	5.00
		3	Frank	I did not receive my order yet.	5.00
		4	Irisa	I've noticed a decline since last year.	4.60
		5	Bob	Not at this time	4.40
		Total N	5	5	5
	1.00	1	Cara	Good products, but confusing website.	4.00
		2	Hank	You guys have a great product.	1.00
		Total N	2	2	2
	Total	N	7	7	7

a. Limited to first 100 cases.

FIGURE 26-5:
A Case
Summaries
showing only
cases with
comments and
sorted.

The following code produces both reports. Just choose Run ⇨ All from the Syntax window.

To take a closer look at the syntax, choose File ⇨ Open ⇨ Data and load the Web Survey2.sav file. Then choose File ⇨ Open ⇨ Syntax and load the Web Survey.sps file. These files can be downloaded from the book's companion website at www.dummies.com/go/spss.

```
DESCRIPTIVES VARIABLES=Sat1 Sat2 Sat3 Sat4 Sat5
/STATISTICS=MEAN MIN MAX
/SORT=MEAN (D).
SORT CASES BY Mean_Sat(D).
TEMPORARY.
SELECT IF length >0.
```

```
SUMMARIZE
/TABLES=Name Comment Mean_Sat BY Any_Ones
/FORMAT=VALIDLIST NOCASENUM TOTAL LIMIT=100
/TITLE='Case Summaries'
/MISSING=VARIABLE
/CELLS=COUNT.
```

At first glance, it may look like you would need a substantial amount of knowledge to put together this code. However, the DESCRIPTIVES command can be pasted as described at the beginning of the chapter. The same is true with SORT and SUMMARIZE. The SUMMARIZE command is found under Analyze ⇨ Reports ⇨ Case Summaries. We typed the other commands, TEMPORARY and SELECT. For more on both commands as well as typing commands in the Syntax window, see the next chapter.

The main point for now is that SPSS will do 80 percent of the typing for you if you use the dialogs. Just remember to use the Paste button to save your work. After you've tested the code, and you know that it works, save the whole thing so you can reuse it at any time.

IN THIS CHAPTER

» Understanding the fundamental
form of Syntax commands

» Controlling the flow of execution
through a program

» Finding some useful commands and
keywords

Chapter **27**

Adding Syntax to Your Toolkit

I n Chapter 26, you see how Syntax can save you time (by avoiding repetitive steps and clearly documenting exactly what you've done for others) and how getting started is pretty easy. When you incorporate Syntax into your routine, you'll want to start expanding your use of Syntax — as long as doing so continues to save you time and effort.

Some Syntax commands can't be pasted from the menus by using the Paste button. And others are easier to type than to paste using the menus. But before you can start typing Syntax, you need to learn a bit more about the grammar and the rules of Syntax, so that is where we begin.

REMEMBER

You can always use the menus for a while before you master Syntax. There's an old saying: "When you're ready, your teacher will appear." So, when you're ready, Syntax — and this chapter — will be waiting for you.

Your Wish Is My Command

A single Syntax language instruction can be simple and on a single line or complex and on multiple lines. A single instruction consists of a command followed by arguments to modify or expand the actions of the command. For example, the following Syntax command generates a report:

```
REPORT /FORMAT=LIST /VARIABLES=MPG.
```

The first thing you probably noticed is that the command is written in all upper-case. That's tradition — not a requirement. You can write in lowercase (or even mixed case) if you want. The old-school way of writing Syntax, dating back to when everything was typed, is to write commands in uppercase and variable names in lowercase. The Syntax window's auto-complete function writes commands in uppercase. Note, too, that the end of the list of arguments is terminated by a single period; the terminator must be there or else SPSS will complain.

Now, about those forward slashes and equal signs: Sometimes you need them, and sometimes they're optional. Always use them and you won't have any trouble. The presence of slashes and equal signs reduces ambiguity for both you and SPSS.

Also, commands can be abbreviated as long as you have at least three letters that uniquely identify the command. Abbreviating commands was a popular strategy when everything was typed, but we can't think of a single reason to abbreviate anything now, especially with the auto-complete feature. Figuring out how to abbreviate a command correctly, using the abbreviations that SPSS will recognize, is more work than just using the entire command, and abbreviations make the program harder for humans to read later.

The command in this example is REPORT, which causes text to be written to SPSS Statistics Viewer. In fact, all output produced by running Syntax programs goes to SPSS Statistics Viewer. The FORMAT specification tells REPORT to make a list of the values. The VARIABLES specification tells REPORT which variables are to be included in the list.

Commands can begin anywhere on a line and continue for as many lines as necessary. That's why SPSS is so persnickety about that terminator (the period) — the period is the primary way SPSS has of detecting the end of a command. If you forget that all-important period, SPSS may think that the additional lines belong to an earlier command.

Table 27-1 lists all the command types and the colors in Syntax Editor. If the syntax turns bright red, it's a bad sign. What you want is for the command to turn blue. Subcommands will be green, and all remaining keywords will be maroon.

Subcommands are optional ways of modifying your command usually placed directly after the slashes. If you choose to leave them out, you get the default settings of the command. *Keyword* is a general term for all the special words in Syntax; we discuss them briefly in the next section. All the stuff that is unique to your program, such as your dataset's variables, will be plain old black text.

TABLE 27-1

Color Coding in the Syntax Editor

Syntax Command Type	Color in the Syntax Editor
Command	Blue
Subcommand	Green
Keyword	Maroon
Other (including variable names)	Black
Error	Red

Understanding Keywords

A *keyword* is simply a word in the Syntax language. All commands in Syntax are keywords. The color-coding in the Syntax window helps you to know if a word has been correctly interpreted by SPSS. For instance, a misspelled keyword won't change color because the misspelling can't be interpreted properly by SPSS. The variable names you define are not keywords, but SPSS can tell which is which by the way you use them. That is, you can name one of your variables the same name as one of the keywords, and SPSS can tell what you mean by how you use the word. Usually.

The names of commands, subcommands, and functions are all keywords — and there are lots of them — but they aren't reserved and you can use them freely. *Reserved* words are a subset of keywords that cannot be used as variable names. For example, you could have variables named format and report, and you could use the following Syntax command to display a list of their values:

```
REPORT /FORMAT=LIST /VARIABLES=REPORT FORMAT.
```

However, using variables names such as report and format is risky, so you want to avoid variable names that could be confused with keywords. Even if you don't confuse SPSS, you might confuse yourself and other users of your program. The safest rule is to avoid words that SPSS could confuse with keywords.

REMEMBER

When a Syntax program executes, the commands will be run on the currently active dataset and uses that dataset's variable names and values. This situation can get confusing when you have more than one dataset open. If SPSS claims that there is no variable with that name, make sure that the correct dataset is active. You can read more about designating the active dataset in Chapter 30.

Declaring Data

You can define variables and their values right in the Syntax window. You might wonder why you would choose this method for loading data. Why not just have a data file? Explicitly listing a bit of data is a great way to ask for advice and to prototype calculations. You can send the DATA LIST command with just a few rows of data when you ask a colleague for help. (Sending both data and commands to others with DATA LIST is still popular in the SPSSX-L community, one of the online resources discussed in Chapter 29.) Just copy and paste the code right into an email along with your question and the code that you're trying to fix.

REMEMBER

Excel doesn't store metadata, so every time you open the file, you need to provide the metadata. That process is tedious the second time you have to do it, and becomes frustrating the third time. If you get new Excel data on a regular basis, prioritize learning how to declare metadata with Syntax.

To do so, create a DATA LIST, which defines the variable names, and follow that opening line of code with the list of values between BEGIN DATA and END DATA commands. The following example creates three variables (ID, SEX, and AGE) and fills them with four instances of data:

```
DATA LIST / ID 1-3 SEX 5 (A) AGE 7-8.
BEGIN DATA.
001 m 28
002 f 29
003 f 41
004 m 32
END DATA.
PRINT / ID SEX AGE.
EXECUTE.
```

The DATA LIST command defines the variables. The first variable is ID. Its values are in the input stream in columns 1 through 3; therefore it's defined as being three digits long. ID has no type definition, so it defaults to numeric. The second variable is named SEX. SEX is one character long, and its values are in column 5 of the input. Its type is declared as alpha (A), so it's declared as a one-character string. The third variable, AGE, is two digits long, is a numeric value, and has its values in columns 7 and 8 of the input.

The BEGIN DATA command comes immediately after the DATA LIST command and marks the beginning of the lines of data — each line is a case. DATA LIST is a bit reminiscent of the old days of loading data using punched cards. The fundamental design of SPSS is that old.

When this list of commands is executed, a normal SPSS window appears, showing a dataset with the variable names and values. You can do all your processing this way, if you prefer. But you don't have to do it by column numbers. You can enter the data in a comma-separated list, as follows:

```
DATA LIST LIST (",")/ ID SEX AGE.
BEGIN DATA.
1,1,28
2,2,29
3,2,41
4,1,32
END DATA.
PRINT / ID SEX AGE.
EXECUTE.
```

These days, the primary motivation for combining DATA LIST with a handful of commands is to provide a quick example to document your work. We don't recommend that you use DATA LIST to analyze anything larger than a trivially sized dataset.

END DATA must begin in the first column of a command line. It's the only command in Syntax that has this requirement.

WARNING

Commenting Your Way to Clarity

You can insert descriptive text, called a *comment,* into your program. This text doesn't do anything except help clarify how the program works when you read (or somebody else reads) your code. You start a comment the same way you start any other command: on its own line. You can use the COMMENT keyword or an asterisk. The comment is terminated by a period. Here's an example:

Separated into two sentences because you don't start "any other command" using the COMMENT keyword.

```
COMMENT This is a comment and will not be executed.
```

An asterisk can be used with the same result, which is the way everyone really does it:

```
* This is a comment placed here for the purpose of
describing what is going on, and it continues until
it is terminated.
```

You can also put comments on the same line as a command by surrounding them with /∗ and ∗/. A comment like this can be inserted anywhere inside the command where you'd normally put a blank. For example, you could put a comment at the end of a command line like this:

```
REPORT /FORMAT=LIST /VARIABLES=AGE /* The comment */.
```

REMEMBER

The command is terminated with a period, but the period comes after the comment because the comment is part of the statement. If you forget, the next line will get swallowed up into the comment and ignored. The following line will not be color-coded correctly either, which may help you catch your mistake. Watch out.

Running Your Code

Commands are executed one at a time, starting from the top of the program. The order is important. You must create a variable before you can use it in a command. For the most part, the order is intuitive; you don't have to think too much about what exists and what doesn't as long as the Syntax is written in a thoughtful sequence.

Some statements don't execute right away. Instead, they're stored for later execution, which makes SPSS run faster. Most people don't know how EXECUTE really works, but this normally doesn't matter because the statements will be executed when their result is needed. You, however, should be aware of the behavior of EXECUTE because the command can cause surprises in some circumstances if you don't understand its subtleties. For example, the PRINT command has a delayed execution:

```
PRINT / ALL.
```

The PRINT command prints the complete list of values for every case in your dataset. It will print all the values, or by naming variables it can be instructed to print values of only the ones you choose. However, the PRINT command isn't executed right away. SPSS stores the instruction for later. Commands like this are called *transformations*. As you might guess, all the commands in the Transform menu, such as COMPUTE, COUNT, and RECODE, are transformations.

When your program comes to a command that executes immediately, the stored commands are executed first. That works fine as long as there's another statement to be executed, but if the PRINT statement is the last one in your program, nothing happens. That is, nothing happens until you run another program, and then the stored statement becomes the first one executed.

There's an easy fix. Simply end your program this way:

```
PRINT / ALL.
EXECUTE.
```

All the EXECUTE command does is execute any statements that have been stored for future execution. You'll see programs written by others who do it this way, but you generally don't want to solve the problem this way. *Procedure commands* (commands that generate output) will accomplish the same thing. So just put any procedure that you have to do anyway after your transformation, such as FREQUENCIES:

```
PRINT / ALL.
FREQUENCIES ALL.
```

For the PRINT command, you have another option. The LIST command does the same thing the PRINT command does, but it executes immediately instead of waiting until the next command:

```
LIST / ALL.
```

TECHNICAL STUFF

A number of commands have a transform version and a procedure version. For instance, SAVE is a procedure, and XSAVE is a transformation. (The Command Syntax Reference, which is located under the Help menu, lists which commands are which.) This execution delay may seem odd at first, but there's a good reason why SPSS behaves this way: If SPSS executed every line one at a time, it would have to reread the data for every line and would be very slow.

TIP

Remember that transformations are delayed, but procedures happen right away. Your Syntax programs will run best (and fastest) when you put all your transformations at the top and all your procedures at the bottom. If you end your program with a transformation, you'll get a `Transformations Pending` error.

Controlling Flow and Executing Conditionals

Unless you specify otherwise, SPSS starts at the top of a program and executes one statement at a time through the program until it reaches the bottom, where it stops. But you can change that. Situations come up where you need to execute a few statements repeatedly, or maybe you want to conditionally skip one or more statements. In either case, you want program execution to jump from one place to another under your control. What you're really trying to do is say that certain cases will be treated one way (by certain lines) and other cases will be treated another way (by other lines).

IF

You use the `IF` command when you have a single statement you want to execute only if conditions are right. For example:

```
IF (AGE > 20) GROUP=2.
```

This statement asks the simple question of whether `AGE` is greater than 20. If so, the value of `GROUP` is set to 2. We could have used the `GT` keyword in place of the `>` symbol. Table 27-2 lists the relational operators you can use to compare numbers.

TABLE 27-2

Relational Operators

Symbol	Alpha	Definition
=	EQ	Is equal to
<	LT	Is less than
>	GT	Is greater than
<>	NE	Is not equal to
<=	LE	Is less than or equal to
>=	GE	Is greater than or equal to

You can also combine the relational expressions with logical operators to ask longer and more complex questions. Here's an example:

```
IF (AGE > 20 AND SEX = 1) GROUP=2.
```

This statement asks whether AGE is greater than 20 and SEX is equal to 1. If so, GROUP is set to 2. The logical operators are listed in Table 27-3.

TABLE 27-3

Logical Operators

Symbol	Alpha	Definition
&	AND	Both relational operators must be true
|	OR	Either relational operator can be true
~	NOT	Reverses the result of a relational operator

TIP

When you construct a complicated conditional expression, you should use parentheses so there is no ambiguity about what is being compared.

Write your expressions so that both the computer and other humans know what you intend. Spell them out. For example, IF (A LT B OR GT 5) is not easy to understand. The same instruction can be written IF ((A LT B) OR (A GT 5)), which is longer but has a clearer meaning.

You can compare strings to strings and numbers to numbers, but you can't compare strings to numbers.

DO IF

The DO IF statement works the same way as the IF statement, but with DO IF you can execute several statements instead of just one. Because you can enter several statements before the terminating END IF, the END IF is required to tell SPSS when the DO IF is over. The following is an example with two statements:

```
DO IF (AGE < 5).
COMPUTE YOUNG = 1.
COMPUTE SCHOOL = 0.
END IF.
```

In addition to having the option of including a number of statements at once, you can use DO IF to test several conditions in a series — and execute only the statements of the first true condition(s) by using ELSE IF:

```
DO IF (AGE < 5).
COMPUTE YOUNG = 1.
ELSE IF (AGE < 9).
COMPUTE YOUNG = 2.
ELSE IF (AGE < 12).
COMPUTE YOUNG = 3.
END IF.
```

SELECT IF

Although the SELECT IF statement was not intended for flow control, you can use it in that way. You can use SELECT IF to remove specific cases, and, as a result, include only the cases you want in your analysis. For example, the following sequence of commands prints only AGE values greater than 40:

```
SELECT IF (AGE > 40).
PRINT / AGE.
EXECUTE.
```

WARNING

Watch out, though. If you save your dataset right after this command, you'll lose data! Any of the logical operators and relational operators that can be used in other IF statements can be used in SELECT IF statements. To prevent accidently losing data, use the TEMPORARY command:

```
TEMPORARY.
SELECT IF (AGE > 40).
PRINT / AGE.
EXECUTE.
```

The SELECT IF will work only until it hits the EXECUTE (or any other procedure). Then SPSS immediately goes back to using all the data. Much better, because it's less risky.

REMEMBER

If you have any procedures that you have to do anyway, you can (and should) delete the EXECUTE command. Just make sure that some procedure — any procedure — comes after the transformation. Pretty much any command that generates output (a table or a graph) is a procedure.

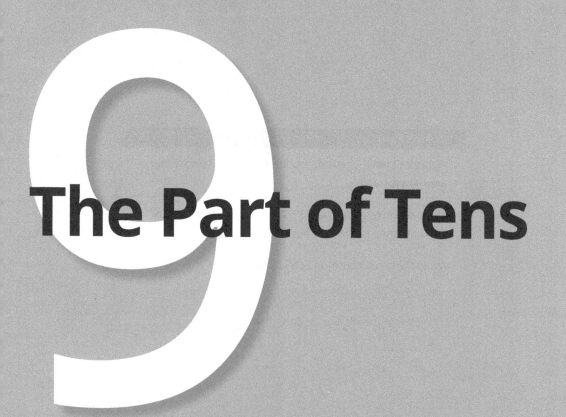

The Part of Tens

Chapter **28**

Ten (or So) Modules You Can Add to SPSS

BM SPSS Statistics comes in the form of a base system, but you can acquire additional modules to add to that system. We discuss the campus editions, subscription plans, and commercial editions of SPSS in Chapter 2. Although the pricing and various bundles differ for each, they all enable you to include the same add-on modules.

If you're using a copy of SPSS at work or in a university setting that someone else installed, you might have some of these add-ons without realizing it because most are so fully integrated into the menus that they look like integral parts of the base system. If you notice that your menus are shorter or longer than someone else's copy of SPSS, this is probably due to add-on modules.

Some add-ons might be of no interest to you; while others could become indispensable. Note that if you have a trial copy of SPSS, it likely has all the modules, including those that you might lose access to when you acquire your own copy. This chapter introduces you to the modules that can be added to SPSS and what they do; refer to the documentation that comes with each module for a full tutorial.

WARNING

You'll likely come across the names *IBM SPSS Amos* and *IBM SPSS Modeler*. Although *SPSS* appears in the names, you purchase these programs separately, not as add-ons. Amos is used for Structural Equation Modeling (SEM) and SPSS Modeler is a predictive analytics and machine learning workbench.

The Advanced Statistics Module

Following is a list of the statistical techniques that are part of the Advanced Statistics module:

>> General linear models (GLM)

>> Generalized linear models (GENLIN)

>> Linear mixed models

>> Generalized estimating equations (GEE) procedures

>> Generalized linear mixed models (GLMM)

>> Survival analysis procedures

Although these procedures are among the most advanced in SPSS, some are quite popular. For instance, hierarchical linear modeling (HLM), part of linear mixed models, is common in educational research. HLM models are statistical models in which parameters vary at more than one level. For instance, you may have data that includes information for both students and schools, and in an HLM model you can simultaneously incorporate information from both levels.

The key point is that this Advanced Statistical module contains specialized techniques that you need to use if you don't meet the assumptions of plain-vanilla regression and analysis of variance (ANOVA). These techniques are more of an ANOVA flavor. Survival analysis is so-called time-to-event modeling, such as estimating time to death after diagnosis.

The Custom Tables Module

The Custom Tables module has been the most popular module for years, and for good reason. If you need to squeeze a lot of information into a report, you need this module. For instance, if you do survey research and want to report on the entire survey in tabular form, the Custom Tables module can come to your rescue because it allows you to easily present vast information.

Get a free trial copy of SPSS Statistics with all the modules, and force yourself to spend a solid day using the modules you don't have. See if any aspect of reporting you're already doing could be done faster with the Custom Tables module. Reproduce a recent report, and see how much time you might save.

In Figure 28-1, you see a simple Frequency table displaying two variables. Note that the categories for both variables are the same. Figure 28-2 is the same data, but here the table was created using the SPSS Custom Tables module and is a much better table.

Frequency Table

Speaker_Discount

		Frequency	Percent	Valid Percent	Cumulative Percent
Valid	Discount	2464	49.3	49.3	49.3
	Regular	2539	50.7	50.7	100.0
	Total	5003	100.0	100.0	

Stereo_Discount

		Frequency	Percent	Valid Percent	Cumulative Percent
Valid	Discount	1545	30.9	30.9	30.9
	Regular	3458	69.1	69.1	100.0
	Total	5003	100.0	100.0	

FIGURE 28-1: Frequencies table of the discount variables.

Custom Tables

	Discount	Regular	Total
Speaker_Discount	49.3%	50.7%	5003
Stereo_Discount	30.9%	69.1%	5003

FIGURE 28-2: Custom table of the discount variables.

If you're producing the table for yourself, presentation may not matter. But if you're putting the table in a report that will be sent to others, you need the SPSS Custom Tables module. By the way, with practice, it takes only a few seconds to make the custom version, and you can use Syntax to further customize the table!

As discussed in Chapter 2, starting in version 27, the Custom Tables module is part of the standard edition.

The Regression Module

The following is a list of the statistical techniques that are part of the Regression module:

>> Multinomial and binary logistic regression

>> Nonlinear regression (NLR) and constrained nonlinear regression (CNLR)

>> Weighted least squares regression and two-stage least squares regression

>> Probit analysis

In some ways, the Regression module is like the Advanced Statistics module — you use these techniques when you don't meet the standard assumptions. However, with the Regression module, the techniques are fancy variants of regression when you can't do ordinary least squares regression. Binary logistic regression is popular and used when the dependent variable has two categories — for example, stay or go (churn), buy or not buy, or get a disease or not get a disease.

The Categories Module

The Categories module enables you to reveal relationships among your categorical data. To help you understand your data, the Categories module uses perceptual mapping, optimal scaling, preference scaling, and dimension reduction. Using these techniques, you can visually interpret the relationships among your rows and columns.

The Categories module performs its analysis on ordinal and nominal data. It uses procedures similar to conventional regression, principal components, and canonical correlation. It performs regression using nominal or ordinal categorical predictor or outcome variables.

The procedures of the Categories module make it possible to perform statistical operations on categorical data:

>> Using the scaling procedures, you can assign units of measurement and zero-points to your categorical data, which gives you access to new groups of statistical functions because you can analyze variables using mixed measurement levels.

>> Using correspondence analysis, you can numerically evaluate similarities among nominal variables and summarize your data according to components you select.

>> Using nonlinear canonical correlation analysis, you can collect variables of different measurement levels into sets of their own, and then analyze the sets.

You can use this module to produce a couple of useful tools:

>> **Perceptual map:** A high-resolution summary chart that serves as a graphic display of similar variables or categories. A perceptual map gives you insights into relationships among more than two categorical variables.

>> **Biplot:** A summary chart that makes it possible to look at the relationships among products, customers, and demographic characteristics.

The Data Preparation Module

Let's face it: Data preparation is no fun. We'll take all the help we can get. No module will eliminate all the work for the human in this human–computer partnership, but the Data Preparation module will eliminate some routine, predictable aspects.

This module helps you process rows and columns of data. For rows of data, it helps you identify outliers that might distort your data. As for variables, it helps you identify the best ones, and lets you know that you could improve some by transforming them. It also enables you to create special validation rules to speed up your data checks and avoid a lot of manual work. Finally, it helps you identify patterns in your missing data.

TIP

As discussed in Chapter 2, starting in version 27, the Data Preparation and Bootstrapping modules are part the base edition.

The Decision Trees Module

Decision trees are, by far, the most popular and well known data mining technique. In fact, entire software products are dedicated to this approach. If you aren't sure whether you need to do data mining but you want to try it out, using the Decision Trees module would be one of the best ways to attempt data mining because you already know your way around SPSS Statistics. The Decision Trees module doesn't have all the features of the decision trees in SPSS Modeler (an entire software package dedicated to data mining), but there is plenty here to give you a good start.

What are decision trees? Well, the idea is that you have something you want to predict (the target variable) and lots of variables that could possibly help you do that, but you don't know which ones are most important. SPSS indicates which variables are most important and how the variables interact, and helps you predict the target variable in the future.

SPSS supports four of the most popular decision tree algorithms: CHAID, Exhaustive CHAID, C&RT, and QUEST.

The Forecasting Module

You can use the Forecasting module to rapidly construct expert time-series forecasts. This module includes statistical algorithms for analyzing historical data and predicting trends. You can set it up to analyze hundreds of different time series at once instead of running a separate procedure for each one.

The software is designed to handle the special situations that arise in trend analysis. It automatically determines the best-fitting autoregressive integrated moving average (ARIMA) or exponential smoothing model. It automatically tests data for seasonality, intermittency, and missing values. The software detects outliers and prevents them from unduly influencing the results. The generated graphs include confidence intervals and indicate the model's goodness of fit.

As you gain experience at forecasting, the Forecasting module gives you more control over every parameter when you're building your data model. You can use the expert modeler in the Forecasting module to recommend starting points or to check calculations you've done by hand.

In addition, an algorithm called Temporal Causal Modeling (TCM) attempts to discover key causal relationships in time-series data by including only inputs that have a causal relationship with the target. This differs from traditional time-series modeling, where you must explicitly specify the predictors for a target series.

The Missing Values Module

The Data Preparation module seems to have missing values covered, but the Missing Values module and the Data Preparation module are quite different. The Data Preparation module is about finding data errors; its validation rules will tell you whether a data point just isn't right. The Missing Values module, on the other hand, is focused on when there is no data value. It attempts to estimate the missing piece of information using other data you do have. This process is called *imputation*, or replacing values with an educated guess. All kinds of data miners, statisticians, and researchers — especially survey researchers — can benefit from the Missing Values module.

TIP

This module is not the same as the discussion of missing data in Chapters 4 and 10. In Chapters 4 and 10 you declared and identified missing data. The Missing Values module replaces missing values.

The Bootstrapping Module

Hang on tight because we're going to get a little technical. *Bootstrapping* is a technique that involves resampling with replacement. The Bootstrapping module chooses a case at random, makes notes about it, replaces it, and chooses another. In this way, it's possible to choose a case more than once or not at all. The net result is another version of your data that is similar but not identical. If you do this 1,000 times (the default), you can do some powerful things indeed.

The Bootstrapping module allows you to build more stable models by overcoming the effect of outliers and other problems in your data. Traditional statistics assumes that your data has a particular distribution, but this technique avoids that assumption. The result is a more accurate sense of what's going on in the population. Bootstrapping, in a sense, is a simple idea, but because bootstrapping takes a lot of computer horsepower, it's more popular now than when computers were slower.

Bootstrapping is a popular technique outside SPSS as well, so you can find articles on the web about the concept. The Bootstrapping module lets you apply this powerful concept to your data in SPSS Statistics.

The Complex Samples Module

Sampling is a big part of statistics. A *simple random sample* is what we usually think of as a sample — like choosing names out of a hat. The hat is your population, and the scraps of paper you choose belong to your sample. Each slip of paper has an equal chance of being chosen. Research is often more complicated than that. The Complex Sample module is about more complicated forms of sampling: two stage, stratified, and so on.

Most often, survey researchers need this module, although many kinds of experimental researchers may benefit from it too. The Complex Samples module helps you design the data collection, and then takes the design into account when calculating your statistics. Nearly all statistics in SPSS are calculated with the assumption that the data is a simple random sample. Your calculations can be distorted when this assumption is not met.

The Conjoint Module

The Conjoint module provides a way for you to determine how each of your product's attributes affect consumer preference. When you combine conjoint analysis with competitive market product research, it's easier to zero in on product characteristics that are important to your customers.

With this research, you can determine which product attributes your customers care about, which ones they care about most, and how you can do useful studies of pricing and brand equity. And you can do all this *before* incurring the expense of bringing new products to market.

The Direct Marketing Module

The Direct Marketing module is a little different from the others. It's a bundle of related features in a wizardlike environment. The module is designed to be one-stop shopping for marketers. The main features are recency, frequency, and monetary (RFM) analysis, cluster analysis, and profiling:

>> **RFM analysis:** RFM analysis reports back to you about how recently, how often, and how much your customers spent on your business. Obviously, customers who are currently active, spend a lot, and spend often, are your best customers.

- ≫ **Cluster analysis:** Cluster analysis is a way of segmenting your customers into different customer segments. Typically, you use this approach to match different marketing campaigns to different customers. For example, a cruise line may try different covers on the travel catalog going out to customers, with the adventurous types getting Alaska or Norway on the cover, and the umbrella-drink crowd getting pictures of the Caribbean.

- ≫ **Profiling:** Profiling helps you see which customer characteristics are associated with specific outcomes. In this way, you can calculate the propensity score that a particular customer will respond to a specific campaign. Virtually all these features can be found in other areas of SPSS, but the wizardlike environment of the Direct Marketing module makes it easy for marketing analysts to produce useful results when they don't have extensive training in the statistics behind the techniques.

The Exact Tests Module

The Exact Tests module makes it possible to be more accurate in your analysis of small datasets and datasets that contain rare occurrences. It gives you the tools you need to analyze such data conditions with more accuracy than would otherwise be possible.

When only a small sample size is available, you can use the Exact Tests module to analyze the smaller sample and have more confidence in the results. Here, the idea is to perform more analyses in a shorter period of time. This module allows you to conduct different surveys rather than spend time gathering samples to enlarge your base of surveys.

The processes you use, and the forms of the results, are the same as those in the base SPSS system, but the internal algorithms are tuned to work with smaller datasets. The Exact Tests module provides more than 30 tests covering all the nonparametric and categorical tests you normally use for larger datasets. Included are one-sample, two-sample, and k-sample tests with independent or related samples, goodness-of-fit tests, tests of independence, and measures of association.

The Neural Networks Module

A *neural net* is a latticelike network of neuronlike nodes, set up within SPSS to act something like the neurons in a living brain. The connections between these nodes have associated *weights* (degrees of relative effect), which are adjustable. When you adjust the weight of a connection, the network is said to learn.

In the Neural Networks module, a training algorithm iteratively adjusts the weights to closely match the actual relationships among the data. The idea is to minimize errors and maximize accurate predictions. The computational neural network has one layer of neurons for inputs and another for outputs, with one or more hidden layers between them. The neural network can be used with other statistical procedures to provide clearer insight.

Using the familiar SPSS interface, you can mine your data for relationships. After selecting a procedure, you specify the dependent variables, which may be any combination of continuous and categorical types. To prepare for processing, you lay out the neural network architecture, including the computational resources you want to apply. To complete preparation, you choose what to do with the output:

>> List the results in tables.

>> Graphically display the results in charts.

>> Place the results in temporary variables in the dataset.

>> Export models in XML-formatted files.

IN THIS CHAPTER

» Connecting with other SPSS users on the Internet

» Discovering the information you need online

» Continuing your journey by finding more advanced content

Chapter **29**

Ten Useful SPSS Resources

BM SPSS Statistics users are all over the world. The Internet is a powerful medium through which you can join the SPSS community, and this chapter points you in the right direction.

Supporting Websites for This Book

You can visit two websites specific to this book. The first is Wiley's own website, where you can download supporting files for this book. Go to www.dummies.com/go/spss4e.

The second website is keithmccormick.com/SSFD4E. The authors will keep this current with the latest news, updates, and how best to reach out to us with questions.

LinkedIn and LinkedIn Groups

Currently, three SPSS groups are on LinkedIn:

>> SPSS Users

>> SPSS Power Users

>> IBM SPSS Users Forum

Groups wax and wane in popularity, so in LinkedIn it's a good idea to search groups, content, and people for #*SPSS*. Figure 29-1 displays a button for each of the categories you can search, so you can indicate that you want to search specifically for groups. If you also search for content, you'll see recent posts by LinkedIn members in their feed.

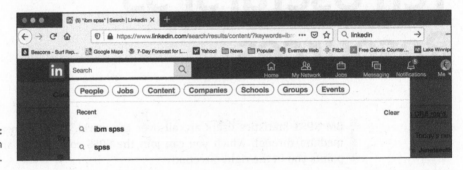

FIGURE 29-1:
A LinkedIn
search.

If you find a post that is particularly interesting, consider following that person. On LinkedIn, following is not the same as connecting. Forming a connection requires mutual agreement, but following does not. The follow option is not as prominent in the interface as the connect option, but follow is the better choice if the person whose feed you want to follow doesn't know you.

LinkedIn has hundreds of millions of members worldwide. You can follow your authors Jesus and Keith at their LinkedIn addresses:

    www.linkedin.com/in/jesus-salcedo-1482a24/

    www.linkedin.com/in/keithmccormick/

IBM SPSS Statistics Certification

If you're in a corporate setting or looking to get a corporate job that involves using SPSS, it may help to get certified in SPSS. For more on IBM's certification program, go to www.ibm.com/certify/certs.html and search for *SPSS* to see specific certification programs.

Having this certification listed on your LinkedIn profile or résumé may help when you're ready to transition to another role or organization. This book will get you well on your way to passing the Level 1 exam, but try the practice questions to get a sense of what you need to review.

Currently, you can find details, including practice questions, about the IBM SPSS Statistics Level 1 certification exam at www.ibm.com/certify/exam?id=C2090-011.

IBM Data Science Community

If you go to the Help menu in SPSS, you'll find a link inviting you to register and join the IBM Data Science Community (or the IBM SPSS Predictive Analytics Community). Make sure to locate and join the SPSS Stats group, which is the official IBM community for SPSS users, by choosing the appropriate topic group. You can also use the following URL: https://community.ibm.com/community/user/datascience/communities/community-home to sign up or log in.

You can import your LinkedIn details to create a profile and link with other social media accounts. A wealth of information is available, including announcements about helpful information, such as webinars. You can also post questions to the forum.

SPSSX-L

SPSSX-L is a listserv, which is an email-based posting system. You send an email to ask questions, and the posts come back to you in the form of email. SPSSX-L predates most of the other resources you'll find on the Internet. You can subscribe at https://listserv.uga.edu/cgi-bin/wa.

You may find the listserv format surprising if you're young enough to have always had the Internet. Even if the idea of a listserv is quaint, you don't want to miss out on the wisdom available through this group. Some of the most knowledgeable and veteran SPSS users are active in SPSSX-L, and they sincerely want to help other users.

To ask a question, simply send an email (instructions are given on the home page) and the system will forward your email to all members. There are instructions on how to cancel if you find that the flow of email is more than you like. You might want to set up an email filter where all the messages from this listserv go to a special folder in your email system, so you can read them when you have the time.

Online Videos

You can find an almost overwhelming number of free and for-fee videos online. Here are some that we have produced ourselves or have seen and recommend. These are for-fee, but can be accessed through both a subscription option or by paying for individual courses:

>> **Packt** (www.packtpub.com):

- "Learning IBM SPSS Statistics" by Keith McCormick and Jesus Salcedo closely aligns with the content in this book, so check it out if you want to reinforce your learning with video demonstrations.

- "Basic Statistics and Data Mining for Data Science" by Jesus Salcedo goes deeper into the theory introduced in Part 5.

- "Advanced Statistics and Data Mining for Data Science" by Jesus Salcedo goes deeper into the theory introduced in Part 5 and beyond with some machine learning topics.

- "Hands-on Statistical Predictive Modeling" by Jesus Salcedo covers linear regression, logistic regression, and discriminant analysis.

>> **LinkedIn Learning** (www.linkedin.com/learning):

- "SPSS Statistics Essential Training (2019)," by Bart Poulson, is popular, well done, recently updated, and extensive at six hours.

- "SPSS for Academic Research" by Yash Patel provides opportunities for practice with the challenge (and solution) at the end of each chapter.

- "Machine Learning and AI Foundations: Linear Regression" by Keith McCormick is an almost four-hour review of regression features in SPSS, with plenty of discussion of theory and the interpretation of results.

Twitter

Twitter might seem like a strange suggestion at first. After all, what can you learn about SPSS in just 280 characters? A tweet won't help much, but you can find thought leaders in the SPSS community and the latest and greatest information on SPSS.

TIP

Here are some recommendations on whom to follow for IBM and SPSS news:

>> **IBM Training (@IBMTraining):** Official news on IBM training, including SPSS training.

>> **IBM Data Science (@IBMDataScience):** Official related IBM tweets.

>> **IBM Live (@IBMLive):** Tweets about the big annual IBM conferences. The relevant conference for SPSSers is called Think.

>> **Keith McCormick (@KMcCormickBlog):** Keith, one of the authors of this book, follows several hundred accounts, more than half of which are stats, AI, and machine learning related, so checking out his follow list is a great way to get up-to-date recommendations.

Here are some Twitter accounts that are great for data visualization and analytics in general to get you started:

>> **The American Statistical Association (@AmstatNews):** The world's largest community of statisticians.

>> **SignificanceAp Magazine (@signmagazine):** A joint statistics magazine from @RoyalStatSoc and @AmstatNews. Great source for interesting articles in the magazine and elsewhere.

>> **Simply Statistics (@simplystats):** Blog by Jeff Leek, Roger Peng, and Rafael Irizarry.

>> **Nathan Yau (@flowingdata):** Influential author and blogger specializing in data visualization.

>> **Edward Tufte (@EdwardTufte):** Famous for his data visualization books and harsh critique of PowerPoint presentations.

>> **Gregory Piatetsky (@kdnuggets):** A data scientist, co-founder of KDD conferences and ACM SIGKDD association for Knowledge Discovery and Data Mining, and president of KDnuggets, a leading site on business analytics, data mining, and data science.

>> **Meta Brown (@metabrown312):** Author of *Data Mining For Dummies* and a thought leader in predictive analytics.

- **Hans Rosling (@HansRosling):** Brilliant lecturer famous for his TED talks. Rosling passed away in 2017 but the account is still active and run by his son Ola (@OlaRosling).

- **Nancy Duarte (@nancyduarte):** Author of *Slideology* and owner of a successful company that polishes corporate presentations. She became famous when she helped Al Gore with his slide presentations.

- **Dean Abbott (@DeanAbb):** Well-known data miner who speaks at the Predictive Analytics World conferences.

- **Andrew Ng (@AndrewYNg):** Chief scientist of Baidu, chairman and co-founder of Coursera, and Stanford CS faculty.

- **Gil Press (@GilPress):** Tech journalist; everything he writes is worth a quick read.

- **TED Talks (@TEDTalks):** Tweets from the same folks who bring you those great 18-minute video talks.

Live Instruction

You can find plenty of instructors waiting to teach you a live class. Many of these classes are reasonably priced. Both Jesus Salcedo and Keith McCormick (your authors) regularly teach online, sometimes to audiences halfway around the world. For more on current trends in SPSS training, go to http://keithmccormick.com/SPSSTraining.

An entire economy of SPSS software instruction is out there. Following are commonly taught IBM SPSS courses:

- **Introduction to SPSS:** Similar to this book and where most would start. After reading this book, this course might be a review.

- **Introduction to Statistical Analysis:** Focuses on the theory with a bit more detail than Part 5.

- **Data Management and Manipulation with SPSS:** A sequel to Introduction to SPSS but with more focus on preparing data, calculating new variables, and merging files.

- **Advanced Statistical Analysis Using SPSS:** A sequel to Introduction to Statistical Analysis that uses some of the techniques in the add-on modules discussed in Chapter 28.

TIP

Find out who's teaching the class, and don't be shy about emailing or chatting with the person before you choose a class. We know most members of the SPSS community, and you can email us (keith@keithmccormick.com and jesussalcedo@yahoo.com) for advice.

If you're taking a course alone, joining a public class might be the most cost-effective, but if two or three people are studying together, a private class might make more sense because you can use your own data and focus on your specific issues. Don't rush. Do your research.

Asynchronous Instruction and Tutorials

One interesting option for learning SPSS Statistics, especially more advanced topics, is a brown-bag lunch format offered by the Analysis Factor (www.theanalysisfactor.com). They cover advanced topics in non-threatening, shorter formats and also offer more extensive seminars on a variety of topics. The training isn't limited to SPSS Statistics, but SPSS content is common.

Another option with an extensive list of courses awaits you at Statistics.com (www.statistics.com). These courses are like university short courses, including homework. The classes are typically asynchronous, so you might see recordings of lectures but will also have access to the instructor during the multiple weeks of the course. A long list of statistics professors and textbook authors are among their ranks. Statistics.com offers serious, in-depth classes, which may be just what you're looking for. We can't guarantee that SPSS Statistics will be the software tool of choice, so if that's important to you, check before you enroll. If the class sounds perfect but is taught using another software tool such as Python or R, don't rule it out.

Finding free SPSS content on the Internet isn't difficult. The challenge is finding *good* free content. The folks at UCLA have maintained great SPSS content for years and we highly recommend UCLA's tutorial. Here are two URLs you should check out:

https://stats.idre.ucla.edu/spss/

https://stats.idre.ucla.edu/other/mult-pkg/whatstat/

SPSS Statistics for Data Analysis and Visualization

Your authors, Jesus and Keith, collaborated on *SPSS Statistics for Data Analysis and Visualization* (Wiley) with their colleagues Jon Peck and Andrew Wheeler. It was explicitly developed to pick up where this book leaves off. By tapping into the wisdom of our coauthors, we managed to have over 100 years of SPSS experience involved in this book.

The book covers the following four major topics:

>> **Advanced SPSS techniques in the add-on modules:** Includes topics such as AMOS, categorical regression, and hierarchical linear models, which are usually not found in other SPSS books but are useful

>> **Data visualization:** Covers advanced charting techniques, including geospatial analysis and techniques requiring the Categories module, such as perceptual mapping

>> **Predictive analytics and machine learning:** Explains neural networks, decision trees, and the basics of predictive analytics using SPSS Statistics

>> **SPSS programming:** Provides 100 pages on topics versus the 20 or so pages in this book

The book doesn't cover topics you would find in a typical multivariate statistics textbook because many books like that are available, some written for SPSS users. From the start, we attempted to cover the topics that we felt were not covered well elsewhere, so intermediate-level regression, ANOVA, and the basics of experimental design are not covered. If you're new to statistics theory, you'll also need a good intermediate-level statistics book; one recommendation is *Using Multivariate Statistics*, 7th Edition by Barbara Tabachnick and Linda Fidell (Pearson).

You can find out more about the book, including a sample chapter, at the following two websites:

>> www.wiley.com/en-us/SPSS+Statistics+for+Data+Analysis+and+Visualization-p-9781119003557

>> keithmccormick.com/SPSSDAV

Chapter **30**

Ten SPSS Statistics Gotchas

O ur ten gotchas serve as a checklist of potential causes of your SPSS woes. Some just waste your time, but others can both waste your time and ruin your analysis. Most of these issues are addressed in the book, but this chapter gives us one more chance to reinforce the importance of avoiding these common issues so you can efficiently use SPSS.

Some of these ten gotchas can be confusing at first. Others are straightforward, but new users might not attribute to them the importance they deserve. What they all have in common is that ignorance of them can get you into hot water. Whenever something seems to be amiss in SPSS, double-check this list. To earn its way onto this list, these gotchas must have generated hundreds of real-world problems as witnessed by us in our client interactions.

Failing to Declare Level of Measurement

To many new users of SPSS, declaring Level of Measurement seems like a nuisance. You can safely ignore it for a while, but our advice is to not wait until the day that it starts causing problems. Here are just a few noteworthy situations where you will regret a decision to procrastinate getting your datasets set up properly:

>> A variable that you need might not appear in a dialog.

>> Features that rely on metadata, such as Codebook, will produce poor results.

>> The chart dialogs won't offer you the options you need for a particular variable.

>> The Custom Tables add-on module will behave strangely.

Proper metadata is a must for the efficient use of SPSS. Those who attempt to save time by skipping the step of setting up their datasets properly will never succeed because they'll waste time in the long run trying to figure out why SPSS is not behaving as it should.

Conflating String Values with Labels

In Chapter 4, we discuss variable types such as numeric, currency, and string. Avoid using the string type. Instead, use a combination of values and value labels. Back in the '60s and '70s, RAM and hard drive space were expensive and limited. Strings use many more characters and bytes than numerics, and back then SPSS couldn't perform calculations using RAM alone, so it needed to use the hard drive as we might use a scratch pad. Now, it might seems quaint to worry about such things, but avoiding strings is still core to the design philosophy of SPSS.

So what kinds of variables should be stored as strings? Addresses, open-ended comments in survey data, and the names of people and companies are good examples of string variables. There aren't many more. The names of the 50 states, the names of products, product categories and SKUs, and most other nominal variables should be set up as pairs of values and value labels.

In the past, leading zeros in data such as zip codes posed a problem, so the data would be declared as string. Now, however, the restricted numeric variable type adds leading zeros padded to the maximum width of the variable, so a zip code variable no longer needs to be declared as a string. Also, Autorecode makes conversions from string to numeric easy. Keep string variables to a minimum.

REMEMBER

Excel files do not allow for metadata, so Excel does not support value and value label pairs. When frequently importing string data from Excel, consider learning the syntax commands (see Chapter 27) as well as autorecode transformation (see Chapter 8) because these techniques might be helpful.

Failing to Declare Missing Data

Years ago, an SPSS user in one of our classes experienced the following situation. He had a 1 through 10 scale, with 10 as the highest satisfaction rating and 1 as the lowest satisfaction rating. He needed a code to represent "refused to answer" and chose 11. When he learned about missing data in class, he wondered if just leaving the 11s in the data would be okay because he had already completed the analysis and the number of refusals was fairly low.

You bet it caused a big problem! It could move the average satisfaction quite far towards 11 even with a 1 to 2 percent nonresponse. What was striking about this example was that the most common answer, 1, was very far from the coded-value for nonresponse. That fact should have made the analysis obviously wrong and easy to spot. Worse, it is well understood in survey research that refusals often reflect respondents who are highly dissatisfied but reluctant to share their opinion. The choice of 11 made their opinion look highly satisfied, not highly dissatisfied, distorting the results even more.

Sadly, folks forget to declare missing quite often, and the error often persists through the final steps of the analysis and is never uncovered. In the example, the problem could have been fixed with one simple step: Declare 11 as user-defined missing, as discussed in Chapter 3. Be vigilant about declaring missing data values in your metadata.

Failing to Find Add-On Modules and Plug-Ins

What can go wrong with add-on modules? The problem that we observe often with clients is that they read about features in add-on modules and then can't find the modules. This might seem odd. Wouldn't everyone know which SPSS functions they own? But you, too, could be confused for several reasons:

>> Someone else paid for your copy of SPSS, often a copy that you access at school or work.

>> The paperwork for your copy of SPSS says Standard or Premium, but it's not clear what this means.

>> You try to find the module in the menus, referring to an image in a book or blog post, and your screen doesn't look like the image.

>> You borrow some working SPSS syntax from a colleague or book, but it fails to work on your copy of SPSS.

SPSS implements add-on modules by adding them to your menus, typically in the Analyze main menu. In Figure 30-1, you can see the Analyze menu from the screen of an SPSS Subscription trial. The trial version always has all modules. So if your menu is shorter than the one you see in the image, you know you don't have the full complement of add-on modules.

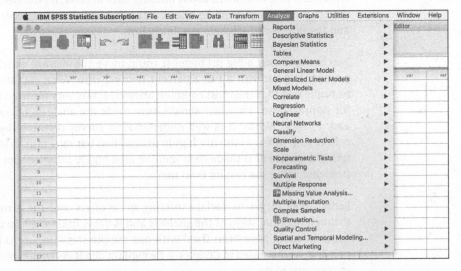

FIGURE 30-1:
The Analyze menu with all modules available.

Nothing is wrong with your copy of SPSS. You just don't have access to all features, including via SPSS Syntax. Some believe that if you know the necessary code and bypass the graphical user interface, you can run any command, but that is not true. To run the syntax for an add-on module, you must own the module. (We explain how bundles are structured in Chapter 2 and the functionality of each add-on in Chapter 28.) We stress this point because we have seen people borrow Syntax from a source, colleague, or book, and try to copy and paste the code into the Syntax window. The syntax code will not work if you lack the proper licensing.

Another common source of confusion is that many SPSS users don't realize that they have access to add-on modules at work or school. This is unfortunate because the modules can be extremely useful. We always recommend the Custom Tables module to clients for greater efficiency in their analysis. Countless times, clients have thought that they had no modules only to discover that Custom Tables was visible in the menus and functioning.

Finally, "plug-ins" are a little different than add-on modules. Features can be added to SPSS by using Python and R. If you're a programmer, you could consider doing this task yourself. However, many of these extensions are already available. All you have to do is download them, and they will appear as additional menu items, with a plus symbol next to the menu entry (see the margin icon). Retired

SPSSer Jon Peck was instrumental in adding this programmability feature to SPSS, and wrote a chapter in *SPSS for Data Analysis and Visualization* (Wiley) about plug-ins and extensions.

Failing to Meet Statistical and Software Assumptions

SPSS is not that smart. SPSS will do whatever you ask it to do. So if you have a variable like Marital Status, with the values: 1= Married, 2=Divorced, 3=Separated, 4=Widowed, and 5=Single, and you ask SPSS to give you a mean for Marital Status, SPSS will give you a mean. However a mean of 2.33 for a nominal variable like Marital Status is not useful. Similarly, if you analyze your data and find that 100% of your friends whom you surveyed think that more monetary resources should be devoted to the tennis center at your country club, but you only interviewed tennis players, then you cannot pass off your results as a random sample of country club members, nor can you be surprised with your findings.

It is important that you have reliable and valid data. SPSS assumes that your data comes from a random sample; if this is not the case, you can still obtain descriptive information; however, you will not be able to generalize your results to a population (review Chapter 15 for more details). You will also need to know what information you can glean from your data. Chapter 14 discusses level of measurement and their appropriate summary statistics.

Additionally, it is important to remember that every statistical test has assumptions. Some statistical tests in SPSS, like the independent samples t-test, automatically assess some of the test assumptions; however, most of the time you will have to run additional checks to assess test assumptions. Remember that the better you meet test assumptions, the more you can trust the results of a test.

TECHNICAL STUFF

You may hear that a test is sensitive to violations of assumptions or robust to violations of assumptions. When a test is *sensitive*, you have to be especially careful to meet the assumptions. When a test is *robust*, there is more wiggle room with the assumptions. Robust tests are mentioned in Chapters 18 and 20.

Confusing Pasting Syntax with Copy and Paste

Virtually all SPSS users start by learning SPSS via the Graphical User Interface and many find SPSS Syntax to be a bit arcane. The confusion arises when a colleague shares a bit of syntax code and offers it up as a shortcut, but it can all look very intimidating. The fear is that you will have to have a big book open on your desk and that you will be typing the commands letter by letter. This is simply not true.

Even if a well-meaning colleague exclaims, "It's easy, just paste it," it might not be clear what they mean. "Pasting" in SPSS, in regards to SPSS Syntax, means to let the SPSS dialogs generate the syntax code for you by giving the instructions via point and click. The syntax is then generated and sent to the Syntax Window. You can think of it as converting clicks into code. It is not the copy, paste maneuver (Control-C, Control-V in Windows) that we do in most software.

So there is no need to skip chapters with Syntax in the name because of the fear that Syntax is difficult to use. One, you can use the menus and dialogs and you'll be just fine for 99 percent of the tasks you have to do. Two, if you invest just an hour or so you can learn the very basics of Syntax and how to generate code automatically from the menus. The first step is to spend some time with Chapters 9 and 10. If you can handle functions, you can handle Syntax. Syntax takes you a step further but it will be a good indication that you are ready for Syntax if Chapters 9 and 10 make sense. Next move on to Chapter 26, and when you are ready tackle Chapter 27.

Thinking You Create Variables in SPSS as You Do in Excel

Almost everyone who learns SPSS brings prior exposure to Excel to the learning experience. There is a critical function in both which is handled quite differently in the two interfaces. In Excel, when you want to implement a formula you work directly in a cell of the spreadsheet and the formula is saved in that same location when you save the spreadsheet. In SPSS, you must use the Compute Variable dialog (or the equivalent in SPSS Syntax) and your formula is not saved in the dataset — only the result is saved in the dataset.

At first, it might seem highly desirable for everyone to save formulas in the dataset, but it might not be clear the high price that is paid for this feature in Excel. SPSS is built to be scalable to large datasets, sometimes 100s of millions of rows of data. In Excel, the spreadsheet must be constantly scanned to update the values of formulas. That scanning, passively and automatically in the background, consumes resources and makes Excel less scalable to very large datasets. Excel becomes noticeably sluggish when datasets are very large for this reason, but Excel was never designed for huge datasets. In SPSS, the data remains constant unless an action prompts a change. To force calculations to update, either the menus must be used again or SPSS Syntax must be run again. Each system is designed with its primary audience in mind.

If you are more familiar with how Excel automatically updates calculations, how should you acclimate to SPSS? If most of your data is read in from a file and you proceed directly to analysis then you will probably be quite content using the Graphical User Interface. If you have very large files or if you have a large number of calculations that are made after the data is read in from a file, you will need to learn SPSS Syntax to be productive. By saving those calculations, perhaps dozens or hundreds of them, in the form of SPSS Syntax you can rerun them all quite easily.

TECHNICAL STUFF

Excel currently has a limit of 1,000,000 rows of data, but just a few years ago the limit was much smaller. This is rarely an issue for Excel users as that many rows is usually sufficient. Excel experts can often find a way around this limit, but it is rarely necessary. The technical reason for this limit is that the entire spreadsheet must be accessible to a computer's memory. SPSS does not require the entire dataset to fit in the computer's memory. This is important to many SPSS users because thousands of companies with datasets larger than the million row limit need to analyze their large datasets in SPSS. The IRS is a notable example of an organization that uses SPSS that has datasets much larger than the million row limit.

Getting Confused by Listwise Deletion

Missing data has often been treated as a chapter-length (or even book-length) topic, but a discussion of that length is not possible in this book. You can handle missing data in many ways, one of which is to use listwise deletion. And being familiar with the term *listwise deletion* may alert you to what would otherwise seem like strange behavior in SPSS. Imagine that you have a large dataset, with thousands of rows. But when you run a multivariate analysis, SPSS behaves as if you have no data at all. You check the steps multiple times, but all you see in the results are messages that indicate that you have "no valid cases." What could be happening?

Listwise deletion is one method for determining which cases in the dataset are used by SPSS for multivariate analysis. When this method is applied, only cases that are valid for *all* variables in the analysis are used. Missing just a single cell of information in the case row will cause the entire case to be removed. Why is this common? Imagine that you're collating data on airline passengers. One column records if a passenger chose to purchase an inflight meal, which applies to only coach passengers. Another column records which of two meal choices the person chose during the first class meal, which applies to only first class passengers. Every row in the dataset will be missing one or the other, resulting in zero rows of data being presented to the multivariate analysis. This situation is common.

This short discussion is not sufficient to weigh the pros and cons of using listwise deletion. However, you will now be aware of it when you run into the problem of zero cases being analyzed. Also be on the lookout for times when many fewer cases than you were expecting are analyzed. Figure 30-2 shows the Options dialog of the Linear Regression dialog. In the Options dialog, listwise deletion is the default. Be careful not to haphazardly choose among the other choices until the regression works. Instead, understand the other options before you try them.

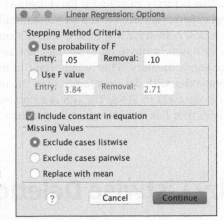

FIGURE 30-2:
The Linear
Regression:
Options dialog.

Losing Track of Your Active Dataset

Your SPSS skills are progressing along nicely and you decide that it's time to try SPSS Syntax. You double-check your work, run the syntax, and encounter the warning shown in Figure 30-3. You confirm that you have the necessary dataset and the necessary variable. What has happened?

FIGURE 30-3:
Warning:
Necessary
variables are
missing.

Almost certainly, you have two (or more) datasets open and you've lost track of which one is active. When you're working in the graphical user interface, it's virtually impossible to get confused because when you access the menus and dialogs you're generally doing so from the Data Editor window. When you're using SPSS Syntax, however, you're running code and there's no guarantee that the necessary data elements are present. Here's what you need to do: Check to see if you have more than one dataset open, and ensure that the dataset you need is the active dataset. The Syntax window has the following indicator:

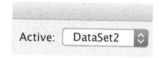

DataSet1 is simply the dataset you opened first. To switch to DataSet2, simply click the arrows and select it. You can assign the dataset that you need also by using the following bit of syntax: DATASET ACTIVATE DataSet1.

Forgetting to Turn Off Select and Split and Weight

A common mistake occurs when you're dealing with a command that stays in effect until you explicitly instruct SPSS to turn it off. Three of these commands are Select, Split, and Weight, which are somewhat unusual in SPSS because they're typically associated with a temporary adjustment to an analysis, not with a permanent change to the data. We discuss Select and Split in Chapter 8. Weight is more technical and is more often associated with survey analysis. Here is a quick explanation of each:

>> **Select:** Indicates which cases you want to include or exclude from your analysis

>> **Split:** Separates the dataset by a grouping variable and analyzes each group separately

>> **Weight:** Adjusts underrepresented groups as if they were fully represented, and applies the reverse adjustment to overrepresented groups

Effective use of all three requires more than just a quick definition. However, checking to see if they're still on is easy, due to an indicator in the lower-right corner of the Data Editor window (see Figure 30-4). The Filter indicator refers to operations in the Select Cases dialog. The Weight and Split By indicators refer to the Weight and Split dialogs, respectively. (Unicode refers to the encoding system used by SPSS, which is typically not temporary, although you can change this in the Edit⇨Options menu.)

FIGURE 30-4:
The Filter, Weight, and Split indicators.

If SPSS is behaving strangely and you're not getting the results you expect, check these indicators. To turn an indicator off, return to the dialog where you gave the original instruction.

WARNING

A common mistake is to accidentally use Select and Split at the same time. (Power users of SPSS might do this intentionally, but only rarely.) In particular, it's never a good idea to use Select and Split on the same variable at the same time. If you do, numerous warnings will appear in the SPSS Output Viewer window.

Index

Symbols

$CASENUM system variable, 125
$DATE system variable, 125
$DATE11 system variable, 125
$JDATE system variable, 125
$LENGTH system variable, 125
$SYSMIS system variable, 125–127
$TIME system variable, 125
$WIDTH system variable, 125

Numbers

3-D bar chart, 178–182
3-D plot, 197
5% trimmed mean, 216
32-bit versions, 18
64 bit versions, 18

A

Abbott, Dean, 430
abbreviating commands, 404
accessibility, screen reader, 361
Add Cases merge operation, 147–151
Add Variables merge operation, 152–159
add-on modules, 415–424
  Advanced Statistics module
    overview, 416
    subscription plans, 20, 21, 23
  advanced techniques, 350
  Bootstrapping module
    overview, 421
    subscription plans, 20, 21, 23
  Categories module
    overview, 418–419
    subscription plans, 20, 22, 23
  Complex Sample module
    overview, 422
    subscription plans, 20, 22, 23

Conjoint module
  overview, 422
  subscription plans, 20, 22, 23
Custom Tables module
  overview, 416–417
  subscription plans, 20, 21, 23
Data Preparation module
  overview, 419
  subscription plans, 20, 21, 23
Decision Trees module
  overview, 419–420
  subscription plans, 20, 22, 23
Direct Marketing module
  overview, 422–423
  subscription plans, 20, 22, 23
Exact Tests module
  overview, 423
  subscription plans, 20, 22, 23
finding, 435–437
Forecasting module
  overview, 420
  subscription plans, 20, 22, 23
with licensing options
  campus editions, 20
  commercial editions, 23
  free trial, 18
  subscription plans, 21
Missing Values module
  overview, 421
  subscription plans, 20, 22, 23
Neural Network module
  overview, 424
  subscription plans, 20, 22, 23
nonparametric tests with, 328
Regression module
  overview, 418
  subscription plans, 20, 21, 23
addresses, 51
adjusted R Square, 296

binary variable, 143–144

binning cases, 113–118

   optimal binning, 117–118

   overview, 113–116

biplots, 419

bitmap (BMP), 78

bivariate procedures, 288–291

   incorrect use of, 287–288

   overview, 348–349

Bonferroni correction

   compare column proportions test, 260

   nonparametric independent samples test, 335

   overview, 312–313

Boolean variable, 143–144

Bootstrapping module

   overview, 421

   SPSS version 27, 24

   subscription plans, 20, 21, 23

box and whisker plots, 217

Brown, Meta, 429

Brown-Forsythe test, 307, 310

bubble chart, 197

bugs, reporting, 15–16

BY reserved word, 125

C

C&RT decision tree algorithm, 420

campus editions, 19–20

Cars.sav file

   3-D plot, 197

   multiline graphs, 194–196

   pivoting trays, 390–392

   scatterplot, 184

   scatterplot matrix, 198–199

   select cases transformation, 100–102

   sorting cases, 98

   split file transformation, 103–104

   stacked bar chart, 199–200

   Style Output dialog, using, 387–389

   TableLooks, applying, 384–386

Case Processing Summary table, 42

cases, 97–118

   binning, 113–118

      optimal binning, 117–118

      overview, 113–116

combining files by adding, 147–151

counting occurrences, 104–107

general discussion of, 13

overview, 26

recoding variables, 107–113

   automatic, 110–113

   into different variables, 107–110

select cases transformation, 100–102

sorting, 97–100

split file transformation, 103–104

categorical level of measurement, 215

categorical regression, 328, 350

categorical variables

   chi-square goodness of fit test, 240–246

   crosstabulation, 251–265

      adding control variables, 261–263

      chi-square test of independence, 256–259

      clustered bar graphs, 264–265

      compare column proportions test, 260–261

      overview, 38–42

      running procedure for, 252–255

   dependent vs. independent variables, 267–283

      Compare Means dialog, 268–269

      conducting inferential tests, 268

      error bar chart, 275–277

      independent-samples t-test, 269–275

      paired-samples t-test, 280–283

      summary independent-samples t-test, 277–279

   frequencies procedure for, 217–221

   general discussion of, 13

   maps from, 207

   in multiple-response sets, 87

Categories module

   overview, 418–419

   subscription plans, 20, 22, 23

.csv files, 66

Central Limit Theorem, 236

central tendency, 215–216, 224

century range settings, 359

Certification, IBM SPSS Statistics, 427

CHAID decision tree algorithm, 420

character encoding, 356–357

Chart Appearance tab, Chart Builder, 176–177

Chart Builder, 164–178

   Basic Elements tab, 168–169

   Chart Appearance tab, 176–177

N

P

Packt website, 428
paired-samples t-test, 269, 280–283
paneling, 170
panels, 178
parameters, 7
parametric tests
  analysis of variance (ANOVA)
    Advanced Statistical module, 416
    general discussion of, 268
    one-way ANOVA vs., 303–304
    statistic relationship between variables and, 297
  linear regression
    defined, 285
    general discussion of, 268
    listwise deletion option, 440
    procedure, 292–300
    purpose of, 349
  Pearson correlation
    assumptions, 291
    defined, 288
    general discussion of, 285
  probablility with, 234
  t-tests
    independent-samples, 231, 232, 269–275, 303–326
    one-sample, 246–250, 269, 348
    overview, 269
    paired-samples, 269, 280–283
    summary independent-samples, 269, 277–279
parentheses, 411
parsing strings, 144–146
pasting
  importance of distinguishing, 438
  SPSS output, 74–75
  Syntax, 396–399
    overview, 396–399
    performing repetitive calculations, 399
PDF (Portable Document Format) documents, 66, 77, 392
Pearson Chi-Square statistic, 257, 258
Pearson correlation
  assumptions, 291
  defined, 288
  general discussion of, 285
Peck, Jon, 437
perceptual maps, 419

period, 404, 408
Piatetsky, Gregory, 429
pie charts, 174, 200–201, 217
pivot tables, 383–392
  pivoting trays, 390–392
  Style Output dialog, 387–389
  TableLooks, 384–387
Pivot Tables tab, Options window, 364–365
pivoting trays, 390–392
Plots dialog, 295
plug-ins, 435–437
PNG (portable network graphics) files, 78
points, data, 378–380
polar charts, 200–201
population pyramids, 191–192
.por files, 66
Portable Document Format (PDF) documents, 66, 77, 392
portable network graphics (PNG) files, 78
portrait orientation, 357
positive relationships, 287
positively skewed distribution, 329
post hoc tests
  for nonparametric independent samples test, 331
  one-way ANOVA procedure, 311–314
postscript (EPS), 78
power analysis, 234
power scale, 172
PowerPoint, 77
.ppt files, 77
precision, 229, 235
predictive analytics, 416
predictor variables, 316
Press, Gil, 430
PRINT command, 409
printing, 80, 392
Privacy tab, Options window, 370
probabilistic sampling, 228
probability tests, 231
  chi-square test of independence
    crosstabulation, 256–259
    with layered variables, 263
  independent-samples t-test, 232
    one-way ANOVA procedure, 303–326
    overview, 269–275
probit analysis, 418

Roles option, 355
Rosling, Hans, 430
rounding numbers, 359
rsvp.sav dataset
    pasting Syntax, 396–399
    recoding into different variables, 108–109
RTF (rich text format) files, 74, 365

S

salaries.sav file, 113–116
Salcedo, Jesus, 4
sampling, 227–229
    Complex Sample module, 422
    Exact Tests module, 423
    overview, 11, 227–228
    sample size
        nonparametric tests and, 328
        overview, 228–229
        precision and, 234–235
    variation within, 304
sampling distribution, 229
SAS file format, 45, 66, 72
.sas7bdat files, 66
SAVE command, 409
Save dialog, 295
saving, 57
    data files, 69
    SELECT IF command and, 412
.sav files, 15, 59–60
scale level of measurement, 56, 215
scale variable
    organizing in bins, 113
    scale level of measurement, 13
scaling procedures, 215, 418
scatterplot matrices, 198–199
scatterplots
    colored, 196–198
    editing data points, 378–380
    linear relationship between variables with, 286–288
    from multiple linear regression model, 325–326
    simple, 184–185
Scheffe test, 312
scientific notation, 48–49, 355, 358
screen reader accessibility, 361
Scripts tab, Options window, 366–367

.sd2 files, 66
.sd7 files, 66
select cases transformation, 100–102
SELECT command, 402, 441–442
SELECT IF command, 412
selection bias, 228
SEM (Structural Equation Modeling), 20, 416
sensitive tests, 437
Session Journal, 365
sessions, 25–42
    creating graphs, 33–37
    interpreting results, 30–32
    investigating data, 37–42
    opening datasets, 25–27
    running analysis, 27–30
settings, 353–370
    Chart tab, 362–363
    Currency tab, 360–361
    Data tab, 358–359
    File Locations tab, 365–366
    General tab, 354–356
    Language tab, 356–357
    Multiple Imputations tab, 368
    Output tab, 361–362
    Pivot Tables tab, 364–365
    Privacy tab, 370
    Scripts tab, 366–367
    Syntax Editor tab, 369–370
    Viewer tab, 357–358
Sidak test, 312
significance value, 243
SignificanceAp Magazine, 429
simple regression, 294
Simply Statistics blog, 429
simulation, 350
64 bit versions, 18
skewed distributions, 328, 329–330
SKU (product codes), 51
slashes, forward, 404
Slideology (Duarte), 430
.slk files, 66
slope (m), 13, 293
S-N-K test, 312
Social Security numbers, 51
sort keys, 97–98

W

Web Survey.sav dataset
  ANY function, 137–138
  LENGTH function, 135–136
  MEAN function, 139–141
  requesting repetitive output with Syntax, 401–402
WEIGHT command, 441–442
weighted least squares regression, 418
weights, 424
Welch test, 307, 310
Welcome dialog, 26, 370
width, variable, 51–52
Wilcoxon signed-rank test, 340–341
Windows operating system, 18
WITH reserved word, 125
within-group variation, 304–305
Word
  exporting data to, 74–80
  settings for copying from, 365
Worldsales.sav file, 207–208
.w files, 66

X

.xlsm files, 66, 77
.xls files, 66, 77
.xlsx files, 66, 77
.xpt files, 66
XSAVE command, 409

Y

Yau, Nathan, 429
Y-axis, adding variable to, 196
y-intercept (*b*), 293

Z

zero, leading, 355
ZIP codes, 51
z-scores, 236–238
z-test, 260–261

About the Authors

Jesus Salcedo is an independent statistical and data mining consultant who has been using SPSS products for over 25 years. He is a former SPSS Curriculum Team Lead and Senior Education Specialist who has written numerous SPSS training courses and trained thousands of users. He earned a PhD in psychometrics from Fordham University. In his free time, Jesus enjoys playing fantasy baseball, hiking, backpacking, and traveling.

Keith McCormick moved to Raleigh-Durham, North Carolina, in the late '90s, planning on graduate school, but a "part-time" SPSS training job turned out to be a career. Keith has been all over the world consulting and conducting training in all things SPSS, statistics, and data mining. Several thousand students later, he has learned a thing or two about how to get folks started in SPSS. Currently, his focus is conference speaking, authoring courses on the LinkedIn Learning platform, and coaching executives on how to effectively manage their analytics teams. An avid consumer of data science and machine learning news, he likes to share his take on his blog atkeithmccormick.com or in his news feed on LinkedIn. In between assignments, Keith likes to travel to out-of-the-way places, try new food, hike around, and find cool souvenirs to bring home.

About the Technical Reviewer

Abram Moats is a data scientist currently working at the Oshkosh Corporation. He graduated with a degree in applied mathematics from Columbia University in May 2020 and continues to expand and deepen his knowledge of data science subjects through practical application and coursework. Abram is the creator of an original series of videos and essays centered on CRISP-DM, a data science process method, which can be found on his LinkedIn and Medium pages. In his free time, he enjoys running, traveling, and practicing his Spanish skills.

Dedication

To all the "legacy SPSS" folks we've known and worked with over the years, some of whom are at IBM now and some of whom have moved onto other things.

Authors' Acknowledgments

We owe our thanks to our friends Meta Brown and Dean Abbott for independently introducing us to the team at John Wiley & Sons, which led not only to our participation in this project but also to *SPSS Statistics for Data Analysis and Visualization*. We would also like to thank Ashley Coffey and Lindsay Lefevere, who helped us overcome obstacles at the beginning of this project. Many thanks to our project editor, Susan Pink, who greatly improved the quality of this book, our technical editor, Abram Moats, and the rest of the *For Dummies* team. We would also like to thank all our friends and colleagues at IBM SPSS.

Jesus would like to thank his partner in crime, Emily, for helping him get through another book and the pandemic.

Finally, there could be no fourth edition without the previous editions. Aaron Poh was instrumental in getting the third edition completed on schedule. We also owe a debt to Arthur Griffith, who wrote the first and second editions. Although we never had an opportunity to meet Arthur, his presence is felt in these pages. Just when we might risk taking ourselves too seriously, we stumble upon a phrase of Arthur's featuring *diddlysquat, jelly beans, Klingon trigonometry,* or a caution to avoid making SPSS grumpy. His wonderful sense of humor has been retained whenever possible in the revision, because we couldn't possibly replicate it.

Publisher's Acknowledgments

Executive Editor: Lindsay Lefevere

Project and Copy Editor: Susan Pink

Technical Editor: Abram Moats

Sr. Editorial Assistant: Cherie Case

Proofreader: Debbye Butler

Production Editor: Siddique Shaik

Cover Image: © loops7/Getty Images